T0178315

Lecture Notes in Computer Science 13749

Eike Kiltz · Vinod Vaikuntanathan (Eds.)

Theory
of Cryptography

20th International Conference, TCC 2022
Chicago, IL, USA, November 7–10, 2022
Proceedings, Part III

 Springer

Editors
Eike Kiltz 🄳
Ruhr University Bochum
Bochum, Germany

Vinod Vaikuntanathan 🄳
Massachusetts Institute of Technology
Cambridge, MA, USA

ISSN 0302-9743   ISSN 1611-3349 (electronic)
Lecture Notes in Computer Science
ISBN 978-3-031-22367-9   ISBN 978-3-031-22368-6 (eBook)
https://doi.org/10.1007/978-3-031-22368-6

This Springer imprint is published by the registered company Springer Nature Switzerland AG
The registered company address is: Gewerbestrasse 11, 6330 Cham, Switzerland

Preface

The 20th Theory of Cryptography Conference (TCC 2022) was held during November 7–10, 2022, at the University of Chicago, USA. It was sponsored by the International Association for Cryptologic Research (IACR). The general chair of the conference was David Cash.

The conference received 139 submissions, of which the Program Committee (PC) selected 60 for presentation giving an acceptance rate of 43%. Each submission was reviewed by at least three PC members in a single-blind process. The 44 PC members (including PC chairs), all top researchers in our field, were helped by 116 external reviewers, who were consulted when appropriate. These proceedings consist of the revised version of the 60 accepted papers. The revisions were not reviewed, and the authors bear full responsibility for the content of their papers.

We are extremely grateful to Kevin McCurley for providing fast and reliable technical support for the HotCRP review software whenever we had any questions. We made extensive use of the interaction feature supported by the review software, where PC members could anonymously interact with authors. This was used to ask specific technical questions, such as those about suspected bugs or unclear connections to prior work. We believe this approach improved our understanding of the papers and the quality of the review process. We also thank Kay McKelly for her fast and meticulous help with the conference website.

This was the eighth year that TCC presented the Test of Time Award to an outstanding paper that was published at TCC at least eight years ago, making a significant contribution to the theory of cryptography, preferably with influence also in other areas of cryptography, theory, and beyond. This year, the Test of Time Award Committee selected the following paper, published at TCC 2011: "Perfectly secure oblivious RAM without random oracles" by Ivan Damgård, Sigurd Meldgaard, and Jesper Buus Nielsen. The award committee recognized this paper for "the first perfectly secure unconditional Oblivious RAM scheme and for setting the stage for future Oblivious RAM and PRAM schemes". The authors were invited to deliver a talk at TCC 2022. The conference also featured two other invited talks, by Rahul Santhanam and by Eran Tromer.

This year, TCC awarded a Best Young Researcher Award for the best paper authored solely by young researchers. The award was given to the paper "A Tight Computational Indistinguishability Bound of Product Distributions" by Nathan Geier.

We are greatly indebted to the many people who were involved in making TCC 2022 a success. A big thanks to the authors who submitted their papers and to the PC members and external reviewers for their hard work, dedication, and diligence in reviewing the papers, verifying their correctness, and discussing the papers in depth. We thank the University of Chicago Computer Science department, Google Research, Algorand Foundation, NTT Research, and Duality Technologies for their generous sponsorship of the conference. A special thanks goes to the general chair David Cash, and to Brian LaMacchia, Kevin McCurley, Kay McKelly, Sandry Quarles, Douglas Stebila, and the

TCC Steering Committee. Finally, we are thankful to the thriving and vibrant community of theoretical cryptographers. Long Live TCC!

September 2022   Eike Kiltz
                                                                      Vinod Vaikuntanathan

Organization

General Chair

David Cash University of Chicago, USA

Program Committee Chairs

Eike Kiltz Ruhr-Universität Bochum, Germany
Vinod Vaikuntanathan MIT, USA

Steering Committee

Jesper Buus Nielsen Aarhus University, Denmark
Krzysztof Pietrzak Institute of Science and Technology, Austria
Huijia (Rachel) Lin UCSB, USA
Yuval Ishai Technion, Israel
Tal Malkin Columbia University, USA
Manoj M. Prabhakaran IIT Bombay, India
Salil Vadhan Harvard University, USA

Program Committee

Gilad Asharov Bar-Ilan University, Israel
Marshall Ball New York University, USA
Amos Beimel Ben Gurion University, Israel
Fabrice Benhamouda Algorand Foundation, USA
Nir Bitansky Tel Aviv University, Israel
Zvika Brakerski Weizmann Institute of Science, Israel
Anne Broadbent University of Ottawa, Canada
Yilei Chen Tsinghua University, China
Ran Cohen Reichman University, Israel
Geoffroy Couteau CNRS, IRIF, Université Paris Cité, France
Nils Fleischhacker Ruhr University Bochum, Germany
Rishab Goyal University of Wisconsin-Madison, USA
Siyao Guo NYU Shanghai, China
Dennis Hofheinz ETH Zurich, Switzerland
Gabe Kaptchuk Boston University, USA
Jonathan Katz University of Maryland, USA

Dakshita Khurana	UIUC, USA
Susumu Kiyoshima	NTT Research, USA
Karen Klein	ETH Zurich, Switzerland
Venkata Koppula	Indian Institute of Technology Delhi, India
Eyal Kushilevitz	Technion, Israel
Alex Lombardi	University of California, Berkeley, USA
Julian Loss	CISPA Helmholtz Center for Information Security, Germany
Fermi Ma	Simons Institute and UC Berkeley, USA
Mohammad Mahmoody	University of Virginia, USA
Ryo Nishimaki	NTT Corporation, Japan
Adam O'Neill	University of Massachusetts Amherst, USA
Emmanuela Orsini	KU Leuven, Belgium
Omer Paneth	Tel Aviv University, Israel
Alon Rosen	Bocconi University, Italy
Lior Rotem	The Hebrew University, Israel
Ron Rothblum	Technion, Israel
Peter Scholl	Aarhus University, Denmark
Sruthi Sekar	UC Berkeley, USA
Katerina Sotiraki	UC Berkeley, USA
Nicholas Spooner	University of Warwick, UK
Noah Stephens-Davidowitz	Cornell University, USA
Stefano Tessaro	University of Washington, USA
Prashant Vasudevan	National University of Singapore, Singapore
David Wu	University of Texas at Austin, USA
Yu Yu	Shanghai Jiao Tong University, China
Mark Zhandry	NTT Research and Princeton University, USA

Additional Reviewers

Damiano Abram	Rohit Chatterjee	Ben Fisch
Amit Agarwal	Arka Rai Choudhuri	Danilo Francati
Shweta Agrawal	Kelong Cong	Tore Frederiksen
Nicolas Alhaddad	Hongrui Cui	Cody Freitag
Benedikt Auerbach	Eric Culf	Rachit Garg
Renas Bacho	Dana Dachman-Soled	Romain Gay
Christian Badertscher	Pratish Datta	Nicholas Genise
Saikrishna Badrinarayanan	Lalita Devadas	Suparno Ghoshal
James Bartusek	Nico Döttling	Aarushi Goel
Gabrielle Beck	Thomas Espitau	Eli Goldin
Alexander Bienstock	Jaiden Fairoze	Shai Halevi
Dung Bui	Oriol Farràs	Mathias Hall-Andersen
Suvradip Chakraborty	Weiqi Feng	Dominik Hartmann

Alexandra Henzinger
Martin Hirt
Viet Tung Hoang
Charlotte Hoffmann
Justin Holmgren
James Hulett
Yuval Ishai
Palak Jain
Ruta Jawale
Zhengzhong Jin
Daniel Jost
Chethan Kamath
Martti Karvonen
Julia Kastner
Shuichi Katsumata
Fuyuki Kitagawa
Sabrina Kunzweiler
Ulysse Lechine
Derek Leung
Hanjun Li
Baiyu Li
Xiao Liang
Yao-Ting Lin
Tianren Liu
Qipeng Liu
Chen-Da Liu-Zhang

Sébastien Lord
George Lu
Takahiro Matsuda
Pierre Meyer
Pratyush Mishra
Tamer Mour
Marta Mularczyk
Alice Murphy
Varun Narayanan
Hai Nguyen
Maciej Obremski
Michele Orrù
Hussien Othman
Tapas Pal
Giorgos Panagiotakos
Dimitris Papachristoudis
Guillermo Pascual Perez
Anat Paskin-Cherniavsky
Robi Pedersen
Luowen Qian
Willy Quach
Nicholas Resch
Lawrence Roy
Yusuke Sakai
Pratik Sarkar
Benjamin Schlosser

Akash Shah
Yixin Shen
Omri Shmueli
Min Jae Song
Fang Song
Pratik Soni
Shravan Srinivasan
Igors Stepanovs
Dominique Unruh
Neekon Vafa
Benedikt Wagner
Hendrik Waldner
Mingyuan Wang
Hoeteck Wee
Ke Wu
Zhiye Xie
Sophia Yakoubov
Takashi Yamakawa
Eylon Yogev
Peter Yuen
Rachel Zhang
Jiaheng Zhang
Vassilis Zikas
Leo de Castro
Akin Ünal

Contents – Part III

ORAM, OT and PIR

Verifiable Private Information Retrieval

Shany Ben-David[1][✉], Yael Tauman Kalai[2], and Omer Paneth[1]

[1] Tel Aviv University, Tel Aviv-Yafo, Israel
shanygabizon@gmail.com
[2] Microsoft Research and MIT, Cambridge, USA

Abstract. A computational PIR scheme allows a client to privately query a database hosted on a single server without downloading the entire database. We introduce the notion of verifiable PIR (vPIR) where the server can convince the client that the database satisfies certain properties without additional rounds and while keeping the communication sub-linear. For example, the server can prove that the number of rows in the database that satisfy a predicate P is exactly n.

We define security by modeling vPIR as an ideal functionality and following the real-ideal paradigm. Starting from a standard PIR scheme, we construct a vPIR scheme for any database property that can be verified by a machine that reads the database once and maintains a bounded size state between rows. We also construct vPIR with public verification based on LWE or on DLIN. The main technical hurdle is to demonstrate a simulator that extracts a long input from an adversary that sends a single short message.

Our vPIR constructions are based on the notion of batch argument for NP. As contribution of independent interest, we show that batch arguments are equivalent to quasi-arguments—a relaxation of SNARKs which is known to imply succinct argument for various sub-classes of NP.

1 Introduction

A single-server computational private information retrieval (PIR) scheme [13] allows clients to query a database privately, without revealing to the server any information about their query. Such a PIR scheme is non-trivial if the server's message is shorter than the database. In the standard notion of PIR, the server is free to use any database to answer the clients query. In this work, we introduce a variant of PIR that we call *verifiable PIR* (vPIR). In vPIR, the server can prove to the client that the database it is using to answer the query satisfies some property, for example: the database entries are sorted, or the database does not contain some value X more than n times. As before, in a non-trivial scheme the server's answer *including the proof* should be shorter than the database.

In this work we focus on *one round* vPIR schemes: the client sends a query and the server responds with a single message that includes both the PIR answer and a proof that the database satisfies the required property. Indeed, one-round is the standard when constructing PIR schemes, and it is required for many applications.[1]

vPIR via Secure Computation. In plain PIR the only standard security requirement is that the client's message hides its query. However, in the setting of vPIR, defining security against malicious servers that may not use a valid database requires more care. One natural approach is to define vPIR as a special case of secure two-party computation for the vPIR functionality. The vPIR functionality takes a query i from the client and a database D from the server, and returns $D[i]$ to the client if D satisfies the required property, or $\perp$ otherwise.

The problem with this approach is that non-trivial one-round vPIR schemes require secure computation with very strong properties. Specifically, we need a one-round secure computation protocol (also known as non-interactive secure computation [8]) with security against a malicious server where the server's communication is sub-linear in its input. Currently, such protocols are only known in the CRS model based on succinct non-interactive arguments of knowledge (SNARKs) for NP.[2] In all known constructions of SNARKs for NP, soundness is either heuristic, or based on so-called non-falsifiable knowledge assumptions. SNARK constructions with an explicit knowledge extractor are not known and are subject to strong barriers [3]. We note that even if we relax security and allow for super-polynomial, or even unbounded simulation, we do not know of any solutions that do not use SNARKs. In light of this barrier, in this work we propose alternative formulations of vPIR and realize them under standard assumptions.

1.1 Our Contribution

Our first contribution is proposing two definitions of vPIR that relax the security definition based on secure computation: A game-based definition for *local* database properties that only depends on a small number of entries, and a simulation-based definition for *global* properties that depends the entire database. We explore possible applications and discuss the limitations of each definition. Then, we show how to construct vPIR schemes that satisfy our definitions for a rich class of properties based on various standard assumptions.[3] Finally, we show that the notion of vPIR is closely connected to the notions of quasi-arguments and batch arguments for NP [4,10] that were recently proposed in relation to delegating computation [6,11]. Based on these connections

---

[1] We expand on the advantages of one-round schemes and discuss solutions with more rounds at the end of this introduction.

[2] Since for vPIR we do not require any security against a corrupted client, the client can send the CRS as part of its message.

[3] We mention that succinct non-interactive arguments (SNARGs) for certain subclasses of NP, including the class of properties supported by our constructions, are known under standard assumptions [1,6,11,16]. Such SNARGs, however, do not give succinct non-interactive secure computation for the vPIR functionality for any non-trivial property since they lack an efficient knowledge extractor. We elaborate on this below where we state our result in more detail.

we derive new results and simplify existing results in the area of delegation. In what follows, we elaborate on our contributions.

Definitions of vPIR. Before presenting our security definitions, we elaborate on the syntax of a vPIR scheme. In a standard PIR scheme the client generates, together with its query, a secret key dk used to decode the answer. In a vPIR scheme the client also generates a verification key vk. The server answers the query using a database that satisfies a property P and its answer includes a proof of this fact. The client verifies the server's answer using vk, and if the answer is accepted, the client decodes it using dk.

In the setting where multiple queries are answered with the same database we may need to verify, not only that each query was answered using some database that satisfies P, but also that all queries where answered using the same database. To this end, we first verify each answer with its own verification key, and then verify the consistency of all the answers together. We require that verifying the consistency of the answers can be done without any verification key. This feature is particularly useful in settings where the queries are generated by multiple clients since it does not require clients to share their verification key.

We consider two flavors of vPIR schemes: publicly verifiable vPIR where vk can be made public, and designated verifier vPIR where vk must be kept secret. In the designated verifier setting, a cheating server that learns vk may be able to break soundness. However, we require that the client's query remains hidden even if vk becomes public. This, in particular, guarantees that by revealing its decision to accept or reject, the client may compromise its verification key and lose soundness, but it does not compromise the secrecy of its query.

We emphasize that even if verification requires only a public key, decoding the server's answer always requires the secret key dk. Nonetheless, public verification has several advantages: First, it allows any user (an not just the client) to audit the server. Furthermore, it allows to reuse the same vPIR query many times without compromising soundness, even if the verification results are made public. Finally, in what follows, we use public verifiability for composition and to derive new results on publicly verifiable delegation.

Next we describe two definitions of vPIR security, for local and for global properties. Each of these security requirements is made in combination with the standard PIR privacy requirement that the client's query completely hides the database location queried.

vPIR for Local Properties. Our first security notion for vPIR deals with local database properties that depend only on a small number of entries. In more detail, we model an ℓ-local property as an efficient program P that takes as input ℓ locations $q_1, \ldots, q_\ell$ and the corresponding database entries $a_1, \ldots, a_\ell$ and produces a binary output. A server holding a database D can prove that it satisfies the ℓ-local property P if the property is satisfied by any ℓ locations. That is, for every $q_1, \ldots, q_\ell$, the property P accepts $q_1, \ldots, q_\ell$ and $a_1, \ldots, a_\ell$ where $\mathbf{a}_i = D[\mathbf{q}_i]$.

Intuitively, our security requirement states that if we query the server on any ℓ locations and the server's answers pass verification then the decoded entries must satisfy the ℓ-local property P. In more detail, we consider the following game between a challenger and an adversary playing the role of the server. The challenger generates ℓ queries for locations $q_1, \ldots, q_\ell$, sends them to the server and obtains ℓ answers. The challenger then checks that each answer passes the verification with its own verification key, and that all ℓ answers together are consistent (this check does not require the verification keys). Finally, the challenger decodes each answer using its own decoding key and obtains the entries $a_1, \ldots, a_\ell$. The adversary wins the game if all the answers are found to be valid and consistent, but the property P rejects $q_1, \ldots, q_\ell$ and $a_1, \ldots, a_\ell$. The requirement is that for any ℓ locations, the adversary wins with negligible probability.

Use Cases. We discuss some examples of using the above definition. Starting with the simple case of 1-local properties, consider a server that offers its clients private access to a database of articles. The server claims that all the articles in its database have been fact-checked and digitally signed by a trusted third party. To prove this claim, we can use a vPIR for the 1-local property checking that a given entry contains a valid digital signature. By the vPIR security the client is guaranteed that if the answer passes verification, the decoded entry will contain a valid signature.

Note that instead of verifying the answer, the client can simply decode it and check if it contains a valid signature. However, in this case, simply revealing the fact that the server is cheating may compromise the secrecy of the clients query. To see that, consider a database that contains a single unsigned article. If the client detects cheating then its query location is completely revealed. In contrast, using vPIR, if the server's database contains even one unsigned article, then, since the client's query is hiding, and since this hiding holds even given the verification key, the server's answer will be rejected with all but negligible probability, regardless of the client's query location. In particular, the verification result does not compromise the client's privacy.

Another important use-case of vPIR for local properties is in the setting of multiple clients. Consider, for example a cheating server that claims to use the same database of articles when interacting with all of its clients, but, in reality, clients asking for the same article may get different content (or no content) based on their identifying information. As in the previous example, clients accusing the server of cheating may be exposing their secret query location. Moreover, in this example, even detecting that the server answers are inconsistent requires the clients to reveal their secret query location to *each other*. Using vPIR two or more clients can guarantee the consistency of their answers, that is, they can verify that if they made the same query they also received the same answer, while keeping their query completely private, even from each other.

Going beyond consistency checking, clients can use vPIR to verify more complicated relations between their answers. For example, if the query locations correspond to the nodes of a graph and the database contains a valid coloring of the graph, then clients can check that their answers verify the coloring constraints (again, while keeping their query location completely hidden, even from each other) by verifying the following 2-local property: given locations q_1, q_2 and colors a_1, a_2 the property rejects if and only if (q_1, q_2) is an edge but $a_1 = a_2$.

vPIR for Global Properties. Next we consider setting where the server would like to prove to its clients something that be expressed as a local property of the client's queries and server's answers. For example, consider again our server that is holding a database of fact-checked and digitally signed articles. Now, suppose that the articles in the server's database update frequently and, as a result, at any given moment a small fraction of the articles, say 10%, have yet to be checked and signed by the third party. Since the database always contains some unsigned articles, the server can no longer prove that the database satisfies the 1-local property. Instead, the server would like to prove that the database satisfies a global property: at least 90% of the entries contain a valid signature.

With this motivation in mind, we propose another security notion for vPIR dealing with global properties that may depend on the entire database. We model a global property P as an efficient program that takes as input the entire database D and produces a binary output. When defining security for global properties, we observe that simply requiring that an accepting answer is consistent with *some* database that satisfies P is insufficient. For example, if the property P asserts that 90% of the entries contain a valid signature, then any answer, whether it is signed or not, is always consistent with some database that satisfies P. Intuitively, the issue with this naive definition is that it does not guarantee that server uses a database that is independent of the query location. To resolve this issue, we propose a simulation based security definition for vPIR with global properties. Our definition is a relaxation of secure computation for the vPIR functionality (where the adversary corrupts the server). Looking ahead, this relaxation will be crucial for our analysis. Nonetheless, we argue that our definition still provides meaningful security in the setting of vPIR and demonstrate its applications.

The definition follows the real-ideal paradigm. In the real experiment, we send the adversary, playing the role of the server, a query for location q and obtain an answer. The output is either the decoded entry or $\perp$ if the answer fails to verify. In the ideal experiment, the simulator submits an entire database to the trusted party that computes the output: either the value at location q or $\perp$ if the database does not satisfy the property P. We require that for any adversarial server there exists an efficient simulator such that for every location q, the output of the two experiments are indistinguishable. We will also consider a variant of this definition where the simulator is allowed to run in super-polynomial time.

vPIR vs. Secure Computation. The above definition is similar to the definition of secure computation for the vPIR functionality with one important relaxation: In the definition of secure computation, the output of the real and ideal experiments contain both the output of the honest client and the output of the adversary/simulator. In our definition, however, only the client's output is included in the output of the experiments. Recall that in addition to the above security requirement, we also require explicitly that client's query is hiding. Therefore, we can always simulate the view of the adversary by generating a query for an arbitrary location. However, while we can simulate the output of the client and the server individually, we may not be able to simulate the joint distribution of the outputs as required for secure computation.

Intuitively, since we simulate the client's output, our definition guarantees that a malicious server skew the client's output distribution. However, since we do not simulate the adversary's view together with the client's output, it may be possible for the adversary to learn something that be simulated in the ideal experiment (as long as the query location remains hidden). For example, going back to our server proving that 90% of the entries in its database are signed, if the client queries a random location, then the ideal experiment's output is either $\perp$, or it contains a signed entry with probability at least 0.9 (this holds even if the simulator is computationally unbounded). Therefore, the same is guaranteed also in the real experiment. However, we cannot guarantee that a malicious server cannot learn, for example, whether the client's answer is signed or not.

Constructions of vPIR. We next provide an overview of our vPIR constructions both for local and for global properties under standard assumptions.

vPIR for Local Properties. Our first result is a designated verifier vPIR for all ℓ-local properties for any constant ℓ under the minimal assumption that PIR schemes exist.

Theorem 1 (Informal). *Assuming poly-logarithmic PIR scheme exists, for any constant ℓ there exists a designated verifier poly-logarithmic vPIR scheme for all ℓ-local properties decidable in polynomial-time. For security parameter κ and a database with m rows, each of length w, the communication complexity and verification time are $w \cdot \text{poly}(\kappa, \log m)$.*

For $\ell > 1$ the vPIR scheme requires public parameters that contain the description of a collision-resistant hash.

Theorem 1 is stated based on poly-logarithmic PIR where the communication complexity is $\text{poly}(\kappa, \log m)$ for a databases of m bits. More generally, assuming PIR with communication complexity $C(m, \kappa)$ we get vPIR with communication complexity $C \cdot w \cdot \text{poly}(\kappa, \log m)$.

In the publicly verifiable setting, we construct vPIR for the same properties under LWE or under bilinear paring.

Theorem 2 (Informal). *Under the LWE assumption, for any constant ℓ there exists a publicly verifiable vPIR scheme for all ℓ-local properties decidable in polynomial-time with communication complexity and verification time $w \cdot \text{poly}(\kappa, \log m)$.*

Theorem 3 (Informal). *Under the DLIN assumption in a prime-order pairing group, for any constants ℓ, ϵ there exists a publicly verifiable vPIR scheme for all ℓ-local properties decidable in polynomial-time T with communication complexity and verification time $(w + T^\epsilon) \cdot 2^{\sqrt{O(\log \kappa \log m)}}$.*

The main tool we use in our construction of vPIR for local properties is a batch argument for NP [4]. We give a generic construction based on any batch argument that satisfies certain properties [6] (see the technical overview for more details). Theorems 2 and 3 are based the batch arguments from [6] and [16] respectively. Theorem 1 is based by the batch argument constructed in [4] that we modify to meet our requirements.

Beyond Constant Locality. The vPIR schemes in the theorems above can only handle properties with constant locality ℓ. To justify this limitation observe that when ℓ is super-constant, a vPIR scheme with an efficient client and server for all ℓ-local properties is unlikely. This is the case since deciding if a given database D satisfies an ℓ-local property P (for every ℓ locations) may require time exponential in ℓ. In contrast, if we had a vPIR scheme for P with an efficient client and server we could also decide if D satisfies P efficiently, by running the honest vPIR server on ℓ queries (for arbitrary locations) and checking if the answers pass verification. If D satisfies P the answers should be accepted. However, if there exist ℓ locations that do not satisfy P then no efficient algorithm queried on these locations should be able to produce answers that pass verification with non-negligible probability. Therefore, since the queries are hiding (even given the verification key) verification must also fail when the queries are for arbitrary locations.

vPIR for Global Properties. Before stating our results on vPIR with global properties, we start by mentioning some barriers. We observe that vPIR for *all* efficiently testable global properties implies SNARKs and, therefore, we do not expect to realize such vPIR under standard assumptions. In more detail, a designated verifier vPIR scheme implies designated verifier SNARKs, while publicly verifiable vPIR implies full-fledged SNARKs. Moreover, vPIR with inefficient simulation implies succinct non-interactive arguments (SNARGs) for NP. None of these notions are known based on any falsifiable assumption, and such constructions are subject to barriers [3,7]. We can transform a vPIR scheme into a SNARK as follows: the CRS contains a query for an arbitrary location. To prove some NP statement, the prover views the witness as a database of bits and proves that it satisfies the global property testing the witness validity. The verifier accepts if the vPIR answer passes verification. If the vPIR scheme is non-trivial then the proof is succinct. To argue knowledge soundness, consider an adversary that convinces the verifier with non-negligible probability. It follows that in the ideal experiment the simulator must submit a database that contains a valid witness to the trusted party and, therefore, it can be used as an extractor.

In light of this barrier, we focus on constructing vPIR for a restricted, yet useful class of global properties. Specifically, we consider the class of properties decidable by a Turing machine that reads the database once and maintains a state of bounded length between rows. In more detail, each property in the class can be tested by a machine P that maintains a state of length S (shorter than the database). For every row in the database, the machine P updates its state by applying an arbitrary efficient function to the current state and database row. (We emphasize the length of the database row or the space of the update function may not be bound by S.) For example, for any efficiently computable predicate Q, we can verify that the number of database rows that satisfy Q is exactly n using a state of size $S = \log(n)$. As another example, verifying that the database is sorted can be done with a state of size $S = w + 1$, where w is the length of each row.

We are ready to state our results on vPIR for global properties, starting with the designated verifier setting.

Theorem 4 (Informal). *Let $\Lambda(\kappa)$ be a function of the security parameter. Assuming Λ-secure poly-logarithmic PIR scheme exists, there exists a designated verifier vPIR scheme for any global property decidable by a polynomial-time read-once Turing machine P with description and state of length at most $\log \Lambda$. The communication complexity and verification time are as in Theorem 1. For every constant $c \in \mathbb{N}$ there exists a simulator running in time $\Lambda^{O(c)}$ such that every $\text{poly}(\Lambda)$-size distinguisher has advantage at most $\Lambda^{-O(c)}$.*

In the publicly verifiable setting, we construct vPIR for the same class of global properties and with the same simulation time under the Λ-hardness of LWE or DLIN. The communication complexity and verification time are as in Theorem 2 and Theorem 3 respectively.

Note that in Theorem 4 we allow the description size of the machine P to grow with the security parameter as long as $|P| \leq \log \Lambda$. If we restrict attention to the non-adaptive setting where the machine P is fixed before the query then we can prove a stronger result where the description size of P is not bounded. We emphasize that even in the non-adaptive setting, the adversary may still choose its database adaptively.

On the Simulation Time. For a bound $\Lambda = \text{poly}(\kappa)$, our result gives a vPIR scheme with polynomial time simulation (with inverse polynomial accuracy). For a super-polynomial Λ, the result captures a larger set of properties, however, with simulation that runs in super-polynomial time (and based on super-polynomial hardness assumptions). However, as argued above, vPIR with super-polynomial, or even unbounded, simulation still provides meaningful security. (Intuitively, it still guarantees that adversary's database is independent of the query location.) Theorem 4 leaves open the possibility of constructing a vPIR scheme where the running time of the simulation does not grow exponentially with the length of the machine's state and description. We discuss some barriers towards such improvements.

As argued above, vPIR for arbitrary global properties implies a SNARKs for NP. We show that this implication can be extended also to vPIR that only supports properties decidable by a read-once Turing machine as long as the simulation time is sub-exponential in the length of the machine's state (and assuming sufficiently strong collision-resistant hashing). As before, we construct a SNARK by letting the prover encode its NP witness in the database. However now, to allow for verification by a read-once machine with a succinct state, we first encode the witness so that each row contains the next bit required by the NP verification procedure. If the same witness bit is used multiple times it will appear in multiple rows. To verify that all occurrences of the same witness bit are consistent we compute a hash tree over the entire witness, adding the root to the machine's state and adding to each row the authentication path for the next witness bit. To argue knowledge soundness, consider an adversary that convinces the verifier with non-negligible probability. It follows that in the ideal experiment the simulator must submit a database that contains either a valid witness or a hash collision. If the simulation time is sub-exponential in the length of the machine's state (or, the length of the hash root) and assuming the hash is sufficiently strong, then the simulator cannot find collisions and, therefore, it can be used as an extractor.

We can further extend this argument to vPIR where the simulation time is sub-exponential in the length of the machine's description. The idea is to hard-code the root into the machine's description instead of adding it to the machine's state. Note that this requires vPIR with adaptive security. Indeed, in the non-adaptive setting we do get vPIR where the simulation time does not grow with the machine's description under standard assumptions.

On vPIR from SNARKs for Sub-classes of NP. As mentioned above, a vPIR scheme can be constructed based on SNARKs for NP by compiling a semi-honest protocol based on any standard PIR scheme. Therefore, a natural approach to proving Theorem 4 is to construct a vPIR based on SNARKs for a sub-class of NP. Specifically, observe that vPIR for any global property decidable by a read-once machine with state of length S can be constructed by combining a standard PIR scheme where the honest server is implemented by a read-once machine with state of length $\text{poly}(\kappa)$ (such PIR schemes are known under various standard assumptions) with a SNARK for NP languages decidable by a read-once machine with state of length $S' = S + \text{poly}(\kappa)$. Currently, however, SNARKs for languages decidable by a read-once machine with super-logarithmic state are not known under any falsifiable assumption. The work of [1] constructed designated verifier *SNARGs* for the same class under $2^{S'}$-hardness assumption,[4] In particular however, we do not know how to compile a standard PIR scheme into a vPIR scheme without relying on the SNARK's efficient knowledge extractor. While the SNARGs of [1] do not directly imply vPIR, the simulation strategy we use to prove Theorem 4 is based on techniques from the analysis of [1].

While the above construction instantiated with the SNARGs of [1] may not satisfy our notion of vPIR for global properties, we can, nonetheless, use it to get a vPIR for 1-local properties where simulation is not required. This is based on the fact that verifying that a databases satisfies a 1-local property can be done by a read-once machine with state of length 1. The advantage of the vPIR

---

[4] The work of [1] constructed a SNARG for a slightly more restricted class: languages decidable by read-one non-deterministic Turing machines with bounded space. However, based on standard techniques, their result can be extended to the case where only the length of the state between rows is bounded.

scheme given in Theorem 1 is that it can be based on polynomial PIR rather than sub-exponential.

vPIR and Delegation. As our final contribution we demonstrate connections between the notion of vPIR and other notions recently introduced in the context of delegating computation. Based on these connections we reinterpret and simplify recent results and prove new results in this area.

Our first connection is between vPIR and the notion of batch arguments for NP [4]. Batch arguments allows us to verify many NP statements with the same complexity as verifying a single statement. They have several applications including SNARGs for P [4–6,11,16]. Specifically, we observe that a vPIR for 1-local properties is equivalent to a stronger variant of batch arguments introduced by [6] known as batch arguments for the index language satisfying the somewhere argument of knowledge property. This equivalence holds in both the designated verifier and the publicly verifiable settings.

We also show a connection between vPIR and quasi-arguments for NP [10, 14]. Quasi-arguments are succinct non interactive arguments for NP satisfying a weak soundness property known as local non-signaling knowledge extraction. They are known to imply SNARGs for P, batch NP, and several other subclasses of NP [1,4,5,9]. We show that vPIR for 3-local properties is equivalent to quasi-arguments satisfying a natural property that we call PIR-friendliness (satisfied by all known constructions). This equivalence as well holds in both the designated verifier and the publicly verifiable settings.

As part of the proof of Theorem 1 we give a transformation from vPIR for 1-local properties to vPIR for ℓ-local properties for any constant ℓ. As a corollary we get a new equivalence between the notions of batch arguments for the index language and PIR friendly quasi-arguments. Based on the recent batch arguments from [6,16] we get new constructions of quasi-arguments under LWE or DLIN. We also get the first quasi-argument with a sublinear CRS. Moreover, since quasi-arguments are known to imply SNARGs for P, we get an alternative construction of SNARGs for P based on batch arguments [6] that is simple and modular. We can also rederive the applications in [11] as direct applications of quasi-arguments and without relying on non-signaling MIPs or sub-exponential security.

We also use the above connections to give a new bootstrapping theorem for quasi-argument. The work of [10] constructs quasi-arguments with a long CRS. Then they used a variant of the bootstrapping technique [2,13,15] to construct SNARGs for P with a sub-linear CRS. However, there were not able to use their technique to bootstrap their quasi-arguments directly. We give a new bootstrapping theorem for vPIR for 1-local properties, similar to bootstrapping theorems proved in previous work [10,16]. Using the connection between vPIR and quasi argument we also get a bootstrapping theorem for quasi-arguments.

1.2   On the Round Complexity of vPIR

In this work we construct vPIR schemes which consist of one round, which is the standard when constructing PIR schemes. Compared to solutions with multiple rounds, one round schemes have several advantages that make them appealing in applications. First, they allow to reuse the same query to produce multiple answers. Another advantage of one-round schemes is that the server can fix its database right before producing its answer. This may be useful, for example, in settings where the client and server are communicating asynchronously (e.g., they are not online simultaneously) and there might be a significant delay between the query and answer. This also allows the server to fix its database as a function of any incoming communication from the client that might be transmitted with the query. Finally, we mention that some techniques such PIR composition [13] require one-round schemes.

We mention that a vPIR scheme with multiple rounds can be constructed based on any succinct interactive argument of knowledge [12]. A scheme with 3 messages can be constructed based on known results on delegating RAM computations under various standard assumptions [4,6,9,10,16]. In this scheme the server's first message is a short commitment to its database. Therefore, when receiving the clients query the server can no longer change its database.

1.3   Open Questions

Our results on vPIR for global properties leaves open several important questions. One natural question is to identify other interesting class of global properties can be proven based on standard assumptions. Another important direction is to construct vPIR that satisfies the full secure computation definition where we simulate the view of both the client and the server together. A related question is to identify other non-trivial functionalities (beyond vPIR) that can be securely realized based on standard assumptions in a single round and with communication complexity that is sub-linear in the input length of the malicious party (perhaps settling for our relaxed notion of simulation).

Our last question deals with simulation security for multiple queries. While our simulation definition for vPIR naturally extends to multiple queries, the proof techniques behind Theorem 4 do not seem to go beyond a single query. In fact we do not know if simulating the answers to multiple queries is possible even for the plain PIR functionality where there are no restrictions on the database used.

2   Technical Overview

In this section we overview our vPIR constructions for local and for global properties.

2.1 vPIR for Local Properties

We describe our construction of vPIR for ℓ-local properties for any constant ℓ in both the designated verifier and the publicly verifiable settings. Our construction proceeds in two steps: first we construct a vPIR scheme for one local properties and then we transform it into a vPIR scheme for properties with constant locality.

Batch Arguments. The main tool we use are batch arguments for the index language [6]. We start from either designated verifier or publicly verifiable batch arguments and get vPIR of the same type. Batch arguments are one message arguments relative to a public key (in the designated verifier setting, the public key is generated together with a secret verification key). In batch arguments for NP the prover and verifier share m NP statements $x_1, \ldots, x_m$ and the prover should convince the verifier that all statements are true. The communication complexity and verification time may grow polynomially with the security parameter and with k, the length of a single witness, but they should be independent of the number of statements m. In batch argument for the index language, the statements $x_1, \ldots, x_m$ are replaced by a single polynomial-time machine M. The prover should convince the verifier that for every $i \in [m]$ there exists a witness $w_i \in \{0,1\}^k$ such that $M(i, w_i)$ accepts.

In the adaptive setting, the prover may choose the statement M as a function of the public key. Batch arguments with full-fledged adaptive soundness are known to imply SNARKs for NP [4]. Therefore, we focus on a weaker notion of adaptive soundness known as somewhere argument of knowledge [6]. The soundness requirement is that for every index $i \in [m]$, we can generate a "programmed" public key for i together with a secret extraction key such that the programmed public key is indistinguishable from an honestly generated key (in particular it hides i). Moreover, given any accepting proof we can use the extraction key to recover a witness w_i such that $M(i, w_i)$ accepts with overwhelming probability.

vPIR for 1-Local Properties. Our vPIR scheme for a 1-local property P is as follows. The client's query for location $q \in [m]$ contains a public key for the batch argument programmed with the index q. The vPIR verification key is the verification key of the batch argument and the vPIR decryption key is the secret extraction key. Given a database D that satisfies P (that is, $P(i, D[i])$ accepts for every $i \in [m]$), the server computes a batch argument proof for the machine P using the witness $D[1], \ldots, D[m]$ and sends it as the vPIR answer. To verify the proof, the client simply verifies the batch argument. To decrypt the answer the client uses the extraction key to recover the witness $D[q]$. The resulting vPIR is non-trivial because the communication complexity of the batch argument does not grow with the database size m. The vPIR query hides the location q since the programmed public key is indistinguishable from an honestly generated key. The security of the vPIR follows directly from the somewhere argument of knowledge property of the batch argument.

In the publicly verifiable setting we can instantiate the construction under LWE or DLIN based on the batch arguments from [6,16]. In the designated verifier setting our starting point is the batch arguments for NP based on PIR from [4]. Their work did not construct batch argument for the index language and security was only proved in the non-adaptive setting. We modify their construction to work for the index language. In a nutshell, to get batch argument for the index language we need to show that the batch NP statement given by a machine M can be described as a 3CNF formula that has a short algebraic representation independent of the number of statements m.

Better Complexity via Composition. We show that the communication complexity and verification time of the a vPIR scheme for 1-local properties can be made sublinear (or even independent) in the running time of the property P by composing it with any SNARG for P. The idea is to add to each database row a SNARG proving that the row satisfies the property P and to prove that the database satisfies the 1-local property P' that each row contains an accepting SNARG. A similar construction was suggested in [6] in the context of batch arguments.

We also show how to transform any publicly verifiable vPIR scheme for 1-local properties with a long query (linear in the database size m]) into a vPIR scheme with sub-linear query length by composing it with itself. The idea follows the standard bootstrapping technique for plain PIR [13]. We divide the database into blocks. We use the vPIR to retrieve one entry from each block and then use the vPIR again to retrieve the PIR answer from one of the blocks. In each invocation of the inner vPIR we prove that each entry in the block satisfies the 1-local property P. In the outer vPIR we prove that the inner vPIR answer of each block satisfies the 1-local property P' that verifies the inner vPIR answer. A similar construction was suggested by [10] in the context of quasi-arguments and by [16] in the context of batch arguments.[5]

vPIR for Properties with Constant Locality. Given a vPIR scheme for 1-local properties we construct a vPIR scheme for ℓ-local properties for any constant ℓ. For simplicity, in this overview we set $\ell = 2$. Our construction requires public parameters that contain a collision-resistant hash key. The server computes a hash tree over the database with root rt. Then, it constructs the database D' with m^2 rows such that row (i,j) contains the pair (r_i, r_j) together with the authentication paths from r_i and from r_j to rt. To query location i of D, the client uses the vPIR scheme for 1-local properties to generate a query q for the location $(i,1)$ in D'. For the security proof to go through, we need to add to q another dummy query q^* for the row $(1,1)$. The server generates the vPIR answer a, a^* for q, q^* using the database D' proving that it satisfies the following 1-local property P'. The property P' has the root rt hard-coded in it and given a location (i,j) and a database row containing a pair (r_i, r_j) and two authentication paths,

---

[5] The construction in [16] composes the batch argument with itself a constant number of times reducing the public key size to m^ϵ for any constant $\epsilon > 0$. We show how to get communication complexity and query generation time that are sub-polynomial in m (under super-polynomial hardness assumptions) by composing the vPIR with itself a super-constant number of times as in [10].

P' checks that the authentication paths are valid with respect to the root rt, and that the 2-local property P accepts the locations (i, j) and rows (r_i, r_j). The server's answer to the query (q, q^*) contains the root rt and the two vPIR answers (a, a^*). To verify the answer (rt, a, a^*), the client verifies both answers a, a^* of the underlying vPIR scheme. To decode the answer, the client decodes the underlying vPIR answer a and retrieves the row r_i. To verify that two answers $(\mathsf{rt}_1, a_1, a_1^*)$ and $(\mathsf{rt}_2, a_2, a_2^*)$ are consistent with the same database we check that $\mathsf{rt}_1 = \mathsf{rt}_2$.

Analysis. Since the queries of the underlying vPIR are hiding, so are the queries of the resulting vPIR. To argue security, consider two sets of queries (q_1, q_1^*) and (q_2, q_2^*) where the queries q_1, q_2 are for locations $(i_1, 1), (i_2, 1)$ respectively, and the dummy queries q_1^*, q_2^* are both for location $(1, 1)$. The adversary, playing the role of the server produces two answers $(\mathsf{rt}_1, a_1, a_1^*)$ and $(\mathsf{rt}_2, a_2, a_2^*)$. We need to show that if the adversary's answers are consistent with each other and each answer passes verification, then the decrypted rows r_{i_1}, r_{i_2} satisfy P. To argue this, we first move to a hybrid experiment where the dummy query q_1^* is for location (i_1, i_2) instead of $(1, 1)$. Since the query q_1^* is generated independently of the queries q_1, q_2, it must remain hiding even given the decryption keys for q_1 and q_2. Moreover, q_1^* is hiding even given the verification keys for all queries. Therefore, it follows that the decrypted rows r_{i_1}, r_{i_2} satisfy P with roughly the same probability in the original security game and in the hybrid experiment. Let $(r_{i_1}^*, r_{i_2}^*)$ be the rows decrypted from the answer a_1^* in the hybrid experiment. If the two answers are consistent with each other then $\mathsf{rt}_1 = \mathsf{rt}_2$. Since each answer passes verification, it follows from the security of the underlying vPIR that the decoded answers a_1, a_2 and a_1^* all satisfy the 1-local property P'. Therefore, it must be that $(r_{i_1}^*, r_{i_2}^*) = (r_{i_1}, r_{i_2})$ or we found a hash collision. Moreover, Since the decoded answer a_1^* satisfies P', the pair $(r_{i_1}^*, r_{i_2}^*)$ satisfies P as required.

2.2   vPIR for Global Properties

Next, we describe our construction of vPIR for any global property decidable by a read-once machine with a bounded length state.

Main Challenge. Before describing our construction, we discuss the main technical challenge in proving simulation security for vPIR. Given an adversary playing the role of the server we need to design a simulator that generates a full database and submits it to the trusted party such that the output of the real and ideal experiments are indistinguishable. If we assume, for simplicity, that the adversary returns an accepting answer with probability 1, then the database submitted by the simulator must always satisfy the global property P. Additionally, for every location i, the distribution of the i-th row in the submitted database must be indistinguishable from the distribution of the adversary's decoded answer given a random query for location i.

In the context of secure computation, the simulator typically extracts the adversary's input (in our case, the database) by using the adversary as a black box. In the case of a vPIR, this approach is problematic: the simulator can execute the adversary with some query, and obtain an answer. However, since the answer is shorter than the database, the simulator cannot possibly extract the entire database from a single answer. It may try to rewind the adversary, execute it with multiple queries and obtain multiple answers. The simulator can extract a small piece of the database from each answer and then try to put these pieces together to create a full database. The problem is that the adversary may use a database that is chosen adaptively, as a function of the query. In particular, the adversary may produce each answer based on a completely different database. In this case, the database reconstructed by the simulator may be different than any database the adversary would ever use and, in particular, it may not satisfy the required property. While we do not know how to extract the "real" database used by the adversary, we show how to carefully put together the extracted pieces and reconstruct some database that makes the output of the real and ideal experiments indistinguishable.

To demonstrate this idea, we start with a warm up: We show that any PIR scheme is also a vPIR scheme for the trivial property that accepts any database. In the real experiment, the client queries the adversary on some location j and decodes the answer r_j. In the ideal experiment, our simulator first queries the adversary on every location $i \in [m]$ and decrypts the answer $\tilde{r}_i$. The simulator puts all the answers together in a single database that contains $\tilde{r}_i$ in location i and submits it to the trusted party. Since the property is always satisfied, the trusted party always outputs $\tilde{r}_j$. The simulation is valid since the outputs r_j and $\tilde{r}_j$ are identically distributed.

We highlight that even in this simple warm up, we are already relying on fact that, following our definition of vPIR security, the output of the real experiment includes only the client's output and not the view of the adversary. In the real experiment, the adversary's view contains a random query q_j for location j and the database it uses (in particular, the row r_j) may depend on q_j. The simulator, however, does not know j and therefore it is not clear how it could simulate a query $\tilde{q}$ such that (q_j, r_j) is indistinguishable from $(\tilde{q}, \tilde{r}_j)$.

Simulation for Non-trivial Properties. The argument above clearly fails for non-trivial properties. Indeed, not every PIR scheme is also a vPIR scheme for non-trivial properties and, therefore, we propose a different construction. The main tool we use to construct vPIR for global properties is a vPIR scheme for 2-local properties. We start from either designated verifier or publicly verifiable vPIR scheme and construct a vPIR of the same type.

Fix a property that can be decided by a polynomial-time read-once Turing machine P with state of length S. We assume that our underlying vPIR for 2-local properties is Λ-secure where $|P|, S \leq \log \Lambda$. To query the database at location i, the client uses the underlying vPIR scheme for 2-local properties to generate two queries: a query q for location i and another dummy query q^* for location 1. Given a database $D = (r_1, \ldots, r_m)$ the server emulates the execution of the global property P on D and obtains all the intermediate states of P as it reads D. Let c_0 be the initial state of P and let c_j be the state after reading the first j rows. Then, the server constructs a new database D' with m rows where the j-th row contains c_{j-1} and r_j. The server generates the vPIR answer a, a^* for q, q^* using the database D' proving that it satisfies the following 2-local property P'. Roughly speaking, the property P' checks that each two rows in D' are consistent with a valid execution of P. In more details, given two locations j, j' and two rows $(c, r), (c', r')$ the property P' checks that:

- If $j = 1$ then c is the initial state c_0 of P.
- If $j = m$ then P with state c accepts after reading the row r.
- If $j = j' + 1$ then P with state c' transitions to state c after reading the row r'.

The server's answer to the query (q, q^*) contains the two vPIR answers (a, a^*). To verify the answer, the client verifies that the answers a, a^* of the underlying vPIR scheme are consistent with each other and that each answer passes verification. To decode the answer, the client decodes the underlying vPIR answer a and retrieves the row r_i.

Analysis. Since the queries of the underlying vPIR are hiding, so are the queries of the resulting vPIR. To argue security we demonstrate a simulator. Our simulation strategy is inspired by the analysis of the SNARGs of [1] for NP languages decidable by a read-once machine with state of bounded length. Translating their techniques to our setting, we can show that if the server's answers are accepting then with overwhelming probability there *exists* a database that satisfies the global property P. The additional challenge facing our simulation is to produce a database that, in addition, has the correct distribution.

We start with a high-level description of our simulation strategy. For simplicity, in this overview we assume that the property P is fixed non-adaptively and that the adversary's answers always pass verification. For every location $i < m$, we define a distribution D_i as follows: we generate a pair of queries (q, q^*) of the underlying vPIR scheme for locations i and $i + 1$ respectively. We send the query (q, q^*) to the prover and get back the answer (a, a^*). If the answer passes verification we decode both a and a^* and obtain the decoded answers $(c_{i-1}, r_i), (c_i, r_{i+1})$. The sample consists of (c_{i-1}, r_i, c_i). For $i = m$ we define D_i similarly, except that we set $c_{m+1} = \bot$.

By the security of the underlying vPIR we have that with overwhelming probability, the decoded answers satisfy the 2-local property P' and, therefore, P with state c_{i-1} transitions to state c_i after reading the row r_i. Thus, we can think of a sample (c_{i-1}, r_i, c_i) from D_i as one step of P. Given a step from D_i and a step from D_{i+1} we say that these steps connect if the value of c_i in both steps is the same. Given one step from each D_i, if each two consecutive steps connect then we can reconstruct a full accepting execution of P on some database. Note that if we sample a step from each D_i independently, these samples may not necessarily connect to a full execution of P. Nonetheless, we show how to sample one step from each D_i *in a correlated way* such that the steps connect to each other with high probability, without changing the marginal distribution of each individual step.

In more detail, using the fact that the vPIR queries hide the locations, we show that the marginal distributions of c_i in D_i and in D_{i+1} are close. Therefore, we can *couple* together the distributions $D_1, \ldots, D_m$ and get a joint distribution D over all m steps such that the marginals of D are exactly the distributions $D_1, \ldots, D_m$, and where steps i and $i+1$ connect with high probability for every i. It follows that a sample from D contains, with high probability, a full accepting execution of P on some database $(r_1, \ldots, r_m)$. Since the marginal distribution of the i-th step is exactly D_i it follows that r_i is indistinguishable from output of the client in the real experiment with location i. While it may be hard to sample from D, we show how to sample from a distribution $\tilde{D}$ that is close to it in time $\mathrm{poly}(\Lambda)$. Our simulator samples from $\tilde{D}$, extracts the database $(r_1, \ldots, r_m)$ and submits it to the trusted party.

We proceed to describe the security proof in more detail. For every $i \in [m]$, let (C'_{i-1}, R_i, C_i) denote a random sample from D_i. By the security of the underlying vPIR, we have that except with probability $\Lambda^{-\omega(1)}$:

- C'_0 is the initial state of P.
- P with state C'_{m-1} accepts after reading the row R_m .
- P with state C'_{i-1} transitions to state C_i after reading the row R_i.

We argue that C_i and C'_i are Λ-indistinguishable. In fact, since the length of the state is at most $\log \Lambda$, C_i and C'_i are also $\Lambda^{-\omega(1)}$-close in statistical distance. We argue this in a sequence of hybrid experiments where in each hybrid we change the way the queries q, q^* are generated and the way we decode the state c_i from the answers a, a^*:

- In the first hybrid, (q, q^*) are for locations $(i, i+1)$ respectively, and we decode c_i from a^*. We have that c_i is distributed exactly like C_i.
- In the second hybrid, (q, q^*) are for locations $(i + 1, i + 1)$ respectively, and we decode c_i from a^*. Since the underlying vPIR is Λ-hiding, we have that c_i is Λ-indistinguishable from the previous hybrid.
- In the third hybrid, (q, q^*) are for locations $(i + 1, i + 1)$ respectively, and we decode c_i from a. By the security of the underlying vPIR, since we check that a and a^* are consistent we have that c_i is Λ-indistinguishable from the previous hybrid.
- In the forth hybrid, (q, q^*) are for locations $(i + 1, i + 2)$ respectively, and we decode c_i from a. Since the underlying vPIR is Λ-hiding, we have that c_i is Λ-indistinguishable from the previous hybrid and it is distributed exactly like C'_i.

The simulator works as follows: For every i the simulator first obtains L independent samples from D_i for some sufficiently large L. Let $\tilde{D}_i$ be the empirical distribution that picks one of these L samples at random and let $(\tilde{C}'_{i-1}, \tilde{R}_i, \tilde{C}_i)$ denote a random sample from $\tilde{D}_i$. Let $\epsilon = \Lambda^{-O(1)}$ be the required simulation accuracy and let $\epsilon' = \epsilon/m^2$. Since the length of the states is bounded by $\log \Lambda$, by setting $L = \mathrm{poly}(\Lambda, 1/\epsilon)$ we can guarantee that (C'_{i-1}, C_i) and $(\tilde{C}'_{i-1}, \tilde{C}_i)$ are ϵ'-close, except with probability at most $\mathrm{negl}(\Lambda)$ (over the L samples from D_i). Since we have that C_i and C'_i are $\Lambda^{-\omega(1)}$-close, it follows that

$\tilde{C}_i$ and $\tilde{C}'_i$ must be $O(\epsilon')$-close. Therefore, there exists a joint distribution $\tilde{D}$ over $\tilde{D}_1 \times \cdots \times \tilde{D}_m$ whose marginals are just $\tilde{D}_1, \ldots, \tilde{D}_m$ such that for every i, a sample $(\tilde{C}'_{i-1}, \tilde{R}_i, \tilde{C}_i)_{i \in [m]}$ from $\tilde{D}$ satisfies $\tilde{C}_i = \tilde{C}'_i$ with probability at least $1 - O(\epsilon')$. By the union bound, we have that the database $(\tilde{R}_1, \ldots, \tilde{R}_m)$ satisfies P with probability at least $1 - O(m \cdot \epsilon')$. Moreover, since each distribution $\tilde{D}_i$ is just uniform over a list of length $L = \text{poly}(\Lambda)$, we can also samples from $\tilde{D}$ in time $\text{poly}(\Lambda)$. Finally, the simulator samples $(\tilde{C}'_{i-1}, \tilde{R}_i, \tilde{C}_i)_{i \in [m]}$ from $\tilde{D}$ and submits the database $(\tilde{R}_1, \ldots, \tilde{R}_m)$ to the trusted party.

It remains to show that for any location j, the output of the real and ideal experiments are indistinguishable. In the real experiment, the queries (q, q^*) are for locations $(j, 1)$ respectively. The client obtains the answers (a, a^*), decodes (c_{j-1}, r_j) from a and outputs r_j. Since the underlying vPIR is Λ-hiding, r_j is Λ-indistinguishable from R_j.

In the ideal experiment the simulator submits to the trusted party the database $(\tilde{R}_1, \ldots, \tilde{R}_m)$ where $\tilde{R}_j$ is distributed like $\tilde{D}_j$. Since each sample from $\tilde{D}_j$ is itself distributed like D_j we have that $\tilde{R}_j$ and R_j are identically distributed. The output of the ideal experiment is either $\tilde{R}_j$ or $\perp$ in case the database $(\tilde{R}_1, \ldots, \tilde{R}_m)$ does not satisfy P. Since this happens with probability at most $O(m \cdot \epsilon') \leq \epsilon/2$ it follows that any $\text{poly}(\Lambda)$-size distinguish has advantage at most ϵ in distinguishing the output of the real and ideal experiment.

3   Preliminaries

Parts of this section are taken verbatim from [10] and [6].

Vectors. For a set U, vector $\mathbf{v} = (v_1, \ldots, v_n) \in U^n$ and index $t \in [n]$ let $\mathbf{v}_t$ denote the element v_t. For a vector of indexes $\mathbf{t} \in [n]^\ell$ denote $\mathbf{v}[\mathbf{t}]$ be the vector $(\mathbf{v}_{t_1}, \ldots, \mathbf{v}_{t_\ell})$.

The Universal Language. Let $\mathcal{L}_U$ be the language of all triplets (Γ, x, y, T) such that Γ is a description of a Turing machine that on input x outputs y in T steps. We write $(\Gamma, x, T) \in \mathcal{L}_U$ as a shorthand for $(\Gamma, x, 1, T) \in \mathcal{L}_U$, i.e., Γ accepts x in T steps.

3.1   Private Information Retrieval

In this section we define private information retrieval (PIR) schemes.

A private information retrieval scheme consists of the algorithms:

$$(\mathsf{PIR.Q}, \mathsf{PIR.A}, \mathsf{PIR.D}),$$

with the following syntax:

Query: The randomized query algorithm $\mathsf{PIR.Q}$ takes as input the security parameter κ, the number of database rows m, the row size w, and an index $t \in [m]$. It outputs a decryption key dk and a query q.

Answer: The deterministic answer algorithm PIR.A takes as input a database $D \in \{0,1\}^{m \times w}$ and a query q. It outputs an answer a.

Decryption: The deterministic decryption algorithm PIR.D takes as input the decryption key dk and an answer a. It outputs a row $r \in \{0,1\}^w$.

Definition 1. *A Λ-secure poly-logarithmic private information retrieval scheme satisfies the following requirements:*

Completeness. *For every $\kappa \in \mathbb{N}$, $m, w \leq 2^\kappa$, database $D \in \{0,1\}^{m \times w}$, and query $t \in [m]$:*

$$\Pr\left[\mathsf{PIR.D}(\mathsf{dk}, a) = D[t] \;\middle|\; \begin{array}{l} (\mathsf{dk}, q) \leftarrow \mathsf{PIR.Q}(\kappa, m, w, t) \\ a \leftarrow \mathsf{PIR.A}(D, q) \end{array} \right] = 1.$$

Efficiency. *In the completeness experiment above:*
- *The query algorithm runs in time $\mathrm{poly}(\kappa)$.*
- *The answer algorithm runs in time $\mathrm{poly}(\kappa, m, w)$.*
- *The decryption algorithm runs in time $w \cdot \mathrm{poly}(\kappa, \log(m))$.*

Λ-Privacy. *For every $\mathrm{poly}(\Lambda)$-size adversary Adv and functions $m, w \leq \Lambda$ there exist a negligible function μ such that for every $\kappa \in \mathbb{N}$ and $t_0, t_1 \in [m]$:*

$$\Pr\left[b' = b \;\middle|\; \begin{array}{l} b \leftarrow \{0,1\} \\ (\mathsf{dk}_0, q_0) = \mathsf{PIR.Q}(\kappa, m, w, t_0) \\ (\mathsf{dk}_1, q_1) = \mathsf{PIR.Q}(\kappa, m, w, t_1) \\ b' \leftarrow \mathsf{Adv}(\mathsf{pp}, q_b) \end{array} \right] \leq \frac{1}{2} + \mu(\Lambda(\kappa)).$$

3.2 Batch Arguments

In this section we define non-interactive batch arguments for the index language. The definition is adapted from [6] (see discussion following Definition 2). In a batch argument for the index language, the statement is given by a Turing machine M and the number of instances m. The prover convinces the verifier that for every $i \in [m]$ there exists a witness w_i such that $M(i, w_i)$ accepts. We fix the parameter m as well as the running time, description size, and witness length of M in setup time.

A non-interactive batch argument for the index language consist of algorithms:

$$(\mathsf{BA.S}, \mathsf{BA.T}, \mathsf{BA.P}, \mathsf{BA.V}, \mathsf{BA.E}),$$

with the following syntax:

Setup: The randomized setup algorithm BA.S takes as input the security parameter κ, the running time T and size N of a Turing machine, the number of instances m, and the witness length l. It outputs a prover key pk, and a verifier key vk.

Trapdoor Setup: The randomized trapdoor setup algorithm BA.T takes as input the security parameter κ, the running time T and size N of a Turing machine, the number of instances m, the witness length l and an index $i \in [m]$. It outputs prover key pk, verifier key vk, and a decryption key dk.

Prover: The deterministic prover algorithm BA.P takes as input the prover key pk, a Turing machine M and witnesses $w_1, \ldots, w_m \in \{0,1\}^l$. It outputs a proof Π.

Verifier: The deterministic verifier algorithm BA.V takes as input the verifier key vk, a Turing machine M, and a proof Π. It outputs an acceptance bit.

Extractor: The deterministic extraction algorithm BA.E takes as input the decryption key dk and a proof Π. It outputs a witness $w \in \{0,1\}^l$.

Definition 2. *A Λ-secure non-interactive batch argument for the index language satisfies the following requirements:*

Completeness. *For every functions $m, l, T, N \leq 2^\kappa$ there exists a negligible function μ such that for every $\kappa \in \mathbb{N}$, witnesses $w_1, \ldots, w_m \in \{0,1\}^l$, index $t \in [m]$, and Turing machine $M \in \{0,1\}^N$ such that $\forall i \in [m]$: $(M, (i, w_i), T) \in \mathcal{L}_U$:*

$$
\Pr \left[\begin{array}{c} \text{BA.E}(\text{dk}, \Pi) = w_t \\ \text{BA.V}(\text{vk}, M, \Pi) = 1 \end{array} \,\middle|\, \begin{array}{l} (\text{pk}, \text{vk}, \text{dk}) \leftarrow \text{BA.T}(\kappa, T, N, m, l, t) \\ \Pi \leftarrow \text{BA.P}(\text{pk}, M, (w_1, \ldots, w_m)) \end{array} \right] = 1.
$$

Efficiency. *In the completeness experiment above:*

- *The prover algorithm runs in time $\text{poly}(\kappa, T, N, m, l)$.*
- *The extraction algorithm runs in polynomial time in its input length.*
- *The verifier and decryption keys are of size $\text{poly}(\kappa, l)$.*

We define the following efficiency measures of the scheme:

- *Let $T_\text{S}(\kappa, T, N, m, l)$ be the running time of the setup and trapdoor setup algorithms.*
- *Let $T_\text{V}(\kappa, T, N, m, l)$ be the running time of the verification algorithm.*
- *Let $L_\text{pk}(\kappa, T, N, m, l)$ be the size of the prover key.*
- *Let $L_\Pi(\kappa, T, N, m, l)$ be the size of the proof.*

Λ-Key Indistinguishability. *For every $\text{poly}(\Lambda(\kappa))$-size adversary Adv and functions $T, N, m, l \leq \Lambda$ there exists a negligible function μ such that for every $\kappa \in \mathbb{N}$ and index $i \in [m]$:*

$$
\left| \begin{array}{l} \Pr\left[\text{Adv}(\text{pk}, \text{vk}) = 1 \mid (\text{pk}, \text{vk}) \leftarrow \text{BA.S}(\kappa, T, N, m, l)\right] \\ - \Pr\left[\text{Adv}(\text{pk}, \text{vk}) = 1 \mid (\text{pk}, \text{vk}, \text{dk}) \leftarrow \text{BA.T}(\kappa, T, N, m, l, i)\right] \end{array} \right| \leq \mu(\Lambda(\kappa)).
$$

Λ-Somewhere Argument of Knowledge. *For every $\text{poly}(\Lambda(\kappa))$-size adversary Adv and functions $T, N, m, l \leq \Lambda$ there exists a negligible function μ such that for every $\kappa \in \mathbb{N}$ and index $i \in [m]$:*

$$
\Pr \left[\begin{array}{c} \text{BA.V}(\text{vk}, M, \Pi) = 1 \\ (M, (i, w), T) \notin \mathcal{L}_U \end{array} \,\middle|\, \begin{array}{l} (\text{pk}, \text{vk}, \text{dk}) \leftarrow \text{BA.T}(\kappa, T, N, m, l, i) \\ (M, \Pi) \leftarrow \text{Adv}(\text{pk}) \\ w \leftarrow \text{BA.E}(\text{dk}, \Pi) \end{array} \right] \leq \mu(\Lambda(\kappa)).
$$

If the somewhere argument of knowledge holds even when Adv is given the verifier key vk then we say that the batch argument is publicly verifiable.

We discuss some differences between Definition 2 and the definition in [6]:

- Our completeness requirement is stronger than the one in [6]. In addition to the verifier accepting, we also require that the extraction algorithm outputs the same witness used to generate the proof.
- The work of [6] only defines publicly verifiable batch arguments while we also consider a designated verifier version. We emphasize that in both the publicly verifiable and the designated verifier setting, key indistinguishability is required to hold even given the verification key.

We construct batch arguments for the index language based on PIR. This extends the result of [4] that obtain the weaker notion of batch arguments for NP (and not for the index language).

Theorem 5 (Batch Argument from PIR). *If there exists a Λ-secure polylogarithmic PIR, then there exists a Λ-secure non-interactive batch argument for the index language with the following efficiency:*

$$T_S = l \cdot \text{poly}(\kappa, N)$$
$$T_V = (N + l) \cdot \text{poly}(\kappa)$$
$$L_{pk} = (N + l) \cdot \text{poly}(\kappa)$$
$$L_\Pi = (N + l) \cdot \text{poly}(\kappa)$$

The proof of this theorem appears in the full version of this work.

Theorem 6 (Publicly Verifiable Batch Argument from LWE [6]). *If the Learning with Errors problem is Λ-hard, then there exists a Λ-secure publicly verifiable non-interactive batch argument for the index language with the following efficiency:*

$$T_S = \text{poly}(\kappa, l)$$
$$T_V = N \cdot \text{poly}(\kappa, l)$$
$$L_{pk} = \text{poly}(\kappa, l)$$
$$L_\Pi = \text{poly}(\kappa, l)$$

Theorem 7 (Publicly Verifiable Batch Argument from Paring [16]). *If Λ-hardness of the k-Lin assumption (for any $k > 1$) holds in a prime-order pairing group, then for every $\epsilon > 0$ there exists a Λ-secure publicly verifiable non-interactive batch argument for the index language with the following efficiency:*

$$T_S = \text{poly}(\kappa, m)$$
$$T_V = \text{poly}(\kappa, T, N, l)$$
$$L_{pk} = m^\epsilon \cdot \text{poly}(\kappa)$$
$$L_\Pi = \text{poly}(\kappa, T, N, l)$$

We remark that the notion of batch arguments defined and constructed in [16] is slightly different than the notion in Definition 2. We explain how to modify the [16] construction to obtain our notion:

- In [16], the prover and verifier are given a circuit implementing the NP verification procedure, while in our notion, the NP verification procedure is given by a Turing machine. As discussed in [6, Sect. 6], the construction of [16] can be modified to work with a Turing machine verification by composing it with a RAM delegation scheme such as the one constructed in [16] under the k-Lin assumption.
- The construction in [16] has a negligible completeness error. The extraction algorithm may fail to extract the witness with negligible probability over the choice of the public key. However, if we slightly modify the trapdoor setup algorithm to only sample "good" public keys that do not lead to extraction failure we get a construction with perfect completeness.

4 Verifiable PIR

In this section we define the notion of verifiable PIR. We consider two security definition: simulation security and a game-based definition that we call local security.

Let κ be the security parameter. In what follows we consider a database with $m(\kappa)$ rows, where each row is a bit string of length $w(\kappa)$. Let $\mathcal{U} = \mathcal{U}_\kappa$ be a set of constraint-checking Turing machines. Each $U \in \mathcal{U}$ takes as input a constraint description Γ and a database D and outputs 1 if and only if D satisfies the constraint Γ.

A verifiable PIR (vPIR) scheme for $\mathcal{U}$ is given by algorithms:

$$(\mathsf{vPIR.S}, \mathsf{vPIR.Q}, \mathsf{vPIR.A}, \mathsf{vPIR.D}, \mathsf{vPIR.V}),$$

with the following syntax:

Setup: The randomized setup algorithm vPIR.S takes as input a security parameter κ. It outputs public parameters pp. If pp are always empty we say that the protocol has no setup.

Query: The randomized query algorithm vPIR.Q takes as input the security parameter κ, the public parameters pp, a machine $U \in \mathcal{U}$, database dimensions m and w, and an index $t \in [m]$. It outputs a decryption key dk, a verifier key vk, and a query q.

Answer: The deterministic answer algorithm vPIR.A takes as input the public parameters pp, a database $D \in \{0,1\}^{m \times w}$, a constraint Γ, and a query q. It outputs an answer a.

Decryption: The deterministic decryption algorithm vPIR.D takes as input the decryption key dk and an answer a. It outputs a row $r \in \{0,1\}^w$.

Verification: The deterministic verification algorithm vPIR.V takes as input a constraint Γ, a verifier key vk and an answer a. It outputs a bit indicating if it accepts or rejects.

Multiple Queries. We also define a version of the verification algorithm vPIR.V for multiple answers. In this setting we allow multiple users to jointly verify the answers to all their queries without sharing their verification keys. To this end, each user invokes the verification algorithm with all the answers but only its own verification key. The verification algorithm is also given the index of the answer that matches the input verification key.

Verification (multiple queries): The deterministic verification algorithm vPIR.V takes as input a constraint Γ, a verifier key vk, a vector **a** of d answers and an index $i \in [d]$. It outputs a bit indicating if it accepts or rejects.

We also use the following shorthand for working with $d > 1$ queries:

- vPIR.VQ$(\kappa, \mathsf{pp}, U, m, w, \mathbf{t})$ stands for $(\mathbf{dk}, \mathbf{vk}, \mathbf{q})$ such that $\forall i \in [d] :$ $(\mathbf{dk}_i, \mathbf{vk}_i, \mathbf{q}_i) = \mathsf{vPIR.Q}(\kappa, \mathsf{pp}, U, m, w, \mathbf{t}_i)$.
- vPIR.VA$(\mathsf{pp}, \Gamma, D, \mathbf{q})$ stands for **a** such that $\forall i \in [d] :$ $\mathbf{a}_i = \mathsf{vPIR.A}(\mathsf{pp}, \Gamma, D, \mathbf{q}_i)$.
- vPIR.VD$(\mathbf{dk}, \mathbf{a})$ stands for **r** such that $\forall i \in [d] : \mathbf{r}_i = \mathsf{vPIR.D}(\mathbf{dk}_i, \mathbf{a}_i)$.
- vPIR.VV$(\Gamma, \mathbf{vk}, \mathbf{a})$ stands for $\bigwedge_{i \in [d]} \mathsf{vPIR.V}(\Gamma, \mathbf{vk}_i, \mathbf{a}, i)$.

Next we define the properties required by a vPIR scheme. In Definition 3 we give the completeness, efficiency and privacy properties. We consider two different definitions for security against malicious server: a simulation based definition with a single query (Definition 4) and a game based definition for multiple queries (Definition 5).

Definition 3. *Let $\mathcal{U}$ be a set of Turing machines. A vPIR scheme for $\mathcal{U}$ satisfies the following requirements:*

Completeness. *For every $m, w, d \leq 2^\kappa$ there exists a negligible function μ such that for every $\kappa \in \mathbb{N}$, machine $U \in \mathcal{U}$, database $D \in \{0,1\}^{m \times w}$, vector of queries $\mathbf{t} \in [m]^d$, and constraint Γ such that $U(\Gamma, D) = 1$:*

$$\Pr\left[\begin{array}{c|c} \mathsf{vPIR.VD}(\mathbf{dk}, \mathbf{a}) = D[\mathbf{t}] & \mathsf{pp} \leftarrow \mathsf{vPIR.S}(\kappa) \\ \mathsf{vPIR.VV}(\Gamma, \mathbf{vk}, \mathbf{a}) = 1 & (\mathbf{dk}, \mathbf{vk}, \mathbf{q}) \leftarrow \mathsf{vPIR.VQ}(\kappa, \mathsf{pp}, U, m, w, \mathbf{t}) \\ & \mathbf{a} \leftarrow \mathsf{vPIR.VA}(\mathsf{pp}, \Gamma, D, \mathbf{q}) \end{array}\right]$$
$$= 1.$$

Efficiency. *In the completeness experiment above:*
- *The setup algorithm runs in time $\mathrm{poly}(\kappa)$.*
- *The decryption algorithm runs in polynomial time in its input length.*
- *The answer algorithm runs time $\mathrm{poly}(\kappa, m, w, T)$ where T is the running time of $U(\Gamma, D)$.*

We define the following efficiency measures of the scheme:
- *Let $T_Q(\kappa, U, m, w)$ be the running time of the query algorithm.*
- *Let $T_V(\kappa, U, m, w)$ be the running time of the verification algorithm.*
- *Let $L_q(\kappa, U, m, w)$ be the size of the query.*
- *Let $L_{\mathsf{dk}}(\kappa, U, m, w)$ be the size of the decryption key.*

– Let $L_{\mathsf{vk}}(\kappa, U, m, w)$ be the size of the verifier key.
– Let $L_a(\kappa, U, m, w)$ be the size of the answer.

Λ-**Privacy.** For every $\mathrm{poly}(\Lambda)$-size adversary Adv and functions $m, w \leq \Lambda$ there exists a negligible function μ such that for every $\kappa \in \mathbb{N}$, machine $U \in \mathcal{U}$, and $t_1, t_2 \in [m]$:

$$\Pr\left[i' = i \left| \begin{array}{l} i \leftarrow [2] \\ \mathsf{pp} \leftarrow \mathsf{vPIR.S}(\kappa) \\ (\mathbf{dk}, \mathbf{vk}, \mathbf{q}) = \mathsf{vPIR.VQ}(\kappa, \mathsf{pp}, U, m, w, (t_1, t_2)) \\ i' \leftarrow \mathsf{Adv}(\mathsf{pp}, \mathbf{vk}_i, \mathbf{q}_i) \end{array} \right. \right] \leq \frac{1}{2} + \mu(\Lambda(\kappa)).$$

4.1   Simulation Security

We give a simulation based security definition for vPIR. In this work we only consider simulation security for a single query. However, the definition can be extended to multiple queries.

Definition 4 (vPIR Security). *Let $\mathcal{U}$ be a set of Turing machines, let $U = \{U_\kappa \in \mathcal{U}\}_{\kappa \in \mathbb{N}}$ and let $\Lambda(\kappa), m(\kappa), w(\kappa)$ be functions. A vPIR scheme for $\mathcal{U}$ satisfying Definition 3 is Λ-secure with respect to (U, m, w) if for every $\mathrm{poly}(\Lambda)$-size adversary Adv, and polynomial P there exists a $\mathrm{poly}(\Lambda)$-size simulator Sim such that for every $\mathrm{poly}(\Lambda)$-size distinguisher D, $\kappa \in \mathbb{N}$, and $t \in [m]$:*

$$|\Pr[\mathsf{D}(\mathrm{Real}_{\mathsf{Adv}}(\kappa, t) = 1] - \Pr[\mathsf{D}(\mathrm{Ideal}_{\mathsf{Sim}}(\kappa, t)) = 1]| \leq \frac{1}{P(\Lambda(\kappa))}.$$

where the experiments $\mathrm{Real}_{\mathsf{Adv}}(\kappa, t)$ and $\mathrm{Ideal}_{\mathsf{Sim}}(\kappa, t)$ are defined as follows:

$\mathrm{Real}_{\mathsf{Adv}}(\kappa, t)$:
  – *Sample parameters $\mathsf{pp} \leftarrow \mathsf{vPIR.S}(\kappa)$.*
  – *Generate a query $(\mathsf{dk}, \mathsf{vk}, q) \leftarrow \mathsf{vPIR.Q}(\kappa, \mathsf{pp}, U_\kappa, m, w, t)$.*
  – *Run the adversary and obtain $(\Gamma, a) \leftarrow \mathsf{Adv}(\mathsf{pp}, q)$.*
  – *If $\mathsf{vPIR.V}(\Gamma, \mathsf{vk}, a) = 0$ output $(\Gamma, \bot)$. Otherwise output $(\Gamma, \mathsf{vPIR.D}(\mathsf{dk}, a))$.*

$\mathrm{Ideal}_{\mathsf{Sim}}(\kappa, t)$:
  – *Run the simulator and obtain $(\Gamma, D) \leftarrow \mathsf{Sim}(\kappa)$.*
  – *If $D = \bot$ or $U_\kappa(\Gamma, D) = 0$ output $(\Gamma, \bot)$. Otherwise output $(\Gamma, D[t])$.*

If the above holds even when Adv is given the verifier key vk then we say that the vPIR is publicly verifiable.

4.2   Local Security

In the multi-query setting, we introduce the notion of ℓ-local vPIR that satisfies a game-based security definition. In local vPIR, instead of verifying a global constraint on the database, we verify that each set of ℓ database rows satisfy some local constraint. In more detail, we say that the a set of constraint-checking Turing machines $\mathcal{U}$ is ℓ-local if for every $U \in \mathcal{U}$ there exists a machine denoted by $\tilde{U}$, such that $U(\Gamma, D) = 1$ if and only if $\tilde{U}(\Gamma, (\mathbf{t}, D[\mathbf{t}])) = 1$ for every $\mathbf{t} \in [m]^\ell$.

Definition 5 (ℓ-local vPIR security). *Let $\mathcal{U}$ be an ℓ-local set of Turing machines. Let $U = \{U_\kappa \in \mathcal{U}\}_{\kappa \in \mathbb{N}}$ and let $\Lambda(\kappa), m(\kappa), w(\kappa)$ be functions. An ℓ-local vPIR scheme for $\mathcal{U}$ satisfying Definition 3 is Λ-secure for (U, m, w) if for every $\mathrm{poly}(\Lambda)$-size adversary Adv there exist a negligible function μ such that for every $\kappa \in \mathbb{N}$ and for every $\mathbf{t} \in [m]^\ell$:*

$$\Pr\left[\begin{array}{l|l} \mathsf{vPIR.VV}(\Gamma, \mathbf{vk}, \mathbf{a}) = 1 & \mathsf{pp} \leftarrow \mathsf{vPIR.S}(\kappa) \\ \tilde{U}_\kappa(\Gamma, (\mathbf{t}, \mathbf{r})) = 0 & (\mathbf{dk}, \mathbf{vk}, \mathbf{q}) \leftarrow \mathsf{vPIR.VQ}(\kappa, \mathsf{pp}, U_\kappa, m, w, \mathbf{t}) \\ & (\Gamma, \mathbf{a}) \leftarrow \mathsf{Adv}(\mathsf{pp}, \mathbf{q}) \\ & \mathbf{r} \leftarrow \mathsf{vPIR.VD}(\mathbf{dk}, \mathbf{a}) \end{array}\right]$$
$$\leq \mu(\Lambda(\kappa)).$$

If the above holds even when Adv is given the verifier keys $\mathbf{vk}$ then we say that the vPIR is publicly verifiable.

In what follows we consider the set $\mathcal{U}_\kappa^\ell = \{U_{T,N}\}_{T,N \leq 2^\kappa}$ where $\tilde{U}_{T,N}(\Gamma, (\mathbf{t}, D[\mathbf{t}])) = 1$ if and only if Γ is a description of a Turing machine of length N and $(\Gamma, (\mathbf{t}, D[\mathbf{t}]), T) \in \mathcal{L}_U$ for every $\mathbf{t} \in [m]^\ell$. We say that an ℓ-local vPIR for $\mathcal{U}^\ell$ is Λ-secure if for every functions $T, N, m, w \leq \Lambda$ the vPIR is Λ-secure and Λ-private for $(U_{T,N}, m, w)$.

5   From Batch Arguments to 1-Local vPIR

In this section we give a construction of a publicly verifiable 1-local vPIR from batch arguments.

Theorem 8. *If there exists a Λ-secure non-interactive batch argument for the index language with efficiency $(T_\mathsf{S}^\mathsf{BA}, T_\mathsf{V}^\mathsf{BA}, L_\mathsf{pk}^\mathsf{BA}, L_\Pi^\mathsf{BA})$ then there exists a Λ-secure 1-local vPIR for $\mathcal{U}^1$ with no setup and with the following efficiency:*

$$T_\mathsf{Q}(\kappa, U_{T,N}, m, w) = T_\mathsf{S}^\mathsf{BA}(\kappa, T, N, m, w)$$
$$T_\mathsf{V}(\kappa, U_{T,N}, m, w) = T_\mathsf{V}^\mathsf{BA}(\kappa, T, N, m, w)$$
$$L_q(\kappa, U_{T,N}, m, w) = L_\mathsf{pk}^\mathsf{BA}(\kappa, T, N, m, w)$$
$$L_\mathsf{dk}(\kappa, U_{T,N}, m, w) = \mathrm{poly}(\kappa, w)$$
$$L_\mathsf{vk}(\kappa, U_{T,N}, m, w) = \mathrm{poly}(\kappa, w)$$
$$L_a(\kappa, U_{T,N}, m, w) = L_\Pi^\mathsf{BA}(\kappa, T, N, m, w)$$

Moreover, if the non-interactive batch argument is publicly verifiable then the 1-local vPIR is publicly verifiable.

In the full version of this work we show how to transform a publicly verifiable 1-local vPIR into one with shorter query. Combined with Theorems 7 and 8 we get the following theorem.

Theorem 9. *If Λ-hardness of the k-Lin assumption (for any $k > 1$) holds in a prime-order pairing group, then for every $\epsilon > 0$ there exists a Λ-secure 1-local publicly verifiable vPIR for $\mathcal{U}^1$ with no setup and with the following efficiency:*

$$T_Q(\kappa, U_{T,N}, m, w) = \text{poly}(T, N, w) \cdot 2^{\sqrt{O(\log \kappa \log m)}}$$

$$T_V(\kappa, U_{T,N}, m, w) = \text{poly}(N, w) \cdot 2^{\sqrt{O(\log \kappa \log m)}}$$

$$L_q(\kappa, U_{T,N}, m, w) = (\text{poly}(N, w) + T^\epsilon) \cdot 2^{\sqrt{O(\log \kappa \log m)}}$$

$$L_{dk}(\kappa, U_{T,N}, m, w) = \text{poly}(N, w) \cdot 2^{\sqrt{O(\log \kappa \log m)}}$$

$$L_{vk}(\kappa, U_{T,N}, m, w) = \text{poly}(N, w) \cdot 2^{\sqrt{O(\log \kappa \log m)}}$$

$$L_a(\kappa, U_{T,N}, m, w) = \text{poly}(N, w) \cdot 2^{\sqrt{O(\log \kappa \log m)}}$$

The proof of Theorems 8 and Theorem 9 appears in the full version of this work.

6 From 1-Local vPIR to vPIR with Constant Locality

In this section we transform a 1-local vPIR into an ℓ-local vPIR for any constant ℓ.

Theorem 10. *If there exists a Λ-secure family of collision resistant hash functions and a Λ-secure 1-local vPIR for $\mathcal{U}^1$ with efficiency $(T'_Q, T'_V, L'_q, L'_{dk}, L'_{vk}, L'_a)$, then for every $\ell \in \mathbb{N}$ there exists a Λ-secure ℓ-local vPIR for $\mathcal{U}^\ell$ with the following efficiency:*

$$T_Q(\kappa, U_{T,N}, m, w) = 2 \cdot T'_Q(\kappa, U_{T',N'}, m', w') + \text{poly}(\kappa)$$
$$T_V(\kappa, U_{T,N}, m, w) = 2 \cdot T'_V(\kappa, U_{T',N'}, m', w') + w \cdot \text{poly}(\kappa)$$
$$L_q(\kappa, U_{T,N}, m, w) = 2 \cdot L'_q(\kappa, U_{T',N'}, m', w')$$
$$L_{dk}(\kappa, U_{T,N}, m, w) = L'_{dk}(\kappa, U_{T',N'}, m', w')$$
$$L_{vk}(\kappa, U_{T,N}, m, w) = 2 \cdot L'_{vk}(\kappa, U_{T',N'}, m', w') + \text{poly}(\kappa)$$
$$L_a(\kappa, U_{T,N}, m, w) = 2 \cdot L'_a(\kappa, U_{T',N'}, m', w') + w \cdot \text{poly}(\kappa)$$

where:

$$T' = T + \ell \cdot w \cdot \text{poly}(\kappa), \ N' = N + w \cdot \text{poly}(\kappa), \ m' = m^\ell, \ w' = \ell \cdot w \cdot \text{poly}(\kappa).$$

Moreover, if the 1-local vPIR is publicly verifiable then the ℓ-local vPIR is publicly verifiable.

The proof of this theorem appears in the full version of this work.

7   From Local vPIR to Simulation Secure vPIR

In this section we give a vPIR scheme for the set $\mathcal{U}$ of global constraints that read the database once and maintain a bounded size state between rows. In more detail, let $\mathcal{U}_\kappa = \{U_{T,N,S}\}_{T,N,S<2^\kappa}$ where $U_{T,N,S}(\Gamma, D = (r_i)_{i \in [m]}) = 1$ if and only if Γ is a description of a Turing machine of length N and for every $i \in [m]$ there exists $c_i \in \{0,1\}^S$ such that $(\Gamma, (c_{i-1}, r_i), c_i, T) \in \mathcal{L}_U$ where c_0 and c_m are some fixed starting and accepting configuration, respectively.

Theorem 11. *If there exists a Λ-secure 2-local vPIR for $\mathcal{U}^2$ with efficiency $(T'_Q, T'_V, L'_q, L'_{vk}, L'_{dk}, L'_a)$, then for every $N, S = O(\log \Lambda)$ and $m, w, T \leq \Lambda$ there exists a vPIR scheme for $\mathcal{U}$ that is Λ-secure and Λ-private with respect to $(U_{T,N,S}, m, w)$ with the following efficiency:*

$$T_Q(\kappa, U_{T,N,S}, m, w) = 2 \cdot T'_Q(\kappa, U_{N',T'}, m, w')$$
$$T_V(\kappa, U_{T,N,S}, m, w) = 2 \cdot T'_V(\kappa, U_{N',T'}, m, w')$$
$$L_q(\kappa, U_{T,N,S}, m, w) = 2 \cdot L'_q(\kappa, U_{N',T'}, m, w')$$
$$L_{dk}(\kappa, U_{T,N,S}, m, w) = L'_{dk}(\kappa, U_{N',T'}, m, w')$$
$$L_{vk}(\kappa, U_{T,N,S}, m, w) = 2 \cdot L'_{vk}(\kappa, U_{N',T'}, m, w')$$
$$L_a(\kappa, U_{T,N,S}, m, w) = 2 \cdot L'_a(\kappa, U_{N',T'}, m, w')$$

where:

$$N' = N + O(1), \quad T' = T + O(\log(m) + S + w), \quad w' = S + w.$$

Moreover, if the 2-local vPIR is publicly verifiable then the vPIR is publicly verifiable.

The proof of this theorem appears in the full version of this work.

The following is corollary of Theorems 5, 8, 10 and 11.

Corollary 1. *If there exists a Λ-secure PIR, then for every $N, S = O(\log \Lambda)$ and $m, w, T \leq \Lambda$ there exists a vPIR for $\mathcal{U}$ that is Λ-secure and Λ-private and Λ-private with respect to $(U_{T,N,S}, m, w)$ with the following efficiency:*

$$T_Q(\kappa, U_{T,N,S}, m, w) = \mathrm{poly}(\kappa, w)$$
$$T_V(\kappa, U_{T,N,S}, m, w) = w \cdot \mathrm{poly}(\kappa)$$
$$L_q(\kappa, U_{T,N,S}, m, w) = w \cdot \mathrm{poly}(\kappa)$$
$$L_{dk}(\kappa, U_{T,N,S}, m, w) = w \cdot \mathrm{poly}(\kappa)$$
$$L_{vk}(\kappa, U_{T,N,S}, m, w) = w \cdot \mathrm{poly}(\kappa)$$
$$L_a(\kappa, U_{T,N,S}, m, w) = w \cdot \mathrm{poly}(\kappa)$$

The following is corollary of Theorems 6, 8, 10 and 11.

Corollary 2. *If Learning with Errors is Λ-hard, then for every $N, S = O(\log \Lambda)$ and $m, w, T \leq \Lambda$ there exists a publicly verifiable vPIR for $\mathcal{U}$ that is Λ-secure and Λ-private with respect to $(U_{T,N,S}, m, w)$ with the following efficiency:*

$$T_Q(\kappa, U_{T,N,S}, m, w) = \text{poly}(\kappa, w)$$
$$T_V(\kappa, U_{T,N,S}, m, w) = \text{poly}(\kappa, w)$$
$$L_q(\kappa, U_{T,N,S}, m, w) = \text{poly}(\kappa, w)$$
$$L_{dk}(\kappa, U_{T,N,S}, m, w) = \text{poly}(\kappa, w)$$
$$L_{vk}(\kappa, U_{T,N,S}, m, w) = \text{poly}(\kappa, w)$$
$$L_a(\kappa, U_{T,N,S}, m, w) = \text{poly}(\kappa, w)$$

The following is corollary of Theorems 7, 9, 10 and 11.

Corollary 3. *If Λ-hardness of the k-Lin assumption (for any $k > 1$) holds in a prime-order pairing group, then for every $\epsilon > 0$, and for every $N, S = O(\log \Lambda)$ and $m, w, T \leq \Lambda$ there exists a publicly verifiable vPIR for $\mathcal{U}$ that is Λ-secure and Λ-private with respect to $(U_{T,N,S}, m, w)$ with the following efficiency:*

$$T_Q(\kappa, U_{T,N,S}, m, w) = \text{poly}\left(\kappa, T, w\right) \cdot 2^{\sqrt{O(\log \kappa \log m)}}$$

$$T_V(\kappa, U_{T,N,S}, m, w) = \text{poly}\left(\kappa, w\right) \cdot 2^{\sqrt{O(\log \kappa \log m)}}$$

$$L_q(\kappa, U_{T,N,S}, m, w) = \left(\text{poly}(\kappa, w) + (T + w \cdot \text{poly}(\kappa))^\epsilon\right) \cdot 2^{\sqrt{O(\log \kappa \log m)}}$$

$$L_{dk}(\kappa, U_{T,N,S}, m, w) = \text{poly}\left(\kappa, w\right) \cdot 2^{\sqrt{O(\log \kappa \log m)}}$$

$$L_{vk}(\kappa, U_{T,N,S}, m, w) = \text{poly}\left(\kappa, w\right) \cdot 2^{\sqrt{O(\log \kappa \log m)}}$$

$$L_a(\kappa, U_{T,N,S}, m, w) = \text{poly}\left(\kappa, w\right) \cdot 2^{\sqrt{O(\log \kappa \log m)}}$$

Acknowledgements. Yael Tauman Kalai's work is supported by DARPA under Agreement No. HR00112020023. Any opinions, findings and conclusions or recommendations expressed in this material are those of the author(s) and do not necessarily reflect the views of the United States Government or DARPA.

Omer Paneth is member of the checkpoint institute of information security and is supported by an Azrieli Faculty Fellowship, Len Blavatnik and the Blavatnik Foundation, the Blavatnik Interdisciplinary Cyber Research Center at Tel Aviv University, and ISF grant 1789/19.

References

1. Badrinarayanan, S., Kalai, Y.T., Khurana, D., Sahai, A., Wichs, D.: Succinct delegation for low-space non-deterministic computation. In: Diakonikolas, I., Kempe, D., Henzinger, M. (eds.) Proceedings of the 50th Annual ACM SIGACT Symposium on Theory of Computing, STOC 2018, Los Angeles, CA, USA, 25–29 June 2018, pp. 709–721. ACM (2018). https://doi.org/10.1145/3188745.3188924

2. Bitansky, N., Canetti, R., Chiesa, A., Tromer, E.: Recursive composition and boot-strapping for SNARKS and proof-carrying data. In: Boneh, D., Roughgarden, T., Feigenbaum, J. (eds.) Symposium on Theory of Computing Conference, STOC 2013, Palo Alto, CA, USA, 1–4 June 2013, pp. 111–120. ACM (2013). https://doi.org/10.1145/2488608.2488623

3. Bitansky, N., Canetti, R., Paneth, O., Rosen, A.: On the existence of extractable one-way functions. SIAM J. Comput. 45(5), 1910–1952 (2016). https://doi.org/10.1137/140975048

4. Brakerski, Z., Holmgren, J., Kalai, Y.T.: Non-interactive delegation and batch NP verification from standard computational assumptions. In: Hatami, H., McKenzie, P., King, V. (eds.) Proceedings of the 49th Annual ACM SIGACT Symposium on Theory of Computing, STOC 2017, Montreal, QC, Canada, 19–23 June 2017, pp. 474–482. ACM (2017). https://doi.org/10.1145/3055399.3055497

5. Brakerski, Z., Kalai, Y.: Witness indistinguishability for any single-round argument with applications to access control. In: Kiayias, A., Kohlweiss, M., Wallden, P., Zikas, V. (eds.) PKC 2020. LNCS, vol. 12111, pp. 97–123. Springer, Cham (2020). https://doi.org/10.1007/978-3-030-45388-6_4

6. Choudhuri, A.R., Jain, A., Jin, Z.: SNARGs for P from LWE. IACR Cryptology ePrint Archive, p. 808 (2021). https://eprint.iacr.org/2021/808

7. Gentry, C., Wichs, D.: Separating succinct non-interactive arguments from all fal-sifiable assumptions. In: Fortnow, L., Vadhan, S.P. (eds.) Proceedings of the 43rd ACM Symposium on Theory of Computing, STOC 2011, San Jose, CA, USA, 6–8 June 2011, pp. 99–108. ACM (2011). https://doi.org/10.1145/1993636.1993651

8. Ishai, Y., Kushilevitz, E., Ostrovsky, R., Prabhakaran, M., Sahai, A.: Efficient non-interactive secure computation. In: Paterson, K.G. (ed.) EUROCRYPT 2011. LNCS, vol. 6632, pp. 406–425. Springer, Heidelberg (2011). https://doi.org/10.1007/978-3-642-20465-4_23

9. Kalai, Y., Paneth, O.: Delegating RAM computations. In: Hirt, M., Smith, A. (eds.) TCC 2016. LNCS, vol. 9986, pp. 91–118. Springer, Heidelberg (2016). https://doi.org/10.1007/978-3-662-53644-5_4

10. Kalai, Y.T., Paneth, O., Yang, L.: How to delegate computations publicly. In: Charikar, M., Cohen, E. (eds.) Proceedings of the 51st Annual ACM SIGACT Symposium on Theory of Computing, STOC 2019, Phoenix, AZ, USA, 23–26 June 2019, pp. 1115–1124. ACM (2019). https://doi.org/10.1145/3313276.3316411

11. Kalai, Y.T., Vaikuntanathan, V., Zhang, R.Y.: Somewhere statistical soundness, post-quantum security, and SNARGs. In: Nissim, K., Waters, B. (eds.) TCC 2021. LNCS, vol. 13042, pp. 330–368. Springer, Cham (2021). https://doi.org/10.1007/978-3-030-90459-3_12

12. Kilian, J.: A note on efficient zero-knowledge proofs and arguments (extended abstract). In: Kosaraju, S.R., Fellows, M., Wigderson, A., Ellis, J.A. (eds.) Proceedings of the 24th Annual ACM Symposium on Theory of Computing, Victoria, British Columbia, Canada, 4–6 May 1992, pp. 723–732. ACM (1992). https://doi.org/10.1145/129712.129782

13. Kushilevitz, E., Ostrovsky, R.: Replication is NOT needed: SINGLE database, computationally-private information retrieval. In: 38th Annual Symposium on Foundations of Computer Science, FOCS 1997, Miami Beach, Florida, USA, 19–22 October 1997, pp. 364–373. IEEE Computer Society (1997). https://doi.org/10.1109/SFCS.1997.646125

14. Paneth, O., Rothblum, G.N.: On zero-testable homomorphic encryption and publicly verifiable non-interactive arguments. In: Kalai, Y., Reyzin, L. (eds.) TCC 2017. LNCS, vol. 10678, pp. 283–315. Springer, Cham (2017). https://doi.org/10.1007/978-3-319-70503-3_9

15. Valiant, P.: Incrementally verifiable computation or proofs of knowledge imply time/space efficiency. In: Canetti, R. (ed.) TCC 2008. LNCS, vol. 4948, pp. 1–18. Springer, Heidelberg (2008). https://doi.org/10.1007/978-3-540-78524-8_1

16. Waters, B., Wu, D.J.: Batch arguments for NP and more from standard bilinear group assumptions. IACR Cryptology ePrint Archive, p. 336 (2022). https://eprint.iacr.org/2022/336

Random-Index Oblivious RAM

Shai Halevi[1($\boxtimes$)] and Eyal Kushilevitz[2]

[1] Algorand Foundation, Boston, USA
shaih@alum.mit.edu
[2] Computer Science Department, Technion, Haifa, Israel

Abstract. We study the notion of *Random-index ORAM* (RORAM), which is a weak form of ORAM where the Client is limited to asking for (and possibly modifying) random elements of the N-items memory, rather than specific ones. That is, whenever the client issues a request, it gets in return a pair (r, x_r) where $r \in_R [N]$ is a random index and x_r is the content of the r-th memory item. Then, the client can also modify the content to some new value x'_r.

We first argue that the limited functionality of RORAM still suffices for certain applications. These include various applications of sampling (or sub-sampling) and, in particular, the very-large-scale MPC application in the setting of Benhamouda et al. [2]. Clearly, RORAM can be implemented using any ORAM scheme (by the Client selecting the random r's by itself), but the hope is that the limited functionality of RORAM can make it faster and easier to implement than ORAM. Indeed, our main contributions are several RORAM schemes (both of the hierarchical-type and the tree-type) of lighter complexity than that of ORAM.

1 Introduction

Oblivious RAM (ORAM), introduced by Goldreich and Ostrovsky [12,13,19], is a method to compile RAM programs into corresponding "oblivious" programs that keep the same functionality but hide the original access pattern to the memory. This is aimed at preventing leakage of secret information about the data that is revealed by such access patterns and cannot be hidden by merely encrypting the data. The study of ORAM started with software protection motivation in mind, but since then found many applications. In particular, ORAM is used for storing data in cloud applications, where a client stores in a cloud server N data items that it owns and it then accesses them via a sequence of read/write operations. ORAM schemes guarantee that the sequence of physical addresses that are read and written by the client does not leak to the server information about which virtual items the client accesses.

ORAM is the subject of a lot of research, resulting in many schemes (e.g., [1,5,9,12,16,19,20,22,23] and *many* more), with the goal of minimizing the overhead incurred by the RAM to ORAM transformation. This beautiful line of work recently culminated with the OptORAMa scheme [1], whose $O(\log N)$ overhead

© The Author(s), under exclusive license to Springer Nature Switzerland AG 2022
E. Kiltz and V. Vaikuntanathan (Eds.): TCC 2022, LNCS 13749, pp. 33–59, 2022.
https://doi.org/10.1007/978-3-031-22368-6_2

meets the known lower bounds [13,17].[1] ORAM found many uses beyond cloud storage, for example for efficient MPC protocols, enabling simulating computations that are represented by RAM programs rather than the less efficient circuit representation. Modern ORAM constructions are also sufficiently efficient to be useful in practical systems. Other variants of ORAM (not addressed by the current work) were also considered in the literature, motivated by other models and by applications. Examples include Parallel ORAM [3], Distributed ORAM [7,14,18] and others.

To further reduce the overhead below the $\Omega(\log N)$ lower bound (or, alternatively, to reduce the practical cost of ORAM schemes), one may consider restricted variants of ORAM that do not provide the full ORAM functionality. One examples is *Offline ORAM* (where the entire sequence is known to the client in advance), for which Boyle and Naor [4] show an improved construction under some assumption related to sorting circuits (in contrast to the lower bound of [13] for offline ORAM in the "balls-and-bins" setting). Another example is *Read only ORAM*, where Weiss and Wichs [25] show an improved construction, based on an assumption related to the existence of small sorting circuits and assuming very good locally decodable codes (LDCs),[2] while, again, in the "balls-and-bins" setting, the lower bound of [13] still holds.

1.1 Random-Index ORAM

In this work we introduce another variant of ORAM, motivated by applications, which we term Random-index-ORAM (RORAM), that only supports random selection of elements from the memory. As in the ORAM setting, the server stores for the client a memory that contains N items. Differently from standard ORAM, however, access requests by the client do not ask for specific memory locations. Instead, whenever the client issues a request, it receives a random sample from the memory. Namely, the client receives a pair (r, x_r), with r a uniformly random location and x_r the data stored in that location. Crucially, the location r is kept hidden from the server/adversary. (We also allow for Write operations, where the client can replace the selected value x_r by another value x'_r.) This is clearly solvable by using a standard ORAM scheme; namely, by the client picking the location r at random and using the standard ORAM to access the content of the r-th memory item. The goal is to improve efficiency beyond that of standard ORAM schemes. Note that the Goldreich-Ostrovsky "balls-and-bins" lower bound [13] applies to RORAM just as for full ORAM, hence we cannot expect to get asymptotic improvements, but we can get significant practical speed-ups, as we show in the sequel.

---

[1] For now, we concentrate only on the overhead in terms of the number of accesses to the memory and ignore other relevant parameters, such as the overhead in server storage, amount of local memory at the client, size of each memory item, etc.

[2] Such LDCs are not known to exist but are also beyond current lower bound techniques.

RORAM Variants. We consider two main security notions for RORAM schemes, depending on the application. The natural extension of standard ORAM security demands that the index r remains secret, and the adversary should learn no information about the sequence of locations $r_1, r_2, r_3, \ldots$ (A weaker version of this condition allows the adversary to learn information, so long as the sequence retains enough min-entropy.)

In some applications however (see below), the client's use of the returned entries may reveal to the server the indexes that were received in the past. In those cases, we still want *future r_i's* to look random to the server (till they are used), but we do not care about hiding past indexes. We can therefore use a weaker condition, requiring only that the next r_{i+1} should be pseudo-random/unpredictable given the entire history so far. This weakening enables RORAM protocols that intentionally leak information about past indexes to the server, which may improve performance.

All these notions also have *batch* variants, where in each step the client receives a batch of some k items, rather than just one. Clearly, this potentially may be more efficient than asking k times for a single item.

1.2   Applications

Clearly, RORAM is a weaker primitive than ORAM, making it possible to achieve meaningful efficiency gains in applications where the RORAM functionality is sufficient. Indeed, we show in this work how to simplify existing ORAM constructions in this case, e.g. by avoiding the need to build and maintain certain hash tables or recursive structures. We sketch here a few applications where the RORAM functionality is sufficient.

Oblivious Statistics. Consider an information-provider with a huge dataset, stored in the cloud, where customers/users may want to make *statistical queries* on this data. (Such queries are very common in data analysis and in machine learning, see e.g. [15, 21].) Concretely, when a query q comes from a user, the provider samples a *random* set S of items from its dataset (of an appropriate size, depending on the desired accuracy) and estimates the answer to q based on this sample. Using RORAM to sample the set S, ensures that S remains hidden, even if the user and the cloud collude (i.e., it makes it difficult to link the answer to q, known to the user, with specific items in the dataset).

Sub-sampling. RORAM is also useful for simulating randomized algorithms that are based on sub-sampling; namely, where the algorithm samples a set S of $N' \ll N$ of the items in a large database, and then computes on S. A client with very small space—not even enough to keep the sub-sample S—can use RORAM to sample N' items for S (one by one, or in batches), build an *ORAM* data-set of size N' by inserting the items in the sample S, and then execute the computation on S using a standard ORAM scheme. The gain is that this solution pays the more expensive ORAM complexity on a smaller data set of only N' items, and pays the smaller RORAM complexity on the larger data-set of N items.

Large-Scale Secure Computation. Our original motivation for studying RORAM comes from the work of Gentry et al. [10], where they studied a similar notion of random-index PIR (RPIR). That work, like ours, was motivated by an application of these notions to very-large-scale secure MPC, specifically for the secrets-on-blockchain architecture of Benhamouda et al. [2]. The architecture from [2] requires periodic random selection of small committees out of a huge population, without the adversary learning who was selected to each committee until after the fact.

A solution to the sampling problem, proposed by Gentry et al. [10], is to assign to the previous committee the task of choosing the next one, as follows:

- The list of parties (or their public keys) is viewed as a public database, from which we seek to sample random entries obliviously.
- The server state is public, making it possible for members of the previous committee to simulate the server actions in their head.
- The client state is shared among the committee, hence client queries and client output are generated via a secure-MPC protocol.

At the conclusion of the selection protocol, the identity (or keys) of the chosen parties for the next committee are known to the client, i.e., they are shared among the previous committee. The adversary, controlling only a minority of the previous committee, does not know who was chosen. The previous committee can then use anonymous public-key encryption over broadcast to transfer its state to the next committee, thereby "activating" it while keeping the adversary in the dark about who they are (until after they start sending messages).

Using this approach, the communication of the protocol depends only on the client complexity. If the selection protocol features small client circuits, even for large databases, then the overall solution could be sub-linear in the total population size.

Gentry et al. [10] mentioned that RORAM can be used in this fashion instead of RPIR, but did not develop this observation much. In particular, they did not present RORAM constructions (and, moreover, it seems that the RORAM definition from [10] would require implementing a full-fledged ORAM, see more discussion in Sect. 5.1).

A Desirable Property: Bounded History. When using RORAM to implement the above approach, all parties must be able to fully reconstruct the server state when they are called to serve on the committee. It is therefore desirable that this state can be recovered by looking only at the transcript of the last T queries, for some predefined (preferably small) parameter T. This will make it easier for parties to exercise a "lazy" strategy, ignoring the server state when they are not on the committee and reconstructing it only when they are chosen to serve.

1.3   Our Contributions

In this work we study random-index ORAM (RORAM), introduce a few security notions for it, and describe constructions that achieve meaningful speed-ups over full-fledged ORAM.

Our constructions follow the two main types of constructions in the ORAM literature: the *hierarchical*-type ORAM constructions (started from [13,19]) and the *tree*-type ORAM constructions (started from [22]). In each case, we can forgo some ingredients of the constructions, whose purpose is to locate specific items of the dataset, replacing them with lighter mechanisms that still allow random selection.

- In Sect. 3 we describe two simple hierarchical-RORAM protocols, achieving two different notions of security. In both protocols, we dispose of the hashing steps that are needed in standard hierarchical-ORAM protocols in order to find specific elements in the various levels of the hierarchy. We show that for RORAM it is enough to use a much lighter element-fetching mechanism. We still use the reshuffling procedures from [1,6,20] (that already improve over the heavier oblivious sort).
- In Sect. 4 we describe a tree-RORAM protocol, where we can eliminate the recursive construction which is needed for full-fledged ORAM, yielding a $O(\log N)$-factor improvement over standard tree ORAMs.

While the constructions that we describe are all quite simple and they follow the high level design of the corresponding ORAM schemes, in some of them the probabilistic analysis of the scheme is a major challenge. We analyze some variants in this work, and leave the analysis of others to future work. We also note that in the ORAM context the hierarchical type design is the one that enables to achieve the asymptotically optimal schemes, while the tree type design seems to allow for practically superior schemes. Hence, there is a motivation to consider RORAM schemes of both types (in addition to differences in the security guarantees in the RORAM case).

Finally, in Sect. 5 we discuss some questions and directions for future work. One such direction are various possibilities for hybrid ORAM/RORAM schemes that can support the full functionality of ORAM but enjoy the efficiency of RORAM schemes in random selection steps. Other directions include the possibility of constructing ORAM from RORAM (the reverse direction is trivial), issues related to data updates in the context of the application to very-large-scale MPC, and possible directions for improving the analyses.

2   Definitions

Random-index Oblivious-RAM (RORAM) was sketched by Gentry et al. in [10], but our definitions are somewhat different than theirs. A RORAM is a two party protocol between a client and a server, where the server holds the state corresponding to the database, but it does not learn the access pattern of the client. Differently from a full-fledged ORAM, in RORAM the client can only read and write random entries, not specific ones.

Similarly to ORAM, we have procedures for Init, Read, and Write, except that the index to be accessed is not an input to the protocol but an output of it. To allow increasing the database size, we also use Concatenate operation.[3]

Definition 2.1 (RORAM Syntax). *A Random-Index ORAM protocol (RORAM) consists of the following components:*

- Init$(1^\lambda, \mathsf{Db}) \to (\mathsf{cst}; \mathsf{SST})$: *The initialization algorithm takes as input the security parameter and initial database* $\mathsf{Db} \in \{0,1\}^*$ *(that could be empty), and generates an initial secret client state* cst *and a public server state* SST.
- Read$(\mathsf{cst}; \mathsf{SST}) \to ((r, x, \mathsf{cst}'); \mathsf{SST}')$: *The client fetches* (r, x)*, with* x *the element in position* r *in the database (presumably for a uniformly random index* $r \in_R [|\mathsf{Db}|]$*). The client and server states are updated to* $\mathsf{cst}', \mathsf{SST}'$*, respectively.*
- Write$((\mathsf{cst}, x'(\cdot)); \mathsf{SST}) \to ((r, x, \mathsf{cst}'); \mathsf{SST}')$: *Similar to* Read*, except that in addition to returning the index* r *and the previous content* x*, the content of position* r *in the database is replaced by* $x' = x'(r, x)$*. (Note that we let the new value* x' *depend on the old value* x *and its location* r*.[4])*
- Concatenate$((\mathsf{cst}, x); \mathsf{SST}) \to (\mathsf{cst}'; \mathsf{SST}')$: *The database size is increased by one, and the value* x *is inserted in the new entry.*

A RORAM protocol is nontrivial if the client and server work in each of these operations is $o(|\mathsf{Db}|)$*.*

2.1 RORAM Security

We consider two notions of RORAM security in this work.

- The weaker notion, motivated by the application to large-scale secure MPC, is *future-randomness*. It asserts that the next index to be returned to the client is random from the server's point of view, even conditioned on all the indexes and elements that were returned in the past.
- The stronger notion, that we call just *randomness*, requires that both future and past indexes are random from the server's point of view.

To see the difference, consider a RORAM protocol in which the client's next query includes the index that it received previously.[5] Such protocol does not offer randomness, but it may still offer future-randomness.

Similarly to RPIR [10], for RORAM too we can weaken these two notions to only require "high entropy" (or unpredictability) rather than pseudorandomness. We can also look at batch versions, where multiple indexes are returned at once. Below are the formal definitions.

---

[3] We could also have a Drop operation to remove elements from the database, but since we cannot target specific elements then dropping will create holes in the database.

[4] The new x' depends only on (r, x) and not on internals of the RORAM protocol (such as its transcript), since the "higher level" client should not be exposed to these internals.

[5] Indeed, the most efficient hierarchical-RORAM protocol that we describe in Sect. 3 has exactly that structure, each client query must include the index that the client received in the previous step.

Future Randomness. Here we consider a game in which together with each client query q_j, the server also gets the index r_{j-1} that the client received in the previous step. The (semi honest) server answers all queries as prescribed by the protocol, until it decides to end the game. It then outputs both the answer to the last query q_j (from which the client can deduce (r_j, x_{r_j})), as well as a guess r'_j for the index r_j. We call this the future-randomness game.

Definition 2.2 (Future randomness). *A RORAM protocol offers future-randomness if for any sequence of queries and any semi-honest PPT server in the future-randomness game, it holds that* $\Pr[r_j = r'_j] \leq 1/N + \mathsf{negl}(\lambda)$. *Here N is the number of elements in the database after the last step, and the probability is taken over all the randomness used by the parties throughout the game.*

Randomness. In the randomness game, we require that the server cannot distinguish the indexes that the client receives from a uniformly random sequence of indexes. Specifically, at the onset of the randomness game, a bit is chosen at random $b \leftarrow \{0, 1\}$ and kept secret from the server. If $b = 1$ then the game proceeds similarly to the future-randomness game, where after answering each query q_j the server is shown the index r_j that the client received. If $b = 0$, then instead of r_j, the server is given r'_j which is chosen uniformly at random from $[N_j]$ (where N_j is the number of elements in the database after step j). The game proceeds in this manner until the server decides to end it, outputting a guess b' for b.

Definition 2.3 (Randomness). *A RORAM protocol offers randomness if for any sequence of queries and semi-honest PPT server in the randomness game, it holds that* $|\Pr[b = b'] - \frac{1}{2}| \leq \mathsf{negl}(\lambda)$. *The probability is taken over all the randomness used by the parties throughout the game.*

Both these notions can be relaxed by replacing the uniform distribution by other distributions with sufficient min-entropy.

2.2 Batch RORAM

Many RORAM applications need to draw not just one but many random samples in each step, so it makes sense to try and amortize the lookup cost. It is straightforward to extend the definitions above to the case where each access returns exactly k elements, where k is a parameter. We just replace the single index r_j in step j by a vector of indexes $\boldsymbol{r}_j \in [N_j]^k$ (and the corresponding vector of elements $\boldsymbol{x}_j$ that are stored in these positions).

Another useful variant, which we employ in Sect. 4, is where the batch size itself could vary. The syntax is exactly the same as above, except that the batch size k is a random variable, determined by the protocol randomness. We are interested in this new notion in the context of not-quite-random-but-high-entropy distributions, but measuring (min-)entropy in this case is a little awkward. Hence we use a more special-purpose notion of *guessing resilience*, which directly measures what we need in the application to large-scale secure MPC.

This notion, which is a variant of future-randomness, has two parameters $\epsilon \leq \delta$. We consider a server with a "budget" of ϵN elements that it can guess, and bound the probability that this server is able to guess more than a δ-fraction of the samples drawn in the next step.

This security game proceeds similarly to the future-randomness process, where the server gets with each query q_j also all the indexes in R_{j-1} that were received by the client in the previous query. When the server decides to end the game, it outputs a set of indexes $R' \subset [N]$. The server is considered successful if $|R'| \leq \epsilon N$ but $|R \cap R'| \geq \delta|R|$, where R is the set of indexes returned in the last step.

Definition 2.4. *For parameters $\epsilon \leq \delta$, a RORAM protocol offers (ϵ, δ) guessing-resilience if for any sequence of queries and any semi-honest PPT server in the guessing game above, it holds that $\Pr[|R'| \leq \epsilon N$ but $|R \cap R'| \geq \delta|R|] \leq \mathsf{negl}(\lambda)$.*

3 Hierarchical RORAM

In this section, we describe two hierarchical RORAM protocols which are more efficient than full-blown ORAM. Specifically, we try to reduce the use of heavy oblivious sorts and to eliminate the use and maintenance of hash tables in each level of the hierarchy (whose goal, in regular hierarchical ORAM, is to locate the concrete item we search for). We assume that the reader is familiar with the common features of all hierarchical ORAM schemes such as:

- The memory is organized in $O(\log N)$ levels of growing sizes, where the i'th level of size 2^i (the smallest level may correspond to $i \approx \log \log n$, of size $O(\log n)$).
- In each step, one item in each level is accessed (to hide the level in which the accessed item is actually found), and then the accessed item is removed from its level and is re-inserted into the smallest level. In a bit more details, each value that is read from some level and is not the desired item is re-encrypted and re-written, and if the desired item is found it is replaced by an encrypted null value (and dummy items are read from the following levels).
- Every $O(2^i)$ steps the contents of the first i levels are randomly reshuffled into level $i + 1$.

The description below is focused on the new aspects of our protocols.

3.1 Protocol 1 - Future Randomness

We start with a scheme for the future-randomness variant; i.e., where the adversary gets to see the chosen locations *after* they are selected and before the next selection (see Definition 2.2). Since the adversary sees after the fact the actual sequence of locations, then it can also compute which items are contained in what levels of the hierarchy. The only information that is hidden from the adversary is *the order* of items within each level. Whenever a request for a next item comes, the following is executed:

- Server (and Client) know, for each level i, the number of items n_i that reside in this level. But the items in each level are randomly ordered, and this ordering is secret. Client selects the winning level i_0 for this round in proportion to the level size. I.e., each level i is the winner with probability $n_i / \sum_j n_j$.
- Client reads one item from each level (to hide the identity of i_0). For simplicity, say that it reads the last item in the level (i.e., the one at position n_i). It discards all those items except the one read from level i_0.[6]
- After the output is revealed, Server omits this item from level i_0 (simply by decreasing n_{i_0} by one) and adds it to the top (smallest) level.[7] More concretely, this is done by the client reading the entire top level (which is small), randomly permuting its elements, and rewriting it (and updating its size).
- Finally, every 2^i steps, all levels i and above are merged into level $i+1$ (with the client's help), to avoid overflow. As observed in [1,20], this operation (termed "intersperse") does *not* require oblivious sort, since it merges randomly permuted arrays. It just needs to hide, for each item in the resulting array, from what level it came. Moreover, in our case we also do not need to bring each item to a specific location, determined by the hash, and/or to construct a corresponding hash table; we only need the result to maintain a random order.

  The complexity of intersperse was bounded in PanORAMa [20] by $n \log \log n$ (vs. $n \log n$ for Oblivious Sort), and was further reduced to the asymptotically optimal $O(n)$ in OptORAMa [1].

For correctness, the idea is that selecting each level in proportion to its size, together with the random order within each level, ensures uniform probability for each output element.

The Security Argument. Recall that we are in the future-randomness model, where the adversary anyway sees each r_i before r_{i+1} is selected. Given the sequence so far $(r_1, \dots, r_i)$ (which implies the knowledge of what level contains each item), the actions that occur *before* giving r_{i+1} to the Client (namely, obliviously reading the "last" item from each level) give the adversary no information and so each element has probability $1/N$ to be the next item.

---

[6] We can further reduce the time in this step at the cost of a (small) penalty in space. That is, if Client has a little extra memory, it could keep the values of all read items (one from each level) from one invocation to the other, instead of reading them again in the next invocation and only update in the next invocation the single item that is currently used (which by then will anyway be known to the adversary).

[7] Note that in this way we refrain from the need to handle so-called "dummy" items, in standard ORAM constructions.

Theorem 3.1. *Protocol 1 is a RORAM protocol satisfying future-randomness, and overhead of $O(\log N)$.*

3.2   Protocol 2 - Randomness

In the protocol above, the server learns after the fact the level from which the item r_i was selected (as this information can be computed by knowing r_i). In the case of the randomness game (Definition 2.3), where the adversary does not get the r_i's, we must in particular hide the winning label i_0 from the server. Hence, the server no longer knows exactly how many elements are in each level, so it cannot just read "the last item" from each level as it did above.

A naive attempt to fix the protocol is for the server to read "the next item" from each level in each step. Namely, in the first step after levels $i-1$ and above are merged into level i, the server will read the first item from level i, then the second item, then the third, and so on. With this protocol, one could hope that level i will contain enough items, with high probability, so the server will be able to keep reading them for 2^i steps, until that level is merged to the level below. Unfortunately, this is not the case. In fact, it can be shown that no matter the ratio between the level sizes, and no matter how often levels are merged into the levels before, level i will always run out of items before the next time that it is merged into level $i+1$.

Rather than reading one element at a time, we therefore switch to reading a "window of elements" from each level. The idea is that (1) most read elements are not really used, since we read from all levels at each step and only select one (according to level sizes). (2) if the level is of size X, we expect to use it with probability X/n, i.e. once every n/X steps (which overcomes the previous problems when reading a new element in each step). Since this is only in expectation, if we start by reading λ elements from the level and then, every n/X steps read one more element (and maintain the "window" of last λ elements), we will argue that with high probability we will always have enough elements to read. (The client rewrites everything that is read, and the selected item is replaced by "dummy", so the server does not know which one was actually used; if the client reads from some level it takes the first non-dummy element in the corresponding window.)

In more detail, each level i has size 2^i, where we start from level $i \approx \log \lambda$ (of size λ, security parameter) and end in level $L = \log n$ of size n (that contains all elements).

- Every 2^{i+1} steps we empty all levels i and above into level $i+1$. This means that each level i is empty for 2^i steps, and then level $i-1$ and above are emptied into level i. The only exception here is level L which is never emptied and every n steps all elements are coming back to it.
- At each step, a level j is selected with probabilities proportional to level sizes (which are known to the client). One item from the winning level is then accessed and moved to the root; see below for details on which item is read. (Reading from level L is simple: just one-by-one for n steps and then when it is re-filled we start over.)

For each level we maintain a public window of size λ (the security parameter) which are the items that the server will read and send to the client. For each level i we have a public parameter ρ_i which is the rate of advancing the window. (We set ρ_i slightly above $2^i/n$; the exact value to be determined below.) As mentioned, level i is filled in step 2^i and emptied in step 2^{i+1}. Thereafter in each step $2^i + t$ (for $t < 2^i$) we read the window $[s_i, s_i + \lambda - 1]$ from this level, where $s_i = \lfloor \rho_i \cdot t \rfloor$.

We are also keeping for each level i a secret pointer p_i to the next element to read, this pointer is known to the client but not to the server. When the level is filled in step 2^i the pointer is set to $p_i = 1$, and thereafter it is advanced whenever we actually access an item from that level (i.e., when that level was selected), or when p_i lags behind the rear of the window (this ensures that we always have $p_i \geq s_i$).

We note that security of this protocol is completely straightforward, as the server never sees any non-encrypted content and its access pattern is deterministic: In each step it reads from each level i all the items in the window $[s_i, s_i + \lambda - 1]$. The hard part is proving correctness, i.e. that every step indeed returns some item to the client. The rest of this section is devoted to proving it, yielding the following theorem:

Theorem 3.2. *Protocol 2 is a RORAM protocol satisfying the randomness property, and overhead of $O(\log N)$.*

The technical proof, which not quite straightforward, is moved to the appendix to make room in the main text for our tree-based construction.

Bounded History. We note that for both protocols in this section, the entire state of the server can be reconstructed by looking at the recent n operations (or less). Specifically, any history that includes the last intersperse operation from levels $L - 1$ and above to level L, has enough information to reconstruct all the ciphertexts in all the levels.

4   Tree-Based RORAM

Below we introduce a class of simple tree-base RORAM schemes, then describe in detail and analyze one specific scheme in this class.

Recall that in tree-ORAM schemes ([22] and follow-up schemes), data items are held in the nodes of a binary tree. At any point, each data item is assigned to one leaf in the tree, and it can be found somewhere on the path from the root to its assigned leaf. A data-access operation consists of looking up a single root-leaf path in the tree, extracting the relevant data item from it, then assigning that element to a new random leaf and pushing it back at the root of the tree. After each data access, a maintenance process is invoked to push elements down the tree towards their assigned leaves, so as to prevent overflow at the top levels.

Full-fledged tree-ORAM must be able to determine *which root-leaf path to read* in order to find specific data items. This is solved via a recursive structure with smaller and smaller trees, where each tree contains information about where to find data items in the next larger tree (so-called "position map"). This solution, however, adds a $O(\log N)$ factor to the ORAM overhead.

4.1   A Class of Tree-RORAM Schemes

We note that since RORAM schemes do not need to look up specific elements, there is no real need for the recursive construction that stores position maps.[8] Instead, here we consider schemes that employ just one tree with all the data items, and where each step just looks up an arbitrary leaf (either a random one or according to some deterministic order). Each operation therefore consists of the following steps:

1. Determine the leaf to read, and look up the path in the tree from the root to that element;
2. Extract one or more data items from this path and return (their encryption) to the client;
3. Assign a fresh random leaf to each extracted element (keep this information within the element), optionally change the data stored in the element, and then push the element back at the root of the tree;
4. Invoke the maintenance process to push elements down towards their assigned leaves.

This class of schemes has several different variations:

– The next leaf to read can be chosen at random in every step, or the scheme can use a round-robin ordering of leaves;
– When reading a root-leaf path, it can return to the client either one data item from the ones assigned to the target leaf, or a batch of some fixed number of them (a parameter k), or all the data items that are assigned to that leaf;
– The elements that were not returned to the client (if any), could either be left in their place, or extracted and assigned new leaves as well;
– Finally, another source of variation is the maintenance process.

Not a Perfectly Uniform RORAM. It is important to note that RORAM schemes from the class above *do not result in a completely uniformly random choice* of data items from the server's point of view. To see that, notice that choosing a random data item would imply a non-uniform distribution on the leaf which is read next (since some leaves will have more items assigned to them than others). Conversely, choosing a uniform leaf (or using a deterministic ordering) implies a non-uniform probability distribution over the chosen data item.

---

[8] Another example of efficiency improvements that come from eliminating the need to access a position map, in a different context than ours (where there is a restriction on the access pattern due to the particular computation that is performed), can be found in [24].

4.2   The Scheme that We Analyze

In this work, we only present one scheme from the class above that arguably features the easiest analysis. This is a "worst case scheme", where the server is provided with as much information as possible (and hence unfortunately it also has the worse parameters).

Specifically, we consider the variant where the leaves are accessed in a round-robin fashion, where all the data-items that are assigned to the target leaf are extracted and returned to the client, and we consider the forward-randomness game where the server gets to see all these items after they are given to the client.

In terms of the maintenance process, we adopt the process of Gentry et al. from [11], which also use a deterministic leaf traversal, specifically bit-reverse ordering. Namely, with a binary tree on L leaves, we name each leaf by a $\log L$ bit string, describing the path from the root (MSB) to that leaf (LSB). For example with $L = 2^8$, leaf 100 is obtained by the path right-left-left from the root, and leaf 001 is obtained by left-left-right. With this representation, the leaves are accessed in reverse bit ordering, $\mathsf{bitReverse}(0), \mathsf{bitReverse}(1), \ldots, \mathsf{bitReverse}(L-1)$. In the example with $L = 2^3$, the order will be $(000, 100, 010, 110, 001, 101, 011, 111)$, or in numbers $(0, 4, 2, 6, 1, 5, 3, 7)$.

Hence the scheme that we consider for the rest of this section is as follows. It maintains an L-leaf binary tree, holding N items in total, where each node can hold upto m data items. m and L are parameters, TBD later as a function of N and the security parameter, with L a power of two. The i'th data-access operation ($i = 0, 1, 2, \ldots$) is implemented as follows:

1. Let $j = \mathsf{bitReverse}(i \bmod L)$. Read the path from the root to leaf j, extract from it all the data items that are assigned to leaf j, and return them to the client;
2. Assign to each of these data items a fresh uniform leaf in $[L]$, and place them all back at the root of the tree (after possibly updating the data in them);
3. Push each data item on the root-to-j path as far down toward its assigned leaf as it can go along that path (i.e., an item assigned to j' is pushed as far down as $\mathsf{commonPrefix}(j, j')$);
4. Write the updated path back to the tree.

Note that as opposed to the future-randomness hierarchical-RORAM protocol from Sect. 3.1, the protocol here does not rely on the server learning the past indexes. Nonetheless, below we analyze it only in the forward-randomness setting where all these indexes are revealed to the server after the fact.

A Technical Lemma. Underlying most of our analysis in this section is the following simple technical lemma, bounding the probability of finding one specific element in one specific leaf. This lemma is independent of the server's view, or the number of elements that are returned to the client. It depends only on the fact that all the elements are evicted from the leaves that we examine, and are then assigned independently to fresh random leaves.

Lemma 4.1. *Fix N, L, and an arbitrary starting assignment of the N elements into the L leaves. Assume that the first leaf to be examined is leaf zero. Then, for every element, the probability that this element will be assigned to leaf zero the next time that this leaf is examined, is between $1/L$ and e/L.*

Note that the lemma talks about the *next* time that leaf zero is examined, not this time. That is, we consider some initial configuration at step 0 where leaf zero is examined, and assert that in step L, when leaf zero will be examined again, each item has probability between $1/L$ and e/L of being there.

Proof. For $i = 0, 1, \ldots, L - 1$, let p_i be the probability that an element which is currently assigned to leaf i will be assigned to leaf 0 the next time that we look at it (not this time). We can define p_i inductively as follows:

- $p_{L-1} = 1/L$;
- $p_i = 1/L \cdot \sum_{j=i+1}^{L-1} 1/L \cdot p_j$.

Solving this recurrence, we get $p_i = \frac{(1+1/L)^{L-i}}{L}$, hence $1/L \leq p_i \leq e/L$ holds for all i.   □

4.3   Bounding the Prediction Probability

Recalling that the scheme above has a variable batch size, we next analyze its security in terms of Definition 2.4. Namely, motivated by the application to large-scale secure-MPC, we focus below on a setting where the adversary has a "budget" of upto ϵN guesses, and we bound the probability that it guesses more than a δ-fraction of the elements that are returned in the next data access. The rest of this subsection is devoted for proving the following:

Theorem 4.2. *For every constant $\delta > 0$, there is another constant $\epsilon = \Omega(\delta^2)$, such that the RORAM scheme above offers (ϵ, δ)-guessing resilience as per Definition 2.4.*

To simplify the analysis, we assume at first that the nodes have infinite capacity, so we can ignore issues of overflow. As we show in Appendix B, standard analysis shows that for appropriate setting of the node-size m, overflow would only happens with negligible probability. Assuming no overflow, we can ignore the tree altogether and concentrate only on the leaves. That is, we consider a process in which an element which is assigned to some leaf is immediately placed in that leaf. For simplicity below we also ignore the reverse-bit-ordering of leaves (which is only needed to argue about overflow probability). Instead we consider the natural ordering of leaves, $0, 1, 2, \ldots, L - 1$.

Recall again that below we only analyze the "pessimistic" case where the adversary sees all the elements that are extracted from the previous leaves. Other cases where it only sees a few of these elements clearly reduces the server's ability to guess, but we were not able to analyze this improvement. We leave it as an interesting open question.

The Optimal Adversary. When the adversary sees all the extracted elements, it is easy to describe the distribution over the locations of all the elements, conditioned on the adversary's view: Those elements that were last seen $L - 1$ steps ago must all be in the next leaf, elements that were last seen $L - 2$ steps ago are uniformly distributed between the next leaf and the one after that, elements that were last seen $L - 3$ steps ago are uniform over the next three leaves, etc. In general, the location of an element that was last seen $(L - j)$ steps ago is uniformly distributed among the next j leaves. Moreover, the location of the different elements are all independent of each other, even conditioned on the adversary's view.[9]

Hence, the optimal strategy for an adversary that tries to guess the elements placed in the next leaf is as follows: The adversary first guesses all the elements that were seen $L - 1$ steps ago, followed by those that were seen $L - 2$ steps ago, then $L - 3$, etc., until the entire budget of ϵN guesses is exhausted. The success of that strategy is analyzed in Appendix B.

Bounded History. Since the protocol above examines the leaves in a round-robin fashion, then the entire state of the server can be reconstructed by looking only at the last L steps of the protocol.

5   Discussion and Future Directions

Before concluding, we discuss below a few other related topics and point out possible future directions and open problems.

5.1   Hybrid ORAM/RORAM Schemes

An interesting direction is constructing a full-fledged ORAM scheme, but such that accessing a random element costs a lot less than a specific element. This would be used to speed up access-oblivious randomized algorithms (e.g. quick-sort) that interleave random selections with accessing specific elements.

If the underlying dataset is fixed and need not be updated, then a simple solution is to just keep two copies of the dataset, one in RORAM for the random selections and the other in a full-fledged ORAM for fetching specific elements.

If updates are needed, however, then keeping such separate structures no longer works, since we will not be able to update specific elements in the RORAM structure. In that case, we can still offer some savings by keeping in each structure enough extra information with each element to find that element in the other structure. For example, if the other structure is a hierarchical ORAM then we can keep information about which level it is found at and where in that level, thus avoiding the need to consult the hash tables.

---

[9] When the adversary only sees a few of the extracted elements, the location of the different elements may not be independent when conditioned on the view. One example is provided in Fig. 1 in the appendix.

Similarly, if the other structure is a (recursive) tree ORAM, then we can keep information about which leaf that element in assigned to (in all the recursive levels). This way, once we locate an element in the non-recursive RORAM tree, we can update all the recursive trees in a full ORAM in one round, rather than having to interact for $O(\log N)$ communication rounds to find it.

Note, however, that keeping the two structures synchronized in this way means that we have to update the heavier ORAM structure every time we read from the lighter RORAM structure, thereby negating much of the RORAM savings.

5.2   Refreshing Keys in Large-Scale MPC

Using RORAM for large-scale MPC as sketched in the introduction brings up the question of how to handle key-refresh by parties. Recall that in that application, the RORAM structure is holding the public keys of all the parties. Since RORAM cannot fetch/update specific elements, it is not clear how can parties refresh their keys and get the new key into the RORAM.[10]

One solution is to only let parties refresh their keys when they are selected to the committee, using the RORAM write operation. This may be sensible in setting where parties serve on committees often enough.[11]

Another option is to handle periodic key-refresh by keeping two structures at any point, the current RORAM that we use and the next one that we are building. The next-RORAM will be called on the entire new database of keys, running the Init operation (and it can do this operation "in the background", a little bit at a time). Once the new RORAM is fully built, we switch to it as the one in use, discard the old one, and begin building the next RORAM after that.

5.3   Improved Schemes and Analysis

Regarding the tree constructions, it is very likely that giving the adversary less information will result in much better parameters (in terms of the dependence of ϵ, δ). For example, instead of revealing all the elements that were extracted from the last leaf, we can reveal (say) only half of them, but still extract and re-assign all the elements from the current leaf. Or maybe even, only extract and re-assign half the elements from the current leaf, leaving the rest of them in place. In all of these options, it is not longer easy to describe the probability distribution over the location of elements, conditioned on the server's view, or to figure out the optimal server guessing strategy. Moreover, the locations of different elements are no longer independent of each other conditioned on this view, complicating

---

[10] Most likely, this is the reason why the RORAM definition from [10] features random reads but writes of specific elements, which seem to require the hybrid RORAM/ORAM solution.

[11] For example, in the realistic threat model where fail-stop attacks are easy to mount but real compromise rarely happens, it may be okay to have parties refresh their keys very rarely, when they are selected to the committee.

the analysis further. (See one example in Fig. 1 in the appendix.) Getting a good handle over the whole class of protocols of this form is an interesting open problem.

5.4   From RORAM to ORAM

One natural question is whether we can construct full-fledged ORAM scheme from RORAM in a black-box manner. For RPIR, Gentry et al. described a RPIR-to-PIR black box transformation, but it requires $O(N)$ work for the server so we cannot use it in the RORAM/ORAM world. Finding such black-box constructions (or an argument why they are unlikely) is still an open problem.

5.5   Miscellaneous

Many other questions can also be asked. For example, [17] expanded the ORAM lower bound from the restricted "balls-and-bins" model of [13] to general schemes. Can a similar result be shown for RORAM? The technique of [17] is based on considering carefully structured access patterns, hence it does not seem to immediately apply for RORAM. Can such a lower bound still be proved or, alternatively, can an upper bound that circumvents the "balls-and-bins" model be designed (possibly, under additional assumptions)? Since the RORAM model is weaker, such a lower bound, if true, may be more difficult to prove.

A   Hierarchical-RORAM: More Details

We now proceed to prove our main theorem:

Theorem 3.2. *Protocol 2 is a RORAM protocol satisfying the randomness property, and overhead of $O(\log N)$.*

Invariants. Recall that for each level i we have at any point a public window $[s_i, s_i + \lambda - 1]$, and a secret pointer p_i (all indexes into the i'th level). What we need to prove is that in every step, some element in indeed returned to the client. A sufficient condition for this method to work, is maintaining these two conditions:

1. The front of the window never exceeds the number of elements in the level, until the level is emptied to the next one. Denoting by S_i the number of items in level i when it is filled in step 2^i, we show that whp we have $S_i \geq \lfloor \rho_i \cdot 2^i \rfloor + \lambda$, which ensures that we have enough elements for 2^i steps.
2. The pointer p_i is always included in the current window $[s_i, s_i + \lambda - 1]$. Since $p_i \geq s_i$ by definition, this is reduced to showing that whp we always have $p_i < s_i + \lambda$.

Analysis of Size Behavior

- Level L is of size n: it starts with all n elements, and every n steps all elements are back and we start another such phase.
- Level $i < L$ has capacity 2^i. Every 2^{i+1} steps it is being emptied to the level below (together with all levels above it), and every 2^i steps it is being filled from the levels above. This means that, if we look at 2^{i+1} consecutive steps, during the first 2^i steps this level is empty, and then we insert into it everything from above. This can be at most 2^i elements, if in all 2^i steps the selected elements are taken from levels below i. After another 2^i steps, this level is emptied again.

Let's consider an interval that begins when level i is emptied, so all the elements are at lower levels. Let us compute the expected number of elements that *remain below levels* i during the 2^i steps before that level is filled. (These are the elements that *will not be* in level i when it is filled.)

For each element $j \in [n]$, let X_j be a characteristic random variable of the event that j was never chosen in any of the 2^i steps (so it remained below level i). Then, the expected value of each X_j is $E[X_j] = \Pr[X_j = 1] = (1 - 1/n)^{2^i}$. The size of level i when it is filled is exactly $n - \sum_j X_j$, so the expected size of level i is $n - \sum_j E[X_j] = n(1 - (1 - 1/n)^{2^i})$.

Recalling that $(1 - 1/n)^{2^i} = \left((1 - 1/n)^n\right)^{2^i/n} \leq (1/e)^{2^i/n}$, the expected size of level $L - i$ when it is filled is therefore bounded from below by (and very close to) $n(1 - (1/e)^{2^{-i}})$. To give a few example, denote by S_i the size of level i when it is filled, and its expected value by $\mu_i = E[S_i]$, then we have

- $\mu_{L-1} \geq n\left(1 - \sqrt{1/e}\right) \approx 0.393n \approx n/2.5$
- $\mu_{L-2} \geq n\left(1 - \sqrt[4]{1/e}\right) \approx 0.221n \approx n/4.5$
- $\mu_{L-3} \geq n\left(1 - \sqrt[8]{1/e}\right) \approx 0.118n \approx n/8.5$
- $\mu_{L-4} \geq n\left(1 - \sqrt[16]{1/e}\right) \approx 0.061n \approx n/16.5$
- ...

It is not hard to see that $\mu_{L-i} < 2^{-i}n$: By symmetry, all elements $j \in [n]$ have the same probability of being chosen at least once, so we might as well look at the probability that a *random element* is chosen at least once. We have 2^{L-i} steps until we fill level $L - i$, so we can choose at most 2^{L-i} distinct elements. Hence for a random element, the probability of it being chosen (at least once) cannot be more than $2^{L-i}/n = 2^{L-i}/2^L = 2^{-i}$.

By a similar argument, μ_{L-i} gets closer to $2^{-i}n$ as i grows: Let #col$_i$ be the expected number of collisions when choosing 2^{L-i} elements at random with repetitions (i.e., the number of times we've chosen an element that was already chosen before). Considering again a random element, we have $\mu_{L-i} = 2^{-i}n - $#col$_i$. Increasing i by one (so halving the number of elements chosen) decreases the expected number of collisions by more than a factor of two (roughly by a factor of four). Hence $\mu_{L-i} = 2^{-i}n(1 - \epsilon_i)$ with ϵ_i monotonically decreasing in

i. We saw above that already for $i = 2$ we have $\mu_{L-2} \geq 2^{-2}n \cdot 0.88$, and it gets closer to $2^{-i}n$ as i increases.

Beyond computing the expected value of the size S_i of level i, we need to also get high-probability bounds on S_i. To that end, we would like to use the fact that $S_i = \sum_j X_j$ (with X_j the characteristic random variables from above) and apply Chernoff bound, but the X_j's are not quite independent.

Luckily, we can use the results from [8] to argue that they are negatively associated, and therefore the Chernoff bound apply to them as well. Specifically, [8, Theorem 13] shows that the random variables N_j =#-of-times-element-i-was-chosen are negatively associated. Then, Proposition 7 implies that also the indicators X_j are negatively associated (since each X_j is a monotonic function of the corresponding N_j). Finally, Proposition 5 says that Chernoff/Hoeffding bounds therefore apply to the sum of the X_j's. We conclude that for all i and every $0 < \delta \leq 1$:

$$\Pr[S_i > \mu_i(1 + \delta)] < \exp\left(-\delta^2 \mu_i/3\right). \tag{1}$$

$$\Pr[S_i < \mu_i(1 - \delta)] < \exp\left(-\delta^2 \mu_i/2\right) \tag{2}$$

We will use the first equation to prove Invariant 1 and the second equation to prove Invariant 2. Let us set the rate of advancing the window at level i to:

$$\rho_i = 3/2 \cdot 2^i/n \text{ for } i \leq L - 2, \text{ and } r_{L-1} = 0.54.$$

With these rates, and assuming that the levels are large enough so that, for all i, we have $2^i > 4\lambda$ and also $n > 25\lambda$, we can conclude the following:

– For $i \leq L-2$, we have $2^i \leq n/4$ and $2^i > \mu_i > 2^i \cdot 0.88$. Together with $2^i \geq 4\lambda$ we get

$$\lfloor \rho_i \cdot 2^i \rfloor + \lambda \leq 3/2 \cdot 2^{2i}/n + \lambda \leq 2^i \cdot (3/2 \cdot 2^i/n + \lambda/2^i)$$
$$\leq 2^i \cdot (3/8 + 1/4) < \mu_i/0.88 \cdot 0.625 < \mu_i(1 - 0.289).$$

Hence

$$\Pr[S_i < \lfloor \rho_i 2^i \rfloor + \lambda] < \exp(-0.289^2 \mu_i/2) < \exp(-0.289^2 \cdot 0.88 \cdot 2^i/2)$$
$$< \exp(-0.289^2 \cdot 0.88 \cdot 2\lambda) < \exp(-\lambda/7).$$

– For $i = L-1$ we have $2^i = n/2$, $\rho_i = 0.54$ and $\mu_i > 0.39n$. Assuming $n > 25\lambda$ we get

$$\lfloor \rho_i 2^i \rfloor + \lambda \leq 0.27n + n/25 = 0.31n < \mu_i(1/4 + 1/24)/0.39 < \mu_i(1 - 0.2).$$

Hence

$$\Pr[S_i < \lfloor \rho_i 2^i \rfloor + \lambda] < \exp(-0.2^2 \mu_i/2) < \exp(-0.2^2 \cdot 0.39n/2) < \exp(-0.2^2 \mu_i/2)$$
$$< \exp(-0.2^2 \cdot 0.39 \cdot 25\lambda/2) < \exp(-\lambda/6).$$

To analyze the 2nd invariant, fix some level i and consider the case where this invariant is violated at some step between 2^i and 2^{i+1}. Let $t_0 < 2^i$ be such that step $2^i + t_0$ was the last time that we advanced the next-element-to-read pointer p_i due to lagging behind the rear of the window ($t_0 = 0$ if it never lagged). Let t_1 be such that step $2^i + t_1$ is the first time that p_i exceeded the front of the window, and note that between steps $2^i + t_0$ and $2^i + t_1$ we only advanced the pointer due to reading elements from level i. Denote $\Delta = t_1 - t_0$.

Hence the number of elements that we read from that level during the interval $[2^i + t_0, 2^i + t_1]$ was $\lambda + \lfloor \rho_i \cdot t_1 \rfloor - \lfloor \rho_i \cdot t_0 \rfloor \geq \lambda + \rho_i \Delta - 1$. Since in each step we read an element with probability at most S_i/n, then the number of elements read is bounded below a binomial random variable with Δ trials and success probability S_i/n. We can bound the probability of violating the 2nd invariant by

$$\Pr[\text{Invariant 2 is violated between steps } 2^i \text{ and } 2^{i+1}]$$
$$\leq \Pr[\exists t_0, \Delta, \text{ s.t. } t_0 + \Delta < 2^i \text{ and } \mathsf{Bin}(S_i/n, \Delta) > \lambda + \rho_i \Delta]$$
$$< 2^{2i} \Pr[\mathsf{Bin}(S_i/n, \Delta) > \lambda + \rho_i \Delta].$$

Obviously for any p, x we have $\mathsf{Bin}(p, x) \leq x$ (with probability one). So $\mathsf{Bin}(S_i/n, \Delta) > \lambda + \rho_i \Delta$ has positive probability only when $\Delta \geq \lambda/(1 - \rho_i)$. Using Inequality (1) and the choice of ρ_i values from above:

– For $i \leq L - 2$, assuming $2^i > 4\lambda$ we have $2^i \geq \mu_i \geq 0.88 \cdot 2^i > 3.52\lambda$, so

$$\Pr[S_i > 5/4 \cdot 2^i] < \Pr[S_i > \mu_i(1 + 1/4)] < \exp(-\mu_i/48) < \exp(-\lambda/14).$$

Moreover, with $\rho_i = 3/2 \cdot 2^i/n$, if $\gamma := S_i/n \leq 5/4 \cdot 2^i/n = \rho_i/1.2$ then we get

$$\Pr[\mathsf{Bin}(\gamma, \Delta) > \lambda + \rho_i \Delta] < \Pr[\mathsf{Bin}(\gamma, \Delta) > \gamma(\lambda/\gamma\Delta + 1.2)\Delta]$$
$$\leq \Pr[\mathsf{Bin}(\gamma, \Delta) > \gamma(16\lambda/5\Delta + 1.2)\Delta],$$

where the last inequality follows since, for $i \leq L - 2$, we have $\gamma = 5/4 \cdot 2^i/n \leq 5/16$. Recalling that $\Delta > \lambda$, we consider three cases:
- $\Delta > \lambda > \Delta/4$: In this case $16\lambda/5\Delta + 1.2 > 2$ and therefore

$$\Pr[\mathsf{Bin}(\gamma, \Delta) > \lambda + \rho_i \Delta] < \Pr[\mathsf{Bin}(\gamma, \Delta) > 2\gamma\Delta]$$
$$< \exp(-\Delta/3) < \exp(-\lambda/3).$$

- $\Delta/4 \geq \lambda > \Delta/16$: In this case $16\lambda/5\Delta + 1.2 > 1.4$ and therefore

$$\Pr[\mathsf{Bin}(\gamma, \Delta) > \lambda + \rho_i \Delta] < \Pr[\mathsf{Bin}(\gamma, \Delta) > 1.4\gamma\Delta]$$
$$< \exp(-0.16\Delta/3) \leq \exp(-\lambda/5).$$

- $\Delta/16 \geq \lambda$: In this case, we trivially have $16\lambda/5\Delta + 1.2 > 1.2$ and therefore

$$\Pr[\mathsf{Bin}(\gamma, \Delta) > \lambda + \rho_i \Delta] < \Pr[\mathsf{Bin}(\gamma, \Delta) > 1.2\gamma\Delta]$$
$$< \exp(-0.04\Delta/3) \leq \exp(-\lambda/5).$$

In any case, we get

$$\Pr[\text{Invariant 2 is violated between steps } 2^i \text{ and } 2^{i+1}]$$
$$< 2^{2i}\big(\exp(-\lambda/14) + \exp(-\lambda/5)\big) < n^2/8 \cdot \exp(-\lambda/14).$$

– For $i = L - 1$ we have $0.39n < \mu_i < 0.4n$ and hence (assuming $n > 25\lambda$)

$$\Pr[S_i > 0.46n] < \Pr[S_i > 0.46 \cdot \mu_i/0.40] < \Pr[S_i > \mu_i(1 + 0.15)]$$
$$< \exp(0.15^2 \mu_i/3) < \exp(0.15^2 \cdot 0.39n/3)$$
$$< \exp(0.15^2 \cdot 0.39 \cdot 25\lambda/3) < \exp(-0.002n) < \exp(-\lambda/14).$$

Moreover, with $\rho_i = 0.54$, if $\gamma := S_i/n \le 0.46 < \rho_i/1.17$ then we get

$$\Pr[\mathrm{Bin}(\gamma, \Delta) > \lambda + \rho_i\Delta] < \Pr[\mathrm{Bin}(\gamma, \Delta) > \gamma(\lambda/\Delta\gamma + 1.17)\Delta].$$

The same case analysis as above (but using 1.17 instead of 1.2) implies that here we have in all cases $\Pr[\mathrm{Bin}(\gamma, \Delta) > \lambda + \rho_i\Delta] < \exp(-\lambda/7)$. Hence for $i = L - 1$ we have

$$\Pr[\text{Invariant 2 is violated between steps } 2^i \text{ and } 2^{i+1}]$$
$$< 2^{2i}\big(\exp(-\lambda/14) + \exp(-\lambda/7)\big) < n^2/2 \cdot \exp(-\lambda/14).$$

This concludes the proof of Theorem 3.2.   □

Improving the Concrete Efficiency by Improved Parameters. The analysis above yields failure probability exponentially small in λ, but the constants are not great (i.e., $\exp(-\lambda/14)$). This can be improved a lot in various ways. Some potential approaches include:

– Making the one-but-last level smaller: The parameters for higher-up levels are much better than for level $L - 1$, if instead we make the level above the leaves of size only $n/4$ rather than $n/2$ then the parameters will improve. (The cost is that merging into the last level will happen twice as often.)
– For the same reason, we can make do with smaller windows at higher levels than we do at lower ones.
– The procedure for advancing the windows could be changed, so that we move it faster at first (when the level has more elements in it) and slower later on.
– Violating the first invariant is not necessarily a failure, what we really care about is the next-element-to-read pointer p_i exceeding S_i, not necessarily the front of the window.

B   Tree-RORAM: More Details

B.1   Analysis of the Optimal Strategy

Recall the optimal adversary strategy: First guesses all the elements that were seen $L - 1$ steps ago, followed by those that were seen $L - 2$ steps ago, then $L - 3$, etc., until their entire budget of ϵN guesses is exhausted.

The number of correct guesses that the optimal strategy yields is a sum of $B = \epsilon N$ Bernoulli random variables, with the ones corresponding to elements seen $(L - j)$ steps ago having success probability of $1/j$. To bound the success probability of this optimal strategy, it remains just to bound the number of elements of each type.

Fix some arbitrary initial configuration from at least $2L$ steps ago, and consider the process starting from that configuration, until the current step. To fix the indexing, assume that the leaf to be examined next is leaf 0. Below we first devise a high-probability upper bound on the number of leaves that the strategy above considers before running out of budget (call that upper-bound J). Then we show an upper bound on the number of elements from these J leaves that will end up in leaf 0, and lower-bound the number of elements from the other $L - J$ leaves, hence getting an upper bound on the fraction of correct guesses.

For $i \in [1, N]$ and $j \in [1, L]$, denote by χ_{ij} the indicator random variable which is one if element i was last seen $L - j$ steps ago (i.e., the last time that we examined leaf $j \mod L$), and zero otherwise. The same analysis as in Lemma 4.1 implies that starting from any arbitrary initial configuration, the probability that element i was found in leaf $j \mod L$ the last time that we examined it, is bounded between $1/L$ and e/L. If it happens to be there, then the probability of not seeing it again until the current step is exactly j/L. Hence we have

- For any i, j, $\Pr[\chi_{ij} = 1] \in [j/L^2, ej/L^2]$.
- Any set of χ_{ij}'s with distinct indexes i are independent, since the locations of different elements are independent.
- For any fixed i the variables $\chi_{i0}, \ldots, \chi_{i,L-1}$ are negatively associated (as they sum up to one).

Given the properties above, we can use the Chernoff bound to reason about sums of these variables. For all the lemmas below, let $\epsilon < 1/4$ be a constant, and let λ be the security parameter.

Fix N, L such that $N > L$, and denote $B = \lfloor \epsilon N \rfloor$. We start by devising an upper-bound on the number of leaves that the adversary considers before running out of guessing budget. That is, we denote by X_j the number of elements that were last seen $L - j$ steps ago (namely $X_j = \sum_{i=1}^{n} \chi_{ij}$), and establish a number J such that whp $\sum_{j=1}^{J} X_i > B$.

Lemma B.1. *Assume that $N > 4\lambda \ln(2)/\epsilon$. Using the notations above and setting $J = \lceil 2L\sqrt{\epsilon} \rceil$ (and noting that $J < L$ since $\epsilon < 1/4$), we have $\Pr[\sum_{j=1}^{J} X_j < B] < 2^{-\lambda}$.*

Proof. The sum $S = \sum_{j=1}^{J} X_j = \sum_{j=1}^{J} \sum_{i=1}^{N} \chi_{ij}$ is a sum of $N \cdot J$ negatively associated Bernoulli random variables, with the success probability of each χ_{ij} between j/L^2 and ej/L^2. Denoting the expected value of the sum by $\mu = E[S]$, we therefore have

$$\mu \geq \sum_{j=1}^{J} \frac{j}{L^2} \cdot N = N \binom{J+1}{2} / L^2 > N/2 \cdot (J/L)^2.$$

Using the Chernoff bound with $\delta = 0.5$, we have $\Pr[S < \mu/2] \leq \exp(-\mu/8)$. The proof now follows just by plugging the values of λ and J: Recall that $J = \lceil 2L\sqrt{\epsilon} \rceil$ and therefore $(J/L)^2 \geq (2L\sqrt{\epsilon}/L)^2 = 4\epsilon$. This implies that $\mu \geq N/2 \cdot (J/L)^2 \geq N/2 \cdot 4\epsilon = 2\epsilon N$.

On the one hand, since $N > 4\lambda \ln(2)/\epsilon$, then $\mu/8 \geq \epsilon N/4 > \lambda \ln(2)$ and hence $\exp(-\mu/8) \leq 2^{-\lambda}$. On the other hand, we have $B \leq \epsilon N \leq \mu/2$. Putting them together, we get

$$\Pr[S < B] \leq \Pr[S < \mu/2] \leq \exp(-\mu/8) \leq 2^{-\lambda},$$

as needed.

For the next two lemmas, let $\gamma_{i,j}$ be the indicator random variable which is one if element i was last seen $L - j$ steps ago *and is currently found in leaf 0*, and zero otherwise. As we explain above, if element i was last seen $L - j$ steps ago then the probability of finding it now in leaf 0 is exactly $1/j$. Therefore γ_{ij} is an AND of χ_{ij} and an independent Bernoulli variable with success probability $1/j$, which means that $\Pr[\gamma_{ij} = 1] \in [1/L^2, e/L^2]$. Also, just like for the χ_{ij}'s, γ_{ij} is independent of all the $\gamma_{i'j'}$'s with $i' \neq i$, and negatively associated with the $\gamma_{ij'}$'s for $j' \neq j$. Hence we can use the Chernoff bound on their sums, as we do in the next two lemmas. It will be convenient to denote by Y_j the number of elements that were last seen $L - j$ steps ago and are found in leaf 0, namely $Y_j = \sum_{i=1}^{N} \gamma_{ij}$.

Lemma B.2. *With the setting above, assuming that $N/L > \frac{3\ln(2)}{2\sqrt{\epsilon}} \cdot \lambda$ and letting $\alpha = 12\sqrt{\epsilon} \cdot N/L$, then $\Pr[\sum_{j=1}^{J} Y_j > \alpha] < 2^{-\lambda}$.*

Proof. The sum $S = \sum_{j=1}^{J} Y_j = \sum_{j=1}^{J} \sum_{i=1}^{N} \gamma_{ij}$ is a sum of $N \cdot J$ negatively associated Bernoulli random variables, each with the success probability between $1/L^2$ and e/L^2. Hence the expected value of the sum is $\mu = E[S] \in [JN/L^2, JNe/L^2]$, and using the Chernoff bound with $\delta = 1$ we have $\Pr[S > 2\mu] \leq \exp(-\mu/3)$.

Substituting $J = \lceil 2L\sqrt{\epsilon} \rceil$ we have $\mu \geq JN/L^2 \geq 2\sqrt{\epsilon}N/L$, and also $\mu \leq JNe/L^2 \leq 6\sqrt{\epsilon}N/L$. On the one hand, since $N/L > \frac{3\ln(2)}{2\sqrt{\epsilon}} \cdot \lambda$, then $\mu/3 \geq 2\sqrt{\epsilon}N/3L \geq \lambda \ln(2)$ so $\exp(-\mu/3) \leq 2^{-\lambda}$. On the other hand, we have $\alpha = 12\sqrt{\epsilon} \cdot N/L \geq 2\mu$. Putting them together, we get

$$\Pr[S > \alpha] \leq \Pr[S > 2\mu] \leq \exp(-\mu/3) \leq 2^{-\lambda},$$

as needed.

Lemma B.3. *With the setting above, assuming that $N/L \geq \frac{8\ln(2)}{(1-3\sqrt{\epsilon})} \cdot \lambda$ and letting $\beta = \frac{(1-3\sqrt{\epsilon})}{2} \cdot N/L$, then $\Pr[\sum_{j=J+1}^{L} Y_j < \beta] < 2^{-\lambda}$.*

Proof. The sum $S = \sum_{j=J+1}^{L} Y_j = \sum_{j=J+1}^{L} \sum_{i=1}^{N} \gamma_{ij}$ is a sum of $N \cdot (L - J)$ negatively associated Bernoulli random variables, each with success probability between $1/L^2$ and e/L^2. Hence the expected value of the sum is $\mu = E[S] \in [(L-J)N/L^2, (L-J)Ne/L^2]$, and using the Chernoff bound with $\delta = 0.5$ we have $\Pr[S < \mu/2] \le \exp(-\mu/8)$.

Substituting $J = \lceil 2L\sqrt{\epsilon} \rceil$ we have $\mu \ge (L-J)N/L^2 \ge (1-3\sqrt{\epsilon})N/L$. On the one hand, since $N/L \ge \frac{8\ln(2)}{(1-3\sqrt{\epsilon})} \cdot \lambda$, then $\mu/8 \ge (1-3\sqrt{\epsilon})N/8L \ge \lambda\ln(2)$ so $\exp(-\mu/8) \le 2^{-\lambda}$. On the other hand, we have $\beta = \frac{(1-3\sqrt{\epsilon})}{2} \cdot N/L \le \mu/2$. Putting them together, we get

$$\Pr[S < \beta] \le \Pr[S < \mu/2] \le \exp(-\mu/8) \le 2^{-\lambda},$$

as needed.

The next lemma concludes the proof of Theorem 4.2.

Lemma B.4. *Let $\epsilon \le 1/9$ be a constant and λ the security parameter. Fix N, L such that $L > \frac{3}{8\sqrt{\epsilon}}$ and $N/L \ge \max\{\frac{3\ln(2)}{2\sqrt{\epsilon}}, \frac{8\ln(2)}{(1-3\sqrt{\epsilon})}\} \cdot \lambda$. Also, fix some arbitrary initial configuration from at least $2L$ steps ago, and consider the process starting from that configuration, until the current step. Denote $\delta = \frac{24\sqrt{\epsilon}}{1+21\sqrt{\epsilon}} < 1$.*

Then, an adversary that sees all the elements that were extracted in previous steps and can guess upto ϵN elements, has probability at most $3 \cdot 2^{-\lambda}$ of guessing more than an δ-fraction of the elements that will be extracted in the current step.

Proof. The conditions on the quantities N, L, ϵ, λ ensure that all the conditions in Lemmas B.1, B.2, and B.3 are satisfied. Hence the conclusions in all these lemmas hold, except perhaps with probability of $3 \cdot 2^{-\lambda}$.

By Lemma B.1 for the optimal adversary strategy above, the adversary exhausts all the guessing budget on elements that were last seen $L - j$ steps ago, for $j = 1, 2, \ldots, J$. By Lemma B.2, at most α of the elements that were last seen in those steps will be found in the next leaf, and by Lemma B.3 at least β other elements will be found there. Hence the fraction of elements that the adversary guesses is at most

$$\frac{\alpha}{\alpha + \beta} = \frac{12\sqrt{\epsilon} \cdot N/L}{12\sqrt{\epsilon} \cdot N/L + \frac{(1-3\sqrt{\epsilon})}{2} \cdot N/L} = \frac{24\sqrt{\epsilon}}{1 + 21\sqrt{\epsilon}} = \delta.$$

A Remark About Constants. The analysis above is very loose, giving up on many constants (on top of using the rather loose Chernoff bound). For example, to ensure that the adversary cannot guess more than $\delta = 1/2$ the elements in the leaf, the theorem above requires that the adversary's budget be limited to only $N/729$. In any real application, the constants will of course be determined by simulation rather than by the above. Some initial simulations that we ran indicate that the real number is something like $\epsilon \approx 2\delta^2$ (so to get $\delta = 1/2$ we need $\epsilon \approx 1/8$).

C   Non-independence for a Tree-RORAM Construction

As mentioned in Sect. 5.3, we show in Fig. 1 an example of a tree-RORAM scheme where the location of the different elements is *not independent* when conditioned on the server's view. Specifically, in this variant we still evict and re-assign all the elements from the current leaf at every step, but the server is only shown one of these elements.

First step (sees #1)	Second step (sees #2)	Pr[this history]	Pr[#3 in leaf1 | this history]	Pr[#1, #2 in leaf2 | this history]
[1,2,3][·]	[1,3] [2]	$\frac{1}{8}\cdot\frac{1}{3}\cdot\frac{1}{8}\cdot 1 = \frac{1}{192}$	1	0
[1,2,3][·]	[1] [2,3]	$\frac{1}{8}\cdot\frac{1}{3}\cdot\frac{1}{8}\cdot\frac{1}{2} = \frac{1}{384}$	1/2	0
[1,2,3][·]	[3] [1,2]	$\frac{1}{8}\cdot\frac{1}{3}\cdot\frac{1}{8}\cdot\frac{1}{2} = \frac{1}{384}$	1	1/4
[1,2,3][·]	[·][1,2,3]	$\frac{1}{8}\cdot\frac{1}{3}\cdot\frac{1}{8}\cdot\frac{1}{3} = \frac{1}{576}$	1/2	1/4
[1,2] [3]	[1] [2,3]	$\frac{1}{8}\cdot\frac{1}{2}\cdot\frac{1}{4}\cdot\frac{1}{2} = \frac{1}{128}$	1/2	0
[1,2] [3]	[·][1,2,3]	$\frac{1}{8}\cdot\frac{1}{2}\cdot\frac{1}{4}\cdot\frac{1}{3} = \frac{1}{192}$	1/2	1/4
[1,3] [2]	[1,3] [2]	$\frac{1}{8}\cdot\frac{1}{2}\cdot\frac{1}{4}\cdot 1 = \frac{1}{64}$	1	0
[1,3] [2]	[1] [2,3]	$\frac{1}{8}\cdot\frac{1}{2}\cdot\frac{1}{4}\cdot\frac{1}{2} = \frac{1}{128}$	1/2	0
[1,3] [2]	[3] [1,2]	$\frac{1}{8}\cdot\frac{1}{2}\cdot\frac{1}{4}\cdot\frac{1}{2} = \frac{1}{128}$	1	1/4
[1,3] [2]	[·][1,2,3]	$\frac{1}{8}\cdot\frac{1}{2}\cdot\frac{1}{4}\cdot\frac{1}{3} = \frac{1}{192}$	1/2	1/4
[1] [2,3]	[1] [2,3]	$\frac{1}{8}\cdot 1\cdot\frac{1}{2}\cdot\frac{1}{2} = \frac{1}{32}$	1/2	0
[1] [2,3]	[·][1,2,3]	$\frac{1}{8}\cdot 1\cdot\frac{1}{2}\cdot\frac{1}{3} = \frac{1}{48}$	1/2	1/4
Pr[#3 in leaf1 | view] = 0.6374			Pr[#3 in leaf1 | #1, #2 in leaf2, view] = 0.62	

A 2-step process with 3 elements and 2 leaves, starting from a random placement, where the adversary sees element #1 coming out of leaf1 and element #2 coming out of leaf2.

Fig. 1. An example of dependence between different elements.

References

1. Asharov, G., Komargodski, I., Lin, W.-K., Nayak, K., Peserico, E., Shi, E.: OptORAMa: optimal oblivious RAM. In: Canteaut, A., Ishai, Y. (eds.) EUROCRYPT 2020. LNCS, vol. 12106, pp. 403–432. Springer, Cham (2020). https://doi.org/10.1007/978-3-030-45724-2_14

2. Benhamouda, F., et al.: Can a public blockchain keep a secret? In: Pass, R., Pietrzak, K. (eds.) TCC 2020. LNCS, vol. 12550, pp. 260–290. Springer, Cham (2020). https://doi.org/10.1007/978-3-030-64375-1_10

3. Boyle, E., Chung, K.-M., Pass, R.: Oblivious parallel RAM and applications. In: Kushilevitz, E., Malkin, T. (eds.) TCC 2016. LNCS, vol. 9563, pp. 175–204. Springer, Heidelberg (2016). https://doi.org/10.1007/978-3-662-49099-0_7

4. Boyle, E., Naor, M.: Is there an oblivious RAM lower bound? In: Sudan, M. (ed.) Proceedings of the 2016 ACM Conference on Innovations in Theoretical Computer Science, Cambridge, MA, USA, 14–16 January 2016, pp. 357–368. ACM (2016). https://doi.org/10.1145/2840728.2840761

5. Devadas, S., van Dijk, M., Fletcher, C.W., Ren, L., Shi, E., Wichs, D.: Onion ORAM: a constant bandwidth blowup oblivious RAM. In: Kushilevitz, E., Malkin, T. (eds.) TCC 2016. LNCS, vol. 9563, pp. 145–174. Springer, Heidelberg (2016). https://doi.org/10.1007/978-3-662-49099-0_6

6. Dittmer, S., Ostrovsky, R.: Oblivious tight compaction In $O(n)$ time with smaller constant. In: Galdi, C., Kolesnikov, V. (eds.) SCN 2020. LNCS, vol. 12238, pp. 253–274. Springer, Cham (2020). https://doi.org/10.1007/978-3-030-57990-6_13

7. Doerner, J., Shelat, A.: Scaling ORAM for secure computation. In: Thuraisingham, B.M., Evans, D., Malkin, T., Xu, D. (eds.) Proceedings of the 2017 ACM SIGSAC Conference on Computer and Communications Security, CCS 2017, Dallas, TX, USA, 30 October–03 November 2017, pp. 523–535. ACM (2017). https://doi.org/10.1145/3133956.3133967

8. Dubhashi, D.P., Ranjan, D.: Balls and bins: a study in negative dependence. Random Struct. Algorithms **13**(2), 99–124 (1998). https://doi.org/10.1002/(SICI)1098-2418(199809)13:2⟨99::AID-RSA1⟩3.0.CO;2-M. https://www.brics.dk/RS/96/25/BRICS-RS-96-25.pdf

9. Gentry, C., Goldman, K.A., Halevi, S., Julta, C., Raykova, M., Wichs, D.: Optimizing ORAM and using it efficiently for secure computation. In: De Cristofaro, E., Wright, M. (eds.) PETS 2013. LNCS, vol. 7981, pp. 1–18. Springer, Heidelberg (2013). https://doi.org/10.1007/978-3-642-39077-7_1

10. Gentry, C., Halevi, S., Magri, B., Nielsen, J.B., Yakoubov, S.: Random-index PIR and applications. In: Nissim, K., Waters, B. (eds.) TCC 2021. LNCS, vol. 13044, pp. 32–61. Springer, Cham (2021). https://doi.org/10.1007/978-3-030-90456-2_2

11. Gentry, C., Halevi, S., Raykova, M., Wichs, D.: Outsourcing private RAM computation. In: 55th IEEE Annual Symposium on Foundations of Computer Science, FOCS 2014, Philadelphia, PA, USA, 18–21 October 2014, pp. 404–413. IEEE Computer Society (2014). https://doi.org/10.1109/FOCS.2014.50

12. Goldreich, O.: Towards a theory of software protection and simulation by oblivious rams. In: Aho, A.V. (ed.) Proceedings of the 19th Annual ACM Symposium on Theory of Computing, New York, USA, pp. 182–194. ACM (1987). https://doi.org/10.1145/28395.28416

13. Goldreich, O., Ostrovsky, R.: Software protection and simulation on oblivious RAMs. J. ACM **43**(3), 431–473 (1996). https://doi.org/10.1145/233551.233553

14. Gordon, S.D., Katz, J., Wang, X.: Simple and efficient two-server ORAM. In: Peyrin, T., Galbraith, S. (eds.) ASIACRYPT 2018. LNCS, vol. 11274, pp. 141–157. Springer, Cham (2018). https://doi.org/10.1007/978-3-030-03332-3_6

15. Kearns, M.J.: Efficient noise-tolerant learning from statistical queries. J. ACM **45**(6), 983–1006 (1998). https://doi.org/10.1145/293347.293351

16. Kushilevitz, E., Lu, S., Ostrovsky, R.: On the (in)security of hash-based oblivious RAM and a new balancing scheme. In: Rabani, Y. (ed.) Proceedings of the Twenty-Third Annual ACM-SIAM Symposium on Discrete Algorithms, SODA 2012, Kyoto, Japan, 17–19 January 2012, pp. 143–156. SIAM (2012). https://doi.org/10.1137/1.9781611973099.13

17. Larsen, K.G., Nielsen, J.B.: Yes, there is an oblivious RAM lower bound! In: Shacham, H., Boldyreva, A. (eds.) CRYPTO 2018. LNCS, vol. 10992, pp. 523–542. Springer, Cham (2018). https://doi.org/10.1007/978-3-319-96881-0_18

18. Lu, S., Ostrovsky, R.: Distributed oblivious RAM for secure two-party computation. In: Sahai, A. (ed.) TCC 2013. LNCS, vol. 7785, pp. 377–396. Springer, Heidelberg (2013). https://doi.org/10.1007/978-3-642-36594-2_22

19. Ostrovsky, R.: Efficient computation on oblivious RAMs. In: Ortiz, H. (ed.) Proceedings of the 22nd Annual ACM Symposium on Theory of Computing, Baltimore, Maryland, USA, 13–17 May 1990, pp. 514–523. ACM (1990). https://doi.org/10.1145/100216.100289

20. Patel, S., Persiano, G., Raykova, M., Yeo, K.: Panorama: oblivious RAM with logarithmic overhead. In: Thorup, M. (ed.) 59th IEEE Annual Symposium on Foundations of Computer Science, FOCS 2018, Paris, France, 7–9 October 2018, pp. 871–882. IEEE Computer Society (2018). https://doi.org/10.1109/FOCS.2018.00087

21. Reyzin, L.: Statistical queries and statistical algorithms: foundations and applications. CoRR abs/2004.00557 (2020). https://arxiv.org/abs/2004.00557

22. Stefanov, E., et al.: Path ORAM: an extremely simple oblivious RAM protocol. In: Sadeghi, A., Gligor, V.D., Yung, M. (eds.) 2013 ACM SIGSAC Conference on Computer and Communications Security, CCS 2013, Berlin, Germany, 4–8 November 2013, pp. 299–310. ACM (2013). https://doi.org/10.1145/2508859.2516660

23. Wang, X., Chan, T.H., Shi, E.: Circuit ORAM: on tightness of the Goldreich-Ostrovsky lower bound. In: Ray, I., Li, N., Kruegel, C. (eds.) Proceedings of the 22nd ACM SIGSAC Conference on Computer and Communications Security, Denver, CO, USA, 12–16 October 2015, pp. 850–861. ACM (2015). https://doi.org/10.1145/2810103.2813634

24. Wang, X.S., Huang, Y., Chan, T.H., Shelat, A., Shi, E.: SCORAM: oblivious RAM for secure computation. In: Ahn, G., Yung, M., Li, N. (eds.) Proceedings of the 2014 ACM SIGSAC Conference on Computer and Communications Security, Scottsdale, AZ, USA, 3–7 November 2014, pp. 191–202. ACM (2014). https://doi.org/10.1145/2660267.2660365

25. Weiss, M., Wichs, D.: Is there an oblivious RAM lower bound for online reads? In: Beimel, A., Dziembowski, S. (eds.) TCC 2018. LNCS, vol. 11240, pp. 603–635. Springer, Cham (2018). https://doi.org/10.1007/978-3-030-03810-6_22

On the Optimal Communication Complexity of Error-Correcting Multi-server PIR

Reo Eriguchi[1,4]([✉]), Kaoru Kurosawa[2,4], and Koji Nuida[3,4]

[1] Graduate School of Information Science and Technology, The University of Tokyo,
Tokyo, Japan
reo-eriguchi@g.ecc.u-tokyo.ac.jp
[2] Research and Development Initiative, Chuo University, Tokyo, Japan
kaoru.kurosawa.kk@vc.ibaraki.ac.jp
[3] Institute of Mathematics for Industry, Kyushu University, Fukuoka, Japan
nuida@imi.kyushu-u.ac.jp
[4] National Institute of Advanced Industrial Science and Technology, Tokyo, Japan

Abstract. An ℓ-server Private Information Retrieval (PIR) scheme
enables a client to retrieve a data item from a database replicated
among ℓ servers while hiding the identity of the item. It is called b-
error-correcting if a client can correctly compute the data item even in
the presence of b malicious servers. It is known that b-error correction
is possible if and only if $\ell > 2b$. In this paper, we first prove that if
error correction is perfect, i.e., the client always corrects errors, the minimum communication cost of b-error-correcting ℓ-server PIR is asymptotically equal to that of regular $(\ell - 2b)$-server PIR as a function of
the database size n. Secondly, we formalize a relaxed notion of statistical b-error-correcting PIR, which allows non-zero failure probability. We
show that as a function of n, the minimum communication cost of statistical b-error-correcting ℓ-server PIR is asymptotically equal to that of
regular $(\ell - b)$-server one, which is at most that of $(\ell - 2b)$-server one.
Our main technical contribution is a generic construction of statistical
b-error-correcting ℓ-server PIR for any $\ell > 2b$ from regular $(\ell - b)$-server
PIR. We can therefore reduce the problem of determining the optimal
communication complexity of error-correcting PIR to determining that of
regular PIR. In particular, our construction instantiated with the state-
of-the-art PIR schemes and the previous lower bound for single-server
PIR result in a separation in terms of communication cost between perfect and statistical error correction for any $\ell > 2b$.

1 Introduction

Private Information Retrieval (PIR) scheme [8] involves a client holding a search
index $\tau \in [n]$ and ℓ servers sharing a database $\boldsymbol{a} = (a_1, \ldots, a_n) \in \{0, 1\}^n$. The
scheme enables the client to fetch its desired bit a_τ from the database while
hiding the client's index τ from the servers. A trivial solution is to ask a server

E. Kiltz and V. Vaikuntanathan (Eds.): TCC 2022, LNCS 13749, pp. 60–88, 2022.
https://doi.org/10.1007/978-3-031-22368-6_3

to send the entire database $\boldsymbol{a}$, which has communication cost $\Theta(n)$. When $\ell = 1$, the trivial solution cannot be improved since it was shown in [8] that a single-server PIR must have communication cost $\Omega(n)$. To achieve communication cost $o(n)$, Chor et al. [8] considered ℓ-server PIR schemes for $\ell \geq 2$ in which servers do not collude. More generally, a PIR scheme is called t-private if any coalition of t servers learns no information on τ. Since then, many ℓ-server PIR schemes have been developed to improve communication cost [1,3,4,7–10,13,21].

As more servers are involved, there is a higher possibility that servers are malicious or faulty, or that the databases are not updated simultaneously. It
♦ is then important to enable a client to correct errors when part of the servers return false answers. Beimel and Stahl [5] introduced b-error-correcting PIR, in which a client can obtain a correct value a_τ even if b (or less) servers return false answers. Note that they only considered perfect error correction, which requires that a client corrects errors with probability 1. They showed that perfect b-error correction is possible if and only if $\ell > 2b$. In particular, they proposed a generic construction of a perfect b-error-correcting ℓ-server PIR scheme from any $(\ell - 2b)$-server PIR scheme for any $\ell > 2b$.

It has remained an open problem: what is the optimal communication complexity of b-error-correcting ℓ-server PIR as a function of n? For perfect error correction, since the previous construction [5] preserves t-privacy and asymptotic communication cost, the optimal communication complexity of b-error-correcting ℓ-server PIR is asymptotically upper bounded by that of $(\ell - 2b)$-server one. To the best of our knowledge, we have not seen work that studies the optimal communication complexity of *statistical* error-correcting PIR, in which non-zero failure probability is allowed.[1] It is unknown whether we can realize statistical error-correcting PIR with strictly lower communication cost than the perfect one. In this paper, we concern the following problems: (1) Is the minimum communication cost of perfect b-error-correcting ℓ-server PIR asymptotically equal to that of $(\ell - 2b)$-server PIR? (2) What if small failure probability is allowed?

1.1 Our Results

We show answers to the above problems.

1. The optimal communication complexity of perfect b-error-correcting ℓ-server PIR is asymptotically equal to that of $(\ell - 2b)$-server PIR as a function of the database size n.
2. We formalize a relaxed notion of statistical b-error-correcting PIR. The optimal communication complexity of statistical b-error-correcting ℓ-server PIR is asymptotically equal to that of $(\ell - b)$-server PIR as a function of n.

In conclusion, we can reduce the problem of determining the optimal communication complexity of error-correcting PIR to determining that of regular PIR.

---

[1] For regular PIR, the authors of [12,18] introduced the statistical analogue of perfect correctness to derive lower bounds for the communication cost of two-server PIR. Statistical correctness allows a client to output an incorrect value with small probability even if all servers behave honestly (Definition 2).

As a corollary, we obtain a separation in terms of communication cost between perfect and statistical error correction. For $\ell > 2b$,

- The minimum communication cost of perfect b-error-correcting $(\ell-2b)$-private ℓ-server PIR is $\Omega(n)$ since it is equal to that of $(\ell - 2b)$-private $(\ell - 2b)$-server one, which is $\Omega(n)$ [8].[2]
- The minimum communication cost of statistical b-error-correcting $(\ell - 2b)$-private ℓ-server PIR is $o(n)$ since it is equal to that of $(\ell - 2b)$-private $(\ell - b)$-server one, which can be instantiated with the scheme [19].

Optimal Communication Complexity for Perfect Error Correction. We show that perfect b-error-correcting ℓ-server PIR implies regular $(\ell - 2b)$-server PIR with the same communication cost (Theorem 4). Combined with the results of [5], the optimal communication complexity of perfect b-error-correcting ℓ-server PIR is asymptotically equal to that of regular $(\ell - 2b)$-server PIR as a function of n (Corollary 2).

Optimal Communication Complexity for Statistical Error Correction. We show that even statistical b-error-correcting ℓ-server PIR is impossible if $\ell \leq 2b$ (Theorem 5). For $\ell > 2b$, we show that as a function of n, the optimal communication complexity of statistical b-error-correcting ℓ-server PIR is asymptotically equal to that of regular $(\ell - b)$-server PIR with statistical correctness (Corollary 4).

Technically, it follows from our generic transformations preserving t-privacy and asymptotic communication complexity between regular, error-detecting, and error-correcting PIR. Error-detecting PIR [11] is a relaxed notion of error-correcting one in a sense that a client can only detect the existence of errors. We first provide a transformation from statistical regular k-server PIR to statistical b-error-detecting k-server one for any $k > b$ with communication overhead $(\log \epsilon^{-1})^2 k^{4+o(1)}$, where ϵ is the failure probability (Corollary 1). Next, we transform b-error-detecting $(\ell - b)$-server PIR to statistical b-error-correcting ℓ-server one with communication overhead $\binom{\ell}{b}$ (Theorem 3). We therefore obtain a transformation from statistical regular $(\ell-b)$-server PIR to statistical b-error-correcting ℓ-server one with communication overhead $(\log \epsilon^{-1})^2 2^{\ell+o(\ell)}$ (Corollary 3). Since the overhead is independent of n, our transformation preserves asymptotic communication cost as a function of n. Although it is exponential in ℓ, the overhead is not significant from a practical point of view since the number of servers is typically small, e.g., $\ell = 3$ [7,10,13,21]. Finally, we show that statistical b-error-correcting ℓ-server PIR implies statistical regular $(\ell - b)$-server one with the same communication cost (Theorem 6).

Instantiation of Our Transformation. Since all of the state-of-the-art schemes satisfy perfect correctness, we show a more communication-efficient

---

[2] Note that ℓ-private ℓ-server PIR is equivalent to single-server PIR since all the ℓ servers are allowed to collude and hence can be viewed as a single server.

transformation that is tailored to perfect regular PIR than Corollary 3 (see Corollary 6). Applying it to [9], we obtain a 1-private statistical b-error-correcting ℓ-server scheme with communication cost $\mathcal{L}_n[r^{-1}, v_k] \cdot \log \epsilon^{-1}$, where $k = \ell - b$, $r = \lfloor \log k \rfloor + 1$ and v_k is a constant depending on k.[3] Based on [19], we obtain a t-private statistical b-error-correcting ℓ-server scheme with communication cost $n^{\lfloor (2k-1)/t \rfloor^{-1}} (\log \epsilon^{-1}) 2^{\ell + o(\ell)}$ for any $t \geq 1$. We also provide a non-generic construction of error-correcting PIR tailored to the ones satisfying a certain algebraic property (Theorem 7). We then obtain a t-private error-correcting scheme with communication cost $n^{\lfloor (2k-1)/t \rfloor^{-1}} (\log n + \log \epsilon^{-1}) \ell^{O(1)}$ for any $t \geq 1$. Note that these t-private schemes are incomparable since the complexity of the latter is polynomial in ℓ while as a function of n, it is larger than the former by a factor of $\log n$.

For any $\ell > 2b$, Corollary 7 gives statistical b-error-correcting $(\ell - 2b)$-private schemes with $o(n)$ communication, while any perfect b-error-correcting $(\ell - 2b)$-private scheme has $\Omega(n)$ communication since we show that it must be based on single-server PIR. This shows a separation in terms of communication cost.

Table 1. Our statistical b-error-correcting t-private ℓ-server PIR schemes for $\ell > 2b$. Let n denote the database size and ϵ denote the failure probability. Let $k = \ell - b$, $r = \lfloor \log k \rfloor + 1$ and v_k denote a constant depending on k.

Method	Communication	t-privacy	Reference
Corollary 6 + [9]	$\mathcal{L}_n[r^{-1}, v_k] \cdot \log \epsilon^{-1}$	$t = 1$	Corollary 7
Corollary 6 + [19]	$n^{\lfloor (2k-1)/t \rfloor^{-1}} (\log \epsilon^{-1}) 2^{\ell + o(\ell)}$	$t \geq 1$	Corollary 7
Theorem 7 + [19]	$n^{\lfloor (2k-1)/t \rfloor^{-1}} (\log n + \log \epsilon^{-1}) \ell^{O(1)}$	$t \geq 1$	Corollary 8

1.2 Related Work

The scheme [19] is a t-private perfect b-error-correcting PIR scheme with communication cost $n^{\lfloor (2k-1)/t \rfloor^{-1}} \ell^{O(1)}$, where $k = \ell - 2b$. Kurosawa [14] proposed a more time-efficient error correction algorithm for the scheme [19]. On the other hand, the generic construction of [5] instantiated with [19] leads to a perfect error-correcting scheme with communication cost $n^{\lfloor (2k-1)/t \rfloor^{-1}} 2^{O(k)} \ell^{O(1)}$. Although the former has smaller communication cost, they have the same complexity as a function of n.

Error-correcting PIR schemes are considered in the setting where the size of each block of a database is large (see [2,16,17,20] and references therein). Since only the download cost is of interest, the schemes are incomparable with those considered in this paper, where total communication cost is of interest.

Eriguchi et al. [11] considered t-private b-error-detecting PIR in a model in which t out of b malicious servers can collude, while we consider a stronger model in which all b malicious servers can collude, which is the same as the one in [5].

---

[3] We define $\mathcal{L}_n[s, c] = \exp(c(\log n)^s (\log \log n)^{1-s})$ for $0 \leq s \leq 1$ and $c > 0$ (see Sect. 3).

The authors of [12,18] considered regular PIR with statistical correctness and derived lower bounds for the communication cost of two-server PIR. We note that there is no known separation in terms of communication cost between perfect and statistical regular PIR in contrast to our separation for error-correcting PIR.

2 Technical Overview

In this section, we provide an overview of our techniques. We give more detailed descriptions and formal proofs in the following sections.

2.1 Optimal Communication Complexity of Error-Correcting PIR

The Case of Perfect Error Correction. First, we consider perfect error-correcting PIR. Beimel and Stahl [5] showed a generic construction of perfect b-error-correcting ℓ-server PIR from any k-server PIR preserving asymptotic communication complexity, where $k = \ell - 2b$. To determine the optimal communication complexity, we prove the converse of their results: any perfect b-error-correcting ℓ-server PIR scheme Π implies a regular k-server PIR scheme Π' with the same communication cost (Theorem 4).

Let C denote a client with a search index τ and $S_1, \ldots, S_\ell$ denote ℓ servers sharing a database $a \in \{0,1\}^n$. For simplicity, we here set $\ell = 3$ and $b = 1$, and assume that S_1 is honest. For a fixed query by C in Π, let $\mathsf{ans}_i(a')$ denote the (deterministic) answer that is generated by S_i when S_i is honest and has database a'. We can see that the two sets $\mathcal{X}_h := \{\mathsf{ans}_1(a') \mid a' \text{ satisfies } a'_\tau = h\}$ ($h \in \{0,1\}$) have empty intersection. Then C can determine a_τ solely from a given $\mathsf{ans}_1(a)$, which implies single-server PIR, since only the $\mathcal{X}_{a_\tau}$ contains $\mathsf{ans}_1(a)$. To see that $\mathcal{X}_0 \cap \mathcal{X}_1 = \emptyset$, assume the contrary, i.e., $\alpha := \mathsf{ans}_1(a') = \mathsf{ans}_1(a'')$ with $a'_\tau = 0$ and $a''_\tau = 1$. Then a malicious server S_2 with database a' can falsely answer $\mathsf{ans}_2(a'')$, yielding the tuple of answers $\mathbf{ans} := (\alpha, \mathsf{ans}_2(a''), \mathsf{ans}_3(a'))$. On the other hand, a malicious server S_3 with database a'' can falsely answer $\mathsf{ans}_3(a')$, yielding the same tuple of answers $\mathbf{ans}$. Now C cannot determine with certainty from $\mathbf{ans}$ which of a' or a'' was actually used, contradicting the perfect error correction of Π. See Sect. 7.1 for the details.

The Case of Statistical Error Correction. Next, we consider statistical b-error-correcting PIR. We show equivalence among statistical regular k-server PIR, statistical b-error-detecting k-server PIR, and statistical b-error-correcting ℓ-server PIR, where $k = \ell - b$. We mean by equivalence that a PIR scheme can be transformed to another preserving asymptotic communication complexity as a function of the database size n, and vice versa. Our results on the optimal communication complexity immediately follow from the equivalence between regular k-server PIR and statistical b-error-correcting ℓ-server PIR.

From Regular to Error-Detecting PIR. Our transformation from any statistical k-server PIR scheme Π_0 to a statistical b-error-detecting k-server PIR scheme Π' (Corollary 1) is obtained by composing the following three transformations:

1. From a statistical k-server PIR scheme Π_0 to a k-server PIR scheme Π_1 with sufficiently small error probability (Lemma 1). This is done by repeating Π_0 λ times for some λ and taking the majority of the outputs; now the error probability is negligible in λ due to the Chernoff bound.
2. From Π_1 to a b-error-detecting k-server PIR scheme Π_2 where the correctness error probability (i.e., for the case of all honest servers) is sufficiently small and the error detection failure probability is smaller than 1 (see below).
3. From Π_2 to Π' where the error detection failure probability is also negligible (Theorem 2). This is done by repeating Π_2 λ' times for some λ' and letting the final output be a bit h if all the λ' outputs are h, otherwise $\perp$ meaning "error detected". Now, to fool Π', a malicious adversary needs to fool all the λ' instances of Π_2; due to the structure of Π_2, it is possible with exponentially small probability in λ' (when ignoring the negligible correctness error probability of Π_2).

We explain the second transformation from Π_1 to Π_2 (Theorem 1), for simplicity with $k = 2$ and $b = 1$. Assume that S_1 is honest. In Π_2, the client C first randomly guess which of S_1 and S_2 is honest. Suppose that C correctly guesses (with probability $1/2$) that S_1 is honest. Secondly, together with a *true* instance of Π_1, C runs a *dummy* instance of Π_1 where the query for S_1 is replaced with the same query as S_2. In the dummy instance, an answer returned by a honest server S_1 tells C the correct answer which S_2 should provide if she is honest (we note that each honest server's answer is supposed to be deterministic). Then C runs the two instances in a random order; given servers' answers, C first checks if S_2's answer in the dummy instance is correct (otherwise outputs $\perp$) and then outputs the output in the true instance. Now a malicious server S_2 who wants to fool Π_2 has to correctly guess which is the dummy instance, honestly behave in the dummy instance, and modify the answer in the true instance. Since the two instances are executed in a random order and are indistinguishable from S_2's viewpoint, S_2 can guess correctly with probability at most $1/2$. In summary, C can detect error with probability at least $(1/2) \cdot (1/2) = 1/4$ (when ignoring the negligible correctness error probability of Π_1), while the correctness error probability of Π_2 is almost the same as that of Π_1 since Π_2 runs only two instances of Π_1. See Sect. 5.1 for the details of the above method.

By carefully adjusting the parameters λ and λ' in the above transformations, we can make the error probability of the final scheme Π' bounded by a given value $\epsilon_{ED} > 0$. If the communication cost of the initial scheme Π_0 is c_0, that of Π' is $c = c_0 (\log \epsilon_{ED}^{-1})^2 \cdot \text{POLY}[k]$, which is asymptotically equal to c_0 as a function of n. See Sect. 5.2 for the details.

From Error-Detecting to Error-Correcting PIR. Our transformation from any statistical b-error-detecting k-server PIR scheme Π' to a statistical b-error-correcting ℓ-server PIR scheme Π simply executes $N := \binom{\ell}{\ell-b}$ independent instances of Π', each interacting with one of the N subsets of $k = \ell - b$ servers (Theorem 3). The output of Π is any bit contained in the N outputs by Π' if it exists; otherwise $\bot$. Now when all the N instances of Π' work correctly, the N outputs contain at least one true bit a_τ in the instance with k honest servers, due to the correctness of Π'; and do not contain the opposite bit due to the error-detection capability of the other $N - 1$ instances. Therefore Π fails only if some of the N instances of Π' fails, which happens with probability at most N times larger than the failure probability of Π'. Note that we can make the failure probability of Π arbitrarily small by starting from Π' with sufficiently small failure probability. See Sect. 6 for the details.

From Error-Correcting to Regular PIR. Finally, we prove that any statistical b-error-correcting ℓ-server PIR scheme Π implies a statistical regular k-server PIR scheme with the same error probability and communication complexity (Theorem 6). This is simply done as follows: When the client C receives correct answers in Π from $k = \ell - b$ honest servers only, C feds b arbitrary answers to the reconstruction algorithm of Π. Since those b answers can be viewed as false answers by the remaining b malicious servers, C correctly retrieves an item due to the error correction capability of Π. See Sect. 7.2 for the details.

2.2   Instantiation of Our Transformation

We instantiate our transformation from regular to statistical error-correcting PIR with the state-of-the-art schemes [9,19]. Although the above transformation (Corollary 3) can be used, we show a construction tailored to regular PIR with perfect correctness since the schemes [9,19] are perfectly correct. We observe that if a regular scheme is perfect, we do not need to make correctness error negligible at the first step of our construction of error-detecting PIR. We show a more communication-efficient construction than the above one (Corollary 6). Instantiated with [9,19], it gives the statistical error-correcting schemes shown in the first and second rows of Table 1. Note that if a statistical regular PIR scheme advances state of the art in the future, we should use the transformation in Corollary 3 instead of that in Corollary 6.

The third scheme can be obtained as follows. The construction follows the framework of the Rabin-BenOr robust secret sharing scheme [15]. Their scheme uses tags produced by a message authentication code (MAC, for short) to verify the integrity of shares. Since a client needs to verify the authenticity of *computations* by servers in PIR, we use a homomorphic MAC of [6]. The answer computed by any honest server is accepted by all honest servers while any incorrect answer is detected by them. If $\ell > 2b$, at least $\ell - b$ answers are declared to be correct after verification procedures. A client runs the reconstruction algorithm of $(\ell - b)$-server PIR on them and obtains a correct value. Note that the tag size of [6] grows linearly in the depth of the evaluated arithmetic circuit. The above construction is non-generic in a sense that it requires that server-side computation is represented by a shallow arithmetic circuit. Since the scheme [19] satisfies it, we obtain the third scheme of Table 1. See Sect. 8.1 for the details.

3   Preliminaries

For $m \in \mathbb{N}$, define $[m] = \{1, \ldots, m\}$. For a subset X of a set Y, we define $\overline{X} = \{y \in Y : y \notin X\}$ if Y is clear from the context. We write $u \leftarrow_{\$} Y$ if u is chosen uniformly at random from a set Y. Define $\binom{[m]}{k}$ as the set of all subsets of $[m]$ of size k. Let $\mathfrak{R}_{\mathcal{A}}$ denote the set of all random strings for a probabilistic algorithm $\mathcal{A}$. Namely, on input x, $\mathcal{A}$ outputs $\mathcal{A}(x; r)$ for $r \leftarrow_{\$} \mathfrak{R}_{\mathcal{A}}$. For a vector $\boldsymbol{x}$, let x_i denote the i-th entry of $\boldsymbol{x}$. Let $\log x$ denote the base-2 logarithm of x and $\ln x$ denote the base-e logarithm of x, where e denotes the Napier's constant. Let $\mathcal{L}_n[s, c]$ denote the function of n defined as $\mathcal{L}_n[s, c] = \exp(c(\log n)^s (\log \log n)^{1-s})$, where $0 \leq s \leq 1$ and $c > 0$.

4   Private Information Retrieval (PIR)

4.1   Definitions.

Definition 1 (Syntax). *An ℓ-server PIR scheme Π for a universe of databases $\{0, 1\}^n$ consists of three algorithms $\Pi = (\mathcal{Q}, \mathcal{A}, \mathcal{D})$, where $\mathcal{Q}$ is probabilistic while $\mathcal{A}$ and $\mathcal{D}$ are deterministic:*

- *A query algorithm $\mathcal{Q}$ takes a search index $\tau \in [n]$ as input. It then samples a random string $r \leftarrow_{\$} \mathfrak{R}_{\mathcal{Q}}$ and outputs $\mathsf{que}_i \in \{0, 1\}^{c_{\mathsf{que}}}$ for $i \in [\ell]$ and $\mathsf{aux} \in \{0, 1\}^{c_{\mathsf{aux}}}$. That is, $\mathcal{Q}(\tau; r) = (\mathsf{que}_1, \ldots, \mathsf{que}_\ell; \mathsf{aux})$.*
- *An answer algorithm $\mathcal{A}$ takes $i \in [\ell]$, $\mathsf{que}_i \in \{0, 1\}^{c_{\mathsf{que}}}$ and $\boldsymbol{a} = (a_1, \ldots, a_n) \in \{0, 1\}^n$ as input and outputs $\mathsf{ans}_i \in \{0, 1\}^{c_{\mathsf{ans}}}$. That is, $\mathcal{A}(i, \mathsf{que}_i, \boldsymbol{a}) = \mathsf{ans}_i$.*
- *A reconstruction algorithm $\mathcal{D}$ takes $(\mathsf{ans}_1, \ldots, \mathsf{ans}_\ell) \in (\{0, 1\}^{c_{\mathsf{ans}}})^\ell$ and $\mathsf{aux} \in \{0, 1\}^{c_{\mathsf{aux}}}$ as input, and outputs $y \in \{0, 1\}$. That is, $\mathcal{D}(\mathsf{ans}_1, \ldots, \mathsf{ans}_\ell; \mathsf{aux}) = y$.*

The (total) communication complexity of Π is given by $\ell(c_{\mathsf{que}} + c_{\mathsf{ans}})$.

Definition 2 (Statistical correctness). *An ℓ-server PIR scheme $\Pi = (\mathcal{Q}, \mathcal{A}, \mathcal{D})$ is said to be $(1 - \epsilon)$-correct if for any $\boldsymbol{a} = (a_1, \ldots, a_n) \in \{0, 1\}^n$ and any $\tau \in [n]$, it holds that $\Pr[r \leftarrow_{\$} \mathfrak{R}_{\mathcal{Q}} : \mathcal{D}(\mathsf{ans}_1, \ldots, \mathsf{ans}_\ell; \mathsf{aux}) = a_\tau] \geq 1 - \epsilon$, where $(\mathsf{que}_1, \ldots, \mathsf{que}_\ell; \mathsf{aux}) = \mathcal{Q}(\tau; r)$ and $\mathsf{ans}_i = \mathcal{A}(i, \mathsf{que}_i, \boldsymbol{a})$ for $i \in [\ell]$.*

Remark 1. In the literature, a PIR scheme is usually required to satisfy perfect correctness, i.e., $\epsilon = 0$. We use the above generalized notion of $(1 - \epsilon)$-correctness for $\epsilon \geq 0$ to show the equivalence between $(1 - \epsilon)$-correct $(\ell - b)$-server PIR and $(b; 1 - \epsilon)$-error-correcting ℓ-server PIR.

Definition 3 (t-Privacy). *An ℓ-server PIR scheme $\Pi = (\mathcal{Q}, \mathcal{A}, \mathcal{D})$ is said to be t-private if for any $X \in \binom{[\ell]}{t}$ and any $\tau, \tau' \in [n]$, the distributions of $(\mathsf{que}_i)_{i \in X}$ and $(\mathsf{que}'_i)_{i \in X}$ are perfectly identical, where $r, r' \leftarrow_{\$} \mathfrak{R}_{\mathcal{Q}}$, $(\mathsf{que}_1, \ldots, \mathsf{que}_\ell; \mathsf{aux}) = \mathcal{Q}(\tau; r)$ and $(\mathsf{que}'_1, \ldots, \mathsf{que}'_\ell; \mathsf{aux}') = \mathcal{Q}(\tau'; r')$.*

4.2   Robust PIR

(k, ℓ)-Robust PIR [5] guarantees that a client can compute a_τ from answers of any k out of ℓ servers. We provide a general notion of $(k, \ell; 1 - \epsilon)$-robust PIR with statistical correctness.

Definition 4. *A PIR scheme $\Pi = (\mathcal{Q}, \mathcal{A}, \mathcal{D})$ is said to be $(k, \ell; 1 - \epsilon)$-robust if*

- *$\mathcal{D}$ takes $X \in \binom{[\ell]}{k}$, $(\mathsf{ans}_i)_{i \in X} \in (\{0,1\}^{c_{\mathsf{ans}}})^k$ and $\mathsf{aux} \in \{0,1\}^{c_{\mathsf{aux}}}$ as input, and outputs $y \in \{0,1\}$;*
- *It holds that $\Pr[r \leftarrow_{\$} \mathfrak{R}_{\mathcal{Q}} : \mathcal{D}(X, (\mathsf{ans}_i)_{i \in X}; \mathsf{aux}) = a_\tau] \geq 1 - \epsilon$ for any $a \in \{0,1\}^n$, any $\tau \in [n]$ and any $X \in \binom{[\ell]}{k}$, where $(\mathsf{que}_1, \ldots, \mathsf{que}_\ell; \mathsf{aux}) = \mathcal{Q}(\tau; r)$ and $\mathsf{ans}_i = \mathcal{A}(i, \mathsf{que}_i, a)$ for $i \in [\ell]$.*

4.3   Error-Correcting and Error-Detecting PIR

We can identify an ℓ-server PIR scheme Π with a protocol $(\Pi; \mathsf{C}, \mathsf{S}_1, \ldots, \mathsf{S}_\ell)$ between a client C and ℓ servers $\mathsf{S}_1, \ldots, \mathsf{S}_\ell$ as follows:

Query. On input $\tau \in [n]$, C chooses $r \leftarrow_{\$} \mathfrak{R}_{\mathcal{Q}}$ and computes $(\mathsf{que}_1, \ldots, \mathsf{que}_\ell; \mathsf{aux}) = \mathcal{Q}(\tau; r)$. Then, C sends que_i to S_i for $i \in [\ell]$.
Answer. On input $a \in \{0,1\}^n$, each S_i returns $\mathsf{ans}_i = \mathcal{A}(i, \mathsf{que}_i, a)$ to C.
Reconstruction. C outputs $y = \mathcal{D}(\mathsf{ans}_1, \ldots, \mathsf{ans}_\ell; \mathsf{aux})$.

We consider a malicious adversary $\mathcal{B}$ who corrupts a set B of at most b servers and returns a possibly modified answer $\widetilde{\mathsf{ans}}_i$ to C instead of ans_i for each $i \in B$.[4]

Definition 5 (Error-correcting PIR). *A PIR scheme Π is said to be $(b; 1 - \epsilon_{\mathrm{EC}})$-error-correcting if for any $a \in \{0,1\}^n$, any $\tau \in [n]$ and any malicious adversary $\mathcal{B}$ who corrupts at most b servers, it holds that $\Pr[\mathsf{C} \text{ outputs } a_\tau] \geq 1 - \epsilon_{\mathrm{EC}}$ in the protocol $(\Pi; \mathsf{C}, \mathsf{S}_1, \ldots, \mathsf{S}_\ell)$.*

Remark 2. In the definition, in order to achieve stronger error correction capability, we allow the modified answers to depend on all of the b queries even if $b > t$ for t-privacy (though now b queries may leak some information on the client's index). This model follows the original definition in [5].

Definition 6 (Error-detecting PIR). *A PIR scheme Π is said to be $(b; 1 - \epsilon_{\mathrm{ED}})$-error-detecting if the following conditions hold:*

- *Π is $(1 - \epsilon_{\mathrm{ED}})$-correct.*
- *C is allowed to output a special symbol $\bot$ and for any $a \in \{0,1\}^n$, any $\tau \in [n]$ and any malicious adversary $\mathcal{B}$ who corrupts at most b servers, it holds that $\Pr[\mathsf{C} \text{ outputs } a_\tau] \geq 1 - \epsilon_{\mathrm{ED}}$ in the protocol $(\Pi; \mathsf{C}, \mathsf{S}_1, \ldots, \mathsf{S}_\ell)$.*

---

[4] More formally, we formalize $\mathcal{B}$ by using a *tampering function* [11]. See [11] or Appendix A for the details.

5   Transformation from Regular to Error-Detecting PIR

We show a generic transformation from any t-private k-server PIR scheme $\Pi_0 = (\mathcal{Q}_0, \mathcal{A}_0, \mathcal{D}_0)$ to a t-private $(k - 1; 1 - \epsilon_{\text{ED}})$-error-detecting k-server PIR scheme Π. The communication overhead is independent of the database size n.

We first give our transformation for larger ϵ_{ED} in Sect. 5.1, which is then reduced to arbitrarily small $\epsilon_{\text{ED}} > 0$ in Sect. 5.2.

5.1   Basic Transformation

Given $\Pi_0 = (\mathcal{Q}_0, \mathcal{A}_0, \mathcal{D}_0)$, we consider the following two query algorithms Π_0^{Compute} and $\Pi_0^{\mathsf{Verify},(i,j)}$. Π_0^{Compute} is used to actually compute a_τ and $\Pi_0^{\mathsf{Verify},(i,j)}$ is used to verify whether S_j correctly computes her answer assuming that S_i is honest.

Π_0^{Compute}: On input $\tau \in [n]$, C chooses $r \leftarrow_\$ \mathfrak{R}_{\mathcal{Q}_0}$ and computes $\mathcal{Q}_0(\tau; r) = (\mathsf{que}_1, \ldots, \mathsf{que}_k; \mathsf{aux})$. Then, he sends (m, que_m) to S_m for $m \in [k]$.

$\Pi_0^{\mathsf{Verify},(i,j)}$: On input $\tau \in [n]$, C chooses $r \leftarrow_\$ \mathfrak{R}_{\mathcal{Q}_0}$ and computes $\mathcal{Q}_0(\tau; r) = (\mathsf{que}_1, \ldots, \mathsf{que}_k; \mathsf{aux})$. Then, he sends (m, que_m) to S_m for $m \in [k] \setminus \{i\}$, and (j, que_j) to S_i.

Now we consider a k-server PIR scheme $\Pi_1 = (\mathcal{Q}, \mathcal{A}, \mathcal{D})$ as shown in Fig. 1, where the client C chooses $i \neq j \in [k]$ uniformly at random, randomly permutes two instances of Π_0^{Compute} and $\Pi_0^{\mathsf{Verify},(i,j)}$, and executes them in parallel with $\mathsf{S}_1, \ldots, \mathsf{S}_k$. C verifies that S_j correctly computes her answer using $\Pi_0^{\mathsf{Verify},(i,j)}$ and then he runs $\mathcal{D}_0$ on the answers obtained during the execution of Π_0^{Compute}.

We obtain the following theorem. We sketch the proof here. The formal proof is given in Appendix B, where a more general result (Theorem 2) is proved.

Theorem 1. *If Π_0 is t-private and $(1 - \epsilon)$-correct, then Π_1 is t-private and $(k - 1; 1 - \epsilon_{\text{ED}})$-error-detecting for $\epsilon_{\text{ED}} = 1 - 1/(2k(k - 1)) + 2\epsilon$. Furthermore, if Π_0 has communication cost c_0, then Π_1 has communication cost $O(c_0 + k \log k)$.*

Proof (Sketch). It is easy to see that Π_1 is $(1 - \epsilon)$-correct. It is also easy to see that Π_1 is t-private and has the communication complexity $2c_0 + O(k \log k) = O(c_0 + k \log k)$. We will prove that Π_1 is $(k - 1; 1 - \epsilon_{\text{ED}})$-error-detecting.

First, we assume that $\epsilon = 0$. Without loss of generality, we suppose that S_1 is honest and a malicious adversary $\mathcal{B}$ corrupts $\mathsf{S}_2, \ldots, \mathsf{S}_k$. Clearly, if $\mathsf{S}_2, \ldots, \mathsf{S}_k$ return correct answers, the client C obtains the correct value a_τ. We may assume that at least one malicious server, say S_2, modifies her answer.

Consider the case where C chooses $(i, j) = (1, 2)$ at Step 1(a) in Fig. 1, which occurs with probability $1/(k(k - 1))$. To make C output the incorrect value $1 - a_\tau$, S_2 needs to honestly behave in the instance $\Pi_0^{\mathsf{Verify},(1,2)}$ and to modify her answer in the other instance Π_0^{Compute}. Note that $\mathcal{B}$ cannot distinguish between two instances $\Pi_0^{\mathsf{Compute}}, \Pi_0^{\mathsf{Verify},(1,2)}$ since the distributions of queries

---

Components.
- A k-server PIR scheme $\Pi_0 = (\mathcal{Q}_0, \mathcal{A}_0, \mathcal{D}_0)$.
- Query algorithms Π_0^{Compute} and $\Pi_0^{\mathsf{Verify},(i,j)}$

Query. On input $\tau \in [n]$, C chooses $i \neq j \in [k]$ uniformly at random and executes $\Pi_0^{\mathsf{Compute}}, \Pi_0^{\mathsf{Verify},(i,j)}$ in a random order. Specifically, C does the following:
1. He chooses $i \neq j \in [k]$ uniformly at random.
2. He randomly permutes two protocols $\Pi_0^{\mathsf{Compute}}, \Pi_0^{\mathsf{Verify},(i,j)}$. Let $\Pi_0^{(1)}, \Pi_0^{(2)}$ denote the resulting sequence.
3. He generates queries for $\Pi_0^{(1)}, \Pi_0^{(2)}$. Let $\mathsf{que}_m^{(\alpha)}$ and $\mathsf{aux}^{(\alpha)}$ denote the query sent to S_m and auxiliary information obtained during the execution of $\Pi_0^{(\alpha)}$, respectively.
4. He sends $\mathsf{que}_m = (\mathsf{que}_m^{(1)}, \mathsf{que}_m^{(2)})$ to each S_m.

Answer. On input $\boldsymbol{a} \in \{0,1\}^n$, each S_m does the following:
1. For each $\mathsf{que}_m^{(\alpha)} = (x, \mathsf{que}_x)$, she computes $\mathsf{ans}_m^{(\alpha)} = \mathcal{A}_0(x, \mathsf{que}_x, \boldsymbol{a})$.
2. She returns $\mathsf{ans}_m^{(\alpha)}$ to C for $\alpha \in \{1,2\}$.

Error detection. If he receives $\widetilde{\mathsf{ans}}_m^{(\alpha)}$ from S_m as $\mathsf{ans}_m^{(\alpha)}$, C does the following:
1. For $\alpha \in \{1,2\}$ with $\Pi_0^{(\alpha)} = \Pi_0^{\mathsf{Compute}}$, he sets $z \leftarrow \mathcal{D}_0(\widetilde{\mathsf{ans}}_1^{(\alpha)}, \dots, \widetilde{\mathsf{ans}}_k^{(\alpha)}; \mathsf{aux}^{(\alpha)})$.
2. For $\alpha \in \{1,2\}$ with $\Pi_0^{(\alpha)} = \Pi_0^{\mathsf{Verify},(i,j)}$, he verifies whether $\widetilde{\mathsf{ans}}_j^{(\alpha)} = \widetilde{\mathsf{ans}}_i^{(\alpha)}$ holds. If it holds, then he outputs z. Otherwise, he outputs $\bot$.

Fig. 1. A basic error-detecting PIR protocol Π_1

that $\mathsf{S}_2, \dots, \mathsf{S}_k$ receive are the same in both cases. Hence, the distribution of an answer returned by S_2 is independent of the permutation chosen by C at Step 1(b). With probability at least $1/2$, S_2 fails to guess the instance $\Pi_0^{\mathsf{Verify},(1,2)}$, in which she has to behave honestly. Therefore, C can detect errors with probability $1/(2k(k-1)) = 1 - \epsilon_{\mathsf{ED}}$. We conclude that Π_1 is $(k-1; 1 - \epsilon_{\mathsf{ED}})$-error-detecting.

In the general case of $\epsilon \geq 0$, the previous argument still holds unless C chooses a *bad* random string such that $\mathcal{D}_0$ outputs $1 - a_\tau$ even if all servers return correct answers. Since Π_1 involves two instances of Π_0 and Π_0 is $(1-\epsilon)$-correct, we can upper bound by 2ϵ the fraction of such bad random strings. Therefore the previous bound for the error probability is increased by 2ϵ, which results in the value of ϵ_{ED} in the statement. $\qquad\square$

5.2 General Transformation

We consider a PIR scheme Π obtained by running sufficiently many independent instances of the basic error-detecting scheme (Fig. 2). We obtain the following theorem. The formal proof is given in Appendix B.

Theorem 2. *Let $b < k$, $\lambda \in \mathbb{N}$, $\epsilon \geq 0$, and $\epsilon_{\mathsf{ED}} = 2\lambda\epsilon + (1 - 1/(2k(k-1)))^\lambda$. If there exists a $(1-\epsilon)$-correct t-private k-server PIR scheme $\Pi_0 = (\mathcal{Q}_0, \mathcal{A}_0, \mathcal{D}_0)$ with communication cost c_0, then there exists a $(b; 1 - \epsilon_{\mathsf{ED}})$-error-detecting t-private k-server PIR scheme with communication cost $c = O(\lambda(c_0 + k \log k))$.*

---

1. For each $\nu \in [\lambda]$, run the protocol Π_1 (Fig. 1) in parallel.
2. Let $z^{(\nu)}$ denote the output of C for $\nu \in [\lambda]$.
3. If $\{z^{(\nu)} : \nu \in [\lambda]\} = \{z\}$ for some $z \in \{0, 1\}$, C outputs z. Otherwise C outputs $\perp$.

Fig. 2. A general error-detecting PIR Protocol Π

Proof (Sketch). Since Π runs λ instances of Π_1, the claim for the communication complexity follows from Theorem 1. When $\epsilon = 0$, a malicious adversary has to fool all the λ independent instances in order to make the client output an incorrect value. Therefore the claimed bound follows from that of Theorem 1. In the general case of $\epsilon \geq 0$, since Π runs Π_0 2λ times in total, the bound is increased by $2\lambda\epsilon$. □

We show that the optimal communication complexity of $(k - 1; 1 - \epsilon_{ED})$-error-detecting k-server PIR is asymptotically upper bounded by that of $(1 - \epsilon_0)$-correct k-server PIR for any $\epsilon_{ED} > 0$ and $\epsilon_0 < 1/2$. Lemma 1 shows that the correctness error of a $(1 - \epsilon_0)$-correct PIR scheme can be made arbitrarily small. We defer the formal proof to Appendix C.

Lemma 1. *Let $0 \leq \epsilon_0 < 1/2$ and $\lambda \in \mathbb{N}$. If there exists a $(1 - \epsilon_0)$-correct t-private k-server PIR scheme Π_0 with communication cost c_0, then there exists a $(1 - \epsilon)$-correct t-private k-server PIR scheme Π with communication cost $c_0\lambda$, where $\epsilon = (2\sqrt{\epsilon_0(1 - \epsilon_0)})^\lambda \leq \exp(-2(1/2 - \epsilon_0)^2\lambda)$.*

Proof (Sketch). We construct Π in a way that it runs λ independent instances of Π_0 and takes the majority of their outputs. Since each instance fails with probability at most ϵ_0, the Chernoff bound implies that the majority fails with probability at most ϵ as in the statement. The claimed upper bound for ϵ is deduced by an elementary analysis. □

Corollary 1 shows a general transformation from any $(1 - \epsilon_0)$-correct k-server PIR scheme to a $(k - 1; 1 - \epsilon_{ED})$-error-detecting PIR scheme.

Corollary 1. *Let $b < k$, $0 \leq \epsilon_0 < 1/2$ and $\epsilon_{ED} > 0$. If there exists a $(1 - \epsilon_0)$-correct t-private k-server PIR scheme with communication cost c_0, then there exists a $(b; 1 - \epsilon_{ED})$-error-detecting t-private k-server PIR scheme with communication cost $c = c_0(\log \epsilon_{ED}^{-1})^2(1/2 - \epsilon_0)^{-2}k^{4+o(1)}$.*

Proof. Let $\lambda, \lambda' \in \mathbb{N}$ be the smallest integers such that $\lambda \geq 2k(k - 1)(\log 3\epsilon_{ED}^{-1})$ and $\lambda' \geq (1/2 - \epsilon_0)^{-2}\lambda$. We have that $\lambda = O(k^2 \log \epsilon_{ED}^{-1})$ and $\lambda' = O((1/2 - \epsilon_0)^{-2}\lambda)$. Let $\epsilon = (2\sqrt{\epsilon_0(1 - \epsilon_0)})^{\lambda'} \leq \exp(-2(1/2-\epsilon_0)^2\lambda') \leq \exp(-2\lambda)$. It follows from Lemma 1 that there exists a $(1 - \epsilon)$-correct t-private k-server PIR scheme with communication cost $c_0' = c_0\lambda'$. Note that

$$2\lambda\epsilon + \left(1 - \frac{1}{2k(k-1)}\right)^\lambda \leq 2\exp(-\lambda) + \left(1 - \frac{1}{2k(k-1)}\right)^\lambda$$

$$\leq 3\exp\left(-\frac{\lambda}{2k(k-1)}\right)$$

$$\leq \epsilon_{ED}.$$

It then follows from Theorem 2 that there exists a $(b; 1 - \epsilon_{ED})$-error-detecting t-private k-server PIR scheme with communication cost $c = O(\lambda(c_0' + k\log k)) = c_0(\log \epsilon_{ED}^{-1})^2(1/2 - \epsilon_0)^{-2}k^{4+o(1)}$.   □

6   Transformation from Error-Detecting to Error-Correcting PIR

We show a transformation from any $(b; 1 - \epsilon_{ED})$-error-detecting $(\ell - b)$-server PIR scheme to a $(b; 1 - \epsilon_{EC})$-error-correcting ℓ-server PIR scheme. Our transformation simply executes $\binom{\ell}{\ell-b}$ independent instances of the error-detecting PIR scheme. In particular, the communication overhead is independent of the database size n. We sketch the proof here but refer to Appendix D for the details.

Theorem 3. *Let $b < \ell/2$, $k = \ell - b$ and $N = \binom{\ell}{k}$. If there exists a $(b; 1 - \epsilon_{ED})$-error-detecting t-private k-server PIR scheme Π_0 with communication cost c, then there exists a $(b; 1 - \epsilon_{EC})$-error-correcting t-private ℓ-server PIR scheme with communication cost Nc for $\epsilon_{EC} = N\epsilon_{ED}$.*

Proof (Sketch). We consider a PIR scheme Π where N independent instances of Π_0 are executed between a client and every subset of k servers. Let $z_1, \ldots, z_N \in \{0, 1, \perp\}$ be the N outcomes. If $\{z_1, \ldots, z_N\}$ is $\{s\}$ or $\{s, \perp\}$ for some $s \in \{0, 1\}$, then the client outputs s and otherwise outputs 0.

Clearly, the communication complexity of Π is Nc. It is also easy to see that Π is t-private since all executions of Π_0 are independent.

For the correctness, a malicious adversary can make the output incorrect only if either the unique instance of Π_0 with k honest servers does not output a_τ (happening with probability at most ϵ_{ED}) or some of the other $N - 1$ instances of Π_0 with possibly corrupted servers fails to detect error (happening with probability at most ϵ_{ED} each). Therefore the error probability is bounded by $\epsilon_{ED} + (N - 1)\epsilon_{ED} = \epsilon_{EC}$.   □

7   Optimal Communication Complexity of Error-Correcting PIR

In this section, we show the relation between the optimum communication complexity of error-correcting PIR and that of regular PIR as a function of the database size n. We use the following notations: For the database size n,

- $\text{PIR}_{k,t;1-\epsilon}(n)$ denotes the minimum communication cost of t-private $(1-\epsilon)$-correct k-server PIR schemes and;
- $\text{EC-PIR}_{\ell,t,b;1-\epsilon}(n)$ denotes the minimum communication cost of t-private $(b; 1-\epsilon)$-error-correcting ℓ-server PIR schemes.

7.1 The Case of Perfect Error Correction

Beimel and Stahl [5] showed a generic transformation from a t-private 1-correct k-server PIR scheme to a t-private 1-correct $(b; 1)$-error-correcting ℓ-server PIR scheme for $b \le (\ell - k)/2$. The communication overhead is $2^{O(k)} \ell \log \ell$, which is independent of the database size n. We show the converse.

Theorem 4. *Let* $b < \ell/2$. *If there exists a* $(b; 1)$-*error-correcting* ℓ-*server PIR scheme* $\Pi = (\mathcal{Q}, \mathcal{A}, \mathcal{D})$, *then there exists a deterministic algorithm* $\mathcal{D}'$ *such that* $\Pi' = (\mathcal{Q}, \mathcal{A}, \mathcal{D}')$ *is a* $(k, \ell; 1)$-*robust PIR scheme, where* $k = \ell - 2b$.

Proof. Let $X \in \binom{[\ell]}{k}$ and $\tau \in [n]$. Below we show that for any possible output $((\mathsf{que}_i)_{i \in [\ell]}; \mathsf{aux})$ of $\mathcal{Q}(\tau)$, if two databases $\boldsymbol{a}'$ and $\boldsymbol{a}''$ satisfy $a'_\tau = 0$ and $a''_\tau = 1$, then we always have $(\mathcal{A}(i, \mathsf{que}_i, \boldsymbol{a}'))_{i \in X} \ne (\mathcal{A}(i, \mathsf{que}_i, \boldsymbol{a}''))_{i \in X}$. Once this is proved, the desired $\mathcal{D}'$ can be constructed as follows: Given $(\mathsf{ans}_i)_{i \in X}$, it first finds (by an exhaustive search) a database $\widehat{\boldsymbol{a}} \in \{0, 1\}^n$ such that $(\mathcal{A}(i, \mathsf{que}_i, \widehat{\boldsymbol{a}}))_{i \in X} = (\mathsf{ans}_i)_{i \in X}$, and then outputs $z = \widehat{a}_\tau$. Note that the actual database $\widehat{\boldsymbol{a}} = \boldsymbol{a}$ indeed satisfies the equality and the uniqueness yields $z = a_\tau$.

Now we show the claim. Assume for the contrary that $(\mathcal{A}(i, \mathsf{que}_i, \boldsymbol{a}'))_{i \in X} = (\mathcal{A}(i, \mathsf{que}_i, \boldsymbol{a}''))_{i \in X}$, which we denote by $(\alpha_i)_{i \in X}$. We fix a partition $[\ell] = X \cup Y \cup Z$ into mutually disjoint parts with $Y, Z \in \binom{[\ell]}{b}$. For each $i \in [\ell]$, define $\widetilde{\alpha}_i \in \{0, 1\}^{C_{\mathrm{ans}}}$ by $\widetilde{\alpha}_i = \alpha_i$ if $i \in X$, $\widetilde{\alpha}_i = \mathcal{A}(i, \mathsf{que}_i, \boldsymbol{a}')$ if $i \in Y$, and $\widetilde{\alpha}_i = \mathcal{A}(i, \mathsf{que}_i, \boldsymbol{a}'')$ if $i \in Z$. Now if Y (resp. Z) is the set of corrupted servers, then a malicious adversary with database $\boldsymbol{a}''$ (resp. $\boldsymbol{a}'$) can let the tuple of answers be $\widetilde{\alpha}$ by setting $\widetilde{\mathsf{ans}}_i = \mathcal{A}(i, \mathsf{que}_i, \boldsymbol{a}')$ for $i \in Y$ (resp. $\mathcal{A}(i, \mathsf{que}_i, \boldsymbol{a}'')$ for $i \in Z$). Therefore, the perfect correctness of Π implies that $\mathcal{D}(\widetilde{\alpha}; \mathsf{aux})$ must output $a''_\tau = 1$ (resp. $a'_\tau = 0$). This is a contradiction. Therefore the claim holds. $\square$

A t-private $(k, \ell; 1)$-robust PIR scheme trivially implies a t-private 1-correct k-server PIR scheme. By combining the results of [5] and Theorem 4, we obtain the following corollary.

Corollary 2. *For any* $b < \ell/2$ *and* $t \ge 1$, *it holds that*

$$\text{EC-PIR}_{\ell,t,b;1}(n) = \Theta_{\ell,b}\left(\text{PIR}_{\ell-2b,t;1}(n)\right),$$

where the notation $\Theta_{\ell,b}(\cdot)$ *hides any constant depending on* ℓ *and* b.

7.2 The Case of Statistical Error Correction

In [5], it is claimed that $(b; 1)$-error-correcting ℓ-server PIR is impossible if $b \ge \ell/2$. We show a more general impossibility result in the case of statistical correctness. The proof is given in Appendix E.

Theorem 5. *Let $b \geq \ell/2$. If there exists a $(b; 1 - \epsilon_{EC})$-error-correcting ℓ-server PIR scheme $\Pi = (\mathcal{Q}, \mathcal{A}, \mathcal{D})$, then $\epsilon_{EC} \geq 1/2$.*

For $b < \ell/2$, we obtain a generic construction of $(b; 1 - \epsilon)$-error-correcting ℓ-server PIR from $(1 - \epsilon)$-correct $(\ell - b)$-server PIR by combining Corollary 1 and Theorem 3.

Corollary 3. *Let $b < \ell/2$, $k = \ell - b$, $0 < \epsilon_0 < 1/2$ and $\epsilon > 0$. If there exists a $(1 - \epsilon_0)$-correct t-private k-server PIR scheme with communication cost c_0, then there exists a $(b; 1 - \epsilon)$-error-correcting t-private ℓ-server PIR scheme with communication cost $c = c_0 (\log \epsilon^{-1})^2 (1/2 - \epsilon_0)^{-2} 2^{\ell + o(\ell)}$.*

Proof. Let $\epsilon_{ED} = \epsilon / \binom{\ell}{b}$. Corollary 1 implies that there exists a $(b; 1 - \epsilon_{ED})$-error-detecting t-private k-server PIR scheme with communication cost $c_1 = c_0 (\log \epsilon_{ED}^{-1})^2 (1/2 - \epsilon_0)^{-2} k^{4 + o(1)} = c_0 (\log \epsilon^{-1})^2 (1/2 - \epsilon_0)^{-2} \ell^{O(1)}$. Then, Theorem 3 implies that there exists a $(b; 1 - \epsilon)$-error-correcting t-private ℓ-server PIR scheme with communication cost $c = c_1 \binom{\ell}{b} = c_0 (\log \epsilon^{-1})^2 (1/2 - \epsilon_0)^{-2} 2^{\ell + o(\ell)}$. □

The following theorem shows the converse of Corollary 3.

Theorem 6. *Let $b < \ell/2$ and $\epsilon_{EC} \geq 0$. If there exists a $(b; 1 - \epsilon_{EC})$-error-correcting ℓ-server PIR scheme $\Pi = (\mathcal{Q}, \mathcal{A}, \mathcal{D})$, there exists an algorithm $\mathcal{D}'$ such that $\Pi' = (\mathcal{Q}, \mathcal{A}, \mathcal{D}')$ is a $(k, \ell; 1 - \epsilon_{EC})$-robust PIR scheme, where $k = \ell - b$.*

Proof. Let $X \in \binom{[\ell]}{k}$, $\tau \in [n]$ and $\boldsymbol{a} \in \{0, 1\}^n$. Given X, $(\widetilde{ans}_i)_{i \in X}$, and aux as input, $\mathcal{D}'$ is defined in a way that it sets $\widetilde{ans}_i = \boldsymbol{0} \in \{0, 1\}^{c_{ans}}$ for $i \in \overline{X}$ and runs $\mathcal{D}((\widetilde{ans}_i)_{i \in [\ell]}; \text{aux})$. Now the input for the internal $\mathcal{D}$ is equivalent to the case of Π where the database is $\boldsymbol{a}$ and a malicious adversary corrupting the servers in $\overline{X}$ has modified each $\widetilde{ans}_i$, $i \in \overline{X}$ to $\boldsymbol{0}$. Therefore the correctness of $\mathcal{D}$ implies that $\mathcal{D}'$ outputs a_τ with probability at least $1 - \epsilon_{EC}$. □

A t-private $(k, \ell; 1 - \epsilon)$-robust PIR scheme trivially implies a t-private $(1 - \epsilon)$-correct k-server PIR scheme. By combining Corollary 3 and Theorem 6, we obtain the following corollary.

Corollary 4. *For any $b < \ell/2$, $t \geq 1$ and $0 < \epsilon < 1/2$, it holds that*

$$\text{EC-PIR}_{\ell, t, b; 1 - \epsilon}(n) = \Theta_{\ell, b, \epsilon}(\text{PIR}_{\ell - b, t; 1 - \epsilon}(n)),$$

where the notation $\Theta_{\ell, b, \epsilon}(\cdot)$ hides any constant depending on ℓ, b and ϵ.

8   Instantiation of Our Transformation

We have shown the generic construction of statistical error-correcting PIR from regular PIR with *statistical* correctness. The reason is that we aim at relating its optimal communication complexity to that of statistical regular PIR. Since all the state-of-the-art schemes satisfy *perfect* correctness, we use a construction tailored to perfect regular PIR in the following instantiations. If an initial scheme is 1-correct, the resulting error-correcting scheme has better communication cost than Corollary 3.

The following corollary shows that if an initial scheme is 1-correct, it is possible to construct a more efficient error-detecting PIR scheme than Corollary 1.

Corollary 5. *Let* $b < k$ *and* $\epsilon_{ED} > 0$. *If there exists a 1-correct* t-*private* k-*server PIR scheme with communication cost* c_0, *then there exists a* $(b; 1 - \epsilon_{ED})$-*error-detecting* t-*private* k-*server PIR scheme with communication cost* $c = O((c_0 + k \log k)k^2(\log \epsilon_{ED}^{-1}))$.

Proof. Let $\lambda \in \mathbb{N}$ be the smallest integer such that $\lambda \geq 2k(k-1)\log \epsilon_{ED}^{-1}$. Observe that $\lambda = O(k^2 \log \epsilon_{ED}^{-1})$. Also, observe that $(1 - 1/(2k(k-1)))^\lambda \leq \exp(-\lambda/(2k(k-1))) \leq \epsilon_{ED}$. The statements then follow from Theorem 2. $\square$

By combining Theorem 3 with Corollary 5, we obtain the following corollary.

Corollary 6. *Let* $b < \ell/2$, $k = \ell - b$ *and* $\epsilon > 0$. *If there exists a 1-correct* t-*private* k-*server PIR scheme with communication cost* c_0, *then there exists a* $(b; 1-\epsilon)$-*error-correcting* t-*private* ℓ-*server PIR scheme with communication cost* $c = c_0(\log \epsilon^{-1})2^{\ell+o(\ell)}$.

Proof. Let $\epsilon_{ED} = \epsilon/\binom{\ell}{b}$. Corollary 5 implies that there exists a $(b; 1 - \epsilon_{ED})$-error-detecting t-private k-server PIR scheme with communication complexity $c_1 = c_0(\log \epsilon_{ED}^{-1})k^{3+o(1)} = c_0(\log \epsilon^{-1})\ell^{O(1)}$. Then, Theorem 3 implies that there exists a $(b; 1 - \epsilon)$-error-correcting t-private ℓ-server PIR scheme with communication complexity $c = c_1\binom{\ell}{b} = c_0(\log \epsilon^{-1})2^{\ell+o(\ell)}$. $\square$

We apply Corollary 6 to the state-of-the-art PIR schemes [9, 19] to obtain the following corollary.

Corollary 7. *Let* $b < \ell/2$, $k = \ell - b$, $t \geq 1$ *and* $\epsilon > 0$. *There exist* $(b; 1 - \epsilon)$-*error-correcting* ℓ-*server PIR schemes* Π_1, Π_2 *such that:*

- Π_1 *is 1-private and has communication cost* $\mathcal{L}_n[(\lfloor \log k \rfloor + 1)^{-1}, v_k] \cdot (\log \epsilon^{-1})2^{\ell+o(\ell)}$, *where* v_k *is a constant depending only on* k *and;*
- Π_2 *is* t-*private and has communication cost* $n^{\lfloor (2k-1)/t \rfloor^{-1}}(\log \epsilon^{-1})2^{\ell+o(\ell)}$.

Observe that if $\ell > b + t$, i.e., $k \geq t + 1 \geq 2$, then Corollary 7 gives t-private $(b; 1 - \epsilon)$-error-correcting ℓ-server PIR with $o(n)$ communication. On the other hand, if $\ell \leq 2b + t$, any $(b; 1)$-error-correcting t-private ℓ-server scheme has communication cost $\Omega(n)$ since it must be based on single-server PIR in view of Corollary 2. Thus, there is a separation in terms of communication cost between perfect and statistical b-error-correcting t-private ℓ-server PIR if $\max\{2b, b+t\} < \ell \leq 2b + t$.

In the next section, we show a non-generic construction assuming a certain algebraic property. If we apply it to the scheme of [19], we obtain a $(b; 1 - \epsilon)$-error-correcting ℓ-server PIR scheme which is more communication-efficient in terms of ℓ than Π_2 in Corollary 7.

8.1 Statistical Error-Correcting PIR Based on Homomorphic MAC

We show a construction of a $(b; 1 - \epsilon)$-error-correcting ℓ-server PIR scheme Π from a $(\ell - b, \ell; 1 - \epsilon')$-robust PIR scheme $\Pi_0 = (\mathcal{Q}_0, \mathcal{A}_0, \mathcal{D}_0)$. Our construction requires that $\mathcal{A}_0$ is represented by low-degree polynomials. The communication overhead is polynomial in ℓ while that of Corollary 3 is exponential in ℓ.

Our construction is based on the framework of the Rabin-BenOr robust secret sharing scheme [15]. Suppose that the client C wants a server S_i to compute a function $F_{a,i}(\cdot) := \mathcal{A}_0(i, \cdot, a)$ on input que_i. Since C does not know a, he verifies the computation of $F_{a,i}(\mathsf{que}_i)$ with help of the other servers S_j $(j \neq i)$. Below we give a specific method to do so based on homomorphic MAC. Our method guarantees that if S_i computes $F_{a,i}$ correctly, her answer is accepted by any honest server S_j. Since the number of honest servers $\ell - b$ is greater than that of dishonest ones b, C then knows that S_i is honest. If S_i does not perform computation correctly, she will be detected with high probability by honest servers. Again, since there are more honest servers than dishonest ones, C can discard the answer returned by S_i. After the above procedures, at least $\ell - b$ answers are declared to be correct. The $(\ell - b, \ell; 1 - \epsilon)$-robustness implies that C can run $\mathcal{D}_0$ based on those answers.

To verify computation of $F_{a,i}$, we uses some techniques for information-theoretic MACs [6]. For simplicity, we assume that $F_{a,i}$ is a single polynomial of degree d over a finite field $\mathbb{F}_p$ and a query is a field element $\mathsf{que}_i \in \mathbb{F}_p$. The client C chooses a random field element α_{ij} from a sufficiently large field $\mathbb{F}_q$, which is used as a secret key to verify the computation of S_i with help of S_j. The authentication tag of the message que_i is a random polynomial $T_{ij}(X)$ of degree 1 over $\mathbb{F}_q$ that evaluates to que_i on the point 0. C sends que_i and T_{ij} to S_i, and $\rho_{ij} = T_{ij}(\alpha_{ij})$ to S_j. Then, S_i computes $\mathsf{ans}_i = F_{a,i}(\mathsf{que}_i)$ and also $G_{ij}(X) = F_{a,i}(T_{ij}(X))$ while S_j computes $\sigma_{ij} = F_{a,i}(\rho_{ij})$. Finally, C verifies whether it holds that $\mathsf{ans}_i = G_{ij}(0)$ and $\sigma_{ij} = G_{ij}(\alpha_{ij})$. Even if S_i sends an incorrect answer $\widetilde{\mathsf{ans}}_i$ along with a modified tag $\widetilde{G}_{ij}(X)$ such that $\widetilde{\mathsf{ans}}_i = \widetilde{G}_{ij}(0)$, C can detect errors unless α_{ij} happens to be a root of a non-zero polynomial $\widetilde{G}_{ij} - G_{ij}$, which occurs with probability roughly $O(d/q)$. The above argument can be generalized into the case where que_i is a vector over $\mathbb{F}_p$ and $F_{a,i}$ is a tuple of multiple polynomials.

Note that the size of each tag grows linearly with the degree of the evaluated polynomial. Since the above verification procedure is performed over every pair of servers, the communication complexity of the resulting scheme Π is $\ell^2 d$ times larger than Π_0 ignoring logarithmic factors of d, ℓ and q. We obtain the following theorem. See the full version for the proof.

Theorem 7. *Let $b < \ell/2$, $k = \ell - b$, $\epsilon_0 \geq 0$ and $\epsilon > \binom{\ell}{b}\epsilon_0$. Let $\Pi_0 = (\mathcal{Q}_0, \mathcal{A}_0, \mathcal{D}_0)$ be a $(k, \ell; 1 - \epsilon_0)$-robust t-private ℓ-server PIR scheme such that:*

- *For any $i \in [\ell]$, a query que_i is an M-dimensional vector over a finite field $\mathbb{F}_p$, i.e., $\mathsf{que}_i \in \mathbb{F}_p^M$;*

– *For any $\boldsymbol{a} \in \{0,1\}^n$ and any $i \in [\ell]$, $\mathcal{A}_0(i, \cdot, \boldsymbol{a})$ is a tuple $(F_{\boldsymbol{a},i}^{(\mu)})_{\mu \in [N]}$ of M-variate polynomials of total degree at most d over $\mathbb{F}_p$, i.e., $\mathcal{A}_0(i, \mathsf{que}_i, \boldsymbol{a}) = (F_{\boldsymbol{a},i}^{(\mu)}(\mathsf{que}_i))_{\mu \in [N]}$ for $\mathsf{que}_i \in \mathbb{F}_p^M$.*

Then there exists a $(b; 1 - \epsilon)$-error-correcting t-private ℓ-server PIR scheme with communication complexity

$$c = O\left(\ell^2(M + Nd) \log \frac{Nd\ell}{\epsilon - \binom{\ell}{b}\epsilon_0}\right).$$

The scheme in [19] satisfies the assumptions of Theorem 7 with $\epsilon_0 = 0$, $p = O(\log \ell)$, $d = \lfloor (2k - 1)/t \rfloor$ and $M, N \in O(dn^{1/d})$. Thus we obtain the following corollary.

Corollary 8. *Let $b < \ell/2$, $k = \ell - b$, $t \geq 1$ and $\epsilon > 0$. There exists a t-private $(b; 1 - \epsilon)$-error-correcting ℓ-server PIR scheme with communication complexity $n^{\lfloor (2k-1)/t \rfloor^{-1}}(\log n + \log \epsilon^{-1})k^{1+o(1)}\ell^{2+o(1)}$.*

Acknowledgement. This research was partially supported by JSPS KAKENHI Grant Numbers JP20J20797 and 19H01109, Japan, JST CREST Grant Number JPMJCR2113, Japan, and JST AIP Acceleration Research JPMJCR22U5, Japan.

A   Definitions

Following [11], we use the notion of tampering functions to formalize a malicious server who corrupts a set of servers and modifies their answers.

Definition 7 (Tampering function). *Let $\Pi = (\mathcal{Q}, \mathcal{A}, \mathcal{D})$ be an ℓ-server PIR scheme. Let $T \subseteq [\ell]$ be a subset. Let f be a function which takes $(\mathsf{que}_1, \ldots, \mathsf{que}_\ell) \in (\{0,1\}^{c_{\mathsf{que}}})^\ell$ and $\boldsymbol{a} \in \{0,1\}^n$ as input, and outputs $(\widetilde{\mathsf{ans}}_1, \ldots, \widetilde{\mathsf{ans}}_\ell) \in (\{0,1\}^{c_{\mathsf{ans}}})^\ell$. We say that f is a tampering function for Π with respect to T if for each $i \in [\ell]$, it holds that*

$$\widetilde{\mathsf{ans}}_i = \begin{cases} \mathcal{A}(i, \mathsf{que}_i, \boldsymbol{a}), & \text{if } i \notin T, \\ f_i(\{\mathsf{que}_{i'}\}_{i' \in T}, \boldsymbol{a}), & \text{if } i \in T, \end{cases}$$

for some function f_i. We denote the family of all such tampering functions by $\mathcal{F}_T^\Pi$.

Definition 8 (Error-correcting PIR). *We say that an ℓ-server PIR scheme $\Pi = (\mathcal{Q}, \mathcal{A}, \mathcal{D})$ is $(1 - \epsilon_{\mathrm{EC}})$-error-correcting with respect to T if for any $\boldsymbol{a} = (a_1, \ldots, a_n) \in \{0,1\}^n$, any $\tau \in [n]$ and any $f \in \mathcal{F}_T^\Pi$, it holds that*

$$\Pr[r \leftarrow_\$ \mathfrak{R}_{\mathcal{Q}} : \mathcal{D}(f(\mathsf{que}_1, \ldots, \mathsf{que}_\ell, \boldsymbol{a}); \mathsf{aux}) = a_\tau] \geq 1 - \epsilon_{\mathrm{EC}},$$

where $(\mathsf{que}_1, \ldots, \mathsf{que}_\ell; \mathsf{aux}) = \mathcal{Q}(\tau; r)$. *We say that an ℓ-server PIR scheme Π is* $(b; 1 - \epsilon_{EC})$-*error-correcting if it is* $(1 - \epsilon_{EC})$-*error-correcting with respect to any* $T \subseteq [\ell]$ *of size* b.

Definition 9 (Error-detecting PIR). *We say that an ℓ-server PIR scheme* $\Pi = (\mathcal{Q}, \mathcal{A}, \mathcal{D})$ *is* $(1 - \epsilon_{ED})$-*error-detecting with respect to* T *if the following conditions hold:*

- *Π is* $(1 - \epsilon_{ED})$-*correct.*
- *$\mathcal{D}$ is allowed to output a special symbol $\perp$ and it holds that for any $\boldsymbol{a} = (a_1, \ldots, a_n) \in \{0, 1\}^n$, any $\tau \in [n]$ and any $f \in \mathcal{F}_T^\Pi$,*

$$\Pr[r \leftarrow_\$ \mathfrak{R}_\mathcal{Q} : \mathcal{D}(f(\mathsf{que}_1, \ldots, \mathsf{que}_\ell, \boldsymbol{a}); \mathsf{aux}) \in \{a_\tau, \perp\}] \geq 1 - \epsilon_{ED},$$

where $(\mathsf{que}_1, \ldots, \mathsf{que}_\ell; \mathsf{aux}) = \mathcal{Q}(\tau; r)$.

We say that an ℓ-server PIR scheme Π is $(b; 1 - \epsilon_{ED})$-*error-detecting if it is* $(1 - \epsilon_{ED})$-*error-detecting with respect to any subset T of size b.*

B   Proof of Theorem 2

Let $\mathcal{I} = \{(i, j) \in [k]^2 : i \neq j\}$. Let Π be a k-server PIR scheme $\Pi = (\mathcal{Q}, \mathcal{A}, \mathcal{D})$ described in Figs. 3, 4 and 5.

Communication complexity. The communication complexity of Π is at most

$$\lambda(2c_0 + O(\log k)) = O(\lambda(c_0 + \log k)).$$

Correctness. Assume that all servers are honest. Let $\boldsymbol{a} \in \{0, 1\}^n$ be a database and $\tau \in [n]$ be a client's index. Let $\nu \in [\lambda]$. We show that the value $z^{(\nu)}$ computed at Step 2(b) of $\mathcal{D}$ is 0 or 1 with probability 1 and is equal to a_τ with probability at least $1 - \epsilon$. If so, the union bound implies that it holds that $\{z^{(\nu)} : \nu \in [\lambda]\} = \{a_\tau\}$ with probability at least $1 - \lambda\epsilon$, which shows the $(1 - \epsilon_{ED})$-correctness of Π.

Assume that $b^{(\nu)} = 0$. We can deal with the other case of $b^{(\nu)} = 1$ similarly. Observe that the first row of $\boldsymbol{Q}^{(\nu)}$ is

$$\mathsf{row}_1^{(j)} = \left((1, \mathsf{que}_{1,1}^{(\nu)}), \ldots, (k, \mathsf{que}_{1,k}^{(\nu)}) \right).$$

Since all servers are honest, the first row of $\boldsymbol{A}^{(\nu)}$ is

$$(\widetilde{\mathsf{ans}}_{1,1}^{(\nu)}, \ldots, \widetilde{\mathsf{ans}}_{1,k}^{(\nu)}; \mathsf{aux}_1^{(\nu)}) = \left(\mathcal{A}(1, \mathsf{que}_{1,1}^{(\nu)}, \boldsymbol{a}), \ldots, \mathcal{A}(k, \mathsf{que}_{1,k}^{(\nu)}, \boldsymbol{a}); \mathsf{aux}_1^{(\nu)} \right).$$

Notations.
- A $(1 - \epsilon)$-correct k-server PIR scheme $\Pi_0 = (\mathcal{Q}_0, \mathcal{A}_0, \mathcal{D}_0)$
- $\mathcal{I} = \{(i,j) \in [k]^2 : i \neq j\}$

$\mathcal{Q}(\tau)$. Given $\tau \in [n]$:
1. For each $\nu \in [\lambda]$, do the following:
    (a) Choose $r^{(\nu)} = (r_m^{(\nu)})_{m \in \{1,2\}} \leftarrow_\$ (\mathfrak{R}_{\mathcal{Q}_0})^2$.
    (b) Choose $(i,j) = (i^{(\nu)}, j^{(\nu)}) \leftarrow_\$ \mathcal{I}$ and $b^{(\nu)} \leftarrow_\$ \{0,1\}$.
    (c) Do the following:
        - If $b^{(\nu)} = 0$, set

$$\mathsf{row}_1^{(\nu)} = \left((1, \mathsf{que}_{1,1}^{(\nu)}), \ldots, (k, \mathsf{que}_{1,k}^{(\nu)}) \right),$$

$$\mathsf{row}_2^{(\nu)} = \left((1, \mathsf{que}_{2,1}^{(\nu)}), \ldots, (j-1, \mathsf{que}_{2,j-1}^{(\nu)}), (i, \mathsf{que}_{2,i}^{(\nu)}), \right.$$
$$\left. (j+1, \mathsf{que}_{2,j+1}^{(\nu)}), \ldots, (k, \mathsf{que}_{2,k}^{(\nu)}) \right),$$

where $(\mathsf{que}_{m,1}^{(\nu)}, \ldots, \mathsf{que}_{m,k}^{(\nu)}; \mathsf{aux}_m^{(\nu)}) = \mathcal{Q}_0(\tau; r_m^{(\nu)})$.
        - If $b^{(\nu)} = 1$, set

$$\mathsf{row}_1^{(\nu)} = \left((1, \mathsf{que}_{1,1}^{(\nu)}), \ldots, (j-1, \mathsf{que}_{1,j-1}^{(\nu)}), (i, \mathsf{que}_{1,i}^{(\nu)}), \right.$$
$$\left. (j+1, \mathsf{que}_{1,j+1}^{(\nu)}), \ldots, (k, \mathsf{que}_{1,k}^{(\nu)}) \right),$$

$$\mathsf{row}_2^{(\nu)} = \left((1, \mathsf{que}_{2,1}^{(\nu)}), \ldots, (k, \mathsf{que}_{2,k}^{(\nu)}) \right),$$

where $(\mathsf{que}_{m,1}^{(\nu)}, \ldots, \mathsf{que}_{m,k}^{(\nu)}; \mathsf{aux}_m^{(\nu)}) = \mathcal{Q}_0(\tau; r_m^{(\nu)})$.
    (d) Construct an 2-by-k matrix $\boldsymbol{Q}^{(\nu)}$ as

$$\boldsymbol{Q}^{(\nu)} = \begin{pmatrix} \mathsf{row}_1^{(\nu)} \\ \mathsf{row}_2^{(\nu)} \end{pmatrix}.$$

    (e) Let $\mathsf{que}_i^{(\nu)}$ be the i-th column of $\boldsymbol{Q}^{(\nu)}$ for $i \in [k]$.
    (f) Let $\mathsf{aux}^{(\nu)} = (\mathsf{aux}_1^{(\nu)}, \mathsf{aux}_2^{(\nu)})$.
2. Let $\mathsf{que}_i = (\mathsf{que}_i^{(\nu)})_{\nu \in [\lambda]}$ for $i \in [k]$.
3. Let $\mathsf{aux} = ((\mathsf{aux}^{(\nu)})_{\nu \in [\lambda]}, (i^{(\nu)}, j^{(\nu)}, b^{(\nu)})_{\nu \in [\lambda]})$.
4. Output $(\mathsf{que}_1, \ldots, \mathsf{que}_k; \mathsf{aux})$.

Fig. 3. The query algorithm of the PIR scheme Π in Theorem 2

$\mathcal{A}(i, \mathsf{que}_i, \boldsymbol{a})$. Given $i \in [k]$, $\mathsf{que}_i = (\mathsf{que}_i^{(\nu)})_{\nu \in [\lambda]}$ and $\boldsymbol{a} \in \{0,1\}^n$:

1. For each $\nu \in [\lambda]$, do the following:
   (a) For each $m = 1, 2$, if the m-th entry of $\mathsf{que}_i^{(\nu)}$ is $(x_m, \mathsf{que}_{m,x_m}^{(\nu)})$, let $\mathsf{ans}_{m,i}^{(\nu)} = \mathcal{A}_0(x_m, \mathsf{que}_{m,x_m}^{(\nu)}, \boldsymbol{a})$.
   (b) Let

$$\mathsf{ans}_i^{(\nu)} = \begin{pmatrix} \mathsf{ans}_{1,i}^{(\nu)} \\ \mathsf{ans}_{2,i}^{(\nu)} \end{pmatrix}.$$

2. Output $\mathsf{ans}_i = (\mathsf{ans}_i^{(\nu)})_{\nu \in [\lambda]}$.

Fig. 4. The answer algorithm of Π

$\mathcal{D}(\widetilde{\mathsf{ans}}_1, \ldots, \widetilde{\mathsf{ans}}_k; \mathsf{aux})$. Given $\widetilde{\mathsf{ans}}_i = (\widetilde{\mathsf{ans}}_i^{(\nu)})_{\nu \in [\lambda]}$ ($i \in [k]$), where $\widetilde{\mathsf{ans}}_i^{(\nu)}$ has the same form as $\mathsf{ans}_i^{(\nu)}$, and $\mathsf{aux} = ((\mathsf{aux}^{(\nu)})_{\nu \in [\lambda]}, (i^{(\nu)}, j^{(\nu)}, b^{(\nu)})_{\nu \in [\lambda]})$:

1. $\mathcal{L} = \emptyset$.
2. For each $\nu \in [\lambda]$, do the following:
   (a) Construct an 2-by-$(k+1)$ matrix $\boldsymbol{A}^{(\nu)}$ as

$$\boldsymbol{A}^{(\nu)} = \left(\widetilde{\mathsf{ans}}_1^{(\nu)} \cdots \widetilde{\mathsf{ans}}_k^{(\nu)} \ \mathsf{aux}^{(\nu)} \right) = \begin{pmatrix} \widetilde{\mathsf{ans}}_{1,1}^{(\nu)} \cdots \widetilde{\mathsf{ans}}_{1,k}^{(\nu)} \ \mathsf{aux}_1^{(\nu)} \\ \widetilde{\mathsf{ans}}_{2,1}^{(\nu)} \cdots \widetilde{\mathsf{ans}}_{2,k}^{(\nu)} \ \mathsf{aux}_2^{(\nu)} \end{pmatrix}.$$

   (b) Do the following:
      − If $b^{(\nu)} = 0$:
        i. Compute

$$y^{(\nu)} = \mathcal{D}_0 \left(\widetilde{\mathsf{ans}}_{1,1}^{(\nu)}, \ldots, \widetilde{\mathsf{ans}}_{1,k}^{(\nu)}; \mathsf{aux}_1^{(\nu)} \right).$$

        ii. Check whether $\widetilde{\mathsf{ans}}_{2,i}^{(\nu)} = \widetilde{\mathsf{ans}}_{2,j}^{(\nu)}$ holds. If the equality holds, set $z^{(\nu)} = y^{(\nu)}$ and otherwise, set $z^{(\nu)} = \bot$.
      − If $b^{(\nu)} = 1$:
        i. Compute

$$y^{(\nu)} = \mathcal{D}_0 \left(\widetilde{\mathsf{ans}}_{2,1}^{(\nu)}, \ldots, \widetilde{\mathsf{ans}}_{2,k}^{(\nu)}; \mathsf{aux}_2^{(\nu)} \right).$$

        ii. Check whether $\widetilde{\mathsf{ans}}_{1,i}^{(\nu)} = \widetilde{\mathsf{ans}}_{1,j}^{(\nu)}$ holds. If the equality holds, set $z^{(\nu)} = y^{(\nu)}$ and otherwise, set $z^{(\nu)} = \bot$.
   (c) Add $z^{(\nu)}$ to $\mathcal{L}$.
3. If $\mathcal{L} = \{z\}$ for some $z \in \{0,1\}$, output z. Otherwise, output $\bot$.

Fig. 5. The reconstruction algorithm of Π

The $(1 - \epsilon)$-correctness of Π_0 implies that

$$y^{(\nu)} = \mathcal{D}_0(\widetilde{\mathsf{ans}}_{1,1}^{(\nu)}, \ldots, \widetilde{\mathsf{ans}}_{1,k}^{(\nu)}; \mathsf{aux}_1^{(\nu)}) = a_\tau$$

with probability $1 - \epsilon$.

If the client chooses $(i, j) \in \mathcal{I}$ at Step 1(b) of $\mathcal{Q}$, the $(2, i)$-th entry of $\boldsymbol{Q}^{(\nu)}$ is equal to the $(2, j)$-th entry of $\boldsymbol{Q}^{(\nu)}$, which is $(j, \mathsf{que}_{2,j}^{(\nu)})$. Since Servers i and j are honest, it holds that

$$\widetilde{\mathsf{ans}}_{2,i}^{(\nu)} = \mathcal{A}_0(j, \mathsf{que}_{2,j}^{(\nu)}, \boldsymbol{a}) = \widetilde{\mathsf{ans}}_{2,j}^{(\nu)}.$$

Hence, at Step 2(b), the equality holds with probability 1.

Therefore, $z^{(\nu)}$ is always set to $y^{(\nu)} \in \{0, 1\}$, which is equal to a_τ with probability $1 - \epsilon$.

Privacy. Observe that a query vector $(\mathsf{que}_i)_{i \in [k]}$ generated by $\mathcal{Q}$ contains nothing more than 2λ independent query vectors $(\mathsf{que}_{m,i}^{(\nu)})_{i \in [k]}$ $(m \in \{1, 2\}, \nu \in [\lambda])$, each generated by $\mathcal{Q}_0$. Therefore, the t-privacy of Π follows from that of Π_0.

Error Detection. We prove that Π is $(b; 1 - \epsilon_{\mathrm{ED}})$-error-detecting. Let $\boldsymbol{a} \in \{0, 1\}^n$ and $\tau \in [n]$. Without loss of generality, we may assume that the server S_1 is honest. Let $T = [k] \setminus \{1\}$ and $f \in \mathcal{F}_T^\Pi$ be a tampering function for Π with respect to T.

Let $\mathcal{I}_0 = \mathcal{I} \times \{0, 1\}$. Let $\mathfrak{R}_\mathcal{Q}$ denote the set of all random strings for $\mathcal{Q}$, that is, $\mathcal{I}_0^\lambda \times (\mathfrak{R}_{\mathcal{Q}_0}^N)^\lambda$. We suppose that any $(\pi, r) \in \mathfrak{R}_\mathcal{Q}$ is decomposed into $\pi = (i^{(\nu)}, j^{(\nu)}, b^{(\nu)})_{\nu \in [\lambda]}$ and $r = (r_m^{(\nu)})_{m \in \{1,2\}, \nu \in [\lambda]}$, where $(i^{(\nu)}, j^{(\nu)}, b^{(\nu)}) \in \mathcal{I}_0$ and $r_m^{(\nu)} \in \mathfrak{R}_{\mathcal{Q}_0}$. We naturally identify any event A with a subset of $\mathfrak{R}_\mathcal{Q}$ consisting of all random strings on which A occurs.

Let E denote the event in which $\mathcal{D}_0$ outputs an incorrect value even if all servers are honest. Formally, we define

$$\mathsf{E} = \left\{ (\pi, r) \in \mathfrak{R}_\mathcal{Q} : \begin{array}{l} \exists \nu \in [\lambda], \exists m \in \{1, 2\}, \\ \mathcal{D}_0((\mathcal{A}_0(i, \mathsf{que}_{m,i}^{(\nu)}, \boldsymbol{a}))_{i \in [k]}; \mathsf{aux}_m^{(\nu)}) = 1 - a_\tau \end{array} \right\},$$

where $((\mathsf{que}_{m,i}^{(\nu)})_{i \in [k]}; \mathsf{aux}_m^{(\nu)}) = \mathcal{Q}_0(\tau; r_m^{(\nu)})$ for any $m \in \{1, 2\}, \nu \in [\lambda]$. The $(1 - \epsilon)$-correctness of Π_0 implies that E occurs with probability at most $2\lambda\epsilon$. Let

$$\mathfrak{R}_\mathsf{E} = \{r \in (\mathfrak{R}_{\mathcal{Q}_0})^\lambda : \exists \pi \in \mathcal{I}_0^\lambda, (\pi, r) \in \mathsf{E}\}.$$

For any $(\pi, r) \in \mathfrak{R}_\mathcal{Q}$, let $w(\pi, r) \in \{0, 1, \bot\}$ denote the value outputted by the client when (π, r) is used to generate queries. Let F denote the set of all (π, r)'s such that $w(\pi, r) = 1 - a_\tau$.

Let R be the random variable representing $r \leftarrow_\$ (\mathfrak{R}_{\mathcal{Q}_0})^\lambda$. We have that

$$\begin{aligned} \Pr[\mathsf{F}] &= \Pr[\mathsf{E} \cap \mathsf{F}] + \Pr[\overline{\mathsf{E}} \cap \mathsf{F}] \\ &\leq \Pr[\mathsf{E}] + \sum_{r \in (\mathfrak{R}_{\mathcal{Q}_0})^\lambda} \Pr[\overline{\mathsf{E}} \cap \mathsf{F} \mid R = r] \cdot \Pr[R = r] \\ &\leq 2\lambda\epsilon + \sum_{r \notin \mathfrak{R}_\mathsf{E}} \Pr[\overline{\mathsf{E}} \cap \mathsf{F} \mid R = r] \cdot \Pr[R = r]. \end{aligned} \tag{1}$$

Fix $r \notin \mathfrak{R}_\mathsf{E}$. For every $\nu \in [\lambda]$, let $\mathsf{F}^{(\nu)}$ be the event conditioned on $R = r$ that $z^{(\nu)} = 1 - a_\tau$ at the ν-th iteration of Step 2 of $\mathcal{D}$. We have that

$$
\Pr\left[\overline{\mathsf{E}} \cap \mathsf{F} \mid R = r\right] \leq \Pr_\pi\left[\mathsf{F}^{(1)} \cap \cdots \cap \mathsf{F}^{(\lambda)}\right]
$$

$$
= \prod_{\nu \in [\lambda]} \Pr_\pi\left[\mathsf{F}^{(\nu)} \mid \mathsf{F}^{(1)} \cap \cdots \cap \mathsf{F}^{(\nu-1)}\right] \tag{2}
$$

Furthermore, we have that

$$
\Pr_\pi\left[\mathsf{F}^{(\nu)} \mid \mathsf{F}^{(1)} \cap \cdots \cap \mathsf{F}^{(\nu-1)}\right]
$$

$$
= \sum_{\substack{\pi^{(1)},\ldots,\pi^{(\nu-1)}, \\ \pi^{(\nu+1)},\ldots,\pi^{(\lambda)}}} \Pr\left[\pi^{(1)},\ldots,\pi^{(\nu-1)},\pi^{(\nu+1)},\ldots,\pi^{(\lambda)}\right]
$$

$$
\times \Pr_{\pi^{(\nu)}}\left[\mathsf{F}^{(\nu)} \mid \mathsf{F}^{(1)} \cap \cdots \cap \mathsf{F}^{(\nu-1)},\pi^{(1)},\ldots,\pi^{(\nu-1)},\pi^{(\nu+1)},\ldots,\pi^{(\lambda)}\right]. \tag{3}
$$

Fix $\pi^{(1)},\ldots,\pi^{(\nu-1)},\pi^{(\nu+1)},\ldots,\pi^{(\lambda)} \in \mathcal{I}_0$. For ease of reading, let COND denote the condition of the probability (3). Define an event BAD that the client picks $\pi^{(\nu)} = (i^{(\nu)}, j^{(\nu)}, b^{(\nu)}) \in \mathcal{I}_0$ such that $i^{(\nu)} \neq 1$. In other words, BAD means that the client fails to guess that S_1 is honest. Then, we have that

$$
\Pr_{\pi^{(\nu)}}\left[\mathsf{F}^{(\nu)} \mid \mathrm{COND}\right]
$$

$$
= \Pr[\mathrm{BAD}] \cdot \Pr_{\pi^{(\nu)}}\left[\mathsf{F}^{(\nu)} \mid \mathrm{COND}, \mathrm{BAD}\right]
$$

$$
+ \Pr\left[\overline{\mathrm{BAD}}\right] \cdot \Pr_{\pi^{(\nu)}}\left[\mathsf{F}^{(\nu)} \mid \mathrm{COND}, \overline{\mathrm{BAD}}\right]
$$

$$
\leq \frac{2k(k-1) - 2(k-1)}{2k(k-1)} + \frac{2(k-1)}{2k(k-1)} \cdot \Pr_{\pi^{(\nu)}}\left[\mathsf{F}^{(\nu)} \mid \mathrm{COND}, \overline{\mathrm{BAD}}\right]
$$

$$
\leq \frac{k-1}{k} + \frac{1}{k} \cdot \Pr_{\pi^{(\nu)}}\left[\mathsf{F}^{(\nu)} \mid \mathrm{COND}, \overline{\mathrm{BAD}}\right]. \tag{4}
$$

We will show that

$$
\Pr_{\pi^{(\nu)}}\left[\mathsf{F}^{(\nu)} \mid \mathrm{COND}, \overline{\mathrm{BAD}}\right] \leq 1 - \frac{1}{2(k-1)}. \tag{5}
$$

Let X denote the set of all $\pi^{(\nu)} \in \mathcal{I}_0$ such that

- $\pi^{(\nu)} \in \overline{\mathrm{BAD}}$, i.e., it has the form of $\pi^{(\nu)} = (1, j^{(\nu)}, b^{(\nu)})$;
- COND occurs on $\pi^{(\nu)}$, i.e., it holds that

$$
\pi := (\pi^{(1)},\ldots,\pi^{(\nu-1)},\pi^{(\nu)},\pi^{(\nu+1)},\ldots,\pi^{(\lambda)}) \in \mathsf{F}^{(1)} \cap \cdots \cap \mathsf{F}^{(\nu-1)}.
$$

Let Y denote a subset consisting of all $\pi^{(\nu)} \in X$ satisfying $\pi \in \mathsf{F}^{(1)} \cap \cdots \cap \mathsf{F}^{(\nu-1)} \cap \mathsf{F}^{(\nu)}$.

If $X = \emptyset$, then (5) clearly holds. If $X \neq \emptyset$, choose $\pi^{(\nu)} = (1, j^{(\nu)}, b^{(\nu)}) \in X$ arbitrarily. Denote the queries sent to the malicious servers $S_2, \ldots, S_k$ when $\pi^{(\nu)}$ is picked at Step 1(b) of $\mathcal{Q}$, by

$$(2, \mathsf{que}_{1,2}^{(\mu)}), \ldots, (k, \mathsf{que}_{1,k}^{(\mu)}), (2, \mathsf{que}_{2,2}^{(\mu)}), \ldots, (k, \mathsf{que}_{2,k}^{(\mu)}), \ \mu \in [\lambda] \tag{6}$$

We can see that if another $(1, j, b) \in \mathcal{I}_0$ is picked, the queries sent to the malicious servers are the same as (6). Since the tampering function f is deterministic, the answers returned by them are also the same regardless of what is picked as $(j^{(\nu)}, b^{(\nu)})$ at Step 1(b) of $\mathcal{Q}$. Therefore, if COND occurs on $\pi^{(\nu)}$, COND occurs on every $(1, j, b) \in \mathcal{I}_0$. In particular, we have that $|X| = 2(k-1)$ if $X \neq \emptyset$.

We have seen that the answers returned by the malicious servers $S_2, \ldots, S_k$ are the same for any $\pi^{(\nu)} \in X$. We denote the answers by

$$\widetilde{\mathsf{ans}}_{1,2}^{(\nu)}, \ldots, \widetilde{\mathsf{ans}}_{1,k}^{(\nu)}, \widetilde{\mathsf{ans}}_{2,2}^{(\nu)}, \ldots, \widetilde{\mathsf{ans}}_{2,k}^{(\nu)}.$$

If all of them are correct, i.e., $\widetilde{\mathsf{ans}}_{m,j}^{(\nu)} = \mathcal{A}_0(j, \mathsf{que}_{m,j}^{(\nu)}, a)$, we obtain that $Y = \emptyset$. This is because at one of the rows of $A^{(\nu)}$, the client computes

$$y^{(\nu)} = \mathcal{D}_0(\widetilde{\mathsf{ans}}_{m,1}^{(\nu)}, \ldots, \widetilde{\mathsf{ans}}_{m,k}^{(\nu)}; \mathsf{aux}_m^{(\nu)}).$$

Since we assume E does not occur, i.e., $r \notin \mathfrak{R}_\mathsf{E}$, an outcome of $\mathcal{D}_0$ never results in $1 - a_r$ and hence $\mathsf{F}^{(\nu)}$ never occurs. Assume that there exist $m \in \{1, 2\}$ and $j \in \{2, 3, \ldots, k\}$ such that

$$\widetilde{\mathsf{ans}}_{m,j}^{(\nu)} \neq \mathcal{A}_0(j, \mathsf{que}_{m,j}^{(\nu)}, a).$$

We can see that $(1, j, 1) \notin Y$ if $m = 1$, and that $(1, j, 0) \notin Y$ if $m = 2$. To see this, consider the case of $m = 1$. If $j^{(\nu)} = j$ and $b^{(\nu)} = 1$ are picked at Step 1(b) of $\mathcal{Q}$, the client detects errors (i.e., outputs $\perp$) since he finds the inconsistency

$$\widetilde{\mathsf{ans}}_{1,1}^{(\nu)} = \mathcal{A}_0(j, \mathsf{que}_{1,j}^{(\nu)}, a) \neq \widetilde{\mathsf{ans}}_{1,j}^{(\nu)}.$$

The other case of $m = 2$ is similar. Therefore, if $X \neq \emptyset$,

$$\Pr_{\pi^{(\nu)}}\left[\mathsf{F}^{(\nu)} \,\middle|\, \mathsf{COND}, \overline{\mathsf{BAD}}\right] = \frac{|Y|}{|X|} \leq \frac{2(k-1) - 1}{2(k-1)} = 1 - \frac{1}{2(k-1)},$$

which implies (5).

Finally, we obtain from (3) and (4) that

$$\Pr_\pi\left[\mathsf{F}^{(\nu)} \,\middle|\, \mathsf{F}^{(1)} \cap \cdots \cap \mathsf{F}^{(\nu-1)}\right]$$

$$\leq \sum_{\substack{\pi^{(1)}, \ldots, \pi^{(\nu-1)}, \\ \pi^{(\nu+1)}, \ldots, \pi^{(\lambda)}}} \Pr\left[\pi^{(1)}, \ldots, \pi^{(\nu-1)}, \pi^{(\nu+1)}, \ldots, \pi^{(\lambda)}\right]$$

$$\times \left(\frac{k-1}{k} + \frac{1}{k} \cdot \left(1 - \frac{1}{2(k-1)}\right)\right)$$

$$\leq 1 - \frac{1}{2k(k-1)}$$

and hence (2) implies that

$$\Pr\left[\overline{\mathsf{E}} \cap \mathsf{F} \mid R = r\right] \le \left(1 - \frac{1}{2k(k-1)}\right)^{\lambda}.$$

Therefore, the $(b; 1 - \epsilon_{\mathrm{ED}})$-error detection follows from (1) and

$$\Pr[\mathsf{F}] \le 2\lambda\epsilon + \left(1 - \frac{1}{2k(k-1)}\right)^{\lambda} = \epsilon_{\mathrm{ED}}.$$

C   Proof of Lemma 1

Define Π as follows:

- Iterate Π_0 λ times in parallel.
- Let $y_i \in \{0,1\}$ be the output of the i-th iteration of Π_0 for $i \in [\lambda]$. If there exists $y \in \{0,1\}$ such that $|\{i : y_i = y\}| > |\{i : y_i = 1 - y\}|$, output y. Otherwise, output 0.

Clearly, the communication complexity of Π is λ times larger than that of Π_0 and the t-privacy of Π directly follows from that of Π_0. Let $\boldsymbol{a} \in \{0,1\}^n$ be a database and $\tau \in [n]$ be a client's index. The outputs of Π_0 are independent and each output is equal to a_τ with probability $1 - \epsilon_0$.

Let X_i be a random variable over $\{0,1\}$ defined as $X_i = 1$ if and only if $y_i = a_\tau$. $X_1, \ldots, X_\lambda$ are i.i.d. random variables such that $p = \mathbb{E}[X_1] = 1 - \epsilon_0$. It then follows from the Chernoff bound that

$$\Pr[\Pi \text{ outputs } 1 - a_\tau] \le \Pr\left[\frac{1}{\lambda}\sum_{i=1}^{\lambda} X_i \le \frac{1}{2}\right]$$

$$= \Pr\left[\frac{1}{\lambda}\sum_{i=1}^{\lambda} X_i \le p + \left(\frac{1}{2} - p\right)\right]$$

$$\le \left(\left(\frac{p}{1/2}\right)^{1/2}\left(\frac{1-p}{1/2}\right)^{1/2}\right)^{\lambda}$$

$$= (4p(1-p))^{\lambda/2}$$

$$= (2\sqrt{\epsilon_0(1-\epsilon_0)})^{\lambda}$$

$$\le \exp\left(-2\left(\frac{1}{2} - \epsilon_0\right)^2 \lambda\right).$$

The last inequality follows from

$$\frac{1}{2}\ln(4\epsilon_0(1-\epsilon_0)) = \frac{1}{2}\ln(1 - 4x^2) \le -2x^2,$$

where $x = 1/2 - \epsilon_0$.

D   Proof of Theorem 3

For $\Pi_0 = (\mathcal{Q}_0, \mathcal{A}_0, \mathcal{D}_0)$, we consider a PIR scheme $\Pi = (\mathcal{Q}, \mathcal{A}, \mathcal{D})$ where $(\mathcal{Q}, \mathcal{A})$ runs N independent instances of $(\mathcal{Q}_0, \mathcal{A}_0)$ between a client and every subset of k servers and $\mathcal{D}$ is defined as follows: For each of N executions of $(\mathcal{Q}_0, \mathcal{A}_0)$, $\mathcal{D}$ runs $\mathcal{D}_0$ on the corresponding input and adds the output to a list $\mathcal{L}$. If $\mathcal{L} = \{s\}$ or $\mathcal{L} = \{s, \perp\}$ for some $s \in \{0,1\}$, then $\mathcal{D}$ outputs s and otherwise outputs 0. The communication complexity of Π is Nc. Since each execution of $\mathcal{Q}_0$ is done independently, Π is also t-private.

We prove that Π is $(b; 1 - \epsilon_{\mathrm{EC}})$-error-correcting for $\epsilon_{\mathrm{EC}} = N\epsilon_{\mathrm{ED}}$. Let $\boldsymbol{a} \in \{0,1\}^n$ and $\tau \in [n]$. Let $H \in \binom{[\ell]}{k}$ be a set of honest servers. Let $f \in \mathcal{F}_{\overline{H}}^{\Pi}$ be a tampering function for Π with respect to $\overline{H}$.

Let $A_1, \ldots, A_N$ be all k-sized subsets of $[\ell]$ such that $A_1 = H$. Let $\Pi_0^{(j)}$ denote the instance of Π_0 executed by the client and servers in A_j. During the execution of $\Pi_0^{(j)}$, the client generates

$$\mathcal{Q}_0(\tau; r_j) = ((\mathsf{que}_i^{(j)})_{i \in A_j}; \mathsf{aux}^{(j)}),$$

where $r_j \in \mathfrak{R}_{\mathcal{Q}_0}$ and $\mathsf{que}_i^{(j)}$ is sent to S_i. Then, S_i receives

$$\mathsf{que}_i' = \{\mathsf{que}_i^{(j)} : j \in [N] \text{ with } i \in A_j\}.$$

In $\Pi_0^{(1)}$, for any $i \in A_1$, S_i returns

$$\widetilde{\mathsf{ans}}_i^{(1)} = \mathsf{ans}_i^{(1)} = \mathcal{A}_0(i, \mathsf{que}_i^{(1)}, \boldsymbol{a}).$$

In each $\Pi_0^{(j)}$ for $j \neq 1$, any server S_i in A_j returns

$$\widetilde{\mathsf{ans}}_i^{(j)} = \begin{cases} \mathsf{ans}_i^{(j)} = \mathcal{A}_0(i, \mathsf{que}_i^{(j)}, \boldsymbol{a}), & \text{if } i \in H, \\ f_i^{(j)}(\{\mathsf{que}_{i'}'\}_{i' \in \overline{H}}, \boldsymbol{a}), & \text{otherwise,} \end{cases}$$

where $f_i^{(j)}$ is a function determined by f. It then follows from our definition of $\mathcal{D}$ that

$$\Pr[\mathcal{D} \text{ outputs } y \neq a_\tau]$$
$$\leq \Pr\left[\mathcal{D}_0((\mathsf{ans}_i^{(1)})_{i \in H}; \mathsf{aux}^{(1)}) \neq a_\tau\right]$$
$$+ \sum_{j=2}^{N} \Pr\left[\mathcal{D}_0((\mathsf{ans}_i^{(j)})_{i \in H \cap A_j}, (\widetilde{\mathsf{ans}}_i^{(j)})_{i \in \overline{H} \cap A_j}; \mathsf{aux}^{(j)}) \notin \{a_\tau, \perp\}\right]$$
$$\leq \epsilon_{\mathrm{ED}} + \sum_{j=2}^{N} \Pr\left[\mathcal{D}_0((\mathsf{ans}_i^{(j)})_{i \in H \cap A_j}, (\widetilde{\mathsf{ans}}_i^{(j)})_{i \in \overline{H} \cap A_j}; \mathsf{aux}^{(j)}) \notin \{a_\tau, \perp\}\right].$$

Therefore it is enough to show that

$$p_0 := \Pr\left[\mathcal{D}_0((\mathsf{ans}_i^{(j)})_{i \in H \cap A_j}, (\widetilde{\mathsf{ans}}_i^{(j)})_{i \in \overline{H} \cap A_j}; \mathsf{aux}^{(j)}) \notin \{a_\tau, \perp\}\right] \leq \epsilon_{\mathrm{ED}}$$

for any $j \in [N] \setminus \{1\}$.

Let $j \in [N] \setminus \{1\}$. Fix $r_{-j} = (r_m)_{m \in [N] \setminus \{j\}}$ arbitrarily. Then $\mathsf{que}_i^{(m)}$ is a fixed constant for any $m \in [N] \setminus \{j\}$ and $i \in A_m$. Therefore for $i \in A_j$, we can write

$$\widetilde{\mathsf{ans}}_i^{(j)} = f_i^{(j)}(\{\mathsf{que}_{i'}'\}_{i' \in \overline{H}}, a) = g_{i, r_{-j}}(\{\mathsf{que}_{i'}^{(j)}\}_{i' \in \overline{H} \cap S_j}, a)$$

using some function $g_{i, r_{-j}}$. Let $\mathcal{X}_{-j}$ denote the random variable which represents r_{-j}. Since $|\overline{H} \cap A_j| \le b$ and Π_0 is $(b, t; 1 - \epsilon_{\mathsf{ED}})$-error-detecting, we have that

$$
\begin{aligned}
p_0 &= \Pr_{r_j, r_{-j}}\left[\mathcal{D}_0((\mathsf{ans}_i^{(j)})_{i \in H \cap A_j}, (\widetilde{\mathsf{ans}}_i^{(j)})_{i \in \overline{H} \cap A_j}; \mathsf{aux}^{(j)}) \notin \{a_\tau, \bot\}\right] \\
&= \sum_{r_{-j}} \Pr[\mathcal{X}_{-j} = r_{-j}] \Pr_{r_j}\left[\mathcal{D}_0((\mathsf{ans}_i^{(j)})_{i \in H \cap A_j}, (\widetilde{\mathsf{ans}}_i^{(j)})_{i \in \overline{H} \cap A_j}; \mathsf{aux}^{(j)}) \notin \{a_\tau, \bot\}\right] \\
&\le \sum_{r_{-j}} \Pr[\mathcal{X}_{-j} = r_{-j}] \times \epsilon_{\mathsf{ED}} \\
&= \epsilon_{\mathsf{ED}}.
\end{aligned}
$$

E   Proof of Theorem 5

For $a = (a_1, \ldots, a_n) \in \{0, 1\}^n$, define $a^* = (a_1^*, \ldots, a_n^*) \in \{0, 1\}^n$ as the same database as a except that $a_1^* = 1 - a_1$. Let $B \subseteq [\ell]$ be a subset of size b and let $B' = [\ell] \setminus B$. Let f be a tampering function such that $f(\mathsf{que}_1, \ldots, \mathsf{que}_\ell, a) = (\widetilde{\mathsf{ans}}_i)_{i \in [\ell]}$, where

$$\widetilde{\mathsf{ans}}_i = \begin{cases} \mathcal{A}(i, \mathsf{que}_i, a), & \text{if } i \notin B, \\ \mathcal{A}(i, \mathsf{que}_i, a^*), & \text{if } i \in B. \end{cases}$$

for any $i \in [\ell]$ and $\mathsf{que}_i \in \{0, 1\}^{c_{\mathsf{que}}}$. Also, let f' be a tampering function such that $f'(\mathsf{que}_1, \ldots, \mathsf{que}_\ell, a) = (\widetilde{\mathsf{ans}}_i')_{i \in [\ell]}$, where

$$\widetilde{\mathsf{ans}}_i' = \begin{cases} \mathcal{A}(i, \mathsf{que}_i, a), & \text{if } i \notin B', \\ \mathcal{A}(i, \mathsf{que}_i, a^*), & \text{if } i \in B' \end{cases}$$

for any $i \in [\ell]$ and $\mathsf{que}_i \in \{0, 1\}^{c_{\mathsf{que}}}$. Note that $f \in \mathcal{F}_B^{\Pi}$ and $f' \in \mathcal{F}_{B'}^{\Pi}$. Also note that $(a^*)^* = a$ and that $i \notin B$ is equivalent to $i \in B'$. Thus, we have that

$$f(\mathsf{que}_1, \ldots, \mathsf{que}_\ell, a) = f'(\mathsf{que}_1, \ldots, \mathsf{que}_\ell, a^*) \tag{7}$$

for any $a \in \{0, 1\}^n$ and $\mathsf{que}_1, \ldots, \mathsf{que}_\ell \in \{0, 1\}^{c_{\mathsf{que}}}$.

Fix $a \in \{0, 1\}^n$ arbitrarily. Define a subset S (resp. S') of $\mathfrak{R}_\mathcal{Q}$ as

$$
\begin{aligned}
S &= \{r \in \mathfrak{R}_\mathcal{Q} : \mathcal{D}(f(\mathsf{que}_1, \ldots, \mathsf{que}_\ell, a); \mathsf{aux}) = a_1\}, \\
S' &= \{r \in \mathfrak{R}_\mathcal{Q} : \mathcal{D}(f'(\mathsf{que}_1, \ldots, \mathsf{que}_\ell, a^*); \mathsf{aux}) = a_1^*\},
\end{aligned}
$$

where $(\mathsf{que}_1, \ldots, \mathsf{que}_\ell; \mathsf{aux}) = \mathcal{Q}(1; r)$. It follows from Eq. (7) and $a_1^* = 1 - a_1 \ne a_1$ that $S \cap S' = \emptyset$. On the other hand, since $|B| = b$ and $|B'| = \ell - b \le b$, the $(b; 1 - \epsilon_{EC})$-error correction of Π implies that $|S| \geq (1 - \epsilon_{EC})|\mathfrak{R}_Q|$ and $|S'| \geq (1 - \epsilon_{EC})|\mathfrak{R}_Q|$. Therefore, we have that

$$|\mathfrak{R}_Q| \geq |S \cup S'| = |S| + |S'| \geq 2(1 - \epsilon_{EC})|\mathfrak{R}_Q|$$

and $\epsilon_{EC} \geq 1/2$.

References

1. Ambainis, A.: Upper bound on the communication complexity of private information retrieval. In: Degano, P., Gorrieri, R., Marchetti-Spaccamela, A. (eds.) ICALP 1997. LNCS, vol. 1256, pp. 401–407. Springer, Heidelberg (1997). https://doi.org/10.1007/3-540-63165-8_196
2. Banawan, K., Ulukus, S.: The capacity of private information retrieval from byzantine and colluding databases. IEEE Trans. Inf. Theory **65**(2), 1206–1219 (2019)
3. Beimel, A., Ishai, Y., Kushilevitz, E., Raymond, J.F.: Breaking the o(n/sup 1/(2k–1)/) barrier for information-theoretic private information retrieval. In: Proceedings of the 43rd Annual IEEE Symposium on Foundations of Computer Science, pp. 261–270 (2002)
4. Beimel, A., Ishai, Y.: Information-theoretic private information retrieval: a unified construction. In: Orejas, F., Spirakis, P.G., van Leeuwen, J. (eds.) ICALP 2001. LNCS, vol. 2076, pp. 912–926. Springer, Heidelberg (2001). https://doi.org/10.1007/3-540-48224-5_74
5. Beimel, A., Stahl, Y.: Robust information-theoretic private information retrieval. J. Cryptol. **20**(3), 295–321 (2007)
6. Catalano, D., Fiore, D.: Practical homomorphic MACs for arithmetic circuits. In: Johansson, T., Nguyen, P.Q. (eds.) EUROCRYPT 2013. LNCS, vol. 7881, pp. 336–352. Springer, Heidelberg (2013). https://doi.org/10.1007/978-3-642-38348-9_21
7. Chee, Y.M., Feng, T., Ling, S., Wang, H., Zhang, L.F.: Query-efficient locally decodable codes of subexponential length. Comput. Complex. **22**(1), 159–189 (2013)
8. Chor, B., Goldreich, O., Kushilevitz, E., Sudan, M.: Private information retrieval. J. ACM **45**(6), 965–982 (1998)
9. Dvir, Z., Gopi, S.: 2-server PIR with subpolynomial communication. J. ACM **63**(4), 1–15 (2016)
10. Efremenko, K.: 3-query locally decodable codes of subexponential length. SIAM J. Comput. **41**(6), 1694–1703 (2012)
11. Eriguchi, R., Kurosawa, K., Nuida, K.: Multi-server PIR with full error detection and limited error correction. In: 3rd Conference on Information-Theoretic Cryptography (ITC 2022), pp. 1:1–1:20 (2022)
12. Goldreich, O., Karloff, H., Schulman, L., Trevisan, L.: Lower bounds for linear locally decodable codes and private information retrieval. Comput. Complex. **15**(3), 263–296 (2006)
13. Itoh, T., Suzuki, Y.: Improved constructions for query-efficient locally decodable codes of subexponential length. IEICE Trans. Inf. Syst. **E93.D**(2), 263–270 (2010)
14. Kurosawa, K.: How to correct errors in multi-server PIR. In: Galbraith, S.D., Moriai, S. (eds.) ASIACRYPT 2019. LNCS, vol. 11922, pp. 564–574. Springer, Cham (2019). https://doi.org/10.1007/978-3-030-34621-8_20

15. Rabin, T., Ben-Or, M.: Verifiable secret sharing and multiparty protocols with honest majority. In: Proceedings of the Twenty-First Annual ACM Symposium on Theory of Computing, STOC 1989, pp. 73–85 (1989)
16. Sun, H., Jafar, S.A.: The capacity of private information retrieval. IEEE Trans. Inf. Theory **63**(7), 4075–4088 (2017)
17. Sun, H., Jafar, S.A.: The capacity of robust private information retrieval with colluding databases. IEEE Trans. Inf. Theory **64**(4), 2361–2370 (2018)
18. Wehner, S., de Wolf, R.: Improved lower bounds for locally decodable codes and private information retrieval. In: Caires, L., Italiano, G.F., Monteiro, L., Palamidessi, C., Yung, M. (eds.) ICALP 2005. LNCS, vol. 3580, pp. 1424–1436. Springer, Heidelberg (2005). https://doi.org/10.1007/11523468_115
19. Woodruff, D., Yekhanin, S.: A geometric approach to information-theoretic private information retrieval. In: 20th Annual IEEE Conference on Computational Complexity (CCC 2005), pp. 275–284 (2005)
20. Yang, E., Xu, J., Bennett, K.: Private information retrieval in the presence of malicious failures. In: Proceedings 26th Annual International Computer Software and Applications, pp. 805–810 (2002)
21. Yekhanin, S.: Towards 3-query locally decodable codes of subexponential length. J. ACM (JACM) **55**(1), 1–16 (2008)

Oblivious-Transfer Complexity of Noisy Coin-Toss via Secure Zero Communication Reductions

Saumya Goyal[1(✉)], Varun Narayanan[2], and Manoj Prabhakaran[3]

[1] Stanford University, Stanford, USA
`saumyagoyal01@gmail.com`
[2] IIT Bombay, Mumbai, India
[3] Technion, Haifa, Israel
`mp@cse.iitb.ac.in`

Abstract. In p-noisy coin-tossing, Alice and Bob obtain fair coins which are of opposite values with probability p. Its Oblivious-Transfer (OT) complexity refers to the least number of OTs required by a semi-honest perfectly secure 2-party protocol for this task. We show a tight bound of $\Theta(\log 1/p)$ for the OT complexity of p-noisy coin-tossing. This is the first instance of a lower bound for OT complexity that is independent of the input/output length of the function.

We obtain our result by providing a general connection between the OT complexity of randomized functions and the complexity of Secure Zero Communication Reductions (SZCR), as recently defined by Narayanan et al. (TCC 2020), and then showing a lower bound for the complexity of an SZCR from noisy coin-tossing to (a predicate corresponding to) OT.

1 Introduction

Consider two parties trying to do a "p-noisy coin-toss" such that each one gets a uniformly random bit, but with probability $p < 1/2$ the bits they obtain are different.[1] They would like to do this with semi-honest information-theoretic security (so that each one has no information about the other's bit, beyond what it learns from its own bit), using as few instances of Oblivious Transfer (OT) as possible.

An easy upper bound on the number of OTs needed is $O(\log 1/p)$, because they can obtain the desired outputs by evaluating a boolean circuit with that many binary gates on $O(\log 1/p)$ uniformly random bits from each party; the

---

[1] This functionality is sometimes referred to as sampling from a *binary symmetric source*. Note that for semi-honest security, as we consider, this is a cryptographically trivial task without any noise (i.e., when $p = 0$).

S. Goyal—Work done while at IIT Bombay

V. Narayanan—Supported by ERC Project NTSC (742754) and ISF Grants 1709/14 & 2774/20.

M. Prabhakaran—Supported by IITB Trust Lab.

E. Kiltz and V. Vaikuntanathan (Eds.): TCC 2022, LNCS 13749, pp. 89–118, 2022.
https://doi.org/10.1007/978-3-031-22368-6_4

upper bound follows from the semi-honest GMW protocol [12–14] (requiring a couple of OTs for each non-linear gate). But it is *a priori* not at all clear if this is the only way to carry out this computation. In particular, a protocol can rely on the semi-honest parties to sample non-uniform bits and use them as inputs in a protocol, and more generally, employ a protocol that does not involve a circuit evaluation at all.

Information-theoretic measures have been used to reason about the complexity of randomized functions in cryptographic and non-cryptographic settings. The most relevant technique to lower bound the OT complexity of general randomized functions is to use the "tension" of the resulting correlation [23]. However, it only yields a lower bound of *one* OT for sampling a noisy coin. Further, for the amortized setting, the lower bound on the rate degrades as the noise decreases.

In this work, we present for the first time an OT complexity lower bound that goes beyond the input/output length of a function, by showing that the number of OTs required for noisy coin-tossing is $\Theta(\log 1/p)$. Further, our lower bound also has a "direct sum" version, showing that tossing n such coins has OT complexity $\Theta(n \log 1/p)$. Remarkably – and in contrast to the information-theoretically derived lower bounds – our result shows that *OT complexity increases as p decreases*, although at the limit when $p = 0$, the OT complexity is 0. Indeed, an information-theoretic complexity measure like tension is unlikely to uncover this non-monotonic behavior of OT complexity.

Our main tool is *Secure Zero Communication Reductions* (SZCR) as defined recently in [22]. We extend the connection between SZCR complexity and OT complexity to randomized functions (in [22] this was limited to deterministic functions), and then show that the noisy coin-flip functionality has a large SZCR complexity of $\Omega(\log 1/p)$. Along the way, we develop a relaxation of SZCR complexity – which we term the *balanced embedding complexity* of a function – which is easier to interpret (especially for randomized functions) and which is sufficient to derive our lower bound.

OT Complexity and Randomized Functions. OT complexity of a (two-input) function – namely, the minimum number of instances of OT that is required by an information-theoretically secure[2] two-party computation protocol for evaluating the function – is a fundamental complexity measure. It follows from the results in the pioneering work in the 80's [12–14] that the OT complexity is upper bounded by the circuit complexity of the function. More recently, Beimel et al. [5] gave non-trivial upper bounds on OT complexity of all functions based on Private Information Retrieval (PIR) protocols, which become sub-exponential when instantiated using state-of-the art PIR results [11]. On the other hand, the few lower bounds that we do have – in terms of communication complexity [6] and "tension" [23] – are no larger than the (smaller) input and output length. Making further progress on OT complexity lower bounds faces major barriers, by implying lower bounds for circuit complexity (for explicit functions) or PIR

---

[2] Throughout this paper, we consider semi-honest and perfect security, which arguably gives the cleanest notion of OT complexity.

(even existentially). Showing an existential lower bound that is super polynomial in the input length will imply super-logarithmic lower bounds for the client computational complexity of 2-server PIR [5], and consequently lower bounds for codes on which PIR can be based. However, these barriers do not apply to *randomized functions*, motivating the current work.

Unfortunately, secure computation of randomized functions is relatively less well-understood, compared to deterministic functions. Indeed, even the characterization of which randomized functions are trivial (i.e., have 0 OT complexity) remains open.

While upper bounds on OT complexity of randomized functions can be obtained via upper bounds on OT complexity of appropriate deterministic functions (evaluated on randomized inputs), *this connection does not apply to lower bounds*. As an illustrative example, we present an inputless randomized function f which corresponds to evaluating a deterministic function g on random inputs, such that g has a positive OT complexity and f has 0 OT complexity![3] For $x, y \in [3]$, let $g(x, y) = M_{x,y}$ where $M = \begin{bmatrix} 1 & 1 & 2 \\ 4 & 5 & 2 \\ 4 & 3 & 3 \end{bmatrix}$. One way to compute this function would be for Alice and Bob to pick x and y respectively, and then use secure function evaluation to compute $g(x, y)$. Now, being an "undecomposable function", the function g cannot be securely computed without using any OTs [3,20]. However, f has a protocol that uses no OTs at all: one party can sample $M_{x,y}$ (without sampling x, y) and send it to the other one; then, independently, Alice samples x and Bob samples y conditioned on $M_{x,y}$.

Our result establishes, for the first time, a non-trivial lower bound technique for OT complexity of randomized functions. While this possibility was alluded to as a motivation in [22], the actual connection between SZCR and OT complexity established there was restricted to deterministic functions.

Our Contributions. We summarize our contributions as follows:

- The main result of this work is to show, for the first time, that the OT complexity of a randomized function can grow independent of the input/output size of the function. Specifically, we show that the OT complexity of securely sampling a noisy coin with flip probability p is $\Theta(\log 1/p)$. Further, this result has a "direct sum" version, so that sampling n independent copies of such a coin has OT complexity $\Theta(n \log 1/p)$.
- While proving this, we develop a more generally applicable tool, which shows that the complexity of an SZCR for a randomized function is a lower bound on the OT complexity of that function (denoted as $|f|_{\text{SZCR}} \leq |f|_{\text{OT}}$). We do this by carefully generalizing the analysis in [22] where the same result was shown for deterministic functions.
- As a contribution towards facilitating future work on SZCR, we present a relaxation of SZCR complexity of randomized functions, namely, *balanced embedding* complexity, so that our result can be summarized as

$$|f|_{\text{EMB}} \leq |f|_{\text{SZCR}} \lesssim |f|_{\text{OT}},$$

---

[3] This phenomenon occurs whenever g is undecomposable [20] but "simple" [21].

where the balanced embedding complexity $|f|_{\text{EMB}}$ is simpler to reason about. Indeed, our tight result on noisy coin-tossing is obtained by establishing a lower bound for balanced embedding complexity.

Related Work. There is a rich line of work in information-theoretic cryptography that studies the complexity of functions through the lens of secure 2-party computation. Starting with the seminal results in the 80's [19,20], complete and trivial functionalities for 2-party computation have been thoroughly characterized, for various levels of security (semi-honest, standalone, UC-secure) (see [21] for a survey). However, quantitative complexity results have been much sparser. The question of OT complexity was explicitly discussed by [4]. [6] presented a general lower bound in terms of the one-way communication complexity of the function. Important upper bounds of OT complexity follow from the semi-honest GMW protocol [12–14] and via PIR protocols [5]. Separate from the lower bound arguments in [6], a long line of works used information-theoretic tools for showing various complexity lower bounds for reductions in information-theoretic cryptography [4,9,10,15–18,23–26]; however, we may not expect such information-theoretic tools to uncover the non-monotonic behavior of OT complexity that we report here.

A similar sounding concept, called *Secure Non-Interactive Reduction* (SNIR) was introduced in [1] (also called Secure Non-Interactive Simulation or SNIS in [2]). It is instructive to compare both SNIR and SZCR with the standard notion of (semi-honest) secure reduction (SR) to a correlation like OT (i.e., the notion of OT complexity). Roughly put,

$$\text{SNIR} \Rightarrow \text{SR} \Rightarrow \text{SZCR}$$

indicating that SNIR is a "stronger" primitive than SR, which is in turn stronger than SZCR. While every function has an SR to the OT correlation (i.e., it is a complete correlation), that is not the case for SNIR: Indeed, there are no complete correlations for SNIR [1]. Both SNIR and SZCR are motivated by approaching the notoriously hard lower bound questions for SR, but they do it in different ways.

– Lower bounds (or impossibility results) for SNIR are an "easier" target than those for SR, and would provide a platform for nurturing new techniques; as and when we completely settle a question for SNIR (as is done in [7]),we can approach SR by relaxing the model (e.g., allow one-directional communication).
– Lower bounds for SZCR are formally (but not necessarily conceptually) harder than those for SR. In this case, one seeks to develop new techniques by asking simpler variants of the lower bound question: e.g., existential questions (a la the "invertible rank conjecture" of [22]) or lower bounds for randomized functions (as in this work) Also, the new perspective provided by SZCR may lead to fresh approaches to the original hard lower bound problems of SR.

2   Technical Overview

Our overall plan to obtain a lower bound on the OT complexity of a randomized function is to show that $|f|_{\mathsf{EMB}} \lesssim |f|_{\mathsf{OT}}$, where $|f|_{\mathsf{EMB}}$ is a new "balanced embedding complexity" that we define for functions, and then directly derive a lower bound for $|f|_{\mathsf{EMB}}$. The significance of this connection is that, *a priori*, OT complexity is difficult to lower bound due to the complex possibilities in a protocol. On the other hand, a balanced embedding has a relatively simple structure that could allow us to easily derive a lower bound on $|f|_{\mathsf{EMB}}$.

As such, the main technical contribution of this work is to define $|f|_{\mathsf{EMB}}$ and to show that $|f|_{\mathsf{EMB}} \lesssim |f|_{\mathsf{OT}}$. This involves a few different steps:

- Defining balanced embedding.
- Obtaining an easy lower bound on $|f|_{\mathsf{EMB}}$, where f is the p-noisy coin-tossing functionality.
- Showing that $|f|_{\mathsf{EMB}} \leq |f|_{\mathsf{SZCR}}$, where $|f|_{\mathsf{SZCR}}$ refers to the "SZCR complexity" of f.
- The final (and main) technical challenge is to show $|f|_{\mathsf{SZCR}} \lesssim |f|_{\mathsf{OT}}$.

Below, we expand on each of these steps.

Balanced Embedding. Identifying randomized functions as weighted bipartite graphs, we define a form of weighted embedding of one such graph into another. The embedding is a "fuzzy" embedding that assigns weights relating how much one node in one graph is associated with a node in the other graph. In fact, there are two such weights (π and θ) which "balance" each other – hence the name balanced embedding.

Definition 1. *Let $G = (\mathcal{S}, \mathcal{T}, \omega)$ be a weighted bipartite graph, where $\mathcal{S}, \mathcal{T}$ form a bi-partition of the nodes of G and $\omega : \mathcal{S} \times \mathcal{T} \to \mathbb{R}_{\geq 0}$ is the weight function. We define a* balanced embedding *of G into another bipartite graph $H = (\mathcal{U}, \mathcal{V}, \phi)$ as (π, θ) where $\pi, \theta : (\mathcal{U} \times \mathcal{S}) \cup (\mathcal{V} \times \mathcal{T}) \to \mathbb{R}_{\geq 0}$ are weight functions such that the following hold, for all $(\alpha, \beta) \in \mathcal{S} \times \mathcal{T}$:*

$$\sum_{v \in \mathcal{V}} \pi(v, \beta) \cdot \phi(u, v) = \theta(u, \alpha) \cdot \omega(\alpha, \beta) \qquad \forall u \in \mathcal{U} \quad (1)$$

$$\sum_{u \in \mathcal{U}} \pi(u, \alpha) \cdot \phi(u, v) = \theta(v, \beta) \cdot \omega(\alpha, \beta) \qquad \forall v \in \mathcal{V} \quad (2)$$

$$\sum_{u \in \mathcal{U}} \pi(u, \alpha) \cdot \theta(u, \alpha) = 1 \qquad \sum_{v \in \mathcal{V}} \pi(v, \beta) \cdot \theta(v, \beta) = 1 \quad \text{if } \omega(\alpha, \beta) > 0 \quad (3)$$

Given a randomized function $f : \mathcal{X} \times \mathcal{Y} \to \mathcal{A} \times \mathcal{B}$, we define its characteristic bipartite graph as $G_f = (\mathcal{X} \times \mathcal{A}, \mathcal{Y} \times \mathcal{B}, \omega)$, where $\omega((x, a), (y, b)) = \Pr[f(x, y) = (a, b)]$. We will be interested in the balanced embedding of G_f into the weighted graph $H_\phi := (\mathcal{U}, \mathcal{V}, \phi)$, where $\phi : \mathcal{U} \times \mathcal{V} \to \{0, 1\}$ is a predicate. In fact, we are specifically interested in predicates that correspond to multiple copies of OT:

$$\phi_{\mathsf{OT}}^m((u_1, \ldots, u_m), (v_1, \ldots, v_m)) = \bigwedge_{i=1}^{m} \phi_{\mathsf{OT}}(u_i, v_i)$$

where $\phi_{OT}(u,v) = 1$ iff $\exists (x_0, x_1, b) \in \{0,1\}^3$ such that $u = (x_0, x_1)$ and $v = (b, x_b)$.

Definition 2. *The* balanced embedding complexity *of* f, $|f|_{EMB}$ *is the smallest* m *such that* G_f *has a balanced embedding into* $H_{\phi_{OT}^m}$.

We remark that for our current result, the lower bound on the balanced embedding complexity of noisy coin-toss (sketched below) does not need to fully exploit all the conditions of a balanced embedding (e.g., in (3), = 1 can be replaced by > 0). However, for facilitating potential applications to other functions in the future, we retain the above version. For the sake of explicitness, we detail two constructions of balanced embedding of any Boolean function to OT predicate–from its truth table and from a Boolean circuit of the function–in Appendix A.

A Lower Bound for a Balanced Embedding of Noisy Coin-Tossing. Below we summarize the short argument to show that $|f|_{EMB} = \Omega(\log 1/p)$, where f is the p-noisy coin-toss functionality with $p < \frac{1}{2}$; i.e., if G_f has a balanced embedding into $H_{\phi_{OT}^m}$, then $m = \Omega(\log 1/p)$.

Let $G_f = (\{0_A, 1_A\}, \{0_B, 1_B\}, \omega)$, where $\omega(b_A, b_B) = (1-p)/2$ and $\omega(b_A, (1-b)_B) = p/2$ for all $b \in \{0,1\}$. Let $H_{\phi_{OT}^m} = (\mathcal{U}, \mathcal{V}, \phi_{OT}^m)$. Suppose (π, θ) is a balanced embedding of G_f to $H_{\phi_{OT}^m}$.

Now, we choose $(u^*, \alpha^*) \in \mathcal{U} \times \{0_A, 1_A\}$ such that $\pi(u^*, \alpha^*) \geq \pi(u, \alpha)$ for all (u, α). W.l.o.g, let $\alpha^* = 0_A$ (as the other case is symmetric). Using (1)–(3) we can argue that for some $v^* \in \mathcal{V}$ such that $\phi_{OT}^m(u^*, v^*) = 1$, $\theta(v^*, 1_B) > 0$. Then, applying (2) to both $(\alpha, \beta) = (1_A, 1_B)$ and $(0_A, 1_B)$, and taking their ratio, we get

$$\frac{\sum_u \pi(u, 1_A) \cdot \phi_{OT}^m(u, v^*)}{\sum_u \pi(u, 0_A) \cdot \phi_{OT}^m(u, v^*)} = \frac{\omega(1_A, 1_B)}{\omega(0_A, 1_B)} = \frac{1-p}{p}.$$

Since $\pi(u, 1_A) \leq \pi(u^*, 0_A)$ for all u, and since $\phi_{OT}^m(u^*, v^*) = 1$,

$$|\{u : \phi_{OT}^m(u, v^*)\}| \geq \frac{\sum_u \pi(u, 1_A) \cdot \phi_{OT}^m(u, v^*)}{\sum_u \pi(u, 0_A) \cdot \phi_{OT}^m(u, v^*)} = \frac{1-p}{p}.$$

Since $|\{u : \phi_{OT}^m(u, v^*)\}| = 2^m$, we have $m \geq \log(1/p) - 1$.

Virtually the same argument holds for the case of n noisy coin-flips, but with the ratio of probabilities used to obtain the bound being $\left(\frac{1-p}{p}\right)^n$, leading to a bound of $m = \Omega(n \log 1/p)$.

Recap of SZCR. We start with a quick recap of SZCR, as introduced in [22]. A μ-SZCR from a 2-party function f (which takes two inputs and produces two outputs, possibly randomized) to a predicate ϕ, is a minimalistic computation model, in which Alice and Bob, on being given respective inputs x and y, produce respective outputs (a, u) and (b, v) *without any communication*, with the guarantee that (a, b) is distributed as $f(x, y)$ (or, in the case of deterministic functions, $(a, b) = f(x, y)$) conditioned on $\phi(u, v) = 1$. It is required that $\phi(u, v) = 1$ with a fixed probability (irrespective of (x, y)) which is at least $2^{-\mu}$. The security condition captures the idea that Alice's view (which is considered to include the predicate's outcome $\phi(u, v)$, as well as her input x and output (a, u)) reveals nothing about Bob's input and output (y, b), beyond what is revealed by (x, a); similarly, Bob's view reveals nothing more about (x, a) than (y, b) itself reveals.

SZCR leads to a pair of natural complexity measures associated with a (possibly randomized) function f: smallest possible μ and m for which there is a μ-SZCR from f to ϕ_{OT}^m. In [22], the minimum such $\mu + m$ was suggested as a convenient complexity measure of a function f. In this work, for simplicity, we shall use the smallest m for which there is a μ-SZCR from f to ϕ_{OT}^m for *any* (finite) μ as the complexity measure $|f|_{\mathsf{SZCR}}$.[4]

Balanced Embedding and SZCR. Given an SZCR that reduces f to ϕ, we obtain a balanced embedding of G_f into H_ϕ. This amounts to assigning weights $\pi(u, \alpha)$ and $\theta(u, \alpha)$ for all $u \in \mathcal{U}$ and $\alpha \in \mathcal{X} \times \mathcal{A}$, and $\pi(v, \beta)$ and $\theta(v, \beta)$ for all $v \in \mathcal{V}$ and $\beta \in \mathcal{Y} \times \mathcal{B}$ in a way that satisfies (1), (2), and (3). Let $\Theta(\mathfrak{A}, \mathfrak{B})$ be an SZCR from f to ϕ. For $\alpha = (x, a)$ and u, we choose $\pi(u, \alpha) \propto \mathsf{Pr}_\mathfrak{A}(u, a|x)$ and $\theta(u, \alpha)$ such that $\pi(u, \alpha) \cdot \theta(u, \alpha) = \mathsf{Pr}_{\hat{S}_A}(u|x, a, D = 1)$, where $\hat{S}_A$ is the simulator for Alice in the SZCR. For $\beta = (y, a)$ and v, $\pi(v, \beta)$ and $\theta(v, \beta)$ are chosen analogously. Having chosen the product of $\pi(u, \alpha)$ and $\theta(u, \alpha)$ in this manner,

$$\sum_u \pi(u, \alpha) \cdot \theta(u, \alpha) = \sum_u \mathsf{Pr}_{\hat{S}_A}(u|x, a, D = 1) = 1,$$

ensuring (3). Since $D = 1$ whenever $\mathfrak{A}$ and $\mathfrak{B}$ choose u and v, respectively, such that $\phi(u, v) = 1$, with π defined as above, and $\alpha = (x, a)$ and $\beta = (y, b)$,

$$\sum_v \pi(v, \beta)\phi(u, v) \propto \mathsf{Pr}_\Theta(D = 1, b|y, x, a, u) = \mathsf{Pr}_\Theta(b|x, y, a) \cdot \frac{\mathsf{Pr}_\Theta(D = 1, u|x, y, a, b)}{\mathsf{Pr}_\Theta(u|x, y, a, b)}.$$

Using the correctness of Θ conditioned on the event $D = 1$ and the fact that (u, a) and (v, b) are sampled depending only on x and y, respectively,

$$\mathsf{Pr}_\Theta(b|x, y, a) \cdot \frac{\mathsf{Pr}_\Theta(D = 1, u|x, y, a, b)}{\mathsf{Pr}_\Theta(u|x, y, a, b)} \propto \frac{\mathsf{Pr}_\Theta(u|x, y, a, b, D = 1)\mathsf{Pr}_f(a, b|x, y)}{\mathsf{Pr}_\mathfrak{A}(u, a|x)}.$$

At this point, noting that $\mathsf{Pr}_\Theta(u|x, y, a, b, D = 1) = \mathsf{Pr}_{\hat{S}_A}(u|x, a, D = 1)$ for all (y, b) and choosing the proportionality constant to be $\sqrt{\mathsf{Pr}_\Theta(D = 1|x, y)}$, we get (1). (2) is shown analogously.

We remark that in translating an SZCR to a balanced embedding, we ignore the SZCR security requirements related to the simulatability of views when the computation is *rejected* by the predicate.

OT Complexity and SZCR. In [22], it was shown that a 2-party secure function evaluation protocol Π^{OT} for a deterministic function f, using m OTs

---

[4] Our connection between SZCR and OT-based 2-PC does extend to both μ and m. But our formulation of balanced embedding complexity $|f|_{\mathsf{EMB}}$ omits μ, and lower bounds on $|f|_{\mathsf{EMB}}$ yield lower bounds on m rather than only on $m + \mu$.

can be transformed into a μ-SZCR from f to the predicate ϕ_{OT} corresponding to m instances of OT,[5] where $\mu = O(m)$. The high-level idea is for Alice and Bob to sample candidate pairs of views in Π^{OT} such that conditioned on ϕ_{OT} accepting the OTs in these views, these views are distributed correctly as in the protocol. Also, it would be ensured that the acceptance probability of the predicate is constant independent of x, y. Then the security guarantee of Π^{OT} translates to the security requirement of SZCR.

Being able to carry out the rejection sampling of views using ϕ_{OT} relies on the fact that protocols (secure or not) admit *transcript factorization*: i.e., the probability of a transcript q occurring in an execution of Π^{OT}, given inputs (x, y) and OT correlation (r, s) to the two parties respectively, can be written as

$$\Pr_{\Pi^{OT}}(q|x, y, r, s) = \rho(x, r, q) \cdot \sigma(y, s, q),$$

for some functions ρ and σ. Given a particular transcript q (say, as a common reference string),[6] each of the two parties can locally sample its views from OTs (r or s, respectively), conditioned on its own input and q, with probability proportional to $\rho(x, r, q)$ or $\sigma(y, s, q)$, respectively with a proportionality constant independent of x or y; then, the probability that the parties end up with a valid joint view in the protocol (for which $\phi_{OT}(r, s) = 1$, and where all such (r, s) have the same probability) is proportional to that in the protocol, conditioned on (x, y, q).

Above, using proportionality constants that are independent of x and y runs into a problem since $\sum_r \rho(x, r, q)$ and $\sum_s \sigma(y, s, q)$ can depend on x, y. To resolve this, the parties are allowed to output an invalid r or s with some probability (implemented by setting $u = (u_0, r)$ and $v = (v_0, s)$, so that Alice or Bob can unilaterally force $\phi_{OT}(u, v) = 0$ by choosing a special value $\perp$ for u_0 or v_0, respectively).

To get a μ-SZCR, with $\mu = O(m)$, it is important to keep the probability with which the parties force aborting bounded. A key aspect in ensuring this turns out to be how the transcript q is chosen. As detailed in [22], if the function is "common-information-free,"–i.e., its characteristic bipartite graph is connected– then a single fixed transcript can be used. But otherwise, if the graph has multiple connected components, a transcript is chosen from among a small set of transcripts $q_1^*, \cdots, q_k^*$, indexed by the different values that the common information can take. An additional rejection step is introduced (see below), corresponding to rejecting a choice of this index that is not consistent with the input-output pair. A somewhat lengthy analysis shows that with appropriately chosen transcripts, the probability of the SZCR accepting is at least $2^{-O(m)}$.

---

[5] That is, $\phi_{OT}(u, v) = 1$ iff $u = (r_1, \cdots, r_m)$, $v = (s_1, \cdots, s_m)$ and each (r_i, s_i) is in the support of the OT correlation. Looking ahead, ϕ_{OT} in fact uses $m + 1$ instances of OT, where the extra instance is used as an "abort switch." Following the notation in [22], later, we denote ϕ_{OT} as $\phi_{\mathsf{supp(OT+)}}$.

[6] The general definition in [22] allowed a CRS, or even more general correlations in an SZCR. For simplicity, we omit this from our adaptation, as we shall not need it for our specific result.

Extending to Randomized Functions. We first notice that the construction in [22] is no longer an SZCR when f is randomized and is not common-information free. To see this, we need to recall more details of the rejection step mentioned above for rejecting the wrong transcript index. Firstly, common information that Alice and Bob obtain when evaluating $f(x,y)$ to obtain outputs a and b respectively, corresponds to the connected component containing the edge $((x,a),(y,b))$ in a bipartite graph G_f representing f.[7] Now, in the SZCR of [22], given x and a common index ℓ, Alice checks if there is at least one a' such that the node (x,a') lies in the component specified by ℓ, and if so she samples r as described above, and computes an output a using the protocol Π on the view (x,r,q_ℓ^*). (Otherwise, she sets $u = (\perp, r)$ to force the predicate to fail.)

But when f is randomized, it is possible that the same transcript, and the same pair of inputs (x,y), could correspond to two different outputs (a_1, b_1) and (a_2, b_2), such that the edges $((x,a_1),(y,b_1))$ and $((x,a_2),(y,b_2))$ are in two different connected components of G_f.[8] So when the parties sample (r, s) conditioned on (x,y,q), it could correspond to either output. This breaks a crucial invariant in the analysis that when the predicate accepts, the outputs produced (a, b) will be such that $((x,a),(y,b))$ is in the connected component corresponding to the common index ℓ.

To fix this, we make a subtle change in the SZCR: Alice and Bob will first sample their respective outputs a and b (rather than computing them from r and s), and then check that the nodes (x,a) and (y,b) are in the connected component corresponding to the common index ℓ. This restores the invariant mentioned above, but necessitates a careful reanalysis. Our new analysis closely follows the original analysis, but needs to accommodate the above modification in the protocol, as well as the fact that G_f can have multiple edges (possibly in multiple connected components) of the form $((x,\cdot),(y,\cdot))$ for the same (x,y).

Our new proof incorporates an additional minor refinement. In [22], the SZCR constructed used a CRS, as this was a part of the model. Here, motivated by simplifying the (already minimalistic) SZCR model further, we restrict ourselves to a version which does not involve a CRS. Instead, the two parties guess a value of the CRS, and use the predicate ϕ_{OT} to check if their guesses match. This does result in a slight quantitative degradation in the acceptance probability (when there are multiple connected components in G_f), but asymptotically, the result remains unchanged.

Finally, we remark that our result (as well as the one in [22]) is not only for an SZCR to OTs, but is shown for any "regular" complete correlation.

---

[7] For randomized functions, G_f is a weighted bipartite graph with the weight of an edge $((x,a),(y,b))$ being $\Pr[f(x,y) = (a,b)]$.

[8] Note that the common information that Alice and Bob obtain in an execution of the protocol Π^{OT} is not solely determined by the transcript, but also by their views of the OT correlation. Indeed, a protocol could use OTs to carry out an information-theoretically secure secret-key agreement protocol, and then use the key as a one-time pad for the rest of the transcript, so that the transcript by itself is distributed identically for all input-output pairs.

3   Preliminaries

Probability Notation. We adhere mostly to the notations used in [22]. In general, we denote a finite set by $\mathcal{X}, \mathcal{Y}, \ldots$ and so on. A member of $\mathcal{X}$ is denoted by x and a random variable taking values in $\mathcal{X}$ is denoted by X. The probability assigned by a distribution D (or a probabilistic process D) to a value x is denoted as $\Pr_D(x)$, or simply $\Pr(x)$, when the distribution is understood. Sampling x according to the distribution D is denoted as $x \leftarrow D$.

Functionalities and Correlations. A (potentially randomized) two party functionality $f : \mathcal{X} \times \mathcal{Y} \rightarrow \mathcal{A} \times \mathcal{B}$ takes inputs x and y, respectively, from Alice and Bob and returns a and b, respectively, to them, where $(a, b) = f(x, y)$. We write $f_A : \mathcal{X} \times \mathcal{Y} \rightarrow \mathcal{A}$ to indicate the function obtained by projecting the output of f to the first coordinate (i.e., retaining only Alice's output). Similarly, $f_B : \mathcal{X} \times \mathcal{Y} \rightarrow \mathcal{B}$ denotes the function obtained from f by retaining only Bob's output.

A correlation ψ over a domain $\mathcal{R} \times \mathcal{S}$ is a 2-party functionality without inputs, i.e., $\psi : \{\perp\} \times \{\perp\} \rightarrow \mathcal{R} \times \mathcal{S}$. The support of ψ is $\mathsf{supp}(\psi) = \{(r, s) | \Pr_\psi(r, s) > 0\}$. A correlation is said to be *regular* if (1) $\forall (r, s) \in \mathsf{supp}(\psi)$, $\Pr_\psi(r, s) = \frac{1}{|\mathsf{supp}(\psi)|}$, (2) $\forall r \in \mathcal{R}$, $\sum_{s \in \mathcal{S}} \Pr_\psi(r, s) = \frac{1}{|\mathcal{R}|}$, and (3) $\forall s \in \mathcal{S}$, $\sum_{r \in \mathcal{R}} \Pr_\psi(r, s) = \frac{1}{|\mathcal{S}|}$. Common examples of regular correlations are those corresponding to Oblivious Transfer (OT) and Oblivious Linear Function Evaluation (OLE), and their n-fold repetitions. For $t \in \mathbb{N}$, t independent copies of a correlation ψ is denoted by ψ^t.

Definition 3. *For a randomized function $f : \mathcal{X} \times \mathcal{Y} \rightarrow \mathcal{A} \times \mathcal{B}$ we define its evaluation graph, G_f as the bipartite graph on vertices $(\mathcal{X} \times \mathcal{A}) \cup (\mathcal{Y} \times \mathcal{B})$ such that the edge weight of an edge $((x, a), (y, b))$ is $\Pr_f(a, b | x, y)$.*

Two vertices u and v in G_f are said to be connected if there is a path from u to v consisting of edges with non-zero edge weight. Let $C \subseteq G_f$ be a connected component of G_f; we define:

$$\mathcal{X}_C = \{x : \exists a, y, b((x, a), (y, b)) \in C\} \quad \mathcal{Y}_C = \{y : \exists b, x, a((x, a), (y, b)) \in C\}$$

Predicates. A predicate is any deterministic function $\phi : \mathcal{U} \times \mathcal{V} \rightarrow \{0, 1\}$ with boolean output. The predicate $\phi_{(=^l)}$ takes a pair of l-bit strings u, v as input and accepts if $u = v$. Given a correlation ψ over $\mathcal{U} \times \mathcal{V}$, we define the predicate $\phi_{\mathsf{supp}(\psi)}$ so that $\phi_{\mathsf{supp}(\psi)}(u, v) = 1$ iff $(u, v) \in \mathsf{supp}(\psi)$. The predicate $\phi_{\mathsf{supp}^*(\psi)}$ is defined identically, except that we allow the domain of $\phi_{\mathsf{supp}^*(\psi)}$ to be $(\mathcal{U} \cup \{\perp\}) \times (\mathcal{V} \cup \{\perp\})$ where $\perp$ is a symbol not in $\mathcal{U} \cup \mathcal{V}$. Specifically, the predicate $\phi_{\mathsf{supp}(\mathsf{OT}^m)}$ allows a domain of $\{0, 1\}^{2m} \times \{0, 1\}^{2m}$ and accepts u, v if $\Pr_{\mathsf{OT}^m}(u, v) > 0$ and rejects otherwise; whereas, $\phi_{\mathsf{supp}^*(\mathsf{OT}^m)}$ behaves the same way but the input domain is now $(\{0, 1\}^{2m} \cup \{\perp\}) \times (\{0, 1\}^{2m} \cup \{\perp\})$.

Let $\phi : \mathcal{U} \times \mathcal{V} \rightarrow \{0, 1\}$ and $\phi' : \mathcal{U}' \times \mathcal{V}' \rightarrow \{0, 1\}$ be two predicates. Their product $\phi \cdot \phi'$ takes $(u, u') \in \mathcal{U} \times \mathcal{U}'$ and $(v, v') \in \mathcal{V} \times \mathcal{V}'$ as inputs and accepts if $\phi(u, v) = 1$ and $\phi'(u', v') = 1$.

Secure 2-Party Communication Protocols. A communication protocol between Alice and Bob using the correlation ψ, denoted by Π^ψ, proceeds as follows: Alice and Bob receive inputs x and y, respectively, and, additionally, they get r and s, respectively, where $(r, s) \leftarrow \psi$. They exchange messages in rounds (message of a party in each round being a randomized function of their current view) to generate a transcript $q \in \mathcal{Q}$. Finally, Alice (resp. Bob) computes their output a (resp. b) by applying a (randomized) map Π_A^{out} (resp. Π_B^{out}) to their final view (x, r, q) (resp. (y, s, q)). Thus, the outcome of an execution of Π^ψ on inputs (x, y) is the joint distribution described by

$$\Pr_{\Pi^\psi}(r, s, q, a, b | x, y)$$
$$= \Pr_\psi(r, s) \cdot \Pr_{\Pi^\psi}(q | x, y, r, s) \cdot \Pr_{\Pi_A^{\text{out}}}(a | x, r, q) \cdot \Pr_{\Pi_B^{\text{out}}}(b | y, s, q), \forall r, s, q, a, b. \tag{4}$$

The protocol Π^ψ is said to compute the functionality $f : \mathcal{X} \times \mathcal{Y} \to \mathcal{A} \times \mathcal{B}$ with perfect security if the distribution $\Pr_{\Pi^\psi}(r, s, q, a, b | x, y)$ described above satisfies the following conditions:

Correctness: For all x, y,

$$\Pr_{\Pi^\psi}(a, b | x, y) = \Pr_f(a, b | x, y), \forall a, b. \tag{5}$$

Privacy against Alice: There exists a randomized simulator $\hat{S}_A : \mathcal{X} \times \mathcal{A} \to \mathcal{R} \times \mathcal{Q}$ such that, for all a, x, y, such that $f_A(a | x, y) > 0$,

$$\Pr_{\Pi^\psi}(r, q | x, y, a) = \Pr_{\hat{S}_A}(r, q | x, a), \forall r, q. \tag{6}$$

Privacy against Bob: There exists a randomized simulator $\hat{S}_B : \mathcal{Y} \times \mathcal{B} \to \mathcal{S} \times \mathcal{Q}$ such that, for all b, x, y, such that $f_B(b | x, y) > 0$,

$$\Pr_{\Pi^\psi}(s, q | x, y, b) = \Pr_{\hat{S}_B}(s, q | y, b), \forall s, q. \tag{7}$$

Transcript Factorization. In any 2-party communication protocol Π^ψ, the probability of generating the transcript, as a randomized function of the inputs (x, y) and the correlation (r, s), can be factorized into separate functions of (x, r) and (y, s). A transcript $q = (m_1, \ldots, m_N)$ is generated by the protocol if Alice produces the message m_1 given (x, r) in round 1, and then Bob produces m_2 given (y, s, m_1) in round 2, and so forth. That is,

$$\Pr_{\Pi^\psi}(m_1, \ldots, m_N | x, y, r, s) = \Pr(m_1 | x, r) \times \Pr(m_2 | y, s, m_1) \times \ldots$$
$$\times \Pr(m_i | y, s, m_1, \ldots, m_{i-1}) \times \ldots.$$

Hence, by collecting the products of odd factors as $\rho(x, r, m_1, \ldots, m_N)$ and even factors as $\sigma(y, s, m_1, \ldots, m_N)$, we can write the transcript as a product of separate functions of (x, r) and (y, s).

Formally, there exist *transcript factorization functions* $\rho : \mathcal{X} \times \mathcal{R} \times \mathcal{Q} \to [0,1]$ and $\sigma : \mathcal{Y} \times \mathcal{S} \times \mathcal{Q} \to [0,1]$, such that

$$\Pr_{\Pi^*}(q|x,y,r,s) = \rho(x,r,q) \cdot \sigma(y,s,q). \tag{8}$$

It is worth noting that, for any x, y, r, s, functions ρ and σ by themselves are not probability mass functions. We shall use this important and well-known transcript factorization property (e.g., [8]) of a protocol in our constructions.

3.1 Zero-Communication Secure Reductions

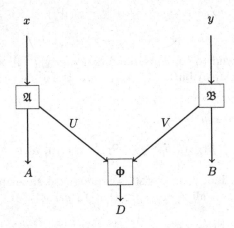

Fig. 1. The random variables involved in a SZCR.

The zero-communication reduction Θ from a functionality f to predicate ϕ is specified by a pair of randomized algorithms $(\mathfrak{A}, \mathfrak{B})$. The random variables involved in the reduction are illustrated in Fig. 1. The reduction proceeds as follows: Alice and Bob receive inputs x, y to the functionality f, respectively. Alice samples $(a, u) \leftarrow \mathfrak{A}(x)$, where a is her proposed output for the functionality f, and u is her input to the predicate ϕ. Similarly, Bob samples $(b, v) \leftarrow \mathfrak{B}(y)$. On receiving u, v from Alice and Bob, respectively, the predicate outputs $d = \phi(u, v)$. Thus, the outcome of an execution of Θ on inputs (x, y) is the joint distribution described by

$$\Pr_{\Theta}(u,v,a,b,d|x,y) = \Pr_{\mathfrak{A}}(u,a|x) \cdot \Pr_{\mathfrak{B}}(v,b|y) \cdot \Pr_{\phi}(d|u,v). \tag{9}$$

Definition 4. *Let* $f : \mathcal{X} \times \mathcal{Y} \to \mathcal{A} \times \mathcal{B}$ *and* $\phi : \mathcal{U} \times \mathcal{V} \to \{0,1\}$ *be randomized functions. For any* $\mu \geq 0$, *a* μ-*secure zero-communication reduction* (μ-SZCR) $\Theta(\mathfrak{A}, \mathfrak{B})$ *from* f *to the predicate* ϕ *is a pair of probabilistic algorithms* $\mathfrak{A} : \mathcal{X} \to \mathcal{U} \times \mathcal{A}$ *and* $\mathfrak{B} : \mathcal{Y} \to \mathcal{V} \times \mathcal{B}$ *such that the following holds for the distribution described in* (9).

Non-triviality and Weak Security. $\exists \mu' \leq \mu, \; \forall (x, y) \in \mathcal{X} \times \mathcal{Y},$

$$\mathsf{Pr}_\Theta(D = 1 | x, y) = 2^{-\mu'}. \tag{10}$$

Correctness. $\forall x, y, a, b \in \mathcal{X} \times \mathcal{Y} \times \mathcal{A} \times \mathcal{B},$

$$\mathsf{Pr}_\Theta(a, b | x, y, D = 1) = \mathsf{Pr}_f(a, b | x, y). \tag{11}$$

Security against Alice. *There exists a randomized function* $S_A : \mathcal{X} \times \mathcal{A} \times \{0, 1\} \rightarrow \mathcal{U}$ *such that* $\forall x, y, a \in \mathcal{X} \times \mathcal{Y} \times \mathcal{A}$ *such that* $\mathsf{Pr}_{f_A}(a | x, y) > 0,$

$$\mathsf{Pr}_\Theta(u | x, y, a, D = 1) = \mathsf{Pr}_{S_A}(u | x, a, 1). \tag{12}$$

$$\mathsf{Pr}_\Theta(u | x, y, D = 0) = \sum_a \mathsf{Pr}_{f_A}(a | x, y) \cdot \mathsf{Pr}_{S_A}(u | x, a, 0). \tag{13}$$

Security against Bob. *There exists a randomized function* $S_B : \mathcal{Y} \times \mathcal{B} \times \{0, 1\} \rightarrow \mathcal{V}$ *such that* $\forall x, y, b \in \mathcal{X} \times \mathcal{Y} \times \mathcal{B}$ *such that* $\mathsf{Pr}_{f_B}(b | x, y) > 0,$

$$\mathsf{Pr}_\Theta(v | x, y, b, D = 1) = \mathsf{Pr}_{S_B}(v | y, b, 1). \tag{14}$$

$$\mathsf{Pr}_\Theta(v | x, y, D = 0) = \sum_b \mathsf{Pr}_{f_B}(b | x, y) \cdot \mathsf{Pr}_{S_B}(v | y, b, 0). \tag{15}$$

In other words, in a SZCR, Alice and Bob compute "candidate outputs" a and b, as well as two messages u and v, respectively, such that correctness (i.e., $f(x, y) = (a, b)$) is required only when ϕ "accepts" (u, v). To be non-trivial, we require a lower bound $2^{-\mu}$ on the probability of ϕ accepting. Weak security requires that an "eavesdropper" who gets to observe whether the predicate ϕ accepts or not learns nothing about the inputs x, y. This is ensured by require the probability of accepting to remain the same as the inputs are changed. Note that as μ increases from 0 to ∞, the non-triviality and weak security constraint gets relaxed.

Finally, the security condition corresponds to security against passive corruption of one of Alice and Bob in a secure computation protocol (using ϕ) that realizes the following functionality f_μ: After computing $(a, b) \leftarrow f(x, y)$, with probability $2^{-\mu}$ the functionality sends the respective outputs to the two parties ("accepting" case); with the remaining probability, it sends the output only to the corrupt party. In the above, (12) and (13) correspond to corrupting Alice, with the first one being the accepting case. Note that in these cases the adversary's view consists of U, in addition to the input x and the boolean variable D (accepting or not), which are given to the environment as well. In the accepting case, the environment also observes the outputs (a, b). In either case, $\hat{S}_A$ is given $(x, f_A(x, y), D)$ as inputs; in the accepting case, we naturally require that the simulated view has the same output a as $f_A(x, y)$ given to $\hat{S}_A$. Security conditions against Bob are interpreted analogously.

4   Balanced Embedding

For a randomized function $f : \mathcal{X} \times \mathcal{Y} \rightarrow \mathcal{A} \times \mathcal{B}$ and a deterministic predicate $\phi : \mathcal{U} \times \mathcal{V} \rightarrow \{0, 1\}$, we study the *balanced embedding*, defined in Definition 1 in Sect. 2 of the evaluation graph G_f into the evaluation graph G_ϕ.

Theorem 1. *If a randomized function* $f : \mathcal{X} \times \mathcal{Y} \to \mathcal{A} \times \mathcal{B}$ *has a* SZCR *to* $\phi : \mathcal{U} \times \mathcal{V} \to \{0,1\}$, *then there is a balanced embedding of the evaluation graph* G_f *into the predicate graph* G_ϕ.

Proof. For each $\alpha = (x, a)$ and $\beta = (y, b)$, define

$$\pi(u, \alpha) = \frac{\mathsf{Pr}_{\mathfrak{A}}(u, a | x)}{\sqrt{\mathsf{Pr}_\Theta(D = 1 | x, y)}} \text{ and } \theta(u, \alpha) = \frac{\mathsf{Pr}_{S_A}(u | x, a, D = 1)}{\pi(u, \alpha)} \forall u \in \mathcal{U}$$

$$\pi(v, \beta) = \frac{\mathsf{Pr}_{\mathfrak{B}}(v, b | y)}{\sqrt{\mathsf{Pr}_\Theta(D = 1 | x, y)}} \text{ and } \theta(v, \beta) = \frac{\mathsf{Pr}_{S_B}(v | y, b, D = 1)}{\pi(v, \beta)} \forall v \in \mathcal{V}$$

Note that we set $\theta(u, \alpha) = 0$ whenever $\pi(u, \alpha) = 0$ and $\theta(v, \beta) = 0$ whenever $\pi(v, \beta) = 0$ since $\Pr(u|x, a)$ and $\Pr(v|y, b)$ are going to be 0 in these cases.
For each $u \in \mathcal{U}$, when $\beta = (y, b)$, and $\alpha = (x, a)$ for any (x, a) such that $\mathsf{Pr}_{\mathfrak{A}}(u, a | x) > 0$,

$$
\begin{aligned}
\sum_{v \in \mathcal{V}} \pi(v, \beta) \cdot \phi(u, v) &\overset{(a)}{=} \frac{\sum_{v : \phi(u,v)=1} \mathsf{Pr}_{\mathfrak{B}}(v | y, b) \mathsf{Pr}_{\mathfrak{B}}(b|y)}{\sqrt{\mathsf{Pr}_\Theta(D = 1|x, y)}} \\
&\overset{(b)}{=} \frac{\mathsf{Pr}_\Theta(D = 1|y, b, x, a, u) \mathsf{Pr}_{\mathfrak{B}}(b|y)}{\sqrt{\mathsf{Pr}_\Theta(D = 1|x, y)}} \\
&\overset{(c)}{=} \frac{\mathsf{Pr}_\Theta(u, D = 1|y, b, x, a) \mathsf{Pr}_{\mathfrak{B}}(b|y)}{\mathsf{Pr}_{\mathfrak{A}}(u|x, a) \sqrt{\mathsf{Pr}_\Theta(D = 1|x, y)}} \\
&= \frac{\mathsf{Pr}_\Theta(u|x, y, a, b, D = 1) \mathsf{Pr}_\Theta(D = 1|x, a, y, b) \mathsf{Pr}_{\mathfrak{B}}(b|y)}{\mathsf{Pr}_{\mathfrak{A}}(u|x, a) \sqrt{\mathsf{Pr}_\Theta(D = 1|x, y)}} \\
&\overset{(d)}{=} \frac{\mathsf{Pr}_{S_A}(u|x, a, D = 1) \mathsf{Pr}_\Theta(D = 1, a, b|x, y) \mathsf{Pr}_{\mathfrak{B}}(b|y)}{\mathsf{Pr}_{\mathfrak{A}}(u|x, a) \mathsf{Pr}_\Theta(a, b|x, y) \sqrt{\mathsf{Pr}_\Theta(D = 1|x, y)}} \\
&\overset{(e)}{=} \frac{\mathsf{Pr}_{S_A}(u|x, a, D = 1) \mathsf{Pr}_\Theta(D = 1|x, y) \mathsf{Pr}_\Theta(a, b|x, y, D = 1)}{\mathsf{Pr}_{\mathfrak{A}}(u|x, a) \mathsf{Pr}_{\mathfrak{A}}(a|x) \sqrt{\mathsf{Pr}_\Theta(D = 1|x, y)}} \\
&\overset{(f)}{=} \frac{\mathsf{Pr}_{S_A}(u|x, a, D = 1) \mathsf{Pr}_f(a, b|x, y)}{\pi(u, \alpha)} \\
&\overset{(g)}{=} \theta(u, \alpha) \cdot \omega(\alpha, \beta).
\end{aligned}
\tag{16}
$$

Here, (a) used the definition of $\pi(v, \beta)$; (b) used the fact that, for all (x, a) such that $\mathsf{Pr}_{\mathfrak{A}}(u, a|x) > 0$,

$$\mathsf{Pr}_\Theta(D = 1|y, b, x, a, u) = \sum_{v : \phi(u,v)=1} \mathsf{Pr}_\Theta(v|y, b, x, a, u) = \sum_{v : \phi(u,v)=1} \mathsf{Pr}_{\mathfrak{B}}(v|y, b);$$

(c) used $\mathsf{Pr}_\Theta(u|x, a, y, b) = \mathsf{Pr}_{\mathfrak{A}}(u|x, a)$ as u is sampled locally by Alice in Θ; (d) follows from the privacy condition (12); (e) used $\mathsf{Pr}_\Theta(a, b|x, y) = \mathsf{Pr}_{\mathfrak{A}}(a|x) \cdot \mathsf{Pr}_{\mathfrak{B}}(b|y)$; (f) follows from (11) - the correctness of Θ, and the definition of $\pi(u, \alpha)$; finally, (g) follows from the definitions of $\theta(u, \alpha)$ and $\omega(\alpha, \beta)$.

Similarly,

$$\sum_{u \in \mathcal{U}} \pi(u, \alpha) \cdot \phi(u, v) = \theta(v, \beta) \cdot \omega(\alpha, \beta) \qquad\qquad \forall v \in \mathcal{V} \qquad (17)$$

And finally, when $\omega(\alpha, \beta) > 0$,

$$\sum_{u \in \mathcal{U}} \pi(u, \alpha) \cdot \theta(u, \alpha) = \sum_{u \in \mathcal{U}} \mathsf{Pr}_{S_A}(u|x, a, D = 1) = 1, \text{ and}$$

$$\sum_{v \in \mathcal{V}} \pi(v, \beta) \cdot \theta(v, \beta) = \sum_{v \in \mathcal{V}} \mathsf{Pr}_{S_B}(v|y, b, D = 1) = 1. \qquad (18)$$

Theorem follows from (16), (17) and (18).   □

Theorem 2. *For the p-noisy coin-toss functionality f, the balanced embedding complexity $|f|_{\mathsf{EMB}} = \Omega(\log 1/p)$, when $p < \frac{1}{2}$; i.e., if G_f has a balanced embedding into $H_{\phi_{OT}^m}$, then $m = \Omega(\log 1/p)$.*

Proof. Let $G_f = (\mathcal{S}, \mathcal{T}, \omega)$, where $\mathcal{S} = \{0_A, 1_A\}$ and $\mathcal{T} = \{0_B, 1_B\}$, and $\omega(b_A, b_B) = (1 - p)/2$ and $\omega(b_A, (1 - b)_B) = p/2$ for all $b \in \{0, 1\}$. Let $H_{\phi_{OT}^m} = (\mathcal{U}, \mathcal{V}, \phi_{OT}^m)$. Suppose (π, θ) is a balanced embedding of G_f to $H_{\phi_{OT}^m}$. Define $(u^*, \alpha^*) \in \mathcal{U} \times \{0_A, 1_A\}$ as

$$(u^*, \alpha^*) = \underset{(u,\alpha):\theta(u,\alpha)>0}{\arg\max} \; \pi(u, \alpha). \qquad (19)$$

Note that $\pi(u^*, \alpha^*) > 0$ since otherwise $\pi(u, \alpha) \cdot \theta(u, \alpha) = 0$ for all (u, α), which violates (3). W.l.o.g., let $\alpha^* = 0_A$ (the other case being symmetric).

Since $\theta(u^*, 0_A) > 0$ and $\omega(0_A, 1_B) > 0$, by (1), $\pi(v^*, 1_B) > 0$ for some $v^* \in \mathcal{V}$ such that $\phi_{OT}^m(u^*, v^*) = 1$. Further, by (2), $\theta(v^*, 1_B) > 0$ since $\pi(u^*, 0_A) > 0$ and $\phi_{OT}^m(u^*, v^*) = 1$. Applying (2) to both $(\alpha, \beta) = (1_A, 1_B)$ and $(0_A, 1_B)$, and taking their ratio, we get

$$\frac{\sum_u \pi(u, 1_A) \cdot \phi_{OT}^m(u, v^*)}{\sum_u \pi(u, 0_A) \cdot \phi_{OT}^m(u, v^*)} = \frac{\omega(1_A, 1_B)}{\omega(0_A, 1_B)} = \frac{1 - p}{p}.$$

By (1), for all u such that $\phi_{OT}^m(u, v^*) = 1$, $\theta(u, 1_A) > 0$ since $\pi(v^*, 0_B) > 0$. But then, by (19), $\pi(u, 1_A) \leq \pi(u^*, 0_A)$ for all u. Therefore, noting that $\phi_{OT}^m(u^*, v^*) = 1$,

$$\sum_u \pi(u, 1_A) \cdot \phi_{OT}^m(u, v^*) \leq \pi(u^*, 0_A)|\{u : \phi_{OT}^m(u, v^*)\}|$$

$$\leq |\{u : \phi_{OT}^m(u, v^*)\}| \sum_u \pi(u, 0_A) \cdot \phi_{OT}^m(u, v^*).$$

Hence,

$$|\{u : \phi_{OT}^m(u, v^*)\}| \geq \frac{\sum_u \pi(u, 1_A) \cdot \phi_{OT}^m(u, v^*)}{\sum_u \pi(u, 0_A) \cdot \phi_{OT}^m(u, v^*)} = \frac{1 - p}{p}.$$

Since $|\{u : \phi_{OT}^m(u, v^*)\}| = 2^m$, we have $m \geq \log(1/p) - 1$.   □

Virtually the same argument holds for the case of n noisy coin-flips, but with the ratio of probabilities used to obtain the bound being $\left(\frac{1-p}{p}\right)^n$, leading to a bound of $m = \Omega(n \log 1/p)$.

5   SZCR from MPC Protocols

In this section, we construct an SZCR from a potentially randomized function to OT check predicate from an MPC protocol for the function using OT; the complexity of the constructed SZCR coincides with the OT complexity of the MPC protocol. We will use this connection to obtain randomized functions that require super-linear OT complexity. The following theorem states more generally for all regular correlations. This is a generalization of one of the main results in [22] that proves this result for *deterministic* functions.

Theorem 3. *If a protocol Π^ψ using a regular correlation ψ distributed over $\mathcal{R} \times \mathcal{S}$ computes a randomised function $f : \mathcal{X} \times \mathcal{Y} \to \mathcal{A} \times \mathcal{B}$ with perfect security, then there exists a μ-SZCR to $\phi_{(=\lceil \log k \rceil)} \cdot \phi_{\mathsf{supp}^*(\psi)}$, where k is the number of connected components in the evaluation graph G_f and $\mu \le \log \frac{|\mathcal{R}||\mathcal{S}||\mathcal{X}|^2|\mathcal{Y}|^2|\mathcal{A}||\mathcal{B}|}{|\mathsf{supp}(\psi)|}$.*

This theorem is proved through Claim 1–Claim 6. In the following section, we make some observations and define some quantities that are used in the construction and analysis of the SZCR we construct.

Let $\mathcal{Q}$ be the set of all transcripts that can be produced in the protocol Π^ψ. We observed that communication protocols admit transcript factorization; i.e., there exist functions $\rho : \mathcal{X} \times \mathcal{R} \times \mathcal{Q} \to [0,1]$ and $\sigma : \mathcal{Y} \times \mathcal{S} \times \mathcal{Q} \to [0,1]$ such that, when x, y are the inputs to Alice and Bob, and (r, s) is the realization of the correlation ψ, for any transcript q,

$$\Pr_{\Pi^\psi}(q|x,y,r,s) = \rho(x,r,q)\sigma(y,s,q).$$

The following set of observations are about a protocol Π^ψ that uses a correlation ψ and computes a given function $f : \mathcal{X} \times \mathcal{Y} \to \mathcal{A} \times \mathcal{B}$ with perfect security. We will exploit the perfect security of the protocol to establish how the protocol behaves in each connected component of the evaluation graph G_f.

Lemma 1. *For each connected component C of the evaluation graph G_f, if $((x_1, a_1), (y_1, b_1))$ and $((x_2, a_2), (y_2, b_2))$ belong to C, then*

$$\Pr_{\Pi^\psi}(q|x_1, y_1, a_1, b_1) = \Pr_{\Pi^\psi}(q|x_2, y_2, a_2, b_2), \forall q \in \mathcal{Q}.$$

Proof. Since Π^ψ is perfectly secure, there exists simulators $\hat{S}_A$ and $\hat{S}_B$ such that, for all x, y, a, b such that $\Pr_f(a, b|x, y) > 0$,

$$\Pr_{\Pi^\psi}(q, r|x, y, a, b) = \Pr_{\hat{S}_A}(q, r|x, a) \quad \Pr_{\Pi^\psi}(q, s|x, y, a, b) = \Pr_{\hat{S}_B}(q, s|y, b).$$

Hence, if edges $((x, a), (y, b))$ and $((x, a), (y', b'))$ belong to C, then, for all $q \in \mathcal{Q}$,

$$\Pr_{\Pi^\psi}(q|x, y, a, b) = \sum_r \Pr_{\hat{S}_A}(q, r|x, a) = \Pr_{\Pi^\psi}(q|x, y', a, b').$$

A similar condition holds for edges $((x, a), (y, b))$ and $((x', a'), (y, b))$ belonging to C. Hence, if edges $((x_1, a_1), (y_1, b_1))$, $((x_2, a_2), (y_2, b_2))$ belong to C, then applying the above two conditions alternatively along a path that begins with the edge $((x_1, a_1), (y_1, b_1))$ and ends with the edge $((x_2, a_2), (y_2, b_2))$, we get the statement of the lemma. □

Lemma 2. *If* $\Pr_{\Pi^\Psi}(a_1, b_1 | x, y, r, s, q) > 0$ *and* $\Pr_{\Pi^\Psi}(a_2, b_2 | x, y, r, s, q) > 0$ *then* $((x, a_1), (y, b_1))$ *and* $((x, a_2), (y, b_2))$ *belong to the same connected component of* G_f.

Proof. For all $(a, b) \in \{(a_1, b_1), (a_2, b_2)\}$, we have

$$\Pr_{\Pi_A^{out}}(a | x, r, q) \cdot \Pr_{\Pi_B^{out}}(b | y, s, q) = \Pr_{\Pi^\Psi}(a, b | x, y, r, s, q) > 0.$$

Hence, $\Pr_{\Pi_A^{out}}(a | x, r, q) > 0$ for $a \in \{a_1, a_2\}$ and $\Pr_{\Pi_B^{out}}(b | y, s, q) > 0$ for $b \in \{b_1, b_2\}$. Thus, by the perfect correctness of Π^Ψ,

$$\Pr(f(x, y) = (a_2, b_1)) > \Pr_{\Pi^\Psi}(a_2, b_1 | x, y, r, s, q)$$
$$= \Pr_{\Pi_A^{out}}(a_2 | x, r, q) \cdot \Pr_{\Pi_B^{out}}(b_1 | y, s, q) > 0.$$

This implies that $((x, a_2), (y, b_1))$ has non-zero weight in G_f, consequently, $(x, a_1) - (y, b_1) - (x, a_2) - (y, b_2)$ is a path in G_f, implying the statement of the lemma. □

In Lemma 1, we showed that for all connected component C of the evaluation graph G_f, and for all edges $((x_1, a_1), (y_1, b_1))$ and $((x_2, a_2), (y_2, b_2))$ belonging to C,

$$\Pr_{\Pi^\Psi}(q | x_1, y_1, a_1, b_1) = \Pr_{\Pi^\Psi}(q | x_2, y_2, a_2, b_2).$$

By an abuse of notation, we denote $\Pr_{\Pi^\Psi}(q | x, y, a, b)$ for all edges $((x, a), (y, b))$ belonging to the connected component C by $\Pr_{\Pi^\Psi}(q | C)$.

To present our SZCR protocol $\Theta(\mathfrak{A}, \mathfrak{B})$ from f to ϕ, that is constructed from the secure computation protocol for f, we need the following quantities.

Definition 5. *For each connected component C in G_f, we define the following quantities:*

$$\rho_C^\dagger(q) = \max_{x \in \mathcal{X}_C} \sum_r \rho(x, r, q) \quad \sigma_C^\dagger(q) = \max_{y \in \mathcal{Y}_C} \sum_s \sigma(v, s, q)$$

Lemma 3. *For every connected component C in G_f, there exists $q^* \in \mathcal{Q}$ such that* $\Pr_{\Pi^\Psi}(q^* | C) > 0$ *and*

$$\rho_C^\dagger(q^*)\sigma_C^\dagger(q^*) \leq |\mathcal{R}||\mathcal{S}||\mathcal{X}_C||\mathcal{Y}_C|\Pr_{\Pi^\Psi}(q^* | C)$$

Proof. Define $\widetilde{\psi}$ to be the uniform distribution over $\mathcal{R} \times \mathcal{S}$. Consider the protocol $\Pi^{\widetilde{\psi}}$ obtained by replacing the correlation ψ in Π^Ψ with $\widetilde{\psi}$. Hence,

$$\Pr_{\Pi^{\widetilde{\psi}}}(q, r, s | x, y) = \Pr_{\widetilde{\psi}}(r, s) \cdot \Pr_{\Pi^{\widetilde{\psi}}}(q | r, s, x, y) = \frac{\rho(x, r, q)\sigma(y, s, q)}{|\mathcal{R}||\mathcal{S}|} \quad (20)$$

Note that ρ, σ induced by Π^{Ψ} is well-defined for $(x, r, q) \in \mathcal{X} \times \mathcal{R} \times \mathcal{Q}$ and $(y, s, q) \in \mathcal{Y} \times \mathcal{S} \times \mathcal{Q}$, respectively.

By imposing a distribution over the inputs, namely the uniform distribution over $\mathcal{X}_C \times \mathcal{Y}_C$, for all $q \in \mathcal{Q}$, define:

$$\Pr_{\Pi^{\tilde{\Psi}}}(q) = \sum_{(x,y)\in\mathcal{X}_C\times\mathcal{Y}_C} \sum_{(r,s)\in\mathcal{R}\times\mathcal{S}} \frac{\Pr_{\Pi^{\tilde{\Psi}}}(q|x,y,r,s)}{|\mathcal{X}_C||\mathcal{Y}_C||\mathcal{R}||\mathcal{S}|}.$$

Since $\Pr_{\Pi^{\Psi}}(q|C)$ and $\Pr_{\Pi^{\tilde{\Psi}}}(q)$ are distributions over $\mathcal{Q}$, there exists $q^* \in \mathcal{Q}$ such that

$$\Pr_{\Pi^{\Psi}}(q^*|C) \geq \Pr_{\Pi^{\tilde{\Psi}}}(q^*) > 0.$$

Hence,

$$\Pr_{\Pi^{\Psi}}(q^*|C) \geq \Pr_{\Pi^{\tilde{\Psi}}}(q^*) = \sum_{(x,y)\in\mathcal{X}_C\times\mathcal{Y}_C} \sum_{(r,s)\in\mathcal{R}\times\mathcal{S}} \frac{\Pr_{\Pi^{\tilde{\Psi}}}(q^*|x,y,r,s)}{|\mathcal{X}_C||\mathcal{Y}_C||\mathcal{R}||\mathcal{S}|}$$

$$\geq \frac{\sum_{(r,s)\in\mathcal{R}\times\mathcal{S}} \Pr_{\Pi^{\tilde{\Psi}}}(q^*|x,y,r,s)}{|\mathcal{X}_C||\mathcal{Y}_C||\mathcal{R}||\mathcal{S}|}, \forall (x,y) \in \mathcal{X}_C \times \mathcal{Y}_C. \tag{21}$$

Choose $(x^*, y^*) \in \mathcal{X}_C \times \mathcal{Y}_C$ such that

$$x^* = \arg\max_{x\in\mathcal{X}_C} \sum_r \rho(x,r,q^*) \quad y^* = \arg\max_{y\in\mathcal{Y}_C} \sum_s \sigma(y,s,q^*).$$

Then, by Definition 5, $\rho_C^{\dagger}(q^*) = \sum_r \rho(x^*, r, q^*)$ and $\sigma_C^{\dagger}(q^*) = \sum_s \rho(y^*, s, q^*)$. Hence,

$$\rho_C^{\dagger}(q^*)\sigma_C^{\dagger}(q^*) = \sum_{r,s} \rho(x^*,r,q^*)\sigma(y^*,s,q^*)$$

$$\overset{(a)}{=} |\mathcal{R}||\mathcal{S}| \sum_{r,s} \Pr_{\Pi^{\tilde{\Psi}}}(q^*,r,s|x^*,y^*)$$

$$\overset{(b)}{\leq} |\mathcal{R}||\mathcal{S}||\mathcal{X}_C||\mathcal{Y}_C| \cdot \Pr_{\Pi^{\Psi}}(q^*|C),$$

where (a) follows from (20) and (b) follows from (21). This concludes the proof. $\square$

Definition 6. *Let $C_1, \ldots, C_k$ be the set of all connected components of the evaluation graph G_f. For each C_i, $i \in [k]$, Lemma 3 guarantees that there exists $q_i^* \in \mathcal{Q}$ such that $\Pr_{\Pi^{\Psi}}(q_i^*|C_i) > 0$ and*

$$\rho_C^{\dagger}(q_i^*)\sigma_C^{\dagger}(q_i^*) \leq |\mathcal{R}||\mathcal{S}||\mathcal{X}_C||\mathcal{Y}_C|\Pr_{\Pi^{\Psi}}(q_i^*|C).$$

We define the distribution λ over $[k]$ as:

$$\Pr_{\lambda}(i) = \frac{\sqrt{c_i}}{\sum_{t\in[k]} \sqrt{c_t}}, \text{ where } c_i = \frac{\rho_{C_i}^{\dagger}(q_i^*) \cdot \sigma_{C_i}^{\dagger}(q_i^*)}{\Pr_{\Pi^{\Psi}}(q_i^*|C_i)}.$$

Let $C_1, \ldots, C_k$ be the connected components in the evaluation graph G_f. Let the inputs to f be $x \in \mathcal{X}$ and $y \in \mathcal{Y}$; for $i \in [k]$, choose $q_i^\star$ as defined in Definition 6 with respect to the protocol Π^ψ; choose $\rho_i^\dagger = \rho_{C_i}^\dagger(q_i^\star)$ and $\sigma_i^\dagger = \sigma_{C_i}^\dagger(q_i^\star)$ as defined in Definition 5; finally, let the distribution λ over $[k]$ be as defined in Definition 6.

$\mathfrak{A}(x)$: Sample $i \leftarrow \lambda$ and $r \in \mathcal{R}$ with probability $\frac{\rho(x, r, q_i^\star)}{\rho_i^\dagger}$, and with remaining probability set $r = \perp$. If $r \neq \perp$, sample $a \leftarrow \Pi_A^{\text{out}}(x, r, q_i^\star)$ and set $A = a$, otherwise $A = \perp$. If $r \neq \perp$ and there exist y', b' such that $((x, a), (y', b')) \in C_i$ then set $U = (I, R)$ to (i, r), else to $(i, \perp)$.

$\mathfrak{B}(y)$: Sample $j \leftarrow \lambda$ and $s \in \mathcal{S}$ with probability $\frac{\sigma(y, s, q_j^\star)}{\sigma_j^\dagger}$, and with remaining probability set $s = \perp$. If $s \neq \perp$, sample $b \leftarrow \Pi_B^{\text{out}}(y, s, q_j^\star)$ and set $B = b$, otherwise set $B = \perp$. If $s \neq \perp$ and there exist x', a' such that $((x', a'), (y, b)) \in C_j$ then set $V = (J, S)$ to (j, s), else to $(j, \perp)$.

$\Phi_{(=\lceil \log k \rceil)} \cdot \Phi_{\text{supp}^*(\psi)}$: Returns $D = 1$ if $\Phi_{(=\lceil \log k \rceil)}(i, j) = 1$ (i.e., $j = i$) and $\Phi_{\text{supp}^*(\psi)}(r, s) = 1$ (i.e., $r \sim s$).

Fig. 2. An SZCR protocol $\Theta(\mathfrak{A}, \mathfrak{B})$ from f to ϕ constructed from the secure computation protocol Π^ψ using the correlation ψ that computes f with perfect security.

Now we present our SZCR protocol in Fig. 2, which is analyzed below.

Proof of Correctness. In the sequel, we will consider x, y, i, j, r, s as defined in Fig. 2. R, S, I, J are the random variables corresponding to r, s, i, j, respectively. Recollect that, we shorten $\Pr(R = r, S = s, I = i, J = j)$ as $\Pr(r, s, i, j)$, whenever there is no scope for confusion. We first make the following claims that will be later used to prove the correctness in Claim 2.

Claim 1. *If $j \neq i$ or $((x, a), (y, b)) \notin C_i$, then $\Pr_\Theta(a, b, D = 1|x, y, i, j) = 0$.*

Proof. Let E be the event $(D = 1, A = a, B = b)$. If $j \neq i$, then $\Phi_{(=\lceil \log k \rceil)}(i, j) = 0$, hence $D = 0$, hence we consider the case where $j = i$. Towards a contradiction, suppose $j = i$ and $((x, a), (y, b)) \notin C_i$ and E occurs with non-zero probability. Event E occurs only if there exist r, s such that $r \sim s$, $\rho(x, r, q_i^\star) > 0$, $\sigma(y, s, q_i^\star) > 0$, $\Pr_{\Pi_A^{\text{out}}}(a|x, r, q_i^\star) > 0$, and $\Pr_{\Pi_B^{\text{out}}}(b|y, s, q_i^\star) > 0$.

$$\Pr_{\Pi^\psi}(a, b|x, y)$$
$$\geq \Pr_{\Pi^\psi}(q_i^\star, a, b, r, s|x, y)$$
$$= \Pr_\psi(r, s) \cdot \Pr_{\Pi^\psi}(q_i^\star|x, y, r, s) \cdot \Pr_{\Pi^\psi}(a, b|x, y, r, s, q_i^\star)$$
$$= \frac{\rho(x, r, q_i^\star) \cdot \sigma(y, s, q_i^\star) \cdot \Pr_{\Pi_A^{\text{out}}}(a|x, r, q_i^\star) \cdot \Pr_{\Pi_B^{\text{out}}}(b|y, s, q_i^\star)}{|\text{supp}(\psi)|} > 0.$$

Thus, by the perfect correctness of Π^ψ, $\Pr_f(a, b|x, y) = \Pr_{\Pi^\psi}(a, b|x, y) > 0$. Additionally, by the construction of Θ, E occurs only if there exist b', y' such that $((x, a), (y', b')) \in C_i$ since, otherwise, Alice would have aborted by sending $\perp$ (instead of sending some $u \in \mathcal{U}$). Hence, the edges $((x, a), (y, b))$ and

$((x, a), (y', b'))$ have non-zero weights in G_f and $((x, a), (y', b')) \in C_i$. But then, $((x, a), (y, b)) \in C_i$, a contradiction. This proves the claim. □

Claim 2. *The probability of acceptance for any inputs x, y is independent of the inputs, and is given by:*

$$\Pr_\Theta(D = 1 | x, y) = \frac{|\mathsf{supp}(\boldsymbol{\Psi})|}{\left(\sum_{l \in [k]} \sqrt{c_l} \right)^2} \tag{22}$$

Proof. Fix inputs x, y. We have,

$$\Pr_\Theta(D = 1 | x, y) = \sum_{i,j,a,b} \Pr_\Theta(D = 1, i, j, a, b | x, y)$$

$$= \sum_{i,j,a,b} \Pr_\Theta(i, j | x, y) \cdot \Pr_\Theta(D = 1, a, b | x, y, i, j).$$

If $j \neq i$, then $D = 0$, furthermore, $\Pr_\Theta(i, j | x, y) = \Pr_\lambda(i) \cdot \Pr_\lambda(j)$. Hence,

$\Pr_\Theta(D = 1 | x, y)$

$$= \sum_{i \in [k], j = i} \sum_{a,b} \Pr_\lambda(i) \cdot \Pr_\lambda(j) \cdot \Pr_\Theta(D = 1, a, b | x, y, i, j)$$

$$= \sum_{i \in [k], j = i} \Pr_\lambda^2(i) \sum_{a,b} \sum_{r \sim s} \Pr_\Theta(r, s | x, y, i, j) \cdot \Pr_\Theta(a, b | x, y, i, j, r, s)$$

$$= \frac{1}{\left(\sum_{t \in [k]} \sqrt{c_t} \right)^2} \sum_{i \in [k]} c_i \sum_{a,b} \sum_{r \sim s} \Pr_{\Pi_A^{out}}(a | x, r, q_i^\star) \cdot \Pr_{\Pi_B^{out}}(b | y, s, q_i^\star) \frac{\rho(x, r, q_i^\star) \cdot \sigma(y, s, q_i^\star)}{\rho_i^\dagger \sigma_i^\dagger}$$

But, $\Pr_{\Pi_A^{out}}(a | x, r, q_i^\star) \cdot \Pr_{\Pi_B^{out}}(b | y, s, q_i^\star) = \Pr_{\Pi^{\Psi}}(a, b | x, y, q_i^\star, r, s)$ and, by transcript factorization property, $\rho(x, r, q_i^\star) \cdot \sigma(y, s, q_i^\star) = \Pr_{\Pi^{\Psi}}(q_i^\star | x, y, r, s)$. Furthermore, $c_i = \frac{\rho_i^\dagger \sigma_i^\dagger}{\Pr_{\Pi^{\Psi}}(q_i^\star | C_i)}$. Applying these observations to the RHS,

$\Pr_\Theta(D = 1 | x, y)$

$$= \frac{1}{\left(\sum_{t \in [k]} \sqrt{c_t} \right)^2} \sum_{i \in [k]} \frac{\rho_i^\dagger \sigma_i^\dagger}{\Pr_{\Pi^{\Psi}}(q_i^\star | C_i)} \sum_{a,b} \sum_{r \sim s} \frac{\Pr_{\Pi^{\Psi}}(a, b | x, y, q_i^\star, r, s) \cdot \Pr_{\Pi^{\Psi}}(q_i^\star | x, y, r, s)}{\rho_i^\dagger \sigma_i^\dagger}.$$

By Claim 1, $\Pr_\Theta(D = 1, a, b | x, y, i, j) = 0$ if $((x, a), (y, b))$ is not an edge in C_i (or $j \neq i$). Furthermore, by definition,

$$0 < \Pr_{\Pi^{\Psi}}(q_i^\star | C_i) = \Pr_{\Pi^{\Psi}}(q_i^\star | x, y, a, b), \text{ for all } ((x, a), (y, b)) \in C_i.$$

Applying both these facts to the RHS,

$\mathsf{Pr}_\Theta(D = 1|x, y)$

$$= \frac{1}{\left(\sum_{t\in[k]} \sqrt{c_t}\right)^2} \sum_{i\in[k]} \sum_{(a,b):((x,a),(y,b))\in C_i} \sum_{r\sim s} \frac{\mathsf{Pr}_{\Pi^*}(a, b, q_i^*|x, y, r, s)}{\mathsf{Pr}_{\Pi^*}(q_i^*|x, y, a, b)}$$

$$= \frac{1}{\left(\sum_{t\in[k]} \sqrt{c_t}\right)^2} \sum_{i\in[k]} \sum_{(a,b):((x,a),(y,b))\in C_i} \sum_{r\sim s} \frac{\mathsf{Pr}_{\Pi^*}(a, b, q_i^*, r, s|x, y)}{\mathsf{Pr}_{\Pi^*}(q_i^*|x, y, a, b)\mathsf{Pr}_{\Pi^*}(r, s|x, y)}$$

For all r, s such that $r \sim s$, $\mathsf{Pr}_\psi(r, s) = \frac{1}{|\mathsf{supp}(\psi)|}$. Applying this to the RHS,

$$\mathsf{Pr}_\Theta(D = 1|x, y) = \frac{|\mathsf{supp}(\psi)|}{\left(\sum_{t\in[k]} \sqrt{c_t}\right)^2} \sum_{i\in[k]} \sum_{(a,b):((x,a),(y,b))\in C_i} \sum_{r\sim s} \frac{\mathsf{Pr}_{\Pi^*}(a, b, q_i^*, r, s|x, y)}{\mathsf{Pr}_{\Pi^*}(q_i^*|x, y, a, b)}$$

$$= \frac{|\mathsf{supp}(\psi)|}{\left(\sum_{t\in[k]} \sqrt{c_t}\right)^2} \sum_{i\in[k]} \sum_{(a,b):((x,a),(y,b))\in C_i} \frac{\mathsf{Pr}_{\Pi^*}(a, b, q_i^*|x, y)}{\mathsf{Pr}_{\Pi^*}(q_i^*|x, y, a, b)}$$

$$= \frac{|\mathsf{supp}(\psi)|}{\left(\sum_{t\in[k]} \sqrt{c_t}\right)^2} \sum_{i\in[k]} \sum_{(a,b):((x,a),(y,b))\in C_i} \mathsf{Pr}_{\Pi^*}(a, b|x, y).$$

Since $\mathsf{Pr}_{\Pi^*}(a, b|x, y) = \mathsf{Pr}_f(a, b|x, y)$ by perfect correctness, and

$$\bigcup_{i\in[k]} \{(a, b) : ((x, a), (y, b)) \in C_i\} = \{(a, b) : \mathsf{Pr}_f(a, b|x, y) > 0\},$$

we get,

$$\mathsf{Pr}_\Theta(D = 1|x, y) = \frac{|\mathsf{supp}(\psi)|}{\left(\sum_{t\in[k]} \sqrt{c_t}\right)^2} \sum_{(a,b)} \mathsf{Pr}_f(a, b|x, y) = \frac{|\mathsf{supp}(\psi)|}{\left(\sum_{t\in[k]} \sqrt{c_t}\right)^2}.$$

This proves the claim.   □

Claim 3. *The reduction Θ is perfectly correct; i.e.,*

$$\mathsf{Pr}_\Theta(a, b|D = 1, x, y) = \mathsf{Pr}_f(a, b|x, y)$$

Proof. Consider (x, y, a, b) such that $\Pr_f(a, b|x, y) > 0$. If $((x, a), (y, b)) \in C_\ell$, by Claim 1, if $i \neq \ell$ or $j \neq \ell$, $\Pr_\Theta(a, b, D = 1|x, y, i, j) = 0$. Hence,

$$
\begin{aligned}
\Pr_\Theta(a, b, D = 1|x, y) &= \sum_{i,j \in [k]} \Pr_\Theta(a, b, D = 1, i, j|x, y) \\
&= \Pr_\Theta(I = J = \ell|x, y) \cdot \Pr_\Theta(a, b, D = 1|x, y, I = J = \ell) \\
&= \Pr_\lambda^2(\ell) \cdot \Pr_\Theta(a, b, D = 1|x, y, I = J = \ell).
\end{aligned}
$$

Expanding this, we get

$$
\begin{aligned}
\Pr_\Theta(a, b, D = 1|x, y) &= \Pr_\lambda^2(\ell) \sum_{r \sim s} \Pr_\Theta(r, s|x, y, I = J = \ell) \cdot \Pr_\Theta(a, b|x, y, r, s, I = J = \ell) \\
&= \Pr_\lambda^2(\ell) \sum_{r \sim s} \frac{\rho(x, r, q_\ell^\star)\sigma(y, s, q_\ell^\star)}{\rho_\ell^\dagger \sigma_\ell^\dagger} \cdot \Pr_{\Pi^\Psi}(a, b|x, y, q_\ell^\star, r, s) \\
&= \Pr_\lambda^2(\ell) \sum_{r \sim s} \frac{\Pr_{\Pi^\Psi}(q_\ell^\star|x, y, r, s)}{\rho_\ell^\dagger \sigma_\ell^\dagger} \cdot \Pr_{\Pi^\Psi}(a, b|x, y, q_\ell^\star, r, s) \\
&= \sum_{r \sim s} \Pr_\lambda^2(\ell) \frac{\Pr_{\Pi^\Psi}(a, b, q_\ell^\star|x, y, r, s)}{\rho_\ell^\dagger \sigma_\ell^\dagger}.
\end{aligned}
$$

Since $\Pr_\Psi(r, s) = \frac{1}{|\text{supp}(\Psi)|}$, multiplying and dividing each term with $\Pr_\Psi(r, s)$, and expanding $\Pr_\lambda^2(\ell)$,

$$
\begin{aligned}
\Pr_\Theta(a, b, D = 1|x, y) &= |\text{supp}(\Psi)| \cdot \Pr_\lambda^2(\ell) \cdot \frac{\displaystyle\sum_{r \sim s} \Pr_{\Pi^\Psi}(a, b, r, s, q_\ell^\star|x, y)}{\rho_\ell^\dagger \sigma_\ell^\dagger} \\
&= \frac{|\text{supp}(\Psi)| \cdot \rho_\ell^\dagger \sigma_\ell^\dagger}{\Pr_{\Pi^\Psi}(q_\ell^\star|C_i) \left(\displaystyle\sum_{t \in [k]} \sqrt{c_t}\right)^2} \cdot \frac{\Pr_{\Pi^\Psi}(a, b, q_\ell^\star|x, y)}{\rho_\ell^\dagger \sigma_\ell^\dagger} \\
&= \frac{|\text{supp}(\Psi)|}{\left(\displaystyle\sum_{t \in [k]} \sqrt{c_t}\right)^2} \frac{\Pr_{\Pi^\Psi}(a, b|x, y) \cdot \Pr_{\Pi^\Psi}(q_\ell^\star|x, y, a, b)}{\Pr_{\Pi^\Psi}(q_\ell^\star|C_i)} \\
&= \frac{|\text{supp}(\Psi)|}{\left(\displaystyle\sum_{t \in [k]} \sqrt{c_t}\right)^2} \Pr_f(a, b|x, y).
\end{aligned} \tag{23}
$$

The final equality follows from the fact that $\Pr_{\Pi^*}(q_\ell^*|C_\ell) = \Pr_{\Pi^*}(q_\ell^*|x, y, a, b)$ since $((x, y), (y, b)) \in C_\ell$. Hence,

$$\Pr_\Theta(a, b|D = 1, x, y) = \frac{\Pr_\Theta(a, b, D = 1|x, y)}{\Pr_\Theta(D = 1|x, y)}$$

$$\overset{(a)}{=} \frac{|\mathrm{supp}(\pmb{\psi})|}{\left(\sum\limits_{t \in [k]} \sqrt{c_t}\right)^2} \Pr_f(a, b|x, y) \cdot \frac{\left(\sum\limits_{t \in [k]} \sqrt{c_t}\right)^2}{|\mathrm{supp}(\pmb{\psi})|} = \Pr_f(a, b|x, y),$$

$$\tag{24}$$

where (a) follows from Claim 2. If $\Pr_f(a, b|x, y) = 0$, then, by Claim 1, $\Pr_{\Pi^*}(a, b, D = 1|x, y) = 0$, and hence $\Pr_\Theta(a, b|D = 1, x, y) = 0$. This concludes the proof.   □

Proof of Security. To prove the security of Θ, we need to show that there exists simulators $S_A' : \mathcal{X} \times \mathcal{A} \times \{0, 1\} \rightarrow (\mathcal{R} \cup \{\perp\}) \times [k]$ and $S_B' : \mathcal{Y} \times \mathcal{B} \times \{0, 1\} \rightarrow (\mathcal{S} \cup \{\perp\}) \times [k]$ such that if $\Pr_f(a, b|x, y) > 0$,

$$\Pr_\Theta(r, i|x, y, a, b, D = 1) = \Pr_{S_A'}(r, i|x, a, D = 1),$$
$$\Pr_\Theta(s, j|x, y, a, b, D = 1) = \Pr_{S_B'}(s, j|y, b, D = 1),$$

and,

$$\Pr_\Theta(r, i|x, y, D = 0) = \sum_a \Pr_{f_A}(a|x, y) \cdot \Pr_{S_A'}(r, i|x, a, D = 0),$$
$$\Pr_\Theta(s, j|x, y, D = 0) = \sum_b \Pr_{f_B}(b|x, y) \cdot \Pr_{S_B'}(s, j|y, b, D = 0).$$

We prove the first two statements in Claim 4 and the last two in Claim 5.

Claim 4. *There exists a randomized function $S_A' : \mathcal{X} \times \mathcal{A} \times \{0, 1\} \rightarrow \mathcal{U} \times [k]$ such that, if $\Pr_f(a, b|x, y) > 0$,*

$$\Pr_\Theta(r, i|x, y, a, b, D = 1) = \Pr_{S_A'}(r, i|x, a, D = 1).$$

Similarly, there exists a randomized function $S_B' : \mathcal{Y} \times \mathcal{B} \times \{0, 1\} \rightarrow \mathcal{V} \times [k]$ such that, if $\Pr_f(a, b|x, y) > 0$,

$$\Pr_\Theta(s, j|x, y, a, b, D = 1) = \Pr_{S_B'}(s, j|y, b, D = 1).$$

Proof. Consider (x, y, a, b) such that $\Pr_f(a, b|x, y) > 0$; let $((x, a), (y, b)) \in C_\ell$. By Claim 1,

$$\Pr_\Theta(r, i, a, b, D = 1|x, y) = 0 \text{ if } i \neq \ell \text{ or } r = \perp. \tag{25}$$

We focus on $\mathsf{Pr}_\Theta(r, i, a, b, D = 1 | x, y)$, when $r \neq \perp$ and $i = \ell$. Noting that $\mathsf{Pr}_\Theta(D = 1, I \neq J | x, y) = 0$,

$$\mathsf{Pr}_\Theta(r, I = \ell, a, b, D = 1 | x, y)$$
$$= \sum_{j \in [k]} \sum_{s: r \sim s} \mathsf{Pr}_\Theta(r, s, I = \ell, j, a, b | x, y)$$
$$= \mathsf{Pr}_\Theta(I = J = \ell | x, y) \sum_{s: r \sim s} \mathsf{Pr}_\Theta(r, s | x, y, I = J = \ell) \cdot \mathsf{Pr}_\Theta(a, b | x, y, r, s, I = J = \ell)$$
$$= \mathsf{Pr}_\lambda^2(\ell) \sum_{s: r \sim s} \frac{\mathsf{Pr}_{\Pi^\Psi}(q_\ell^\star | x, y, r, s)}{\rho_i^\dagger \sigma_i^\dagger} \mathsf{Pr}_\Theta(a, b | x, y, r, s, I = J = \ell).$$

We have,

$$\mathsf{Pr}_\Theta(a, b | x, y, r, s, I = J = \ell) = \mathsf{Pr}_{\Pi_A^{out}}(a | x, r, q_\ell^\star) \cdot \mathsf{Pr}_{\Pi_B^{out}}(b | y, s, q_\ell^\star) = \mathsf{Pr}_{\Pi^\Psi}(a, b | x, y, r, s, q_\ell^\star).$$

Substituting for $\mathsf{Pr}_\lambda(\ell)$ from Definition 6 and noting that $\mathsf{Pr}_{\Pi^\Psi}(q_\ell^\star | C_\ell) = \mathsf{Pr}_{\Pi^\Psi}(q_\ell^\star | x, y, a, b)$ since $((x, a), (y, b)) \in C_\ell$,

$$\mathsf{Pr}_\Theta(r, I = \ell, a, b, D = 1 | x, y) = \sum_{s: r \sim s} \frac{\rho_i^\dagger \sigma_i^\dagger}{\mathsf{Pr}_{\Pi^\Psi}(q_\ell^\star | C_\ell) \left(\sum_{t \in [k]} \sqrt{c_t} \right)^2} \frac{\mathsf{Pr}_{\Pi^\Psi}(a, b, q_\ell^\star | x, y, r, s)}{\rho_i^\dagger \sigma_i^\dagger}$$
$$= \sum_{s: r \sim s} \frac{\mathsf{Pr}_{\Pi^\Psi}(a, b, q_\ell^\star | x, y, r, s)}{\mathsf{Pr}_{\Pi^\Psi}(q_\ell^\star | x, y, a, b) \left(\sum_{t \in [k]} \sqrt{c_t} \right)^2}.$$

Since $\mathsf{Pr}_\Psi(r, s) = \frac{1}{|\mathsf{supp}(\Psi)|}$, multiplying and dividing each term with $\mathsf{Pr}_\Psi(r, s)$,

$$\mathsf{Pr}_\Theta(r, I = \ell, a, b, D = 1 | x, y) = \frac{|\mathsf{supp}(\Psi)|}{\left(\sum_{t \in [k]} \sqrt{c_t} \right)^2} \sum_{s: r \sim s} \frac{\mathsf{Pr}_\Psi(r, s) \cdot \mathsf{Pr}_{\Pi^\Psi}(a, b, q_\ell^\star | x, y, r, s)}{\mathsf{Pr}_{\Pi^\Psi}(q_\ell^\star | x, y, a, b)}$$
$$= \frac{|\mathsf{supp}(\Psi)|}{\left(\sum_{t \in [k]} \sqrt{c_t} \right)^2} \frac{\mathsf{Pr}_{\Pi^\Psi}(a, b, q_\ell^\star, r | x, y)}{\mathsf{Pr}_{\Pi^\Psi}(q_\ell^\star | x, y, a, b)}$$
$$= \frac{|\mathsf{supp}(\Psi)|}{\left(\sum_{t \in [k]} \sqrt{c_t} \right)^2} \mathsf{Pr}_{\Pi^\Psi}(a, b | x, y) \mathsf{Pr}_{\Pi^\Psi}(r | x, y, a, b, q_\ell^\star)$$
$$= \frac{|\mathsf{supp}(\Psi)|}{\left(\sum_{t \in [k]} \sqrt{c_t} \right)^2} \mathsf{Pr}_f(a, b | x, y) \mathsf{Pr}_{\Pi^\Psi}(r | x, y, a, b, q_\ell^\star).$$

Hence, by (23),

$$\mathsf{Pr}_\Theta(r, I = \ell | a, b, x, y, D = 1) = \frac{\mathsf{Pr}_\Theta(r, I = \ell, a, b, D = 1 | x, y)}{\mathsf{Pr}_\Theta(a, b, D = 1 | x, y)} = \mathsf{Pr}_{\Pi^\Psi}(r | x, y, a, b, q_\ell^\star).$$

By perfect privacy of Π^Ψ, there exists a simulator $\hat{S}_A$ such that

$$\mathsf{Pr}_\Theta(r, I = \ell | a, b, x, y, D = 1) = \mathsf{Pr}_{\Pi^\Psi}(r | x, y, a, b, q^\star_\ell) = \mathsf{Pr}_{\hat{S}_A}(r | x, a, q^\star_\ell).$$

Since C_ℓ is determined by (x, a), we can set $\mathsf{Pr}_{S'_A}(x, a, 1) = \mathsf{Pr}_{\hat{S}_A}(r | x, a, q^\star_\ell)$. The first statement in the claim follows from this observation and (25). The second statement can be proved analogously. $\square$

Claim 5. *There exists a randomized function $S'_A : \mathcal{X} \times \mathcal{A} \times \{0, 1\} \to (\mathcal{R} \times \{\perp\}) \times [k]$ such that*

$$\mathsf{Pr}_\Theta(r, i | x, y, D = 0) = \sum_a \mathsf{Pr}_{f_A}(a | x, y) \cdot \mathsf{Pr}_{S'_A}(r, i | x, a, D = 0).$$

Similarly, there exists a randomized function $S'_B : \mathcal{Y} \times \mathcal{B} \times \{0, 1\} \to \mathcal{S} \times [k]$ such that

$$\mathsf{Pr}_\Theta(s, j | x, y, D = 0) = \sum_b \mathsf{Pr}_{f_B}(b | x, y) \cdot \mathsf{Pr}_{S'_B}(s, j | y, b, D = 0).$$

Proof. When $r = \perp$, the predicate always rejects $(D = 0)$, hence, for all i,

$$\mathsf{Pr}_\Theta(R = \perp, i, D = 0 | x, y) = \mathsf{Pr}_\Theta(R = \perp, i | x, y) = \mathsf{Pr}_\Theta(R = \perp, i | x).$$

The predicate accepts $(D = 1)$ if and only if Alice and Bob choose i, j and r, s, respectively, such that $i = j$ and $r \sim s$. Hence,

$$\mathsf{Pr}_\Theta(r, i, D = 0 | x, y)$$

$$= \mathsf{Pr}_\Theta(r, i | x, y) - \mathsf{Pr}_\Theta(i, J = i | x, y) \sum_{s: r \sim s} \mathsf{Pr}_\Theta(r, s | x, y, i, J = i)$$

$$= \mathsf{Pr}_\Theta(r, i | x, y) - \mathsf{Pr}_\Theta(i, J = i | x, y) \sum_{s: r \sim s} \frac{\rho(x, r, q^\star_i) \cdot \sigma(y, s, q^\star_i)}{\rho^\dagger_i \sigma^\dagger_i}$$

$$= \mathsf{Pr}_\Theta(r, i | x, y) - \mathsf{Pr}^2_\lambda(i) \sum_{s: r \sim s} \frac{\mathsf{Pr}_{\Pi^\Psi}(q^\star_i | x, y, r, s)}{\rho^\dagger_i \sigma^\dagger_i}.$$

We focus on the second term in the RHS. Expanding $\mathsf{Pr}^2_\lambda(i)$ using Definition 6,

$$\mathsf{Pr}^2_\lambda(i) \sum_{s: r \sim s} \frac{\mathsf{Pr}_{\Pi^\Psi}(q^\star_i | x, y, r, s)}{\rho^\dagger_i \sigma^\dagger_i} = \sum_{s: r \sim s} \frac{\mathsf{Pr}_{\Pi^\Psi}(q^\star_i | x, y, r, s)}{\mathsf{Pr}_{\Pi^\Psi}(q^\star_i | C_i) \left(\sum_{t \in [k]} \sqrt{c_t} \right)^2}$$

$$= \frac{1}{\mathsf{Pr}_{\Pi^\Psi}(q^\star_i | C_i) \cdot \left(\sum_{t \in [k]} \sqrt{c_t} \right)^2} \sum_{s: r \sim s} \frac{\mathsf{Pr}_{\Pi^\Psi}(q^\star_i, r, s | x, y)}{\mathsf{Pr}_{\Pi^\Psi}(r, s | x, y)}$$

$$= \frac{|\mathsf{supp}(\Psi)|}{\mathsf{Pr}_{\Pi^\Psi}(q^\star_i | C_i) \cdot \left(\sum_{t \in [k]} \sqrt{c_t} \right)^2} \mathsf{Pr}_{\Pi^\Psi}(q^\star_i, r | x, y)$$

The last equality used the fact that $\Pr_\psi(r,s) = \frac{1}{|\mathrm{supp}(\psi)|}$ for all $r \sim s$. Thus, when $\hat{S}_A$ is the simulator for Alice that witnesses the perfect security of Π^ψ,

$$\Pr_\Theta(r, i, D = 0 | x, y)$$

$$= \Pr_\Theta(r, i | x) - \frac{|\mathrm{supp}(\psi)|}{\Pr_{\Pi^\psi}(q_i^\star | C_i) \cdot \left(\sum_{t \in [k]} \sqrt{c_t} \right)^2} \sum_a \Pr_{\Pi^\psi}(q_i^\star, r | x, y, a) \cdot \Pr_{\Pi^\psi}(a | x, y)$$

$$\overset{(a)}{=} \Pr_\Theta(r, i | x) - \frac{|\mathrm{supp}(\psi)|}{\Pr_{\Pi^\psi}(q_i^\star | C_i) \cdot \left(\sum_{t \in [k]} \sqrt{c_t} \right)^2} \sum_a \Pr_{\Pi^\psi}(q_i^\star, r | x, y, a) \cdot \Pr_{f_A}(a | x, y)$$

$$\overset{(b)}{=} \Pr_\Theta(r, i | x) - \frac{|\mathrm{supp}(\psi)|}{\Pr_{\Pi^\psi}(q_i^\star | C_i) \cdot \left(\sum_{t \in [k]} \sqrt{c_t} \right)^2} \sum_a \Pr_{\hat{S}_A}(q_i^\star, r | x, a) \cdot \Pr_{f_A}(a | x, y).$$

Here, (a) and (b) follow from the perfect correctness and perfect security against Alice, respectively. The first statement of the claim now follows from the fact that $\Pr_\Theta(D = 0 | x, y)$ is the same non-zero value for all x, y as established in Claim 2 The corresponding statement for Bob (second statement) can be shown analogously. □

We conclude the proof of security by noting that the properties in Claim 4 and Claim 5 can be satisfied by the same S_A' and S_B'.

Bound on Accept Probability. It remains to upper bound the probability with which the predicate accepts ($D = 1$) for all inputs x, y.

Claim 6. *The protocol Θ accepts with probability $2^{-\mu}$ where $\mu \leq$ $\log \frac{|\mathcal{R}||\mathcal{S}||\mathcal{X}|^2|\mathcal{Y}|^2|\mathcal{A}||\mathcal{B}|}{|\mathrm{supp}(\psi)|}$.*

Proof. By Claim 2, $\Pr_\Theta(D = 1 | x, y) = \frac{|\mathrm{supp}(\psi)|}{\left(\sum_{t \in [k]} \sqrt{c_t} \right)^2}$. By Definition 6, $c_t = \frac{\rho_t^\dagger \sigma_t^\dagger}{\Pr_\Pi(q_t^\star | C_t)}$ and $q_t^\star$ is chosen such that $\rho_t^\dagger \sigma_t^\dagger \leq |\mathcal{R}||\mathcal{S}||\mathcal{X}_{C_t}||\mathcal{Y}_{C_t}| \Pr_{\Pi^\psi}(q_t^\star | C_t)$ and $\Pr_{\Pi^\psi}(q_t^\star) > 0$, hence, $c_t \leq |\mathcal{R}||\mathcal{S}||\mathcal{X}_C||\mathcal{Y}_C|$. Using Cauchy-Schwartz,

$$\sum_{t \in [k]} \sqrt{c_t} \leq \sqrt{\sum_{t \in [k]} c_t} \cdot \sqrt{k} \leq \sqrt{k \cdot |\mathcal{R}||\mathcal{S}| \sum_{t \in [k]} |\mathcal{X}_{C_t}||\mathcal{Y}_{C_t}|} \leq \sqrt{|\mathcal{R}||\mathcal{S}||\mathcal{A}||\mathcal{B}||\mathcal{X}||\mathcal{Y}|}$$

The final inequality used the fact that each (x, a) shows up in at most one of the connected components; hence, $k \leq \sqrt{|\mathcal{X}||\mathcal{Y}||\mathcal{A}||\mathcal{B}|}$ and $\sum_{t \in [k]} |\mathcal{X}_{C_t}||\mathcal{Y}_{C_t}| \leq k \cdot |\mathcal{X}_C||\mathcal{Y}_C| \leq |\mathcal{X}||\mathcal{Y}|\sqrt{|\mathcal{A}||\mathcal{B}|}$.

$$\Pr_\Theta(D = 1 | x, y) \geq \frac{|\mathrm{supp}(\psi)|}{|\mathcal{R}||\mathcal{S}||\mathcal{X}|^2|\mathcal{Y}|^2|\mathcal{A}||\mathcal{B}|} \Rightarrow \mu \leq \log \frac{|\mathcal{R}||\mathcal{S}||\mathcal{X}|^2|\mathcal{Y}|^2|\mathcal{A}||\mathcal{B}|}{|\mathrm{supp}(\psi)|}.$$

□

Corollary 1. *Consider a randomised function* $f : \mathcal{X} \times \mathcal{Y} \to \mathcal{A} \times \mathcal{B}$ *with* k *connected components in its evaluation graph* G_f. *If a protocol* Π^{OT^ℓ} *using* ℓ *copies of* OT *correlation computes* f *with perfect security, then there exists a* μ-SZCR *to* $\phi_{\mathsf{supp}(\mathsf{OT}^{\ell + \lceil \log k \rceil + 1})}$ *such that* $\mu \le \log \frac{|\mathcal{R}||\mathcal{S}||\mathcal{X}|^2|\mathcal{Y}|^2|\mathcal{A}||\mathcal{B}|}{|\mathsf{supp}(\psi)|}$.

Proof. By Theorem 3, f has a μ-SZCR to $\phi_{(=\lceil \log k \rceil)} \cdot \phi_{\mathsf{supp}^*(\mathsf{OT}^m)}$. But, $\phi_{(=\lceil \log k \rceil)}$ can be realized using $\phi_{\mathsf{supp}(\mathsf{OT}^{\lceil \log k \rceil})}$ (since 1-bit equality can be checked with 1 OT) and $\phi_{\mathsf{supp}^*(\mathsf{OT}^m)}$ can be realized using $\phi_{\mathsf{supp}(\mathsf{OT}^{m+1})}$ (by encoding the input symbol $\perp$ in $\phi_{\mathsf{supp}^*(\mathsf{OT}^m)}$ using an extra OT). Consequently, the predicate $\phi_{(=\lceil \log k \rceil)} \cdot \phi_{\mathsf{supp}^*(\mathsf{OT}^m)}$ can be realized using $\phi_{\mathsf{supp}(\mathsf{OT}^{\lceil \log k \rceil})} \cdot \phi_{\mathsf{supp}(\mathsf{OT}^{m+1})} = \phi_{\mathsf{supp}(\mathsf{OT}^{\lceil \log k \rceil + m + 1})}$. This implies the corollary.   □

A   Basic Constructions

In this section, for the sake of explicitness, we detail two basic constructions of Balanced Embedding from any function to the OT predicate – from a truth table and from a boolean circuit of the function. The first construction is implied by the second one, which in turn is implied by the general construction of balanced embedding from SZCR.

A.1   Balanced Embedding from Truth Table

Theorem 4. *For any deterministic function* $f : \{0,1\}^n \times \{0,1\}^n \to \{0,1\} \times \{0,1\}$, *there exists a balanced embedding to* ϕ_{OT}^k *for* $k = 2^{n+1}$.

Proof. To define the balanced embedding (π, θ) we will define inputs u_α and v_β to ϕ_{OT}^k such that $\pi(u, \alpha) = \theta(u, \alpha) = 1$ for $u = u_\alpha$ and 0 for rest; and similarly $\pi(v, \beta) = \theta(v, \beta) = 1$ for $v = v_\beta$ and 0 for rest. u_α and v_β where $\alpha = (x, a)$ and $\beta = (y, b)$ are defined as follows:

- For $0 \le i \le 2^n - 1$, $u_i = (1, a)$, if $i = x$ and $u_i = (0, 0)$ otherwise, whereas $v_i = (0, f_A(i, y))$.
- For $2^n \le i \le 2^{n+1} - 1$, $v_i = (1, b)$, if $i = 2^n + y$ and $v_i = (0, 0)$ otherwise, whereas $u_i = (0, f_B(x, i))$.

It is straight forward to see that this definition satisfies the conditions of a balanced embedding as the only compatible u, v pairs correspond to correct outputs being sampled at both the ends.   □

A.2   Constructing Balanced Embedding from Circuit

Theorem 5. *Given a circuit* C *with NAND gates that computes a function* f, *we can construct a balanced embedding to* $\phi_{\mathsf{OT}}^{2|C|}$.

Proof. Let x and y be the inputs of Alice and Bob, respectively. For each wire w in C, Alice and Bob sample w_A and w_B, respectively, as follows:

(i). If w is an input wire that reads x_i, then $w_A = x_i$ and $w_B = 0$, and if w is an input wire that reads y_i, then $w_A = 0$ and $w_B = y_i$

(ii). If w is the output wire computing $f_A(x, y)$, then $w_A \leftarrow \{0, 1\}$ and $w_B = 0$, and if w is the output wire computing $f_B(x, y)$, then $w_A = 0$, and $w_B \leftarrow \{0, 1\}$.

(iii). Otherwise, $w_A \leftarrow \{0, 1\}$ and $w_B \leftarrow \{0, 1\}$.

For each gate g in C, we denote the two input wires by $\text{In}1^g, \text{In}2^g$ and the output wire by Out^g.

We define sets U_x and V_y corresponding to inputs x, y. Elements of these sets $(u_i \in \{0, 1\}^2 : 1 \leq i \leq 2|C|)$ and $(v_i \in \{0, 1\}^2 : 1 \leq i \leq 2|C|)$ are be sampled as follows:

Enumerate the gates in C as $g_1, g_2, \ldots, g_{|C|}$; for $1 \leq i \leq 2|C|$:

- Set $u_{2i-1} = (\alpha_A^{g_i}, \text{In}1_A^{g_i} \oplus \alpha_A^{g_i})$ and $u_{2i} = (\beta_A^{g_i}, \text{In}2_A^{g_i} \oplus \beta_A^{g_i})$, where $\alpha_A^{g_i}, \beta_A^{g_i}$ are sampled uniformly at random subject to:

$$\alpha_A^{g_i} \oplus \beta_A^{g_i} = \text{Out}_A^{g_i} \oplus (\text{In}1_A^{g_i} \cdot \text{In}1_A^{g_i}) \oplus 1. \tag{26}$$

- Sets $v_{2i-1} = (\text{In}2_B^{g_i}, \alpha_B^{g_i})$ and $u_{2i} = (\text{In}1_B^{g_i}, \beta^{g_i})$, where $\alpha_B^{g_i}, \beta_B^{g_i}$ are sampled uniformly at random subject to:

$$\alpha_B^{g_i} \oplus \beta_B^{g_i} = \text{Out}_B^{g_i} \oplus (\text{In}1_B^{g_i} \cdot \text{In}1_B^{g_i}). \tag{27}$$

Finally, set candidate outputs $a = \hat{w}_B$, where $\hat{w}$ is the wire that outputs $f_A(x, y)$ in C, and $b = \tilde{w}_A$, where $\tilde{w}$ is the wire that outputs $f_B(x, y)$ in C. We use functions $O_A : \mathcal{U} \times X \to \{0, 1\}$ and $O_B : \mathcal{V} \times Y \to \{0, 1\}$ to denote the a and b values generated for specific u, x and y, b pairs respectively.

We then define the embedding (π, θ) for $\alpha = (x, a)$ and $\beta = (y, b)$ as $\pi(u, \alpha) = \theta(u, \alpha) = 2^{-|C|}$ if $u \in U_x$ and $a = O_A(u, x)$ and 0 otherwise. Similarly, $\pi(v, \beta) = \theta(v, \beta) = 2^{-|C|}$ if $v \in V_y$ and $b = O_B(v, y)$ and 0 otherwise. It is easy to check that this construction is indeed correct, owing to the correctness of the circuit C. $\qquad \square$

References

1. Agarwal, P., Narayanan, V., Pathak, S., Prabhakaran, M., Prabhakaran, V.M., Rehan, M.A.: Secure non-interactive reduction and spectral analysis of correlations. In: Dunkelman, O., Dziembowski, S. (eds.) EUROCRYPT 2022. LNCS, vol. 13277, pp. 797–827. Springer, Cham (2022). https://doi.org/10.1007/978-3-031-07082-2_28

2. Amini Khorasgani, H., Maji, H.K., Nguyen, H.H.: Secure non-interactive simulation: feasibility and rate. In: Dunkelman, O., Dziembowski, S. (eds.) EUROCRYPT 2022. LNCS, vol. 13277, pp. 767–796. Springer, Cham (2022). https://doi.org/10.1007/978-3-031-07082-2_27

3. Beaver, D.: Perfect privacy for two-party protocols. In: Feigenbaum, J., Merritt, M. (eds.) Proceedings of DIMACS Workshop on Distributed Computing and Cryptography, vol. 2, pp. 65–77. American Mathematical Society (1989)

4. Beaver, D.: Correlated pseudorandomness and the complexity of private computations. In: STOC, pp. 479–488 (1996)
5. Beimel, A., Ishai, Y., Kumaresan, R., Kushilevitz, E.: On the cryptographic complexity of the worst functions. In: Lindell, Y. (ed.) TCC 2014. LNCS, vol. 8349, pp. 317–342. Springer, Heidelberg (2014). https://doi.org/10.1007/978-3-642-54242-8_14
6. Beimel, A., Malkin, T.: A quantitative approach to reductions in secure computation. In: Naor, M. (ed.) TCC 2004. LNCS, vol. 2951, pp. 238–257. Springer, Heidelberg (2004). https://doi.org/10.1007/978-3-540-24638-1_14
7. Bhushan, K., Misra, A.K., Narayanan, V., Prabhakaran, M.: Secure non-interactive reducibility is decidable. In: These Proceedings (2022)
8. Chor, B., Kushilevitz, E.: A zero-one law for Boolean privacy. SIAM J. Discrete Math. **4**(1), 36–47 (1991)
9. Csiszár, I., Ahlswede, R.: On oblivious transfer capacity. In: International Symposium on Information Theory (ISIT), pp. 2061–2064 (2007)
10. Dodis, Y., Micali, S.: Lower bounds for oblivious transfer reductions. In: Stern, J. (ed.) EUROCRYPT 1999. LNCS, vol. 1592, pp. 42–55. Springer, Heidelberg (1999). https://doi.org/10.1007/3-540-48910-X_4
11. Dvir, Z., Gopi, S.: 2-server PIR with subpolynomial communication. J. ACM **63**(4), 39:1–39:15, 2016
12. Goldreich, O., Micali, S., Wigderson, A.: How to play ANY mental game. In ACM (ed.) STOC, pp. 218–229 (1987). See [12, Chap. 7] for more details
13. Goldrcich, O., Vainish, R.: How to solve any protocol problem - an efficiency improvement (extended abstract). In: Pomerance, C. (ed.) CRYPTO 1987. LNCS, vol. 293, pp. 73–86. Springer, Heidelberg (1988). https://doi.org/10.1007/3-540-48184-2_6
14. Haber, S., Micali, S.: Unpublished manuscript cited by [12] (1986)
15. Imai, H., Morozov, K., Nascimento, A.C.A.: On the oblivious transfer capacity of the erasure channel. In: International Symposium on Information Theory (ISIT), pp. 1428–1431 (2006)
16. Imai, H., Morozov, K., Nascimento, A.C.A.: Efficient oblivious transfer protocols achieving a non-zero rate from any non-trivial noisy correlation. In: International Conference on Information Theoretic Security (ICITS) (2007)
17. Imai, H., Morozov, K., Nascimento, A.C.A., Winter, A.: Efficient protocols achieving the commitment capacity of noisy correlations. In: International Symposium on Information Theory (ISIT), pp. 1432–1436 (2006)
18. Imai, H., Müller-Quade, J., Nascimento, A.C.A., Winter, A.: Rates for bit commitment and coin tossing from noisy correlation. In: International Symposium on Information Theory (ISIT), p. 45 (2004)
19. Kilian, J.: Founding cryptography on oblivious transfer. In: STOC, pp. 20–31 (1988)
20. Kushilevitz, E.: Privacy and communication complexity. In: FOCS, pp. 416–421 (1989)
21. Maji, H., Prabhakaran, M., Rosulek, M.: Complexity of multi-party computation functionalities. Cryptology and Information Security Series, vol. 10, pp. 249–283. IOS Press, Amsterdam (2013)
22. Narayanan, V., Prabhakaran, M., Prabhakaran, V.M.: Zero-communication reductions. In: Pass, R., Pietrzak, K. (eds.) TCC 2020, Part III. LNCS, vol. 12552, pp. 274–304. Springer, Cham (2020). https://doi.org/10.1007/978-3-030-64381-2_10

23. Prabhakaran, V., Prabhakaran, M.: Assisted common information with an application to secure two-party sampling. IEEE Trans. Inf. Theory **60**(6), 3413–3434 (2014). https://doi.org/10.1109/TIT.2014.2316011

24. Winkler, S., Wullschleger, J.: Statistical impossibility results for oblivious transfer reductions. Cryptology ePrint Archive, Report 2009/508 (2009). http://eprint.iacr.org/

25. Winter, A., Nascimento, A.C.A., Imai, H.: Commitment capacity of discrete memoryless channels. In: Paterson, K.G. (ed.) Cryptography and Coding 2003. LNCS, vol. 2898, pp. 35–51. Springer, Heidelberg (2003). https://doi.org/10.1007/978-3-540-40974-8_4

26. Wolf, S., Wullschleger, J.: New monotones and lower bounds in unconditional two-party computation. In: Shoup, V. (ed.) CRYPTO 2005. LNCS, vol. 3621, pp. 467–477. Springer, Heidelberg (2005). https://doi.org/10.1007/11535218_28

Theory II

One-Time Programs from Commodity Hardware

Harry Eldridge[1], Aarushi Goel[2(✉)], Matthew Green[1], Abhishek Jain[1], and Maximilian Zinkus[1]

[1] Johns Hopkins University, Baltimore, USA
{hme,mgreen,abhishek,zinkus}@cs.jhu.edu
[2] NTT Research, Sunnyvale, USA
aarushi.goel@ntt-research.com

Abstract. One-time programs, originally formulated by Goldwasser et al. [26], are a powerful cryptographic primitive with compelling applications. Known solutions for one-time programs, however, require specialized secure hardware that is not widely available (or, alternatively, access to blockchains and very strong cryptographic tools).

In this work we investigate the possibility of realizing one-time programs from a recent and now more commonly available hardware functionality: the *counter lockbox*. A counter lockbox is a stateful functionality that protects an encryption key under a user-specified password, and enforces a limited number of incorrect guesses. Counter lockboxes have become widely available in consumer devices and cloud platforms.

We show that counter lockboxes can be used to realize one-time programs for general functionalities. We develop a number of techniques to reduce the number of counter lockboxes required for our constructions, that may be of independent interest.

1 Introduction

One-time programs, formulated by Goldwasser et al. [26], are a flexible and powerful cryptographic primitive with compelling applications to limited-attempt authentication, fuzzy vaults, limited-query differential-private data analysis, and even autonomous ransomware and beyond. In the standard model, one-time programs are known to be impossible to realize purely in software [13,26]. To evade this impossibility, prior works have examined the problem of building one-time programs from secure hardware tokens [26,30], or alternatively, using blockchains [28].

The works of [26,30] employ tamper-proof hardware that implements *one-time memory* – a simple, stateful functionality that allows anyone to read one location, after which all other locations become inaccessible. While these results are practical and work in a variety of settings, they have mainly garnered theoretical interest. The likely cause is that one-time memory tokens have not been available as a standard feature of popular personal or cloud computing platforms. While it is possible to realize these tokens using programmable smart cards or

© The Author(s), under exclusive license to Springer Nature Switzerland AG 2022
E. Kiltz and V. Vaikuntanathan (Eds.): TCC 2022, LNCS 13749, pp. 121–150, 2022.
https://doi.org/10.1007/978-3-031-22368-6_5

HSMs [17,32,52], such development typically requires expensive equipment and considerable development effort. Moreover, the few affordable platforms that support custom programming may provide weak or limited security guarantees. If portability is not required, tamper-proof hardware tokens can also be realized through virtualization: *secure enclaves* such as Intel SGX [42] and ARM Trust-Zone [46] offer tamper-resilience under relatively strong adversarial assumptions such as operating system (OS) compromise. Indeed, if such an enclave platform is considered trusted, it is likely easier to implement an entire one-time functionality within the enclave. However, implicit trust in an enclave provider is unacceptable in some threat models, and the soundness of this trust regardless of threat model has been repeatedly called into question [14,19,45]. These execution environments also typically place limitations on end-users' ability to deploy arbitrary code [6,33,50].

Counter Lockboxes. Recently, a new generation of device- and cloud-based secure hardware has become available to end users. This includes secure co-processors that are now built into many smartphones and tablets, including the Apple Secure Enclave Processor (SEP) [3] and Google's Titan M2 [27] co-processor. It also includes specialized Hardware Security Modules (HSMs) that have recently been deployed within the data centers of consumer cloud providers; these can be accessed remotely from consumer devices to implement services such as Apple's Cloud Key Vault [39], Android Backup [48], WhatsApp backup [38], and Signal Secure Value Recovery [40]. Notably, these systems are not aimed at enterprise customers; they are configured to protect end-user cryptographic keys, even from attacks that might be launched by the device manufacturer or cloud provider themselves. These systems are now being used across billions of devices, making them more broadly accessible to consumers than any prior secure hardware platform.

Unlike secure enclave environments such as TrustZone or SGX, these consumer-oriented hardware devices do not allow end-devices to securely execute arbitrary programs. Instead, they present a limited interface to the device's application software. Since the primary purpose of these systems is to protect encryption keys under user-selected passwords, the most common interface is a functionality akin to what we describe as a *counter lockbox*.[1] To initialize a lockbox, the application software provides a password to the hardware along with a *maximum attempt limit*. At any later point, the software can retrieve the decryption key by providing the correct password. To protect the key against guessing attacks, the hardware increments a tamper-resistant counter for each incorrect guess: when this counter exceeds the maximum attempt limit, the hardware deletes the stored key. Given that this lockbox functionality has been deployed at massive scale, it represents an attractive building block for constructing more sophisticated cryptographic protocols.

---

[1] The term *counter lockbox* was previously introduced by Apple for its SEP [3]. We use it in this work to refer to a broad class of similar functionalities.

Using Lockboxes to Construct One-Time Programs. The ubiquity of this basic lockbox functionality motivates us to investigate the following question: *can such a simple functionality be used to achieve general secure computation?* In this work, we answer the question in the affirmative: given access to a sufficient number of lockboxes, we show that it is possible to realize the full power of one-time programs.

This result has important practical implications: since lockboxes are increasingly available to consumer hardware, this approach provides a "backdoor" route to constructing obfuscated software, even on hardware that does not directly support this functionality. This capability facilitates many constructive applications. For example, it can be used to build sophisticated attempt-limiting authentication functionalities. A limited-attempt fuzzy vault [34] can release cryptographic secrets when a user provides an input that satisfies some complex approximate function such as biometric matching or inexact string comparison [15]. Obfuscated software also enables privacy-preserving applications such as differentially-private statistical data analysis, where query limits must be enforced to maintain a privacy budget [22]. This functionality has a dark side as well: one-time programs allow for the creation of *autonomous ransomware* [10,20,36], a form of malware with no command-and-control infrastructure: in this paradigm, decryption keys are revealed only when the user provides the malware with proof of payment on a public blockchain. This last concern illustrates how carefully system designers must tread when exposing secure lockbox functionality to users and developers, since as we demonstrate in this work, even this relatively weak primitive can be leveraged into powerful secure computation. The lower bounds for this transformation also raise practical concerns: system designers may wish to know *how many* instances may be safely exposed to users before the power of these constructions can be exploited.

1.1 Our Results

In this work, we show that it is possible to construct secure one-time programs (OTP) using multiple instances of the counter lockbox functionality. Our main result is a construction of OTP for general functionalities based on one-way functions that requires a *constant* number of counter lockboxes per input-bit. This asymptotically matches prior constructions of one-time programs [25] in the number of hardware tokens utilized.

Theorem 1 (Informal). *Assuming the existence of one-way functions, for any functionality F, there exists a construction of one-time programs in the lockbox-hybrid model that makes $\mathcal{O}(1)$ invocations to the lockbox functionality per input bit of F.*

We present our main result with counter lockboxes that allow exactly one password attempt. In practice, lockboxes may allow more attempts. For example, lockboxes may fix the maximum number of attempts to some system-wide constant (*e.g.*, 10 attempts.) To handle such cases, we demonstrate an extension of our main construction that supports lockboxes with *any* number of password attempts. The resulting scheme requires the same number of lockboxes as before.

Reducing The Number of Hardware Tokens. We observe that at the cost of stronger assumptions, it is possible to achieve an asymptotic reduction in the *total* number of counter lockboxes. In particular, by using laconic oblivious transfer (LOT) [18] with malicious receiver security, we can reduce the total number of lockboxes to be *independent* of the input size and to depend only on the security parameter.

Our transformation is *generic*, and is applicable to any OTP construction (including prior known schemes). As such, this might be of independent interest.

Theorem 2 (Informal). *Assuming the existence of malicious receiver laconic oblivious transfer, for any functionality F, there exists a construction of one-time programs that makes $\mathcal{O}(\lambda)$ total invocations to the lockbox functionality (where λ is the security parameter).*

LOT schemes with malicious receiver security can be generically constructed by compiling the receiver message of existing LOT schemes with succinct arguments of knowledge (SNARKs) [11,44] either in the random oracle model, or by relying on knowledge assumptions.

Our Approach. Our starting point is the observation from the work of Goldwasser et al. [26] that garbled circuits [51] are almost like one-time programs, except the seeming need of interactive oblivious transfer (OT) to transmit the wire labels corresponding to an evaluator's input. Fortunately, a one-time memory (OTM) token naturally yields the OT functionality, which paves the way for constructing one-time programs from OTM tokens.

Unlike OTMs, however, a natural use of counter lockboxes yields a "leaky" OT functionality, where the receiver is able to learn *both* sender inputs with some constant probability (we elaborate on this in Sect. 2). By applying standard OT combiner techniques [31,43], the leaky OT functionality can be transformed into secure OT. However, this results in a significant overhead in the number of lockboxes required. Specifically, this approach requires $O(\lambda)$ lockboxes *per input bit* of the functionality, as opposed to $O(1)$ OTMs required in prior works.

Towards obtaining our result in Theorem 1, we observe that $O(1)$ lockboxes per input bit are sufficient to instantiate a leaky "batch" oblivious transfer functionality, where the receiver can learn both sender inputs for an a priori bounded constant fraction of the input bits. We then devise a way to construct a secure (i.e., "non-leaky") batch-OT from leaky batch-OT via *robust garbling* – a form of garbling where security holds even if the receiver learns both labels for a constant fraction of the input wires – for special functions. The secure batch-OT can then be used together with standard garbled circuits to obtain one-time programs for general functions.

Finally, we demonstrate that using laconic OT, the task of designing OTP for general functions with arbitrary input lengths can be reduced to the task of designing an OTP for functions whose input length is a fixed polynomial in the security parameter. As a result of this reduction, we are able to "compress" the effective input size, thereby achieving a reduction in the number of required hardware tokens. As we discuss later, this transformation requires an LOT scheme that achieves simulation-based security against malicious receivers.

Real World Implications. In order to assess the practical feasibility of our one-time programs, we need to consider several cost factors – number of hardware tokens required, cost of each hardware token, time to generate the OTP, and the size of software component of the OTP.

In our first construction, the main consideration is hardware. Indeed, besides the use of lockboxes to implement leaky batch OT, the rest of our construction comprises of robust garbling for special functions – an efficient, information-theoretic gadget, and regular garbled circuits. The efficiency of state-of-the-art constructions of regular garbled circuits is well-established in prior works [47]. In Sect. 8.1, we evaluate the concrete number of lockboxes required to implement one-time programs in practice and observe that there is a notable (albeit, constant factor) expansion from the input length to the number of total lockboxes required due to the use of binary linear error-correcting codes in our scheme. Overall, our results show that one-time programs may be practical for small to modest-sized inputs using a number of lockboxes that may be practical on today's systems or systems that will be available in the near future. Because such one-time programs may allow for destructive applications, our concrete bounds on the number of lockboxes can provide safety guidance for system developers who expose such functionalities to application developers.

Given our current understanding of LOT schemes, our second transformation is primarily of theoretical interest at the moment. We first note that recent works [1,29] have achieved significant improvements in concrete efficiency of LOT by allowing for linear decryption times (as opposed to poly-logarithmic decryption complexity achieved in the initial works). Our transformation only requires the laconic digest property of LOT and is not sensitive to decryption complexity. As such, it can be instantiated using the state-of-the-art LOT schemes with linear decryption complexity. However, the main efficiency bottleneck stems from the fact that our transformation requires a "non-interactive" version of LOT which is obtained by evaluating the LOT sender algorithm *inside a garbled circuit*. For current LOT schemes, this translates to evaluating *public-key* operations inside a garbled circuit for every receiver input bit, which to our current understanding, is quite expensive. Our work, therefore, motivates the design of new LOT schemes (with potentially linear decryption times) with "garbling friendly" sender algorithms.

2   Technical Overview

We now describe our main ideas for constructing a one-time program using counter lockboxes. We first describe a basic construction that relies on a fairly large number of lockboxes with only one attempt allowed (denoted $A = 1$). This approach requires $O(\lambda)$ lockboxes *per bit of input* to the one-time program for security parameter λ. This construction serves as a technical warm-up and high-lights the main challenges in building OTPs from counter lockboxes as opposed to one-time memory (OTM) tokens used by Goldwasser et al. [26].

We then describe our key ideas towards constructing OTPs with many fewer lockboxes, even *constant* per input bit. This asymptotically matches prior constructions based on OTM tokens. Finally, we discuss two extensions. First, we describe a generic method using laconic oblivious transfer [18] (LOT) to reduce the *total* number of lockboxes to be independent of the input size, and to depend only on λ. Second, we describe how our constructions can be extended to support counter lockboxes that allow multiple password attempts.

Initial Ideas. Goldwasser et al. [26] proposed a construction of one-time programs using one-time memory (OTM) tokens. Their construction relies on the observation that garbled circuits are almost like one-time programs, except that the sender needs to interact with the receiver (via oblivious transfer) to securely hand over input wire labels for the garbled circuit corresponding to the receiver's input. This interaction can be replaced with OTMs for each input wire: the sender can embed both the 0-label and the 1-label for each wire inside an OTM, and send all the OTMs together with the garbled circuit in *one shot*. The security of OTM ensures that the receiver learns at most one label from each OTM, which it can then use to evaluate the garbled circuit.

While the above idea is intuitive, the security proof requires a bit more care due to the fact that the adversary can choose its input in an *adaptive* fashion and query the OTM tokens in an arbitrary order. In particular, the proof of security requires garbling schemes with adaptive security. Efficient solutions for such garbling schemes are known in the random oracle model [8].

In this work, we build OTPs using a different kind of hardware token, the *counter lockbox*. A natural approach is to emulate the OTM functionality using counter lockboxes. However, an immediate challenge arises. Recall that a counter lockbox protects a secret value with a pre-configured password and limited attempts; if the number of incorrect attempts reaches the threshold, the secret value is irrevocably deleted. A natural idea is to store the two wire labels for each input bit in two separate lockboxes and devise a mechanism that allows a receiver to unlock only one of the two lockboxes. This, however, seems to require revealing only one of the two passwords to the user, returning to the problem of emulating OTM.

2.1 Basic Protocol

Our first idea is to use the receiver's input bits as passwords to the lockboxes. Concretely, for each input wire, we can use 0 and 1 as the passwords for the lockboxes that hide the 0-label and 1-label, respectively. The two lockboxes for each wire are then shuffled so that the input-to-password mapping is not known to the receiver.

An honest receiver can simply use the same value to attempt to unlock both lockboxes associated with an input wire. This guarantees that they obtain their desired label from one lockbox and consumes the single attempt of the other.

A malicious receiver may attempt to learn both labels by guessing the password for both of the lockboxes. This will give them only a $\frac{1}{2}$ chance of success: at least one label remains hidden with that probability. This idea can be leveraged to reduce the adversary's chances of learning both values: instead of embedding each label in a single lockbox, we "distribute" each label across additional lockboxes.

We now discuss the baseline construction of OTP that results from using lockboxes in this manner. A reader already familiar with the garbling based OTP approach may want to skip the next two paragraphs and directly go to the analysis of this baseline construction.

Generating the OTP. Let C be a Boolean circuit with input length n. The sender first garbles C to obtain a garbled circuit $\tilde{C}$ along with n pairs of wire labels $(\mathsf{label}_0^i, \mathsf{label}_1^i)$. It then performs the following steps:

1. Sample uniform bits $b_1, \ldots, b_{2\ell}$, where ℓ counts the number of lockboxes each label is distributed across.
2. For each $j = 1$ to 2ℓ: first, create an independent lockbox L_j^i using maximum attempt counter $A = 1$ and password $P = b_j$. Receive the corresponding lockbox secret K_j.
3. Next, compute $\mathsf{CT}_0^i = \mathsf{label}_0^i \oplus \bigoplus_{\forall j, b_j = 0} K_j$ and $\mathsf{CT}_1^i = \mathsf{label}_1^i \oplus \bigoplus_{\forall j, b_j = 1} K_j$.

Finally, the sender provides the receiver with the garbled circuit $\tilde{C}$ and the tuples $(\mathsf{CT}_0^1, \mathsf{CT}_1^1), \ldots, (\mathsf{CT}_0^n, \mathsf{CT}_1^n)$ as well as references to the $2\ell \cdot n$ lockboxes.

OTP Evaluation. To evaluate this program on an input $x = (x_1, \ldots, x_n)$, the receiver performs the following steps for $i = 1$ to n:

1. For $j = 1$ to 2ℓ, attempt to open the lockbox L_i with password x_i to retrieve either K_j or an error (in which case, set $K_j = 0$.)
2. Compute $\mathsf{label}_{x_i}^i = \mathsf{CT}_{x_i}^i \bigoplus_{j=1}^{\lambda} K_j$.

The receiver can now evaluate $\tilde{C}$ using the labels $\mathsf{label}_{x_1}^1, \ldots, \mathsf{label}_{x_n}^n$ to obtain a circuit output.

Analysis. It is easy to verify correctness of the above construction. What remains is to show that the protocol achieves security, *i.e.*, that a malicious receiver has a negligible chance of recovering more than one label for any input wire. The argument here is simple: to recover both $(\mathsf{label}_0^i, \mathsf{label}_1^i)$ for some wire i, the attacker must query each of 2ℓ lockboxes L_j^i using exactly the right passwords. However, since the lockboxes do not reveal the password until the attempt to open is made (at which point, the lockbox either reveals the secret or destroys it), the attacker must succeed in distinguishing between the 0 and 1 lockboxes. With an optimal guessing strategy, this happens with probability $\frac{\ell! \ell! \cdot n}{2\ell!} \approx \frac{1}{2^{O(\ell)}}$. Therefore, for λ bits of security, we need $\ell = O(\lambda)$ lockboxes per-input wire.

Limitations. While a decent baseline solution, this simple approach has several limitations. First, the number of lockboxes required grows with $O(\lambda)$, which is significantly worse than the one-time program construction of [26] that requires a constant number of hardware tokens per wire. Moreover, the above solution does not support lockboxes that allow multiple password attempts, and therefore has limited applicability for real-world use. To address these limitations, in the following sections we present techniques to reduce the number of counter lockboxes required. Later, we also describe approaches for supporting lockboxes that allow multiple password attempts.

2.2 Reducing the Number of Lockboxes

Our baseline solution can be seen as implicitly building a secure *combiner* for the OTM functionality. Indeed, the secret-sharing-based approach is also used in prior works that build secure combiners for oblivious transfer (OT) (e.g. [31,43]). It is natural to ask whether one can obtain a reduction in the number of lockboxes by using a more efficient combiner. To the best of our knowledge, however, all existing methods require an overhead of $O(\lambda)$ – the same as our baseline solution – when each component is only secure with constant probability.

We now discuss our key insights towards reducing the number of lockboxes required for one-time programs. To streamline this discussion, we start by defining an abstract "leaky" OT primitive and show how to obtain a one-time program using this primitive. Later, we discuss how counter lockboxes can be used to instantiate such a primitive and also analyse the total number of the lockboxes required for this instantiation.

Insight I: Leaky Batch-OT. Let us assume we have access to a leaky OT functionality, where the receiver can choose to specify: (1) either a choice bit b and get sender input m_b as output, (2) or a special "leakage" option. In this case, it learns both sender inputs m_0 and m_1 with some constant probability, and only one of the these inputs with the remaining probability.

This notion can be generalized to a *leaky batch-OT* functionality, where the receiver is allowed to learn both sender inputs for an a priori bounded *constant fraction* of the OTs. Furthermore, it is easy to see that multiple copies of the leaky OT functionality – one for each input bit – can realize leaky batch-OT. We ask whether it is possible to build one-time programs using leaky batch-OT, *without paying the overhead of standard OT combiners*.

At first, this seems highly unlikely. Indeed, the standard approach to one-time programs – as discussed earlier – involves the use of garbled circuits. Using leaky batch-OT would result in leakage of *both* wire labels for several input wires. The security of standard garbled circuits, however, completely breaks down if both wire labels are leaked even for a single wire (let alone multiple wires).

Insight II: Robust Garbling. We address this challenge by using a notion of *robust* garbling – one where security of the garbled function is ensured even if the receiver learns both labels for a constant fraction of the input wires. If achievable, such a tool would be clearly helpful for our task at hand. However, while intuitively appealing, it is not immediately apparent how to formally define such a notion.

With leakage, the adversary may obtain labels for multiple different inputs – inputs differing at bit locations where both wire labels were obtained. Should the adversary then be allowed to learn multiple outputs, or only a single output? Clearly the former conflicts with the one-time nature of the required functionality, and thus we would like to enforce the latter. This raises a new question: *which* output? For example, if the function is such that each input corresponds to a different output, it is not clear how we can enforce the single-output requirement in a meaningful way. Indeed, achieving our intuitive notion of robustness seems impossible for general functions. We note that previously, Almashaqbeh et al. [2], also considered a notion of robustness in garbled circuits (and more generally in non-interactive secure multiparty computation). However, given their application, they consider a slightly weaker setting, where they are able to assume an a priori fixed output for the adversary and hence do not need to deal with the above issue of "which output to reveal".[2] Since such assumptions are not applicable to our setting, we cannot rely on their definition of robustness.

We therefore weaken our goal and attempt to define robust garbling for a restricted class of functions that have a huge number of collisions, i.e. where inputs have a certain degree of *redundancy*. If we consider functions where multiple inputs with an overlapping subset of input bits have the same output, we could hope to achieve robustness. Even if the receiver learns multiple labels for the remaining (non-overlapping) bits, it will only learn at most one unique output.

As the following example shows, however, we need to be more careful. Consider two n-bit input strings $\mathbf{x}_1$ and $\mathbf{x}_2$ that share the same first $n/2$ bits, and another input string $\mathbf{x}_3$ that shares the same last $n/2$ bits with $\mathbf{x}_2$. Toward the above intuitive description of collisions, if $\mathbf{x}_1$ and $\mathbf{x}_2$ correspond to the same output, and $\mathbf{x}_2$ and $\mathbf{x}_3$ do as well, by transitivity $\mathbf{x}_1$ and $\mathbf{x}_3$ (that do not necessarily share a significant fraction of overlapping bits) also have the same output. Without further specification, this can escalate quickly until all inputs have the same output and we end up with a constant function.

In a pursuit to capture more interesting and non-trivial functions, we specify a class of functions that take inputs of length n, with respect to a parameter γ and try to capture the idea that there is only at most one unique non-$\perp$ output associated with any $n - \gamma$ input bits. Note that this is different from saying that inputs with the same subset of $n - \gamma$ input bits have a unique output. We say that a function is *admissible* if for any $n - \gamma$ input bits, there exists *at most one unique* combination of the remaining γ bits, such that the output of this function on the combined n-bit input is a non-$\perp$ value. Moreover, if such a unique combination of the remaining γ bits exists, then it is *easy* to find them using a deterministic procedure.[3] In this work, we consider robust garbling for such admissible functions.

OTPs from Robust Garbling. Let us now assume that we have robust garbling for this restricted class of functions. We now describe how we can leverage robust garbling to build OTPs for general functions. Let F be the

---

[2] we refer the reader to Sect. 2.5 for a more detailed comparison with their work.

[3] The reason why we need this deterministic procedure will be explained shortly.

intended OTP functionality. Then, consider a new functionality F' such that $F'(\mathsf{enc}(\mathbf{x})) = F(\mathbf{x})$, where F' is an admissible function amenable to robust garbling and enc is some mapping function that allows us to map inputs of F to inputs of F'. Concretely, we can use an error-correcting code (ECC) as the mapping function enc that can introduce redundancy in the mapped input to help ensure that F' satisfies the above conditions of being an amenable function.

This idea can now be used to design an OTP for F as follows: (1) The sender garbles F using a regular garbling scheme. (2) For each input wire i and bit $b \in \{0, 1\}$, it defines $F'_{i,b}$ such that on input $\mathsf{enc}(\mathbf{x})$, $F'_{i,b}$ runs the ECC decoding function dec to decode $\mathbf{x}$ and then if $\mathbf{x}[i] = b$ it outputs the b-label for the i-th wire, and otherwise it outputs $\perp$. For any ECC with distance $\gamma + 1$, there is only one "valid" codeword associated with any $n - \gamma$-bit message, hence, it is easy to see that dec (and as a result $F'_{i,b}$) is an admissible function. (3) The sender garbles each $F'_{i,b}$ using robust garbling. An important point to note is that each $F'_{i,b}$ takes the same input $\mathsf{enc}(\mathbf{x})$. (4) The sender uses this observation to concatenate input labels for each $F'_{i,b}$ and embed them inside the leaky batch-OT.

Constructing Leaky OT. We now describe our idea for constructing leaky OT (and consequently leaky batch-OT). Intuitively, our leaky oblivious transfer functionality allows the receiver to obtain *both* sender inputs with some constant probability.

Our construction of leaky OT is quite natural: in fact, we use the same approach as in the base protocol discussed earlier, where the sender prepares 2ℓ lockboxes (where ℓ is some constant) and distributes the "0" and "1" message across ℓ lockboxes. As before, in order to learn both sender inputs, the adversary must correctly guess the passwords for each of the 2ℓ associated lockboxes. The adversary then succeeds with a constant probability of $\approx \frac{1}{2^{O(\ell)}}$.

For leaky batch-OT, when considering a collection of n such leaky OTs, the probability that an adversary can successfully obtain both sender inputs for a constant fraction of the OTs is $\approx \frac{1}{2^{O(n\ell)}}$. Now, observe that if n is sufficiently large (say $n = O(\lambda)$), then the probability $\approx \frac{1}{2^{O(n\ell)}}$ is negligible in λ, even if ℓ is some constant value. While this analysis is somewhat simplified, it suffices for the purposes of this discussion. More details can be found in the technical sections.

Importantly, the above insight gives us significant improvement in the required number of lockboxes. Specifically, we now only require a constant number of lockboxes per OT (or input wire). However, as discussed before, in order to implement our idea of combining leaky batch-OT with robust garbling, the length of input to this leaky batch-OT is slightly longer than our "real" input. In particular, the input to our leaky batch-OT is an ECC encoding of the receiver's input. If we use binary linear ECCs with constant rate, then the length of this codeword is $n + \gamma$ where $\gamma = O(n)$, and we need a total of $\ell \cdot (n + \gamma)$ lockboxes, which in an amortized sense is a constant number of lockboxes per n-bits.

Handling Adaptivity. We now highlight some important subtleties regarding the security definitions of leaky batch-OT and robust garbling.

In our OTP constructions, we use robust garbling in conjunction with leaky batch-OT. Specifically, the receiver obtains labels for a robust-garbled circuit from the leaky batch-OT. From our prior discussion on leaky batch-OT, it is clear that an adversary can obtain both labels for some (e.g. γ out of n) of the input wires of this robust garbling. Moreover, recall that in above construction of leaky batch OT, given the entire set of lockboxes, an adversary can query them in *any* order of its choosing. In fact, it can "adaptively" decide an order based on the outcomes of previously queried lockboxes. In other words, the adversary can be "fully adaptive". Our definition of leaky batch-OT must allow for this flexibility and our robust garbling must also support this "fully adaptive" setting.

Since the adversary can potentially learn both labels for some of the inputs, for simulation, we need a way to predict the output based only on the input bits for which the adversary gets exactly one label. This is why we require that the set of admissible functions admit a deterministic procedure to predict the only (if any) valid associated output.

Finally, we remark that since the adversary can choose to ask for the *second* label of some input wires in any order, the simulator would not know until the last query which $n - \gamma$ input bits it must consider to predict the output. However, by then it might be "too late" to correctly simulate garbling. To overcome this, we make a crucial observation about our construction of leaky batch-OT from lockboxes: recall that in our construction we have 2ℓ lockboxes associated with every index $i \in [n]$. If an adversarial receiver successfully opens the relevant lockboxes and learns *one of the sender messages* (say msg_i^b) associated with that index, it is easy to predict if the adversary will also be able to learn the *other sender message* (say msg_i^{1-b}) corresponding to that index. Indeed, if the adversary made any incorrect password attempts for any of the ℓ lockboxes associated with msg_i^{1-b}, then the simulator can predict that the adversary will never be able to learn msg_i^{1-b}. However, if no incorrect password attempts were made for those ℓ lockboxes, then the adversary can be certain that the remaining (unopened) lockboxes associated with index-i have password $1-b$ and can always successfully open them and learn msg_i^{1-b}.

Therefore, we model our definition of leaky batch-OT to require the following: whenever the adversary makes a query for a particular index, it must specify whether it plans to query the second message for this index in the future. Moreover, since we only want to allow for some bounded leakage, the number of indices for which the adversary can make this request is bounded by a parameter γ. This observation helps ensure that the simulator of robust garbling does not need to wait until the "last query" to determine which $n - \gamma$ input bits it must consider to predict the output. Instead, this can be determined once the adversary makes at least one query for each of the n indices.

Constructing Robust Garbling. We now discuss robust garbling for a subclass of admissible functions. As discussed earlier, such a construction for a restricted function class suffices for our use in the construction of OTP. In particular, we consider admissible functions of the form $f = (\mathbf{M}, \mathbf{u}, \mathbf{z})$, where

$\mathbf{M} \in \{0,1\}^{k \times n}$, $\mathbf{u} \in \{0,1\}^k$ are public and $\mathbf{z} \in \{0,1\}^k$ is private, such that on any input $\mathbf{x} \in \{0,1\}^n$, $f(\mathbf{x}) = \begin{cases} \mathbf{z} & \text{if } \mathbf{u} = \mathbf{Mx} \\ \mathbf{z}' \xleftarrow{\$} \{0,1\}^k & \text{otherwise} \end{cases}$

While all "invalid" inputs must lead to a $\bot$ output in admissible functions, the above function instead outputs a random $\mathbf{z}'$. We note that this is not a problem in our setting (and the above function is still admissible). This is because in our OTP construction, the value $\mathbf{z}$ will correspond to labels of the garbled circuit that garbles the actual function for which we compute the OTP. In the case that the output of the above function is a random unrelated value instead of a valid label, the receiver will be able to detect this while evaluating and demarcate this output as essentially equivalent to $\bot$. We elaborate more on this in Sect. 6.2.

Benhamouda et al. [9] design a non-interactive *multi-party* computation (NIMPC) protocol for such functions, but where $\mathbf{M}, \mathbf{u}, \mathbf{z}$ could be matrices and vectors in any field and where each party contributes one element of $\mathbf{x}$ as input. This NIMPC protocol can be re-imagined as a robust garbling for such functionalities, when $\mathbf{M}, \mathbf{u}, \mathbf{z}$ are matrices and vectors over the Boolean field. Previously, Almashaqbeh et al. [2] leveraged a similar observation (of combining this NIMPC protocol with a regular garbled circuit) towards designing a garbling scheme that remains robust in the presence of an adversary who gets access to both labels for a fraction of the input-wires. However, there are some important differences between our definition and theirs; see Sect. 2.5 for a discussion).

The NIMPC protocol in [9] is presented in two phases – (1) an *offline pre-processing phase* that outputs private messages to each party and a broadcast message to all parties, and (2) an *online phase* where each party deterministically computes and broadcasts a single message based on its input and the private message output in the pre-processing phase. We observe that when working over a Boolean field, the broadcast message of the offline phase can be viewed as a garbling of the above function. Since there are only two-possible values for each element of the input vector $\mathbf{x}$, we can compute both possible messages corresponding to each element that the parties are expected to send in the online phase, and these may essentially act as the wire labels for the garbled circuit.

More concretely, this robust garbling works as follows: (1) sample a random matrix $\mathbf{s} \xleftarrow{\$} \{0,1\}^{k \times k}$ and compute $\mathbf{s}'_i = \mathbf{s} \cdot \mathbf{M}_{.,i}$ for each $i \in [n]$. (2) For input wire $i \in [n]$, the 0-label $\text{label}_{i,0} \in \{0,1\}^k$ is sampled randomly and the 1-label is computed as $\text{label}_{i,1} = \text{label}_{i,0} \oplus \mathbf{s}'_i$. (3) The garbled function is defined as $\tilde{f} = \mathbf{z} \oplus \mathbf{s} \cdot \mathbf{u} \oplus \bigoplus_{i \in [n]} \text{label}_{i,0}$. To evaluate, the receiver can simply exclusive-or all the appropriate labels with $\tilde{f}$. In Sect. 6.2, we show this construction satisfies the above notion of robust garbling, and that if $\mathbf{x}$ satisfies $\mathbf{u} = \mathbf{Mx}$, then $\mathbf{z} = \tilde{f} \oplus \bigoplus_{i \in [n]} \text{label}_{i,\mathbf{x}[i]}$, otherwise, this evaluation will output random $\mathbf{z}'$.

2.3   Reducing Lockboxes Using Laconic OT

We now describe a generic method for achieving an asymptotic reduction in the total number of counter lockboxes by using laconic oblivious transfer (LOT) [18].

Recall that our previous construction requires a total of $\mathcal{O}(n)$ lockboxes for n-bit inputs. Using LOT, we can reduce the number of lockboxes to be independent of the input size and only depend on the security parameter (as determined by the LOT scheme).

An LOT scheme allows a receiver to commit to a large input $x \in \{0,1\}^n$ via a short *hash* whose size is a fixed polynomial in the security parameter. Subsequently, a sender with inputs (m_0, m_1) and an index i sends a short message to the receiver. Using this message, the receiver can recover $m_{x[i]}$ but $m_{1-x[i]}$ remains computationally hidden.[4] Moreover, the hash value can be reused by the sender to transmit different messages to the receiver, based on different choices of indices i.

At a high-level, we can use LOT to "compress" the effective input size, thereby achieving an asymptotic reduction in the number of lockboxes. More specifically, let C be a circuit with n-bit inputs. We can build a one-time program for C using the following two-step approach:

1. First, we compute an adaptively secure garbled circuit $\tilde{C}$ for C together with a set of wire labels.
2. Now let Send be the next-message sender function in an LOT scheme. Let us consider n different copies $(\text{Send}_1, \ldots, \text{Send}_n)$ of Send, where the i-th copy is hardwired with an index $i \in [n]$ and a pair of labels $(\text{lab}_i^0, \text{lab}_i^1)$. Here, lab_i^b is the b-th label corresponding to the i-th input bit computed in the first step. Now, consider a new circuit **Send** that computes all of the functions $\text{Send}_1, \ldots, \text{Send}_n$ (in parallel). The input to this circuit is the LOT receiver message H – namely, the hash of an input x (to the original circuit C). We now create a one-time program $\widetilde{\text{OTP}}$ for **Send** with $\mathcal{O}(|\text{H}|)$ counter lockboxes using the scheme described in the previous sub-section. The final one-time program OTP for circuit C consists of $\widetilde{\text{OTP}}$ *and* the garbled circuit $\tilde{C}$ computed in the first step.

To evaluate the one-time program OTP on an input x, a receiver first computes an LOT hash H of x and evaluates $\widetilde{\text{OTP}}$ on input H. Using the output values, it evaluates the garbled circuit $\tilde{C}$ and returns its output.

It is easy to verify that the above construction achieves correctness. In order to prove security, we need to be able to *extract* the input of the receiver. However, from the security of $\widetilde{\text{OTP}}$, we can only hope to extract the input to $\widetilde{\text{OTP}}$, namely, H, which is presumably the LOT hash of some input x. In order to extract the actual x, we therefore require an LOT scheme that achieves simulation-based security against malicious receivers.

It is well known that such an LOT scheme cannot be constructed using standard black-box simulation techniques [21]. However, if we rely on random oracles or knowledge assumptions, then such a scheme can be constructed by compiling

---

[4] We emphasize that LOT is non-trivial even without privacy for receivers. While receiver privacy can be generically added [18], we do not require it for our transformation.

an LOT scheme with a succinct argument of knowledge (SNARK) [11,44]. Due to space constraints we defer the formal description of our OTP construction using Laconic OT to the full version of the paper.

2.4 Counter Lockboxes with Multiple Password Attempts

Up to this point we have only considered counter lockboxes that allow for a *single* attempt to guess the password. For some real-world instantiations of counter lockboxes e.g. [39,40], this may not be a valid assumption. We now discuss how our construction of leaky batch-OT can be adapted to support counter lockboxes that allow for *any number* of password attempts.

A natural approach is that the sender may simply "burn" all but one attempt from each lockbox they configure. However, this may be undesirable, especially in a cloud-based lockbox setting or if the sender does not wish to track the state of each lockbox. Therefore, we also provide a subtler approach described in this section and more fully examined in the full version of the paper.

Let z be the number of password attempts allowed by a counter lockbox functionality. We modify the previous construction as follows: once the sender decides that a particular lockbox should be a b-lockbox for a choice bit b, they do not simply set its password to b. Instead, they create z distinct strings $\mathsf{bin}(1)\|b, \ldots, \mathsf{bin}(z)\|b$ – each ending with bit b, where $\mathsf{bin}(i)$ denotes the binary representation of i. The sender then selects one of these z at random and sets it as the password for the counter lockbox.

For any choice bit b, an honest receiver can simply generate and try all of the z potential passwords for any lockbox. This guarantees that it can open all of the required lockboxes to reconstruct the desired label for its choice bit. On the other hand, the adversary gains no new advantage from having z attempts since there are $2z$ potential password choices for any lockbox. In particular, an adversary can do no better in determining whether a lockbox is a b-lockbox than by "committing" to some b and trying b concatenated with each possible prefix string. We can therefore achieve the same parameters for the multiple password attempt case as in the single attempt case. Due to space constraints we defer a formal treatment of this topic to the full version of the paper.

2.5 Related Work

Chaum and Pederson [16] were the first to propose the use of tamper-proof hardware for cryptography purposes, and Goldreich and Ostrovsky [24] explored its application to software protection. Goldwasser, Kalai and Rothblum [26] introduced the notion of one-time programs as well as one-time memory tokens. Further improvements to their construction were investigated by Goyal et al. [30] and Bellare et al. [8]. More recently, Goyal and Goyal [28] investigated the use of blockchains to construct one-time programs.

Prior to our work, Almashaqbeh et al. [2] also leveraged the techniques from [9] to achieve a form of robustness in non-interactive secure computation using garbled circuits in a different context. There are some key differences between

---
Functionality $\mathcal{F}_f^{\mathsf{OTP}}$
___

Create: Upon receiving (create, sid, P_i, P_j, x) from P_i where x is a string do:
1. Send (create, sid, P_i, P_j) to P_j.
2. Store (P_i, P_j, x).

Execute: On receiving (run, sid, P_i, y) from party P_j, find the stored tuple (P_i, P_j, x) (if no such tuple exists, do nothing.) Send $f(x, y)$ to P_j and delete tuple (P_i, P_j, x).

Fig. 1. Ideal functionality for a one-time program (OTP), parameterized with a specific function f, quoted from [30].

our work and theirs: we provide a general definition of robust garbling that accounts for the challenges involved in determining the adversary's input (and output) in our setting involving "leakage". In particular, as discussed earlier, since it is unclear how to define robust garbling for general functions, we define a class of admissible functions and robust garbling for such functions (as discussed in Sect. 2.2). In contrast, their definitions assume an a priori fixed input (and output) for the adversary, and are not applicable to our setting. Further, our definitions (unlike theirs) account for *fully adaptive* adversaries, which is crucial to our setting where the adversary can query the lockboxes in arbitrary order.

3   Preliminaries

We include preliminary definitions and discussion for *computational indistinguishability*, the *UC-Framework*, *adaptive projective garbling schemes*, *linear error-correcting codes* and *succinct non-interactive arguments of knowledge (SNARKs)* in the full version of the paper.

3.1   One-Time Programs

One-time Programs (OTP) were introduced by [26]. At a high level, a one-time program for a function f enables a party to evaluate f on any one input of its choice. The security of a one-time program dictates that no efficient adversary should be able to learn anything about the function f, beyond what can be inferred from its output $f(x)$ on any one input x of its choice.

Similar to Goyal et al. [30], we model one-time programs as a two-party non-interactive protocol that is secure against malicious receivers. We define the ideal functionality for a one-time program in Fig. 1.

4   Counter Lockboxes

In this section, we formalize our notion of *counter lockboxes*. A *counter lockbox*, or just "lockbox," is a stateful abstraction for securely storing cryptographic secrets such that they are protected by a human-memorable password. To create a new lockbox, a requester provides a password P and a maximum attempt counter A. The lockbox then generates random value K and returns K to the requester. The lockbox also stores internally A, some data with which it can re-compute K given P, and some information it can use to check if a future password guess matches P.

At a later point, a requester can provide some password P' to the lockbox, which will use its internal state to check if P' produces a match. If so, the lockbox recomputes and returns K to the requester. If the password does not produce a match, the lockbox decrements A. After A incorrect guesses the lockbox completely erases its internal content, preventing the value of K from ever being retrieved.

We model the lockbox functionality as $\mathcal{F}_\lambda^{\mathsf{Lockbox}}$, described in Fig. 2. In this work, we study cryptography in the $\mathcal{F}_\lambda^{\mathsf{Lockbox}}$-hybrid model.

Functionality $\mathcal{F}_\lambda^{\mathsf{Lockbox}}$

Create: On input (create, P_i, P_j, sid, id, P, A) from party P_i where $A > 0$, send (create, P_i, P_j, sid, id) to P_j. Sample $K \in \{0, 1\}^\lambda$, store the tuple $(P_i, P_j, sid, id, P, A, K, 0)$, and send K to P_i

Open: On input (open, P_i, sid, id, P') from party P_j:
- If a tuple $(P_i, P_j, sid, id, P, A, K, N)$ does not exist, then do nothing.
- If $N = A$ then delete the tuple and return expired.
- Otherwise if $P = P'$ then delete and replace the tuple with $(P_i, P_j, sid, id, P, A, K, 0)$ and return K.
- If $P \neq P'$ then delete and replace the tuple with $(P_i, P_j, sid, id, P, A, K, N+1)$ and return bad_guess.

Fig. 2. Ideal functionality for a counter lockbox. This simplified interface assumes that the lockbox "secret" K is a random string of length λ and that the password guess is directly compared to a stored password.

On the Communication Model. Previous works using secure hardware tokens [26] assume a two-party model in which a *sender* provisions stateful tokens and sends them to the *receiver*, who then uses them to evaluate a one-time program. This model can be directly adapted to cloud-based lockbox functionalities by simply forwarding references to the appropriate online locations. Lockboxes on a fixed device, however, may require adapted usage. For example, unlike hardware tokens, lockboxes implemented within the Apple SEP are an integral component of the device and cannot easily be removed or replaced. Hence our results can rely on the following different usage scenarios:

1. In a cloud-based scenario, the sender provisions a series of lockboxes on a shared (accessible to both parties) server, such as an Apple Cloud Key Vault [39] HSM or Google Titan [48] HSM in a remote data center. The sender then provides the location (IP address or URL) of these lockboxes along with some auxiliary data to the receiver. The receiver accesses these lockboxes to evaluate the one-time program.

2. In a device-based scenario, the sender provisions a device (such as an Apple iOS device with a SEP) with lockboxes and then physically delivers the device to the receiver. Given the physical security of the SEP [3], these lockboxes are designed to resist device forensics. Auxiliary data can be transmitted within the regular device memory, and evaluation could even be facilitated by custom on-device software such as an iOS app if deemed acceptable to the evaluator.
3. In a further device-centric instantiation, the sender and receiver may not be physically co-located. To provision lockboxes on the receiver's secure hardware, the sender employs a cryptographic protocol that enables secure message transmission to the receiver's secure hardware, while entirely bypassing the receiver's ability to observe this provisioning. For example, Apple's SEP supports a cryptographic protocol for communications between the SEP and application processor within a single device. With appropriate key management, this could be repurposed to allow a remote party to communicate securely with a receiver's SEP.

In all three settings, we assume that the hardware itself is secure against logical and physical attacks: this means that the only way to access lockbox secrets is through the password interface the hardware exposes. By contrast we assume that, at least at program execution time, the receiver has full control of the remaining portions of the device processor and can query the lockbox interface arbitrarily.

Discussion. In all prior hardware-token models, the sender physically transmits the device to the receiver and it is assumed that there is no "backward communication channel" to the sender. Indeed, such a channel can lead to privacy loss for the receiver.

However, one could consider a stronger model, where the sender does in fact have the ability to inspect lockboxes after the receiver is done querying them. In such a model, to prevent the sender from learning receiver's input bits, it is important to ensure that the following three states of lockboxes remain indistinguishable – (1) lockboxes with leftover password attempts, (2) lockboxes that were "destroyed" because of failed password attempts and (3) ones that are still presumably "functional" because they were opened using the correct password. For the first kind, we can use a simple defense and ask the receiver to consume all password attempts on each.

For the remaining two forms, our ideal lockbox functionality implicitly assumes that an adversary cannot distinguish between hardware that outputs the secret and one where the secret was destroyed because of failed password attempts. In the above stronger model, hardware that matches this ideal functionality clearly will not "leak" extra information once its attempts have been expired. It simply outputs ⊥, and there is no way to distinguish between "expired during evaluation without producing a secret" and "did output the secret but expired later as a defensive cleanup measure." While in general, real hardware may not behave like an ideal function, our definition of this ideal functionality is inspired by precise technical specifications from vendors such as Apple (see e.g. Apple iOS Security Guide), and there seems to be strong evidence that hardware

Functionality $\mathcal{F}^{OT}_{(n,\gamma)}$

Initialize: Upon receiving (init, sid, id, sen, rec, $\{(\mathsf{m}_{i,0}, \mathsf{m}_{i,1})\}_{i \in [n]}$) from the sender sen, where $\{(\mathsf{m}_{i,0}, \mathsf{m}_{i,1})\}_{i \in [n]} \in \mathcal{M}^{2n}$, send (init, sid, id, sen, rec) to the receiver rec and store the tuple $(sid, id, \text{sen}, \text{rec}, \{(\mathsf{m}_{i,0}, \mathsf{m}_{i,1})\}_{i \in [n]}, \mathcal{S}_1, \mathcal{S}_2, \text{counter})$, where $\mathcal{S}_1 = \mathcal{S}_2 = \emptyset$ and counter $= 0$.

Open: Upon receiving (open, sid, id, sen, rec, i, b, choice) from party rec, where choice $\in$ {both, single}, find the stored tuple $(sid, id, \text{sen}, \text{rec}, \{(\mathsf{m}_{i,0}, \mathsf{m}_{i,1})\}_{i \in [n]}, \mathcal{S}_1, \mathcal{S}_2, \text{counter})$ (if no such tuple exists, do nothing).
- If $i \in \mathcal{S}_1$, do nothing.
- Else if $i \in \mathcal{S}_2$, send $\mathsf{m}_{i,b}$ to rec.
- Else, do the following:
  - If choice = single, send $\mathsf{m}_{i,b}$ to rec, then delete and replace the tuple with $(sid, id, \text{sen}, \text{rec}, \{(\mathsf{m}_{i,0}, \mathsf{m}_{i,1})\}_{i \in [n]}, \mathcal{S}_1 \cup \{i\}, \mathcal{S}_2, \text{counter})$
  - else, if choice = both and counter = γ return forbidden. Else if counter < γ send $\mathsf{m}_{i,b}$ to rec, then delete and replace the tuple with $(sid, id, \text{sen}, \text{rec}, \{(\mathsf{m}_{i,0}, \mathsf{m}_{i,1})\}_{i \in [n]}, \mathcal{S}_1, \mathcal{S}_2 \cup \{i\}, \text{counter} + 1)$.

Fig. 3. Ideal functionality for leaky batch-OT

will satisfy it. As a result, our constructions remain secure in this stronger model as long as the hardware behaves similarly to the ideal functionality.

5   Leaky Batch-OT

In this section, we present and formalize a notion of *leaky batch-OT* and show how it can be realised using counter lockboxes.

5.1   Definition

Leaky batch oblivious transfer is a two-party functionality between a sender and receiver, where the sender initially inputs n pairs of messages $\{(\mathsf{m}_{i,0}, \mathsf{m}_{i,1})\}_{i \in [n]}$ where each $\mathsf{m}_{i,b}$ is in some message domain $\mathcal{M}$. For each $i \in [n]$, the receiver inputs a single bit $b \in \{0, 1\}$ and obtains $\mathsf{m}_{i,b}$. Additionally, at most γ times, the receiver is allowed to input i and obtain $\mathsf{m}_{i,1-b}$, assuming they have previously received $\mathsf{m}_{i,b}$. Our specific formulation is more nuanced. We give a formal definition of this *reactive* functionality in Fig. 3.

5.2   Construction

In this section, we construct a protocol for leaky batch-OT using counter lockboxes. Recall that our definition of leaky batch-OT only allows the receiver to obtain both messages for at most γ indices $i \in [n]$. Therefore, we show that if ℓ is set to $\lceil -\log_2(\frac{\gamma}{n}) \rceil + 1$ then except with some negligible probability in n a malicious receiver can successfully obtain keys of all 2ℓ lockboxes for at most γ indices $i \in [n]$. We give a formal description of this protocol in the $\mathcal{F}^{\text{Lockbox}}_{\lambda}$-hybrid model in Fig. 4. Due to space constraints we defer the formal proof of security to the full version of the paper and include a proof sketch here.

Theorem 3. *There exists a protocol for securely realizing the leaky batch-OT functionality $\mathcal{F}^{OT}_{(n,\gamma)}$ (Fig. 3) against a malicious sender and receiver, in the $\mathcal{F}^{Lockbox}_{\lambda}$-hybrid model, where the sender only sends a single message to receiver, while the receiver does not to send any messages to the sender.*

Proof Sketch. We first present a simulator that in the ideal world simulates sending lockboxes to the adversary as in the protocol. We then show that as long as the adversary is not able to successfully open all 2ℓ lockboxes associated with more than γ input wires, with BAD denoting the event that the adversary succeeds in doing so, the transcript output by the simulator is indistinguishable from that computed in the real world.

We then proceed to show that the probability that the BAD event happens in negligible when $\ell = \lceil -\log_2(\frac{\gamma}{n})\rceil + 1$. For this, we first show that the probability of the adversary successfully opening all 2ℓ lockboxes for one wire is at most $p = (\frac{1}{2})^{\ell} \cdot \frac{\ell!}{(2\ell-1)!!}$. As intuition, the adversary can do no better when guessing passwords than just guessing whatever password is in the majority among the remaining lockboxes. For ℓ of the guesses this gives them a 50% chance of success, producing the $(\frac{1}{2})^{\ell}$ term. The second term follows from a similar but more involved calculation. Following our derivation of p, we use a Chernoff bound to show that the overall probability is negligible in n. We then conclude that when n is large, i.e. $O(\lambda)$, the protocol is secure.

- **Sender:** Let $\ell := \lceil -\log_2(\frac{\gamma}{n})\rceil + 1$. Given inputs $\{(m_{i,0}, m_{i,1})\}_{i\in[n]}$, the sender sen samples a fresh sid. For each $i \in [n]$, do the following:
  1. Sample a random permutation $\pi_i : [2\ell] \to [2\ell]$.
  2. Sample 2ℓ unique ids $\{id_{i,j}\}_{j\in[2\ell]}$.
  3. For each $j \in [2\ell]$,
     - If $\pi_i(j) \leq \ell$, invoke $\mathcal{F}^{Lockbox}_{\lambda}$ on arguments $(\mathsf{create}, \mathsf{sen}, \mathsf{rec}, sid, id_{i,\pi_i(j)}, 0, 1)$ and obtain $K^{\pi_i(j)}_{i,0}$ in return.
     - Else, invoke $\mathcal{F}^{Lockbox}_{\lambda}$ on arguments $(\mathsf{create}, \mathsf{sen}, \mathsf{rec}, sid, id_{i,\pi_i(j)}, 1, 1)$ and get $K^{\pi_i(j)}_{i,1}$ in return.
  4. Compute $C_{i,0} := m_{i,0} \oplus \bigoplus_{j=1}^{\ell} K^j_{i,0}$.
  5. Compute $C_{i,1} := m_{i,1} \oplus \bigoplus_{j=\ell+1}^{2\ell} K^j_{i,1}$.
  6. Send $\{(C_{i,0}, C_{i,1})\}_{i\in[n]}$ to the receiver rec.
- **Receiver.** Given a set of input bits $\{b_i\}_{i\in[n]}$ and upon receiving $\{(sid, id_{i,\pi_i(j)}, \mathsf{sen}, \mathsf{rec})\}_{j\in[2\ell], i\in[n]}$ from the $\mathcal{F}^{Lockbox}_{\lambda}$ functionalities and $\{(C_{i,0}, C_{i,1})\}_{i\in[n]}$ from the sender, the receiver proceeds as follows for each $i \in [n]$:
  1. For each $j \in [2\ell]$, invoke $\mathcal{F}^{Lockbox}_{\lambda}$ on arguments $(\mathsf{open}, \mathsf{sen}, sid, id_{i,\pi_i(j)}, b_i)$ to receive either $K^{\pi_i(j)}_{i,b_i}$ or bad_guess, in which case set $K^{\pi_i(j)}_{i,b_i} = 0$.
  2. Compute $m_{i,b_i} = C_{i,b_i} \oplus \bigoplus_{j=1}^{2\ell} K^{\pi_i(j)}_{i,b_i}$.

Fig. 4. Protocol for leaky batch OT

6   Robust Garbling

In this section, we formalize the notion of robust garbling for a class of admissible functions. We then present a robust garbling scheme for a sub-class of such functions, with fully adaptive, information-theoretic security.

6.1   Definitions

In a robust garbling scheme, we want to capture the requirement that even if the receiver obtains both labels for some of the input wires, it should only be able to learn exactly one output. However, this poses the following conundrum: on the one hand, we are allowing the receiver to obtain labels for *multiple* inputs. On the other hand, we do not want it to learn more than *one* output. How do we reconcile these requirements?

While achieving a reconciliation seems impossible for general functions, we can hope to do so for functions where the inputs have some level of *redundancy*. In other words, if only a subset of the input bits are sufficient to determine the output of the function, we can hope to construct a garbling scheme where even if the receiver learns multiple labels for the remaining bits, it will only learn at most one uniquely defined output.

We now give a formal definition of such a class of functions.

Definition 1 (Function Class $\mathcal{F}^{n,\gamma}$). $\mathcal{F}^{n,\gamma}$ *contains all functions* $f :$ $\{0,1\}^n \to \{0,1\}^* \cup \{\bot\}$ *such that for any set* $\mathcal{S} \subset [n]$ *of size* $(n - \gamma)$ *and any set of bits* $\{x_i\}_{i \in \mathcal{S}}$, *there exists at most one "valid"* $\{x_i\}_{i \in \overline{\mathcal{S}}}$ *such that* $f(x_1, \ldots, x_n) \neq \bot$.

Further, there is an an associated function $\mathsf{Expand} : \{0,1\}^{(n-\gamma)} \to \{0,1\}^n$ *such that for every* $\{x_i\}_{i \in \mathcal{S}}$:

1. *If* $\exists \{x_i\}_{i \in \overline{\mathcal{S}}}$, *such that* $f(x_1, \ldots, x_n) \neq \bot$, *then* $\mathsf{Expand}(\{x_i\}_{i \in \mathcal{S}}) = (x_1, \ldots, x_n)$.
2. *Else,* $f(\mathsf{Expand}(\{x_i\}_{i \in \mathcal{S}})) = \bot$.

At a high level, the above definition implies that it is possible to determine the unique output associated with any $(n - \gamma)$ bits of input.

Next, we formalize the notion of *robust garbling* for this class of functions. In addition to the robustness property discussed above, we also want this garbling scheme to be "fully adaptive". That is, upon receiving the garbled circuit, the adversary should be allowed to choose its input bit-by-bit, depending on the labels received thus far. We note that this is stronger than the standard notion of adaptivity for garbled circuits [7,8,23], where the adversary must specify its *entire input* in one go, after receiving the garbled circuit.

Moreover, as discussed previously, we allow the adversary to receive both labels for some of the input wires. However, in case it plans to obtain the second label for any index, it must specify that at the time of making the first query for that index. This way, once the adversary has received at least one label for each input position, the simulator can determine the output based on the ones for which the adversary is guaranteed to not make a second query and simulate accordingly. Therefore, we model our simulator for robust garbling to essentially consist of three algorithms (SimFunc, SimIn, SimInLast), where SimFunc simulates the garbled circuit using only "public-information" about the circuit (e.g., the size of the circuit). SimIn and SimInLast are used for simulating the input wire labels, where SimInLast is used specifically once the adversary has obtained at least one label for each input wire.

We now present a definition of robust garbling.

Definition 2 (Robust Garbling) *A robust garbling scheme for functions $f \in \mathcal{F}^{n,\gamma}$ consists of a tuple of PPT algorithms (RobGarble, RobGarbleInp, RobEval) such that:*

- $(\tilde{f}, \text{st}) \leftarrow \text{RobGarble}(1^\lambda, f)$: *This is a PPT algorithm that takes as input the security parameter 1^λ and a function $f \in \mathcal{F}^{n,\gamma}$ and outputs a garbling $\tilde{f}$ and some private state information st.*
- $\text{lab}_{i,x_i} \leftarrow \text{RobGarbleInp}(\text{st}, i, x_i)$: *This is a PPT algorithm that takes as input the state information st, an index $i \in [n]$ and an input bit x_i, and outputs the corresponding input label lab_{i,x_i}.*
- $y = \text{RobEval}(\tilde{f}, \{\text{lab}_{i,x_i}\}_{i \in [n]})$: *Given a garbling $\tilde{f}$ and a set of labels $\{\text{lab}_{i,x_i}\}_{i \in [n]}$ it outputs a value $y \in \{0,1\}^k$.*

Correctness. *For every $\lambda \in \mathbb{N}$, $f \in \mathcal{F}^{n,\gamma}$, and for each $\mathbf{x} \in \{0,1\}^n$, it holds that: $\Pr[\text{RobEval}(\tilde{f}, \{\text{lab}_{i,x_i}\}_{i \in [n]}) = f(\mathbf{x})] = 1$, where $(\tilde{f}, \text{st}) \leftarrow \text{RobGarble}(1^\lambda, f)$ and $\forall i \in [n]$, $\text{lab}_{i,x_i} \leftarrow \text{RobGarbleInp}(\text{st}, i, x_i)$.*

γ-Robust Adaptive Security. *There exists a PPT simulator $\text{Sim} = (\text{SimFunc}, \text{SimIn}, \text{SimInLast})$ such that, for any non-uniform PPT adversary $\mathcal{A}$ there exists a negligible function v such that:*

$$\left| \Pr[\text{Exp}_{\mathcal{A},\text{GC},\text{Sim}}^{\text{RobAdp}}(1^\lambda, 0) = 1] - \Pr[\text{Exp}_{\mathcal{A},\text{GC},\text{Sim}}^{\text{RobAdp}}(1^\lambda, 1) = 1] \right| \leq v(\lambda)$$

where the experiment $\text{Exp}_{\mathcal{A},\text{GC},\text{Sim}}^{\text{RobAdp}}$ is defined in Fig. 5

6.2 Construction

In this section, we present an information-theoretically secure construction of robust garbling for functions of the form $f = (\mathbf{M}, \mathbf{u}, \mathbf{z}) \in \mathcal{F}^{n,\gamma}$, where $\mathbf{M} \in \{0,1\}^{k \times n}$, $\mathbf{u} \in \{0,1\}^k$ are public and $\mathbf{z} \in \{0,1\}^k$ is private, such that on any input $\mathbf{x} \in \{0,1\}^n$, $f(\mathbf{x}) = \begin{cases} \mathbf{z} & \text{if } \mathbf{u} = \mathbf{Mx} \\ \mathbf{z}' \xleftarrow{\$} \{0,1\}^k & \text{otherwise} \end{cases}$.

We use $\mathcal{F}_{\text{linear}}^{n,\gamma}$ to denote this subclass of $\mathcal{F}^{n,\gamma}$. While all *invalid* inputs must to lead to a $\perp$ output in any $f \in \mathcal{F}^{n,\gamma}$, functions in $\mathcal{F}_{\text{linear}}^{n,\gamma}$ instead output a random $\mathbf{z}'$. We note that depending on the context, this may not be a problem (and the above function can still be admissible), if the receiver can distinguish a *valid* output $\mathbf{z}$ from an *invalid* random $\mathbf{z}'$ potentially using some "additional

---

Experiment $\mathsf{Exp}_{\mathcal{A},\mathsf{GC},\mathsf{Sim}}^{\mathsf{RobAdp}}$

1. The adversary specifies a function $f \in \mathcal{F}^{n,\gamma}$ and obtains $\tilde{f}$, where $\tilde{f}$ is created as follows:
   - If $b = 0$: $(\tilde{f},\mathsf{st}) \leftarrow \mathsf{RobGarble}(1^\lambda, f)$
   - If $b = 1$: $(\tilde{f},\mathsf{st}) \leftarrow \mathsf{SimFunc}(1^\lambda, 1^{|f|})$ (Here, we implicitly assume that this simulator can get any public information about f, not just its size.)
2. Initialize $\mathcal{S}_1 = \mathcal{S}_2 = \emptyset$ and counter $= 0$. For each $j \in [n + \gamma]$, the adversary $\mathcal{A}$ specifies a tuple $(i_j, x_{i_j}, \mathsf{choice}_i)$, where $\mathsf{choice}_i \in \{\mathsf{single}, \mathsf{both}\}$.
   - If $\mathsf{choice}_i = \mathsf{single}$ and $(i, \cdot) \notin \mathcal{S}_1$, update $\mathcal{S}_1 = \mathcal{S}_1 \cup \{(i, x_{i_j})\}$. Else if $\mathsf{choice}_i = \mathsf{both}$, $i \notin \mathcal{S}_1 \cup \mathcal{S}_2$ and counter $< \gamma$, update $\mathcal{S}_2 = \mathcal{S}_2 \cup \{i\}$ and set counter $=$ counter $+ 1$. In both cases do the following:
     - If $b = 0$, output $\mathsf{lab}_{i_j, x_{i_j}} \leftarrow \mathsf{RobGarbleInp}(\mathsf{st}, i_j, x_{i_j})$.
     - If $b = 1$ and $|\mathcal{S}_1 \cup \mathcal{S}_2| < n$, output $\mathsf{lab}_{i_j, x_{i_j}} \leftarrow \mathsf{SimIn}(\mathsf{st}, i_j, x_{i_j})$.
     - If $b = 1$ and $|\mathcal{S}_1 \cup \mathcal{S}_2| = n$, output $\mathsf{lab}_{i_j, x_{i_j}} \leftarrow \mathsf{SimInLast}(\mathsf{st}, i_j, x_{i_j}, \mathcal{S}, \mathsf{out})$, where $\mathcal{S} \subset [n]$ is the set of indices $i \in [n]$ such that $(i, \cdot) \in \mathcal{S}_1$ and $\mathsf{out} = f(f_{\mathsf{expand}}(\{x_i\}_{i \in \mathcal{S}}))$.
   - Else if $\mathsf{choice}_i = \mathsf{both}$, $i \notin \mathcal{S}_1$ and $i \in \mathcal{S}_2$, do the following.
     - If $b = 0$, output $\mathsf{lab}_{i_j, x_{i_j}} \leftarrow \mathsf{RobGarbleInp}(\mathsf{st}, i_j, x_{i_j})$.
     - If $b = 1$, output $\mathsf{lab}_{i_j, x_{i_j}} \leftarrow \mathsf{SimIn}(\mathsf{st}, i_j, x_{i_j})$.

Finally, the adversary outputs a bit b', which is the output of the experiment.

Fig. 5. γ-robust adaptivity experiment

information." In our OTP construction, the value $\mathbf{z}$ will correspond to labels of the garbled circuit that garbles the actual function for which we compute the OTP. While these labels are also random vectors in $\{0,1\}^k$, the receiver gets "additional information" in the form of the garbled circuit where $\mathbf{z}$ is used as an input wire label. In case the output of the above function is a random unrelated value instead of a valid label, while evaluating, the receiver will be able to detect this and demarcate this output as essentially equivalent to $\perp$.

Garbling Scheme. We now present a construction of robust garbling scheme for the above class of functions. As discussed previously, this is adapted from the non-interactive *multi-party* computation (NIMPC) protocol for such functions proposed by Benhamouda et al. [9].

- $\mathsf{RobGarble}(1^\lambda, f)$:
  1. Sample a random $\mathbf{s} \xleftarrow{\$} \{0,1\}^{k \times k}$.
  2. For each $i \in [n]$, sample a random $\mathbf{r}_i \in \{0,1\}^k$.
  3. Set $\mathsf{st} = \mathbf{s}, \{\mathbf{r}_i\}_{i \in [n]}$.
  4. Output garbling $\tilde{f} = \mathbf{z} \oplus \mathbf{s} \cdot \mathbf{u} \oplus \bigoplus_{i \in [n]} \mathbf{r}_i$.
- $\mathsf{RobGarbleInp}(\mathsf{st}, \mathcal{I}, \{x_i\}_{i \in [n] \setminus \mathcal{I}})$:
  1. Parse $\mathsf{st} = \mathbf{s}, \{\mathbf{r}_i\}_{i \in [n]}$.
  2. For each $i \in [n]$, compute $\mathbf{s}'_i = \mathbf{s} \cdot \mathbf{M}_{.,i}$, where $\mathbf{M}_{.,i}$ denotes the i-th column of $\mathbf{M}$
  3. For each $i \in \mathcal{I}$, compute and output $\mathsf{lab}_{i,0} = \mathbf{r}_i$ and $\mathsf{lab}_{i,1} = \mathbf{r}_i \oplus \mathbf{s}'_i$.
  4. For each $i \in [n] \setminus \mathcal{I}$, output $\mathsf{lab}_{i,x_i} = \mathbf{r}_i \oplus \mathbf{s}'_i \cdot x_i$.
- $\mathsf{RobEval}(\tilde{f}, \{\mathsf{lab}_{i,x_i}\}_{i \in [n]})$: Compute and output $\tilde{f} \oplus \bigoplus_{i \in [n]} \mathsf{lab}_{i,x_i}$.

We prove the following theorem in the full-version of our paper.

Theorem 4 *There exists an information-theoretically secure robust adaptive garbling scheme for each every function $f \in \mathcal{F}_{\text{linear}}^{n,\gamma}$.*

7   One-Time Program

In this section we use the tools built in previous sections to construct a one-time program. In addition to leaky batch-OT and robust garbling for $\mathcal{F}_{\text{linear}}^{n,\gamma}$, we make use of a standard adaptive, projective garbled circuit and linear error-correcting codes over $\mathbb{F}_2$.

We instantiate our one-time program construction using a $[n, k, \gamma+1]_2$-binary linear error-correcting code, where k is the message length, n is the code-word length, and $\gamma+1$ is the distance. We give a formal description of this construction in the $\mathcal{F}_{(n,\gamma)}^{\text{OT}}$-hybrid model. While an honest receiver does not use the "leaky" aspect of our leaky batch-OT to receive both $(\mathsf{lab}'_{j,0}, \mathsf{lab}'_{j,1})$ for any index j, a malicious receiver can certainly try to exploit it. However, since the number of "double-labels" that they can obtain is capped at γ (and our robust garbling is secure as long as double-labels for at most γ input wires are revealed), they will never receive enough to successfully obtain both labels for any input wire of the adaptive garbled circuit. As a result, even a malicious receiver will only be able to learn the output for a single input.

Protocol. We give a formal description of the OTP protocol in Fig. 6, in the $\mathcal{F}_{(n,\gamma)}^{\text{OT}}$-hybrid model, using $[n, k, \gamma + 1]$-binary linear error-correcting codes, an adaptive projective garbled circuit (AdaGarbleCkt, AdaGarbleInp, AdaEvalCkt) and a robust function garbling scheme (RobGarble, RobGarbleInp, RobEval) for $\mathcal{F}_{\text{linear}}^{n,\gamma}$.

Note that for all $i \in [k]$ and $b \in \{0,1\}$, the function $F_{i,b}$ belongs to the $\mathcal{F}_{\text{linear}}^{n,\gamma}$ class of functions described in Sect. 6.2. It is easy to identify when the output is $\bot$, as the output of each function is an input wire label for a garbled circuit. The use of an error-correcting code grants the properties required by $\mathcal{F}_{\text{linear}}^{n,\gamma}$. By the definition of minimum distance, any set of $(n - \gamma)$ fixed bits will define only a single valid codeword, and the Expand function is simply a lookup for the codeword uniquely defined by those bits. Finally, each $F_{i,b}$ clearly meets the linear construction requirement of $\mathcal{F}_{\text{linear}}^{n,\gamma}$. We prove the following theorem in the full-version of our paper.

Theorem 5 *Assuming the existence of one-way functions, there exists a non-interactive protocol for securely realizing $\mathcal{F}_f^{\text{OTP}}$ against a semi-honest sender and malicious receiver in the $\mathcal{F}_{(n,\gamma)}^{\text{OT}}$-hybrid model.*

8   Concrete Analysis

In this section, we present a concrete analysis to investigate the suitability of our schemes for real-world applications. In Sect. 8.1, we estimate the number of lock-boxes required for different input lengths. In Sect. 8.2, we discuss how lockboxes

- **Sender:** Given an input f, the sender sen proceeds as follows:
  1. Express f as a circuit C, then compute $(\tilde{C}, \{\mathsf{lab}_{i,b}\}_{i\in[k],b\in\{0,1\}}) \leftarrow \mathsf{AdaGarbleCkt}(1^\lambda, C)$.
  2. Instantiate a linear error-correcting code with length n, rank k, minimum distance $\gamma + 1$ and generating matrix $\mathbf{G}$.
  3. For each $i \in [k]$, and each $b \in \{0,1\}$, compute a matrix $\mathbf{M}_{i,b}$ and vector $\mathbf{u}_{i,b}$ such that $\mathbf{u}_{i,b} = \mathbf{M}_{i,b} \cdot \mathbf{y}$ if and only if $\mathbf{y}$ is a valid codeword generated using $\mathbf{G}$ and its corresponding word has bit b at position i, i.e. $\mathbf{u}_{i,b} = \mathbf{M}_{i,b} \cdot \mathbf{y} \iff \exists \mathbf{x} \in \{0,1\}^k, \mathbf{y}^\mathsf{T} = \mathbf{x}^\mathsf{T} \cdot G \wedge \mathbf{x}_i = b$. Then, define the following function:

$$F_{i,b}(\mathbf{y}) = \begin{cases} \mathsf{lab}_{i,b} & \text{if } \mathbf{u}_{i,b} = \mathbf{M}_{i,b} \cdot \mathbf{y} \\ \mathbf{z}' \xleftarrow{\$} \{0,1\}^k & \text{otherwise} \end{cases}$$

  Next, compute $(\tilde{F}_{i,b}, \{\mathsf{robustLab}_{j,b'}^{i,b}\}_{j\in[n],b'\in\{0,1\}}) \leftarrow \mathsf{RobGarble}(1^\lambda, F_{i,b})$.
  4. Define $\overrightarrow{\mathsf{robustLab}}_{j,b'} := \{\mathsf{robustLab}_{j,b'}^{i,b}\}_{i\in[k],b\in\{0,1\}}$ for all $j \in [n], b' \in \{0,1\}$.
  5. Sample a fresh sid and id and invoke $\mathcal{F}_{(n,\gamma)}^{\mathsf{OT}}$ on arguments $(\mathsf{init}, sid, id, \mathsf{send}, \mathsf{rec}, \{(\overrightarrow{\mathsf{robustLab}}_{j,0}, \overrightarrow{\mathsf{robustLab}}_{j,1})\}_{j\in[n],b'\in\{0,1\}})$
  6. Send $(\tilde{C}, \{\tilde{F}_{i,b}\}_{i\in[k],b\in\{0,1\}})$ to the receiver rec.
- **Receiver:** Given an input $\mathbf{x}$ and upon receiving $(sid, id, \mathsf{sen}, \mathsf{rec})$ from $\mathcal{F}_{(n,\gamma)}^{\mathsf{OT}}$ and $(\tilde{C}, \{\tilde{F}_{i,b}\}_{i\in[k],b\in\{0,1\}})$ from the sender, the receiver proceeds as follows:
  1. Compute $\mathbf{y} := \mathbf{x}^\mathsf{T} \cdot \mathbf{G}$.
  2. For each $j \in [n]$, invoke $\mathcal{F}_{(n,\gamma)}^{\mathsf{OT}}$ on arguments $(\mathsf{open}, sid, id, \mathsf{sen}, \mathsf{rec}, j, \mathbf{y}[j])$ and get $\overrightarrow{\mathsf{robustLab}}_{j,\mathbf{y}[j]} = \{\mathsf{robustLab}_{j,\mathbf{y}[j]}^{i,b}\}_{i\in[k],b\in\{0,1\}}$ in return.
  3. For each $i \in [k]$, compute $\mathsf{lab}_{i,x_i} = \mathsf{RobEval}(\tilde{F}_{i,\mathbf{x}[i]}, \mathsf{robustLab}_{j,\mathbf{y}[j]}^{i,\mathbf{x}[i]}\}_{j\in[n]})$.
  4. Compute and output $z \leftarrow \mathsf{AdaEvalCkt}(\tilde{C}, \{\mathsf{lab}_{i,\mathbf{x}[i]}\}_{i\in[k]})$.

Fig. 6. OTP protocol

can be instantiated using commodity hardware and the associated costs and finally in Sect. 8.3, we discuss some potential applications of our construction.

8.1   Number of Lockboxes

We use lockboxes to implement the leaky batch-OT functionality and the input to this functionality is an encoding of the "real" input of the receiver. For encoding, we require linear binary ECC with a constant rate. More often than not, finding optimal binary ECC for specific input lengths k typically requires iterating over all possible alphabets in the domain. In our case, the problem of choosing optimal codes, is made worse by the fact that we don't necessarily require codes with optimal distance γ or the smallest codeword length n. Instead, we want a code that gives the smallest value of $2n\ell$, while ensuring that $\left(\frac{e^{(\epsilon/p-1)}}{(\epsilon/p)^{\epsilon/p}}\right)^{np} < \frac{1}{2^{O(\lambda)}}$, where $p = (\frac{1}{2})^\ell \cdot \frac{\ell!}{(2\ell-1)!!}$ and $\epsilon = \gamma/n$ (See Sect. 5.2 for details). To simplify this problem and to get an estimate of how many lockboxes are required, we pick a particular binary ECC with constant rate and find values of n, γ and ℓ that give the smallest value of $2n\ell$ withing this encoding scheme. In particular, we use Justesen codes [35].

Table 1. Lockboxes required for various input lengths with statistical security parameter $\lambda \geq 50$

Input Length (k)	Codeword Length (n)	(n', k', m, γ)	ℓ	Total LB $(2n\ell)$	LB/Bit $(2n\ell/k)$
192	496	(43, 32, 6, 12)	7	7224	37.625
256	752	(47, 32, 8, 16)	7	10528	41.125
560	1302	(93, 80, 7, 14)	7	18228	32.55
5000	14180	(709, 500, 10, 400)	4	113440	22.688
300000	735720	(24524, 20000, 15, 13080)	4	5885760	19.6192

Encoding with Justesen Codes. Justesen codes are derived as the code concatenation of a Reed-Solomon code and the Wozencraft ensemble. The encoding algorithm works as follows – the given binary input string of length k is divided into k' blocks of length m each. This new vector of length k' is encoded using the Reed Solomon code $(n', k', n' - k' + 1)$ over field $GF(2^m)$. Finally, the resulting n' blocks of length m each are encoded using Wozencraft ensemble. We use a particular Wozencraft ensemble [41], that yields a final codeword of length $2mn'$. The minimum distance γ of the resulting code is $\sum_{i \in [g]} i \cdot \binom{2m}{i}$, where g is the smallest integer such that $\sum_{i \in [g]} \binom{2m}{i} \leq n' - k' + 1$.

Estimating the Optimal no. of Lockboxes. Since, n' here can potentially take any value $< 2^m$ (and $m \in [1, k]$), a bruteforce approach to find optimal values even within Justesen code will result in an exponential search. To reduce the search space, we observe that for any given input length k and distance γ, it suffices to only look at the smallest admissible value of n'. Greater values of n' for the same k and γ yield worse security and larger values of $2n\ell$. We use this observation to deploy the following strategy – for any input length k, iterate over all possible values of $m \in [1, k]$, compute all corresponding admissible values of g, γ and set $n' = k' + \left(\sum_{i \in [g]} \binom{2m}{i}\right) - 1$ (this significantly reduces potential domain for n'). For each such combination of (m, n', γ), we calculate security for reasonable values of ℓ and find the combination of $(n', k', m, \gamma, \ell)$ that results in the fewest total number of lockboxes, while ensuring that the security is at least 2^{-50}.

We report the number of lockboxes required for some input lengths in Table 1. As expected, the number of lockboxes per input wire decreases as the number of inputs increase. By replacing Wozencraft ensemble with BCH codes [12], we can hope to get small improvements for larger input lengths; however, for smaller inputs, BCH codes are unlikely to help. Overall, due to the lack of efficient binary linear ECC, the number of required lockboxes are unlikely to be significantly better than the ones computed using Justesen codes. Our laconic OT-based construction offers some relief in this regard: for instance, if the length of digest output by the receiver is 256 bits, we require 10,528 total lockboxes for *any* input length.

8.2 Instantiating Lockboxes

To realize counter lockboxes from the widely-available device- and cloud-based hardware, some implementation considerations arise. In this section, we provide brief background on each candidate lockbox and the practical considerations involving their use.

Cloud-Based Backup Services. Apple's Cloud Key Vault was introduced in 2016 when Apple added functionality to encrypt and store user-controlled encryption keys within hardware security modules (HSM) to remove Apple's own ability to access them. Each iCloud account (registered email address) has access to a Cloud Key Vault record, which corresponds to a password-protected HSM entry which allows up to ten attempts[5] via the Secure Remote Password [4,5] (SRP) protocol. Notably, this requires one email address per lockbox, as Apple allocates a single Cloud Key Vault entry to each user account.

Similar to Apple's Cloud Key Vault, Google introduced HSM-based user-controlled encryption to protect backups even from insider threats [37]. Their system relies on the Titan [48] HSM hardware, and similarly implements a password-based attempt-limited authentication service which can naturally be viewed as a counter lockbox. Akin to Apple's Cloud Key Vault, Google allocates a single backup service instance per user account, and so each lockbox requires a registered Google account (email address) to be deployed. Both iCloud and Google accounts can be acquired for free, but acquiring multiple accounts can require evading anti-spam measures.

Signal, the secure messaging platform, offers users a backup method relying on user-controlled encryption inaccessible to Signal's servers. This service is called Secure Value Recovery, or SVR. SVR allows users to set a PIN, and gives them ten attempts to authenticate to an Intel SGX enclave to retrieve their backup data. As a secure enclave, SGX itself is capable of running one-time programs. However, to end users only a basic API is exposed which allows authentication attempts over a secure connection. Rather than email-based registration, Signal requires phone numbers, specifically to receive a confirmation SMS. Therefore, each SVR lockbox requires a phone number able to receive an SMS; such numbers cost $0.50 USD/month each at scale with a service like Twilio [49].

iOS Devices. Apple also offers the eponymous counter lockbox as hardware within modern iOS devices (smartphones and tablets) available since Fall 2020. This component emerged with the second-generation Secure Enclave Processor [3] (SEP) and was designed to prevent forensic attacks against the passcode

---

[5] In Sect. 2.4, we discuss generic techniques to convert a multiple-attempt (e.g. 10) lockbox into a single-attempt, including simply "burning" $n-1$ attempts of each n-attempt lockbox before transmitting their locations to the receiver.

attempt counter which moderates access to a device and its filesystem. Although there are few official documents, initial exploration seems to imply that iOS devices are able to support up to 1024 counter lockbox instances simultaneously. Since counter lockboxes are intended for use by iOS itself, third-party developers must interact with them directly on jailbroken devices. Finally, a note on monetary costs: currently, iPad air 4th generation can be purchased for about $300. Thus, the average cost of each lockbox can be estimated to be about $0.30 USD.

8.3   Applications

Given the cost of each lockbox and the notable expansion between input length and total lockboxes as seen in Table 1, at present the real-world applicability of our constructions is somewhat limited. However, compelling applications involving small input lengths are within reach: Bitcoin addresses are 160-bit hashes, which could be input into a delegated signature one-time program. Downsampled biometric measurements could be input to fuzzy matching algorithms, or passwords into client-side key derivations for user authentication. Compressed descriptions of aggregations could be input to an offline differentially-private database service to maintain privacy budgets. As lockbox availability grows, these domains will only expand.

Acknowledgements. The first, second and fourth authors were supported in part by NSF CNS-1814919, NSF CAREER 1942789 and Johns Hopkins University Catalyst award. The fourth author was additionally supported in part by AFOSR Award FA9550-19-1-0200 and the Office of Naval Research Grant N00014-19-1-2294. The first, third and fifth authors were supported by the National Science Foundation under awards CNS-1653110 and CNS-1801479 and by DARPA under Agreements No. HR00112020021 and Agreements No. HR001120C0084. The fifth author was additionally supported by a Google Security & Privacy Award. This work was done in part while the second author was a student at Johns Hopkins University and while the second and fourth authors were visiting University of California, Berkeley. Any opinions, findings and conclusions or recommendations expressed in this material are those of the author(s) and do not necessarily reflect the views of the United States Government or DARPA.

References

1. Alamati, N., Branco, P., Döttling, N., Garg, S., Hajiabadi, M., Pu, S.: Laconic private set intersection and applications. Cryptology ePrint Archive, Report 2021/728 (2021). https://eprint.iacr.org/2021/728
2. Almashaqbeh, G., et al.: Gage MPC: bypassing residual function leakage for non-interactive MPC. Proc. Priv. Enhanc. Technol. **2021**(4), 528–548 (2021)
3. Apple Inc., Secure Enclave. https://support.apple.com/guide/security/secure-enclave-sec59b0b31ff/web
4. Apple Inc., Escrow security for iCloud Keychain (2021). https://support.apple.com/guide/security/escrow-security-for-icloud-keychain-sec3e341e75d/web

5. Apple Inc., HomeKit communication security (2021). https://support.apple.com/guide/security/homekit-communication-security-sec3a881ccb1/web

6. ARM Holdings. Trusted Base System Architecture Documents. https://www.arm.com/technologies/trustzone-for-cortex-a/tee-reference-documentation. Subject to Non-Disclosure Agreement

7. Backes, M., Gerling, R.W., Gerling, S., Nürnberger, S., Schröder, D., Simkin, M.: WebTrust – a comprehensive authenticity and integrity framework for HTTP. In: Boureanu, I., Owesarski, P., Vaudenay, S. (eds.) ACNS 2014. LNCS, vol. 8479, pp. 401–418. Springer, Cham (2014). https://doi.org/10.1007/978-3-319-07536-5_24

8. Bellare, M., Hoang, V.T., Rogaway, P.: Adaptively secure garbling with applications to one-time programs and secure outsourcing. In: Wang, X., Sako, K. (eds.) ASIACRYPT 2012. LNCS, vol. 7658, pp. 134–153. Springer, Heidelberg (2012). https://doi.org/10.1007/978-3-642-34961-4_10

9. Benhamouda, F., Krawczyk, H., Rabin, T.: Robust non-interactive multiparty computation against constant-size collusion. In: Katz, J., Shacham, H. (eds.) CRYPTO 2017, Part I. LNCS, vol. 10401, pp. 391–419. Springer, Cham (2017). https://doi.org/10.1007/978-3-319-63688-7_13

10. Bhudia, A., O'Keeffe, D., Sgandurra, D., Hurley-Smith, D.: RansomClave: ransomware key management using SGX. In: The 16th International Conference on Availability, Reliability and Security (2021)

11. Bitansky, N., et al.: The hunting of the SNARK. J. Cryptol. **30**(4), 989–1066 (2017)

12. Bose, R.C., Ray-Chaudhuri, D.K.: On a class of error correcting binary group codes. Inf. Control **3**(1), 68–79 (1960)

13. Broadbent, A., Gutoski, G., Stebila, D.: Quantum one-time programs. In: Canetti, R., Garay, J.A. (eds.) CRYPTO 2013, Part II. LNCS, vol. 8043, pp. 344–360. Springer, Heidelberg (2013). https://doi.org/10.1007/978-3-642-40084-1_20

14. Van Bulck, J., et al.: Breaking virtual memory protection and the SGX ecosystem with foreshadow. IEEE Micro **39**(3), 66–74 (2019)

15. Chatterjee, R., Athayle, A., Akhawe, D., Juels, A., Ristenpart, T.: Password typos and how to correct them securely. In: S&P 2016. IEEE (2016)

16. Chaum, D., Pedersen, T.P.: Wallet databases with observers. In: Brickell, E.F. (ed.) CRYPTO 1992. LNCS, vol. 740, pp. 89–105. Springer, Heidelberg (1993). https://doi.org/10.1007/3-540-48071-4_7

17. Chen, Z.: Java Card Technology for Smart Cards: Architecture and Programmer's Guide. Addison-Wesley Longman Publishing Co., Inc (2000)

18. Cho, C., Döttling, N., Garg, S., Gupta, D., Miao, P., Polychroniadou, A.: Laconic oblivious transfer and its applications. In: Katz, J., Shacham, H. (eds.) CRYPTO 2017, Part II. LNCS, vol. 10402, pp. 33–65. Springer, Cham (2017). https://doi.org/10.1007/978-3-319-63715-0_2

19. Dall, F., et al.: CacheQuote: efficiently recovering long-term secrets of SGX EPID via cache attacks. IACR Trans. Cryptogr. Hardw. Embed. Syst. **2018**(2), 171–191 (2018)

20. Delgado-Mohatar, O., Sierra-Cámara, J.M., Anguiano, E.: Blockchain-based semi-autonomous ransomware. Future Gener. Comput. Syst. **112**, 589–603 (2020)

21. Döttling, N., Garg, S., Goyal, V., Malavolta, G.: Laconic conditional disclosure of secrets and applications. In: Zuckerman, D., (eds.) 60th FOCS, pages 661–685. IEEE Computer Society Press, November 2019

22. Dwork, C., McSherry, F., Nissim, K., Smith, A.: Calibrating noise to sensitivity in private data analysis. In: Theory of Cryptography Conference (2006)

23. Garg, S., Srinivasan, A.: Adaptively secure garbling with near optimal online complexity. In: Nielsen, J.B., Rijmen, V. (eds.) EUROCRYPT 2018, Part II. LNCS, vol. 10821, pp. 535–565. Springer, Cham (2018). https://doi.org/10.1007/978-3-319-78375-8_18

24. Goldreich, O., Ostrovsky, R.: Software protection and simulation on oblivious rams. J. ACM (JACM) **43**(3), 431–473 (1996)

25. Goldwasser, S., Kalai, Y.T., Rothblum, G.N. : Delegating computation: interactive proofs for muggles. In: Ladner, R.E., Dwork, C. (eds.) 40th ACM STOC, pp. 113–122. ACM Press, May 2008

26. Goldwasser, S., Kalai, Y.T., Rothblum, G.N.: One-time programs. In: Annual International Cryptology Conference, pp. 39–56 (2008)

27. Google. Google Tensor debuts on the new Pixel 6 this fall (2021). https://blog. google/products/pixel/google-tensor-debuts-new-pixel-6-fall/

28. Goyal, R., Goyal, V.: Overcoming cryptographic impossibility results using blockchains. In: Kalai, Y., Reyzin, L. (eds.) TCC 2017, Part I. LNCS, vol. 10677, pp. 529–561. Springer, Cham (2017). https://doi.org/10.1007/978-3-319-70500-2_18

29. Goyal, R., Vusirikala, S., Waters, B.: New constructions of hinting PRGs, OWFs with encryption, and more. In: Micciancio, D., Ristenpart, T. (eds.) CRYPTO 2020, Part I. LNCS, vol. 12170, pp. 527–558. Springer, Cham (2020). https://doi. org/10.1007/978-3-030-56784-2_18

30. Goyal, V., Ishai, Y., Sahai, A., Venkatesan, R., Wadia, A.: Founding cryptography on tamper-proof hardware tokens. In: Micciancio, D. (ed.) TCC 2010. LNCS, vol. 5978, pp. 308–326. Springer, Heidelberg (2010). https://doi.org/10.1007/978-3-642-11799-2_19

31. Harnik, D., Kilian, J., Naor, M., Reingold, O., Rosen, A.: On robust combiners for oblivious transfer and other primitives. In: Cramer, R. (ed.) EUROCRYPT 2005. LNCS, vol. 3494, pp. 96–113. Springer, Heidelberg (2005). https://doi.org/ 10.1007/11426639_6

32. Hazay, C., Lindell, Y.: Constructions of truly practical secure protocols using standardsmartcards. In: Ning, P., Syverson, P.F., Jha, S. (eds.) ACM CCS 2008, pp. 491–500. ACM Press, October 2008

33. Intel. Overview on signing and whitelisting for intel software guard extension (SGX) enclaves. https://www.intel.com/content/dam/develop/external/us/ en/documents/overview-signing-whitelisting-intel-sgx-enclaves-737361.pdf

34. Juels, A., Sudan, M.: A fuzzy vault scheme. Des. Codes Cryptogr. **38**(2), 237–257 (2006)

35. Justesen, J.: Class of constructive asymptotically good algebraic codes. IEEE Trans. Inf. Theory **18**(5), 652–656 (1972)

36. Kaptchuk, G., Green, M., Miers, I.: Giving state to the stateless: augmenting trustworthy computation with ledgers. In: NDSS 2019 (2019)

37. Kensinger, T.: Google and Android have your back, by protecting your backups, September 2018. https://security.googleblog.com/2018/10/google-and-android-have-your-back-by.html

38. Krassovsky, S., Cadden, G., et al.: Security of End-To-End Encrypted Backups (2021). https://scontent.whatsapp.net/v/t39.8562-34/241394876_ 546674233234181_8907137889500301879_n.pdf/WhatsApp_Security_Encrypted_ Backups_Whitepaper.pdf?ccb=1-5&_nc_sid=2fbf2a&_nc_ohc=4K040x7GheAAX_-4c-_&_nc_ht=scontent.whatsapp.net&oh=01_AVxDv1cRlVElvg0Fv89URSU_ XOQUupw70bDPw6o2w0LEWg&oe=6211F5FC

39. Krstić, I.: Behind the scenes with iOS security (2016). https://www.blackhat.com/docs/us-16/materials/us-16-Krstic.pdf
40. Lund, J.: December 2019 https://signal.org/blog/secure-value-recovery/. Accessed 2 May 2022
41. MacWilliams, F.J., Sloane, N.J.A.: The Theory of Error-Correcting Codes. North-Holland Pub. Co. (1977)
42. McKeen, F., et al.: Intel® software guard extensions (intel® sgx) support for dynamic memory management inside an enclave. In: HASP 2016. ACM (2016)
43. Meier, R., Przydatek, B., Wullschleger, J.: Robuster combiners for oblivious transfer. In: Vadhan, S.P. (ed.) TCC 2007. LNCS, vol. 4392, pp. 404–418. Springer, Heidelberg (2007). https://doi.org/10.1007/978-3-540-70936-7_22
44. Micali, S.: Computationally sound proofs. SIAM J. Comput. **30**(4), 1253–1298 (2000)
45. Murdock, K., Oswald, D.F., Garcia, F.D., Van Bulck, J., Gruss, D., Piessens, F.: Plundervolt: software-based fault injection attacks against intel SGX. In: S&P 2020. IEEE (2020)
46. Pinto, S., Santos, N.: Demystifying arm trustzone: a comprehensive survey. ACM Comput. Surv. (CSUR) **51**(6) (2019)
47. Rosulek, M., Roy, L.: Three halves make a whole? Beating the half-gates lower bound for garbled circuits. In: Malkin, T., Peikert, C. (eds.) CRYPTO 2021, Part I. LNCS, vol. 12825, pp. 94–124. Springer, Cham (2021). https://doi.org/10.1007/978-3-030-84242-0_5
48. Savagaonkar, U., Porter, N., Taha, N., Serebrin, B., Mueller, N.: Titan in depth: Security in plaintext (2017). https://cloud.google.com/blog/products/identity-security/titan-in-depth-security-in-plaintext
49. Twilio (2022). https://www.twilio.com/sms/pricing/us
50. Xu, Q.: ARM-software/tf-issues (2017). https://github.com/ARM-software/tf-issues/issues/534
51. Yao, A.C.-C.: How to generate and exchange secrets (extended abstract). In: 27th FOCS, pages 162–167. IEEE Computer Society Press, October 1986
52. yubico. YubiHSM 2. https://www.yubico.com/product/yubihsm-2/

Universal Reductions: Reductions Relative to Stateful Oracles

Benjamin Chan[1]([envelope]) [iD], Cody Freitag[1] [iD], and Rafael Pass[1,2]

[1] Cornell Tech, New York, USA
{byc,cfreitag,rafael}@cs.cornell.edu
[2] Tel-Aviv University, Tel Aviv-Yafo, Israel

Abstract. We define a framework for analyzing the security of cryptographic protocols that makes minimal assumptions about what a "realistic model of computation is". In particular, whereas classical models assume that the attacker is a (perhaps non-uniform) probabilistic polynomial-time algorithm, and more recent definitional approaches also consider quantum polynomial-time algorithms, we consider an approach that is more agnostic to what computational model is physically realizable.

Our notion of *universal reductions* models attackers as PPT algorithms having access to some arbitrary unbounded *stateful* Nature that cannot be rewound or restarted when queried multiple times. We also consider a more relaxed notion of *universal reductions w.r.t. time-evolving, k-window, Natures* that makes restrictions on Nature—roughly speaking, Nature's behavior may depend on number of messages it has received and the content of the last $k(\lambda)$-messages (but not on "older" messages).

We present both impossibility results and general feasibility results for our notions, indicating to what extent the extended Church-Turing hypotheses are needed for a well-founded theory of Cryptography.

1 Introduction

Modern Cryptography relies on the principle that cryptographic schemes are proven secure based on mathematically precise assumptions; these can be general—such as the existence of one-way functions—or specific—such as the hardness of factoring products of large primes. The security proof is a *reduction* that "transforms" any attacker A of a scheme (e.g., a pseudorandom generator) into an attacker A' that breaks the underlying assumption (e.g., inverts an alleged one-way function). More formally, cryptographic security of a single primitive or assumption is often defined as an *interactive game* (a.k.a. a *security game*) between a *challenger* C and an *adversary* A. C sends a random challenge (e.g. a product of two large primes) to A, who tries to respond in such a way—potentially over many rounds—to make the challenger accept (e.g. by sending the individual factors). The game is determined by the challenger C and the primitive is said to be secure if no "realistic" adversary can cause the challenger

© The Author(s), under exclusive license to Springer Nature Switzerland AG 2022
E. Kiltz and V. Vaikuntanathan (Eds.): TCC 2022, LNCS 13749, pp. 151–180, 2022.
https://doi.org/10.1007/978-3-031-22368-6_6

to accept with some specified probability. (In the sequel, we will abuse notation and often identify the security game simply by the challenger C.) A reduction R from a game with challenger C (i.e., a security game C) to one with challenger C' provides a way to use a successful adversary A in the game C to construct a successful adversary A' in the game C'. This study has been extremely successful, and during the past four decades many cryptographic tasks have been put under rigorous treatment and numerous constructions realizing these tasks have been proposed under a number of well-studied complexity-theoretic hardness assumptions.

In this paper, we revisit what it means to transform the alleged attacker A for the scheme into an attacker A' for the underlying assumption. In particular, the standard cryptographic treatment explicitly assumes that the attacker A is a (perhaps non-uniform) probabilistic polynomial-time (PPT) Turing machine. Thus, when using the scheme in the "real-world", the security proof is only meaningful if this model of the attacker *correctly captures the computational capabilities of a real-life attacker*—that is, the PPT model correctly captures all "real-life" computation that can be feasibly carried out by an attacker in our physical world. The *extended Church-Turing hypothesis* stipulates that this is the case:

The extended Church-Turing Hypothesis: *A probabilistic Turing machine can efficiently simulate any realistic model of computation.*

But whether this hypothesis holds is strictly speaking a religious, as opposed to scientific, belief.[1] Indeed, the advent of quantum computing directly challenges this hypothesis. Based on exciting developments in quantum computation, it is becoming increasingly clear that viewing an adversary simply as a polynomial-time Turing machine, or polynomial-size circuit, may not be so "realistic". Quantum computers have access to qubits that we believe cannot be described with classical bits or run by a classical, polynomial-sized circuit. Furthermore, by the no-cloning theorem [WZ82, Die82], quantum states cannot be copied or re-used, which is a common technique used by many classical security proofs. We remark that this impacts the security of protocols/primitives even for security games where the challenger C is purely classical (i.e., primitives implemented by a classical algorithm that the attacker interacts with using classical communication). In recent years, there has been a successful line of work that has focused on

---

[1] Without getting too deep into Philosophy, it seems reasonable to argue that the Extended Church-Turing Hypothesis does not pass Popper's falsifiability test [Pop05], as we do not have "shared ways of systematically determining" whether a probabilistic Turing machine cannot perform some task (as testified by the fact that the P v.s. NP problem is still open). As such, the statement of the hypothesis is no different from the classic example of "All men are mortal", which according to Popper's theory is not scientific as we do not have systematic procedures for deducing whether a person is immortal. This is in contrast to assumptions such as "Factoring products of random 1000-bit primes is hard for all physically realizable computation devices", as we do have a systematic way of determining whether some such device manages to complete the task—simply run it.

proving the security of cryptographic protocols against quantum adversaries (see e.g. [Sho94, Gro96, AC02, Wat09, BDF+11, Unr12, Zha12, ARU14, Unr16, Mah18, BS20] for examples of cryptographic attacks, constructions, and techniques in a quantum world). A vast set of new cryptographic techniques have been developed to address the idiosyncrasies of quantum computation and their impact on the security of systems. But, to deduce "real-life" security from such security proofs, we still need to rely on a quantum version of the extended Church-Turing hypothesis (stipulating that quantum polynomial-time algorithms/circuits can simulate all realistic models of computation).

This begs the question: could there be *even more powerful, or even just incomparable, realistic adversaries* beyond quantum polynomial-time adversaries? After all, a hundred years ago, modern computers did not exist, and quantum physics was in its infancy. Consequently, predicting the computational power of an adversary a hundred years into the future seems unreasonable. If the quantum extended Church-Turing hypothesis is wrong, because of the advent of a new type of computation, it would force yet another re-examination of cryptography.

In this work, instead of tailoring security reductions to specific classes of increasingly powerful adversaries, we ask:

> *Can we have a well-founded theory of Cryptography without making assumptions on the limits of "physically realizable models of computation"?*

Concretely, what if some human manages to (repeatedly) break the security of some cryptographic scheme. There is currently a heuristic leap of faith in our cryptography treatment that this human (and any physical phenomena they may be using) can be implemented in PPT/QPT. Can this leap of faith be avoided?

In particular, ideally, we would want a theory of cryptography without making any types of extended Church-Turing hypotheses, where the security of some scheme is *only* based on *falsifiable* assumptions of the type that some computational task cannot be solved by a "physically realizable computation".[2]

Towards this goal, we will focus our attention on *classical primitives* (i.e., security games with challengers C that are classical and where the attacker can communicate with C only by using classical communication), but consider attackers with unknown/unbounded computational capabilities. At first sight, doing to seems to inherently require information-theoretic security (and all the standard limitations thereof). But our approach will instead be to consider a *purely-reduction based framework*: Our framework will provide a way to reduce the security of a game with challenger C to one with a challenger C' without assuming anything about the adversary *other than the fact that it continually*

---

[2] For concreteness, and to simplify notation, we will model attackers as Turing machines so technically we are still relying on the (more reasonable) non-extended Church-Turing hypothesis. But we highlight that nothing in our treatment requires doing so and none of our results would change if we instead allowed any, even non-computable, attackers. See Sect. 3 for more discussion.

wins in C. Now, rather than proving the security of some primitive C w.r.t. PPT attackers based on assumptions of the form "C' cannot be broken by PPT attackers", we will view the reduction from C to C' as the main goal: the existence of such a reduction will then imply the statement *"Security of C with respect to any physically realizable attacker holds as long as security of C' holds with respect to any physically realizable attacker"*, without having to impose any restrictions on what the class of "physically realizable attackers" actually is (as long as they only communicate with the challenger C using classical communication). We note that this reduction-based approach follows intuitions similar to those by Rogaway in his influential "formalizing human ignorance" paper [Rog06], where a purely reduction-based approach is also advocated for (but for a different reason, and where the standard notion of a reduction is employed).

Let us emphasize that whereas our framework is not imposing any upper bounds on the class of feasible computation (hence the name "universal"), we will be assuming a lower bound: in accordance with the standard literature, we will use PPT as a *lower bound* on what can be feasibly done by an attacker.[3] (In other words, polynomial-time computations will be considered realistically feasible, today and forever in the future.) Additionally, we will here focus our attention only on cryptographic primitives where the honest players are standard PPT machines (as opposed to e.g. quantum).

1.1 Universal Reductions in a Nut-shell

Towards defining our reduction-based notion of security, we need to start off by specifying the notion of an attacker we consider. An *augmented adversary* (A, Nat) consists of a uniform PPT interactive Turing machine (ITM) A, known as the *attacker*, and a *stateful*, potentially unbounded ITM Nat, known as the *Nature*. We think of A as the part of the augmented adversary that only uses "standard" computational resources, whereas Nat is a shared resource in the world that may have "magical" computational resources. The stateful nature of Nat is what distinguishes our model from more standard models of "black-box" security used in cryptography. We think of A as some real-life attacker (using today's readily available computing infrastructure) that can interact with a physical Nature Nat. Furthermore, A's interactions with Nature may in turn alter Nature. For instance, if Nat can capture quantum physical phenomena, then by the no-cloning theorem [WZ82, Die82], any type of measurements of Nat may alter it in ways that cannot be reversed (without losing information). Thus, statefulness is key for capturing this.

Roughly speaking, we say that there is a *universal reduction* from a security games C to a game C' if for every PPT A, there exists a "transformed" PPT attacker A' such that for every Nature Nat, if the augmented adversary (A, Nat)

---

[3] This model clearly oversimplifies as, say, n^{100} computation is not actually feasible. But we start off with a standard asymptotic treatment to get a model that is easy to work with. In practice, a more concrete treatment is desirable, but we leave this for future work.

wins in the security game C, then the augmented adversary (A', Nat) wins in the security game C'. In other words, the new transformed attacker A' needs to make use of the same Nature Nat as A.[4] (As the reader may notice, this notion captures an "existential" as opposed to a "constructive" notion of a reduction— that is, we are only required to show that a transformed attacker A' *exists*, as opposed to constructively providing it using an efficient transformation from A; we will also discuss constructive notions of reductions below.) We emphasize that A' may only communicate with Nat; it may not rewind, restart, or see any of the implementation details of Nat. In essence, we require A' to win in C' by making use of Nature, much like the original attacker A did, and taking into account that its interaction with the cosmos may alter it. The reasons we model A and A' as PPT, is that we consider PPT as a *lower bound* on what is currently feasible, and assume that this lower bound is valid not only today but also in the future (i.e., we will be able to only do more computation in the future). Thus we can write security proofs today that hold regardless of how powerful the universe ends up being (i.e. even if the extended Church-Turing hypothesis turns out to be true). All non-PPT computation can be thought of as being inside Nat.

Comparison with Relativized Reductions and UC Security. Before proceeding to further formalizing this notion, let us briefly point out some technical similarities and differences with the notion of a *relativized reduction* (see e.g., [IR95]); roughly speaking, a relativized reduction, and the related notion of a black-box reduction, is a reduction that works even if the attacker has access to some arbitrary (perhaps non-efficiently computable) function (a.k.a. the "oracle"). The main difference between the notion of a universal reduction and that of relativized reductions is that universal reductions can be viewed as reductions that relativize also with respect to an *interactive, stateful* oracle, whereas relativized reductions are only required to work in the presence of a *non-interactive, stateless*, oracle. As we explained above, considering stateful, interactive, Natures is a crucial aspect of our definition; as we shall see shortly, even formalizing how to deal with stateful oracles/Natures will be non-trivial.

We highlight that the idea to consider cryptographic protocols in the presence of an external stateful entity is also not entirely new: the notion of Universally Composable (UC) security [Can01] does exactly this but in a different context— more specifically, in the context of simulation as opposed to in the context of reductions; see Sect. 1.6 for more discussion on the relationship between universal reductions and UC.

---

[4] We refer to such reductions as "universal" because they are agnostic to the computational resources of an attacker (and thus can be "universally" applied, independent of the attacker's computational power). Additionally, on a technical level, and as we discuss in more detail shortly, considering security relative to a stateful entity is related to how security is defined in the framework for Universal Composability of Canetti [Can01].

1.2 Formalizing Universal Reductions

To formalize the notion of a universal reduction we first need to define what it means for (A, Nat) to win in some security game C. The standard notion of winning simply requires the attacker to succeed in convincing C *once* with some probability p. For us, since we consider stateful Natures, this will be too weak. A stateful Nature Nat may decide to be helpful in winning with C just once, and then never again, and such a Nature may not be very helpful in breaking some underlying assumption (at least not repeatedly). In the standard models of reductions, this is not a problem since the attacker can simply be restarted, but this is not allowed in our setting. Consequently, to get a meaningful notion of security, we will restrict our attention to (ruling out) attackers that *repeatedly*, or *"robustly"*, win in the security game, no matter what other communications are taking place with the cosmos. In more detail, we consider any history of interaction ρ that Nat may have seen, where an interaction prefix ρ consists of the messages Nature has received and the random coins it may have tossed. We then require (A, Nat) to succeed in winning for C even if (A, Nat) is fed any such prefix ρ. We denote such an interaction, where entities are provided the security parameter 1^λ, as $\langle C \leftrightarrow A \leftrightarrow \mathsf{Nat}(\rho) \rangle (1^\lambda)$.

In other words, we are considering an attacker A that is interacting with some physical stateful Nature Nat with unknown computational capabilities, but also consider the possibility that there are others in the world (captured by the prefix ρ) that have interacted with Nature in ways that are unknown to the attacker. Still, the attacker needs to succeed in breaking C *no matter what those other prior communications are* (i.e. given any transcript of interactions that previously took place). In fact, this transcript may be of any length, that is, more than just polynomial in λ (noting that Nat may have more than polynomially many interactions in the past).[5]

Definition 1 (Robustly Winning Security Game; Informal). *Let C be a challenger in a security game. We say that an augmented adversary (A, Nat) has robust advantage $a(\cdot)$ in C if, for every prefix view ρ, security parameter $\lambda \in \mathbb{N}$, it holds that C outputs 1 with probability at least $a(\lambda)$ in the interaction $\langle C \leftrightarrow A \leftrightarrow \mathsf{Nat}(\rho) \rangle (1^\lambda)$.*

Given this notion of robust winning, we can now capture the above-mentioned notion of a universal reduction.

Definition 2 (Universal Reduction; Informal). *Let C and C' be security games. We say that there is a ϵ-universal reduction from C to C' if for every PPT A, there exists some PPT A', such that for every Nat, if the augmented adversary (A, Nat) has robust advantage $a(\cdot)$ in C, then (A', Nat) has robust advantage $\epsilon'(\cdot)$ in C' where $\epsilon'(\lambda) = \epsilon(\lambda, a(\lambda))$.*

---

[5] Nevertheless, we note that all our results also hold if restricting the length of ρ to be polynomial.

The function ϵ here quantifies the security degradation of the reduction. Let us briefly mention that one may also consider an *a priori* weaker looking notion of a "win-once" universal reduction, that only requires the *transformed* attacker (A', Nat) to have *non-robust* advantage $\epsilon'(\cdot)$ in C'; that is, (A', Nat) is only required to win once in C' as opposed to robustly/repeatedly (while the original attacker (A, Nat) still needs to have robust advantage). As it turns out, this weaker notion is equivalent to the one provided in Definition 2; see Lemma 1 for more details. We also note that one may consider alternative, seemingly weaker, variants of robustness (e.g., that the attacker only wins an inverse polynomial fraction of the time) but again such a notion turns out to be equivalent (up to a difference in parameters); see the full version [CFP22] of this paper for more details.

Black-Box Reductions and Dummy Adversaries. As mentioned above, the notion of a universal reduction is "existential" as opposed to a "constructive": We do not actually require an efficient transformation taking attackers A to attackers A'; rather, we just need to show that for every attacker A, the attacker A' *exists*. One could also consider an *a-priori* stronger notion of a *universal black-box reduction* where the transformed attacker A' is defined as $A' = R^A$, where R is fixed PPT (that works for any attacker A). As it turns out, this notion is (again) equivalent to the (existential) notion of a universal reduction provided in Definition 2. The reason for this is that to prove the existence of a universal reduction, and actually also a universal black-box reduction, it suffices to show that the reduction applies just to a so-called "dummy" adversary A_{dummy} that essentially just forwards messages between C and Nat; this, intuitively, follows from the fact that we can always push all the work of a prospective attacker A into Nat (more formally, considering a new Nature Nat' that combines Nat and A). We note that a similar phenomena happens for the notion of UC security [Can01], and we are borrowing the term of a "dummy" adversary from there.

Lemma 1 (Dummy Lemma; Informal). *Let C and C' be security games. Assume that there exists some ϵ and some PPT R_{dummy} such that for every Nat, if the augmented adversary A_{dummy} has robust advantage $a(\cdot)$ in C, then $(R_{\mathsf{dummy}}, \mathsf{Nat})$ has robust advantage $\epsilon'(\cdot)$ in C' where $\epsilon'(\lambda) = \epsilon(\lambda, a(\lambda))$. Then, there exists an ϵ-universal black-box reduction from C to C'.*

We highlight that whereas the actual proof of Lemma 1 indeed follows the above intuition, the formalization is quite subtle and quite different from the proof of the dummy lemma in the UC framework—the key obstacle is dealing with the fact that the attacker needs to win robustly.

Note that as a consequence of Lemma 1, we have that to prove the existence of a universal reduction, we may without loss of generality assume that $A = A_{\mathsf{dummy}}$ (i.e., in essence that Nat is directly breaking C), and thus proving the existence of a universal reduction amounts to showing the existence of a PPT "filter" $A' = R_{\mathsf{dummy}}$ between C' and Nat.

Composition. We additionally note that the notion of a universal reduction composes. Namely, if hardness of C_1 can be based on the hardness of C_2, and hardness of C_2 can be based on the hardness of C_3, then hardness of C_1 can be based on hardness of C_3.

Theorem 1 (Composition Theorem; Informal). *Let C_1, C_2, C_3 be security games. Suppose there exists an ϵ_1-universal reduction from C_2 to C_1, and an ϵ_2-universal reduction from C_3 to C_2. Then, there exists an ϵ^*-universal reduction from C_3 to C_1 where $\epsilon^*(\lambda, a) = \epsilon_1(\lambda, \epsilon_2(\lambda, a))$.*

The proof of the composition theorem essentially follows directly from the definition of a universal reduction.

1.3   On the Feasibility of Universal Reductions

We turn to studying the feasibility of universal reductions.

Universal Reductions from Single-Shot, Straightline, Black-Box Reductions. We observe that any *straight-line* black-box reduction between C and C' that only invokes the attacker *once* is also a universal reduction. This should not be a surprise since the stateful nature of the attacker in our model never becomes an issue if the reduction only invokes the attacker once. Nevertheless, our model formally demonstrates why such simple types of reductions are advantageous from a (qualitative) security point of view.

Theorem 2 (Universal Reductions from Single-shot Straightline Black-box Reductions; Informal). *Let C and C' be security games. Suppose there exists an ϵ-straightline black-box reduction from C to C' that interacts with the adversary once. Then there exists an ϵ-universal reduction from C to C'.*

Fortunately, many well-known reductions in cryptography fall into this class of reductions: PRG length extension, the GGM construction of PRFs from PRGs [GGM86], IND-CPA secure encryption from PRFs, Naor's bit commitments from PRGs [Nao91], and Lamport's one-time signatures from OWFs [Lam79]. We note that for Lamport's construction, this is straightforward to see. For the rest of the proofs, we rely on a uniform security analysis for a hybrid argument, which for example is provided in [Gol07] for PRG length extension. For the convenience of the reader, we provide brief sketches for the constructions and proofs for all of these primitives in the full version [CFP22] of this paper .

Combining these classical results with Theorem 2, we thus directly get the following corollaries (formally stated in the full paper [CFP22]):

Corollary 1 (PRG length extension; Informal). *Let m be a polynomial and G be an $\lambda + 1$-bit stretch PRG. There exists a $m(\lambda)$-bit stretch PRG G_m and an ϵ-universal reduction from the PRG security of G_m to the PRG security of G for $\epsilon(\lambda, a) = 1/2 + \delta/m(\lambda)$, where $\delta = a - 1/2$.*

Corollary 2 (PRF from PRGs; Informal). *Let G be any PRG. There exists a PRF F and an ϵ-universal reduction from the PRF security of F to the PRG security of G for $\epsilon(\lambda, a) = 1/2 + \delta/\mathrm{poly}(\lambda)$, where $\delta = a - 1/2$.*

Corollary 3 (IND-CPA secure private-key encryption from PRGs; Informal). *Let G be any PRG. There exists a private-key encryption scheme and an ϵ-universal reduction from the IND-CPA security of the encryption scheme to the PRG security of G for $\epsilon(\lambda, a) = 1/2 + \delta/2 - \mu(\lambda)$ for a negligible function μ, where $\delta = a - 1/2$.*

Corollary 4 (Commitment schemes from PRGs; Informal). *Let G be any PRG. There exists a statistically binding commitment scheme and an ϵ-universal reduction from the hiding of the commitment scheme to the PRG security of G for $\epsilon(\lambda, a) = 1/2 + \delta/2$, where $\delta = a - 1/2$.*

Corollary 5 (One-time Signatures from OWFs; Informal). *Let f be any OWF. There exists a signature scheme and an ϵ-universal reduction from the one-time security of the signature scheme to the OWF security of f for $\epsilon(\lambda, a) = a/(2\lambda)$.*

Universal Reductions from New Single-Shot Straightline Reductions. Often times, security reductions used in the literature do invoke the attacker multiple times, and it may not be clear how such reductions can be translated to work in the setting of universal reductions. We first show that sometimes famous reductions in the literature that require invoking the attacker multiple times can be made single-shot straightline. In particular, we show that the GMW protocol [GMW91] for graph 3-coloring is witness indistinguishable (WI) [FS90] based on a universal reduction to a commitment scheme (and hence PRGs) with a new proof; the standard proof requires rewinding the attacker and would thus not be applicable in our setting. (This proof may be interesting in its own right; as far as we know, the only proof of WI security of GMW with a straight-line reduction is the work of Hofheinz [Hof11] that shows WI security of GMW when the underlying commitment satisfies a notion of selective-opening security. As far as we know, it was an open problem to present a straight-line reduction based just on standard security; this is what we do.)

Theorem 3 (Witness Indistinguishability from PRGs; Informal). *Let G be any PRG. For every language in NP, there exists an interactive proof system (P, V) and an ϵ-universal reduction from the WI of (P, V) to the PRG security of G for $\epsilon(\lambda, a) = 1/2 + \delta/\mathrm{poly}(\lambda)$, where $\delta = a - 1/2$.*

Beyond Single-Shot Straightline Reductions. While Theorem 3 provides some initial hope that more reductions in the literature can be made single-shot straightline, there are other classic reductions that we do not know how to make single-shot. In fact, going one step further, we next show that some classic results in the literature cannot be established with respect to universal reductions.

One of our main results shows that Yao's classic result on hardness amplification of any weak one-way functions via direct product [Yao82] cannot be proven with a universal reduction. In fact, we show that hardness of any arbitrary "black-box" one-way function cannot be amplified essentially *at all* using a n-fold direct product. Given a function f, let $f^{(n)}$ denote the n-fold direct product of f:

Theorem 4 (Impossibility of Hardness Amplification; Informal). *Consider some polynomial n, and some function ϵ. Suppose there is an ϵ-universal black-box reduction from the OWF security of $f^{(n)}$ to the OWF security of f that uses only black-box access of f, and that works for any function f. Then, there exists a negligible function μ such that $\epsilon(\lambda, a) \leq a + \mu(\lambda)$.*

Note that there is a trivial reduction that embeds the challenge $f(x)$ a single time into a random location of the output of $f^{(n)}$ that has advantage $\epsilon(\lambda, a) = a$. The above theorem says that no universal reduction can do noticeably better than this trivial reduction, even if considering attackers that succeed with some fixed constant probability, say $\frac{1}{2}$.[6]

To give some intuition behind the proof of Theorem 4, let us recall on a very high-level how Yao's original proof works: given as input y, the reduction embeds y into a random "position" i—letting $y_i = y$, generates random pre-images x_j for $j \neq i$, and lets $y_j = f(x)$, $\vec{y} = y_1 y_2 \ldots$ and then runs $A(\vec{y})$. If A fails, then we repeat the process (a polynomial number of times), again embedding y into a new random position i. Note that this reduction is thus repeatedly running A on *correlated* inputs—the inputs all contain the same string y (but except for that y, they are independent). An augmented adversary could notice these correlations and may stop working in case it sees correlations of this form (i.e., a substring y that is repeated from a previous query). Note that such an attacker still robustly wins in the security game: the probability that a fresh input from the challenger coincides with any previously seen strings is negligible.[7] Now, an arbitrary reduction may not necessarily work in the same way as Yao's reduction. However, at a high level, we show that if the reduction works for *any* function f (and only uses the function as a black-box), then the reduction has to ask A on inputs that are correlated, and thus we can still use a similar type of attacker.

---

[6] We emphasize that Theorem 4 is ruling out also so-called "parameter-aware" black-box reductions [BBF13], where the reduction may depend on the success probability a of the attacker; note that Yao's original reduction is parameter dependent—more specifically, the number of repetitions is required to be superlinear in the adversary's success probability, and as shown in [LTW05] a dependency on the attackers success probability is inherent for black-box reductions. Theorem 4 rules out also such parameter-aware universal reductions and indeed rules out universal reductions that increase the success probability of the adversary even if assuming that the original attackers success probability is, say, $\frac{1}{2}$.

[7] There is a small subtlety here. Robustness is defined with respect to all previous transcripts, even exponentially long ones, so naively implementing this approach will not work since eventually we can include all possible strings y in the transcripts. Rather, the way we formalize this argument is to consider a Nat that only has "polynomial memory" and checks for repeated strings y in the most recent part of the transcript it is fed.

We additionally show that the universal aspect of Theorem 4 (i.e., that it works for *any* function f) is inherent. If the function f is *rerandomizable* (see the full paper for a formal definition), then we can show a universal reduction for hardness amplification of f—in essence, we show that Yao's reduction directly works. At first sight, this may seem surprising: As mentioned above, Yao's reduction does invoke the attacker multiple time, and does so on correlated inputs (and as discussed above, this correlation lead to problems). Rerandomizability helps overcome this issue and enables the reduction to always feed Nat messages that are independent and have the same distribution.

For our next result, we show that the Goldreich-Levin theorem [GL89] for constructing a OWF with a hardcore predicate from any OWF cannot be turned into a universal reduction, again as long as the underlying OWF is only accessed in a black-box way. For an underlying function g, the Goldreich-Levin theorem shows that the inner product function is hardcore for the "randomized" function $\hat{g}(x,r) = (g(x),r)$. Namely, $\langle x,r \rangle$ cannot be predicted given $(g(x),r)$ where $|x| = |r|$. We extend our impossibility to any predicate h for any length of randomness r (even no randomness).

Theorem 5 (Impossibility of a Goldreich-Levin Theorem; Informal).
Consider some function ϵ and some efficiently computable predicate h. Suppose there is an ϵ-universal black-box reduction from the security of the hardcore predicate h w.r.t. $\hat{g}(x,r) = (g(x),r)$ to the OWF security of g that uses only black-box access to g and that works for function g. Then, there is a negligible function μ such that $\epsilon(\lambda, a) \leq \mu(\lambda)$ for all $a \leq 0.99$.

The proof relies on similar intuitions to the hardness amplifications result.[8] The above theorem gives an indication of why it may be hard to come up with a universal reduction from PRGs to OWFs as known constructions of PRGs from OWFs rely on the Goldreich-Levin theorem. We leave open the question of whether there exists some alternative way to universally reduce PRGs to OWFs.

Concluding, while we can write nice universal reductions in some settings, we also have some pretty severe impossibility results. To overcome these impossibility results, we additionally consider more relaxed—yet, in our eyes, natural—variants of universal reductions.

1.4 Restricted Classes of Natures

While it is natural to assume that an attacker can affect Nature/the Cosmos, it also seems reasonable (at least in some contexts) to make additional assumption on the class of Natures. In particular, we will consider Natures that act *independently of the content of interactions they had "far back" in the past*. Roughly

---

[8] Again, we highlight that Theorem 5 rules out also "parameter-aware" reductions that depend on the success probability of the attacker—in fact, it rules out also reductions that only work if the underlying attacker's success probability is 0.99. (As noted in [BBF13], Goldreich-Levin's standard reduction is parameter-aware, and this is inherent as shown in [LTW05].).

speaking, we allow Nature to change over time, and we will allow Nature to be stateful within a single, or a bounded number of, sessions but assume that the actual content of messages received too farin the past (that is, many messages ago) does not significantly affect the behavior of Nature.

In more detail, choose any polynomial function $k(\cdot)$, and consider those natures whose responses depend only on (a) the *number of queries* it has received in the past, (b) the *last $k(\lambda)$ messages* that it received, and (c) the randomness that it used to respond to those $k(\lambda)$ messages. We call a nature that satisfies these conditions a *time-evolving k-window nature*. We formalize this by requiring that the output of Nature given any two prefixes ρ and ρ' of the *same length* that also share the last $k(\lambda)$ messages and coins, it must be that $\mathsf{Nat}(\rho)$ behaves identically (or ϵ-close to) $\mathsf{Nat}(\rho')$. (The same-length requirement is what allows Nature to evolve over time).

Definition 3 (Time-Evolving k-Window Natures). *Let $k(\cdot)$ be a polynomial function. A Nature machine Nat is said to be a k-window Nature if there exists a negligible function μ s.t. for all machines C, $\lambda \in \mathbb{N}$, and interaction prefixes ρ, ρ', ρ'', where $\|\rho\| = \|\rho'\|$ and $\|\rho''\| = k(\lambda)$, it holds that*

$$\Delta\left(\langle C \leftrightarrow \mathsf{Nat}(\rho \circ \rho'')\rangle(1^\lambda), \langle C \leftrightarrow \mathsf{Nat}(\rho' \circ \rho'')\rangle(1^\lambda)\right) \leq \mu(\lambda).$$

where $\langle C \leftrightarrow S\rangle(1^\lambda)$ denotes the output of C in an interaction with a machine S, Δ denotes statistical distance, $\|\rho\|$ denotes the number of messages contained within ρ, and $\rho \circ \rho''$ denotes prefix concatenation.

Observe that by sending to Nature a sequence of $k(\lambda)$ "dummy messages" $\perp$, we can (roughly speaking) reset the state of a time-evolving k-window Nature, by making it so that its behavior only depends on those dummy messages (and corresponding coins) and the number of messages it received in the past—regardless of the state that Nature started in before receiving those dummy messages. In other words, we can think of an augmented adversary (A, Nat) where Nat is time-evolving k-window (when called repeatedly, each time utilizing the above resetting procedure) as a sequence of attackers $A_1, A_2, \ldots$ such that (1) each individual attacker A_i succeeds in the security game, but (2) the way it succeeds may be different, and (3) the security reduction cannot restart the attacker but may "move on" to the next attacker in the sequence.

As our main result for time-evolving k-window Natures, we show that any *non-adaptive*, straight-line black-box classical reduction can be transformed into a universal reduction, when restricting to time-evolving k-window Natures. In more detail, we refer to a straight-line black-box reduction R as non-adaptive if R interacts with the challenger C and attacker A according to the following pattern:

- R starts by interacting with C for any number of rounds of its choice; at some point it decides that it wants to start communicating with the attacker A.
- At this point, R selects m different PPT machines $M_1, M_2, \ldots, M_m$.

– For each $i \in [m]$, we let M_i communicate (straight-line) with a fresh instance of A, and let a_i denote the output of M_i at the end of the interaction.
– Finally, R gets back the answers $a_1, \ldots, a_m$ and gets to continue interacting with C.

We show:

Theorem 6 (Universal Reductions from Non-adaptive Reductions; Informal). *Let C, C' be challengers. If there exists a non-adaptive straight-line black-box reduction from C to C', then for any polynomial $k(\cdot)$, there exists a universal reduction from C to C' w.r.t. time-evolving k-window Natures.*

At a very high level, the idea behind the proof of Theorem 6 is the following. Recall that (roughly speaking) an augmented adversary, with a time-evolving k-window Nature, can be treated as a sequence of attackers $A_1, A_2, \ldots$ that is fixed ahead of time and utilized in order. Such a sequence of attackers can essentially be turned into a "standard" fully restartable attacker by, at each invocation, choosing a random attacker A_i out of the sequence of attackers. Of course, in a real execution we are forced to utilize $A_1, A_2, \ldots$ in sequence and in order. Fortunately, for any non-adaptive reduction, we can emulate (with inverse polynomial statistical gap) this standard randomized restartable attacker by *permuting* the order of the queries of the reduction, and inserting these queries into a sufficiently long bogus interaction. Note that we here inherently rely on the fact the a time-evolving k-window Nature can be reset so that the last k messages no longer affects its state, so that its behavior depends on only the length of the prefix of messages it receives.

We remark that many (but not all) of the classical reductions in the cryptographic literature are of the non-adaptive type. In particular, these include reductions such as those in Yao's hardness amplification [Yao82] and the Goldreich-Levin Theorem [GL89] (which we proved could not be shown using a "plain" universal reduction). Perhaps surprisingly, our results therefore imply that we can achieve hardness amplification or hard-core bits for attackers that change their behavior across queries (albeit in this limited way).

k-Window Natures. We finally turn our attention to the more restrictive class of simply *k-window Natures* (i.e., not time-evolving), that are identically defined except that we quantify over any two prefixes ρ and ρ' (with the same last $k(\lambda)$ messages and coins), and not just those of equal length. We observe that straight-line black-box reductions, even those that are *adaptive*, that only sequentially invoke the attacker in multiple sessions, directly imply universal reductions w.r.t. k-window Natures; this essentially follows directly from the definition (by using a standard hybrid argument), and by the observation that sending such a Nature k dummy messages resets it to a default state (from which is acts indistinguishably):

Theorem 7 (Universal Reductions from Adaptive Reductions; Informal). *Let C, C' be challengers. If there exists a (possibly adaptive) sequential straight-line black-box reduction from C to C', then for any polynomial $k(\cdot)$, there exists a universal reduction from C to C' w.r.t. k-window Natures.*

1.5   Universal Reductions Imply Standard Reductions

As a sanity check, we finally observe that the existence of a universal reduction from C to C', even one that is only w.r.t. k-window Natures (where $k(\cdot)$ is large enough to bound the number of rounds of interaction with C), implies the existence of a reduction for classic models of attackers such as PPT, non-uniform PPT, quantum polynomial time (QPT), and QPT with non-uniform quantum advice (which we refer to as non-uniform QPT). This follows by noticing that all these models of computations can be captured by a k-window Nature Nat, when used to win a k-round security game C. For the case of PPT, non-uniform PPT, and (uniform) QPT, this is trivial. For non-uniform QPT, it is a bit more problematic since a non-uniform QPT algorithm may make some measurement that ruins the non-uniform advice in a way that makes the algorithm non-restartable. But this issue can be resolved by, for every bound $b(\cdot)$ on the number of restarts, considering a Nat that contains $b(\lambda)$ copies of the non-uniform quantum advice. The resulting attacker (A', Nat) that breaks C' will then still be non-uniform QPT (albeit with longer non-uniform advice than the original attacker breaking C).

Theorem 8 (Classical Reductions from Universal Reductions; Informal). *Let C and C' be security games, and let $k(\cdot)$ be a polynomial function that upper bounds the number of rounds in any interaction with C. Assume there exists a ϵ-universal reduction from C to C' w.r.t. (k, μ)-window Natures, for an arbitrary choice of μ. Then there exists a ϵ-reduction from C to C' w.r.t. PPT, non-uniform PPT, QPT, and non-uniform QPT attackers.*

A Note on Post-quantum Security. Note that Theorem 8 shows that if you can base the security of some (classical) security game C on the security of C' using a universal reduction (even with respect to just k-window Natures), then it implies resilience of C with respect to quantum attackers if assuming that C' is secure with respect to quantum attackers.

Let us highlight, however, that this result only holds true to security games C that themselves are classical. For instance if C is the security game of a PRF and C' is that of a PRG, then we only get quantum security of the PRF with respect to attackers that can get evaluations of the PRF on classical inputs. (As such, the combination of Corollary 2 and Theorem 8 does not subsume the results of Zhandry [Zha12] showing post-quantum PRF security of the GGM construction [GGM86] since Zhandry notably allows the attacker to make quantum queries to the PRF.). In other words, our framework currently only consider primitives where the *honest* players are classical. (Of course, we could extend our model to also deal with quantum security games but we believe it is a more pressing issue to get a "future-proof" notion of security w.r.t., cryptographic primitive and protocols that are run by honest players on classical computers).

1.6   Conclusions, Related and Future Work

Interpreting our Results. Our results demonstrate both limitations and feasibility of universal reductions—that is, the feasibility of a foundation for cryptographic security without making extended Church-Turing type assumptions about the class of physically-realistic computations. This paper is only a first step—we have not done an extensive survey of all the reductions in the literature, and we have not investigated all primitives out there; notably, we have focused only on the most basic primitives/reductions. We leave an exploration of more advanced primitives, such as zero-knowledge proofs and secure computation for future work.

Taken together, our result provide a new qualitative understanding of how different types of restrictions on black-box reductions result in security w.r.t. stronger classes of attacker. In particular, when restricting our attention to straight-line black-box reductions: (1) reductions that only invoke the attacker once, yield the strongest form of "plain" universal reduction, (2) reductions that are non-adaptive yield universal reductions w.r.t. time-evolving k-window Natures, and (3) adaptive ones yield universal reductions w.r.t. k-window Natures, for any choice of polynomial $k(\cdot)$.

So given our three different notions of security (which we have shown all imply standard notions of security), which one should we aim to achieve? Obviously the strongest form of plain universal reduction is the most desirable as it allows us to argue security while making only minimal "religious" assumptions about the class of physically-feasible computation. Our results demonstrate that indeed this notion is achievable for many constructions of interest (e.g., for primitives proven secure using straight-line black-box reduction that call the attacker once, or for some cases even multiple times when the queries are independent). Our impossibility results, however, also demonstrate important limitations, showing that in some situations, stronger types of "religious" assumptions about the class of feasible computation are required. The class of time-evolving k-window Natures seems like a reasonable midpoint between expressivity of the theory and the assumptions made on the class of physically-feasible computation.

More Justification for Time-Evolving k-Window Natures. Let us briefly comment on the recent and independent of work of Bitansky, Brakerski, and Kalai ([BBK22]), who study the quantum security of non-interactive reductions. Similar to us, they propose a framework to deal with stateful attackers, and show that non-adaptive reductions (with a polynomial solution space, including decisional assumptions) imply post-quantum security with a *uniform* reduction. In more detail, [BBK22] leverages the main result of Chiesa et al. [CMSZ21] that shows how to effectively "rewind" quantum attackers for a restricted class of protocols so that they effectively become time-evolving but otherwise stateless (or rather, bounded memory)— [BBK22] refer to such attackers as persistent solvers. Next, [BBK22] rely on a proof that is very similar to the proof of our Theorem 6 to show that non-adaptive black-box straight-line reductions can be applied to such attackers.

Note that our Theorem 8 shows that universal reduction w.r.t. not only time-evolving k-window, but also simply k-window Natures (which by Theorem 7 are implied by also adaptive straight-line black-box reductions) imply quantum security but it requires using a *non-uniform* reduction. By relying on the results of [CMSZ21], [BBK22] effectively show that universal reductions w.r.t. time-evolving k-window Natures have the advantage that the reduction for quantum security—for *specific* security games—becomes fully uniform. Consequently, we take the works of [CMSZ21, BBK22] as further evidence that restricting attention to universal reductions w.r.t. time-evolving k-window Natures is meaningful.

Comparison to Universal Composition (UC). Let us highlight that some of the intuition behind our definition take inspiration from the framework for Universal Composability (UC) by Canetti [Can01]. In particular, a simulator in the UC framework needs to interact with the attacker in a black-box straight line fashion in the presence of any environment, without the power of rewinding or restarting the environment. Clearly, there are many similarities between the notion of an environment and our notion of Nature. As such, one may be tempted to hope that UC protocols automatically have universal reductions. This intuition is misleading (as demonstrated e.g., by our Theorem 4). The reason for this is that whereas the simulator in the UC framework is required to be straight-line (and the attacker/environment is allowed to be fully stateful), the *security proof/reduction* used to argue that the simulation is "correct" (i.e., indistinguishable from the real execution in the eyes of the environment) may very well use rewinding (and in fact often does). In more detail, standard proofs in the UC framework still assume that the environment is a non-uniform PPT machine to reduce security to some assumption (e.g., one-wayness of a function).

It is also worthwhile to compare universal reductions to UC security with an *unbounded environment* (in analogy with how we consider Natures that are unbounded). While such a notion of UC security indeed also would be "future-proof" in the sense that it does not make any assumptions about computational limits on the class of physically realizable computations, the problem with such a notion is that it only enables information-theoretically secure protocols, whereas our goal here is to develop a computational theory of cryptography that is "future-proof". One could consider defining primitives (e.g., one-way functions, PRGs, signatures) as UC functionalities, and consider whether one functionality can be implemented in a UC way using some other functionality with respect to a computationally-unbounded environment; as far as we are aware, such a method has not previously been advocated for and is in line with what we are doing here. However, we highlight that doing this is non trivial for several reasons: (1) it is non trivial to define standard cryptographic primitives as UC functionalities (e.g., how does one define an idealized one-way function); (2) such a treatment would require presenting a *straight-line reduction* that is required to work even if the environment (i.e., Nature in our language) only helps the attacker to succeed *once*; as we have argued above, such a notion is overly strong (and it is trivial to present impossibility results for it). In contrast, by focusing directly on a reduction-based framework, we can (1) define primitives in the standard game-based way, (2) only require the reduction to work for attackers that win *robustly* (i.e., repeatedly) to rule out trivial cases when Nature helps the attacker to win just a single time.

Let us finally mention that a natural way to define protocol security in a both universally-composable and universally-reducible way would be to consider the standard UC definition of security, but requiring that the security reductions used to prove indistinguishability of the simulation are universal. We leave an exploration of such protocols for future work.

Comparison to Abstract Cryptography. We end by noting that the frameworks for *abstract cryptography* [MR11], and *constructive cryptography* [Mau11], among other things also have as a goal of building up a theory of cryptography that is independent of the model of computation used to model an adversary. While these frameworks were used to analyze how to obtain higher-level functionality (e.g., secure channel) from advanced primitives (e.g., secure encryption and MACs) and also used to analyze some building blocks (for instance see [Mau02, MP04, MPR07]), as far as we can tell, they have not been used to understand the underlying most basic building blocks that we study here (e.g., hardness amplification of one-way functions, whether one-way functions have hardcore bits, etc.). At a very high-level, the idea is to view security reductions among primitives as simulations of one system in terms of another; these simulations, just as in the UC framework, need to be straight-line, black-box, and only invoke the attacker once. As far as we can tell, consequently, the same two differences as presented w.r.t. UC with an unbounded environment also apply here. Most notably, since we restrict attention to attackers that win repeatedly/robustly, we can obtain feasibility results using reductions that invoke the attacker multiple times (and this is also what makes it significantly more challenging to present impossibility results).

We highlight that also in the constructive cryptography, *computational* simulation has been defined to consider tasks requiring computational assumption, but this is defined by restricting attention to polynomial-time distinguishers, so such computational definitions still rely on a extended Church-Turing assumption. It would be interesting to extend these works by considering a computational notion of indistinguishability based on universal reductions.

2   Overview of Techniques

We now describe our main technical contributions. We direct the reader to the full paper [CFP22] for full proofs and theorem statements.

2.1   The Dummy Lemma

Universal reductions give universal black-box reductions. (See Lemma 1) Consider a "dummy attacker" A_{dummy} that forwards all messages from C to the Nature Nat, and forwards replies from Nat back to C. The "dummy lemma" says (informally) that if there exists a universal reduction R_{dummy} between two security games that works for augmented adversaries of the form (A_{dummy}, Nat), then there exists a universal reduction that works for any augmented adversary (A, Nat).

Moreover, it is constructive, and the resulting reduction uses A in a black-box way. Here, we briefly provide some intuition for why the "dummy lemma" holds.

The key observation is that since R_{dummy} works for any Nature talking with the dummy attacker A_{dummy}, it must in particular also work for the Nature Nat' that internally simulates an attacker A talking to Nat, for any augmented adversary (A, Nat). If (A, Nat) wins some security game C, then $(A_{\mathsf{dummy}}, \mathsf{Nat}')$ should also win an interaction with C, as Nat' is essentially simulating the augmented adversary (A, Nat) inside. Thus, the reduced attacker $(R_{\mathsf{dummy}}, \mathsf{Nat}')$ should also win the game C'. Finally, consider the reduction R^A that internally runs R_{dummy} and forwarding all its attacker messages to its oracle A. Since R_{dummy} is only talking to Nat' in a straightline fashion, intuitively, the augmented adversary (R^A, Nat) should behave exactly like $(R_{\mathsf{dummy}}, \mathsf{Nat}')$ and thus also win C'. Formalizing this intuition, however, is a bit tricky since we need to make sure that $(A_{\mathsf{dummy}}, \mathsf{Nat}')$ is also *robustly* winning in C, which requires a more complicated construction of Nat'; see the full paper [CFP22].

2.2 Straightline Black-Box Reductions and Witness Indistinguishability

We overview why single-shot, straightline, black-box reductions imply universal reductions, and use this to show a witness indistinguishable proof based on a universal reduction to PRG security.

Single-shot Straightline Reductions imply Universal Reductions. (See Theorem 2) We first argue that "single-shot" straightline black-box reductions imply universal reductions. Suppose there is a *classical* straightline, black-box reduction R that succeeds in some security game C' with probability ϵ when making single-shot usage of an adversary A with advantage a in the game C. That is, R interacts with A a single time without any rewinding or restarting. As we shall observe, any such reduction must also "relativize" with respect to any stateful oracle Nat. In more detail, consider some augmented adversary (B, Nat) that has robust advantage a in a game C, and let B' be an adversary that simulates a communication between R and B: Any time R wants to query its adversary A, we direct that communication to B, and any time B wants to query Nature Nat, we direct that communication to Nat. Since for every prefix ρ, we have that $(B, \mathsf{Nat}(\rho))$ wins in C, we also have that for every prefix ρ, $R^{(B,\mathsf{Nat}(\rho))}$ wins in C and thus $(B', \mathsf{Nat}(\rho))$ (which perfectly emulates $R^{(B,\mathsf{Nat}(\rho))}$) does so as well, so (B', Nat) also has robust advantage in C'. Note that this construction crucially relies on the fact that R only invokes its attacker *once* and without rewinding it (so that communication with Nat can be forwarded).

Let us emphasize, however, that universal reductions are not equivalent with single-shot straightline reductions: as we already discussed, we can obtain universal reductions that do reuse the attacker multiple time—we demonstrate this for the case of hardness amplification for rerandomizable functions—and for this task it is easy to see that a straightline single-shot black-box reductions cannot be used (see the full paper for details).

Universal Reductions from Some Classic Reductions. The above observation shows that if we can construct proofs of security using single-shot, straight-line, black-box reductions, then we immediately can infer the existence of a universal reduction. We observe that indeed some of the classical proofs of security (for e.g. PRG length extension, PRFs from PRGs, encryption from PRFs, commitments from PRGs, one-time signatures from OWFs) fall into this category; see Corollaries 1 through 5.

Universal Reductions from New Classic Reductions: Witness Indistinguishable Proofs. (See Theorem 3) Many classic cryptographic reductions, however, do require rewinding/restarting the adversary. Most notable are reductions/simulations for notions of privacy in interactive proofs like zero-knowledge [GMR89]. As we shall see, we demonstrate that sometimes these can be "de-rewinded". In particular, we will focus our attention on a weakening of zero-knowledge, known as *witness indistinguishability* [FS90], and will show how to provide a new single-shot straightline reduction (and as a consequence, a universal reduction) to PRGs. (We hope that this proof will serve as an example of how classic proofs may be "de-rewinded".)

Recall that an interactive proof system [GMR89], (P, V), for an NP language L specifies an interaction between the prover P with access to a witness w and the verifier V, on common input a security parameter 1^λ and a statement x. It should satisfy completeness, meaning on inputs $x \in L$ and w a valid witness for x, $P(w)$ causes V to accept. The other required property is soundness, meaning on input $x \notin L$, no cheating prover P^* can cause V to accept (with noticeable probability). Sometimes we want additional privacy and security properties for the witness w used. One basic property is witness indistinguishability (WI) [FS90] which requires that no (potentially cheating) verifier V^* can tell if P is using one witness w_0 or another witness w_1. Note that this might seem like a weak property (e.g., it provides no guarantees for languages with unique witnesses), but it has been shown to be extremely useful for broader cryptographic applications (see e.g. [FS90,DN07,BG08]).

We show that the GMW protocol for graph 3-colorability [GMW91] is WI using a single-shot straightline reduction to PRG security. We note that previous classical proofs showing WI of the GMW protocol first showed that GMW is actually zero-knowledge and then use this to conclude that it also satisfies WI. But this approach requires rewinding the adversary; we shall dispense of this rewinding.

We proceed to recalling the GMW protocol. Let $G = (U, E)$ be the input graph where $U = [n]$. Recall that the prover P in this protocol has access to a valid 3-coloring $w: [n] \to [3]$ such that for all $(i, j) \in E$, $w(i) \neq w(j)$. To prove that the graph G is indeed 3-colorable, P samples a random permutation $\pi: [3] \to [3]$ and commits to the colors $c_k = \pi(w(k))$ for all $k \in [n]$. V asks to open a random edge $(i, j) \in E$, and P responds with the openings revealing c_i and c_j. V accepts the interaction if $c_i \neq c_j$ and the openings are valid. Completeness of the protocol can be checked straightforwardly. The protocol has statistical soundness $(1 - 1/|E|)$ (meaning the verifier will catch a cheating prover with probability roughly $1/|E|$) by the statistical binding of the commitment, since at least one edge must be colored incorrectly if G is not 3-colorable. We proceed to argue WI by showing that no cheating verifier V^* can distinguish interactions with $P(w_0)$ or $P(w_1)$ for any two distinct witnesses w_0 and w_1.

To formalize this claim, we model WI as a security game as follows. We allow the adversary A to select a graph G and two valid witnesses w_0 and w_1. The challenger C samples a bit $b \leftarrow \{0, 1\}$ and proceeds to interact as $P(w_b)$ while A acts as the (potentially cheating) verifier V. After the interaction, A outputs a bit b^* and C outputs 1 (so A wins) iff $b = b^*$.

Now suppose that there is an adversary A that distinguishes $P(w_0)$ and $P(w_1)$ with probability $1/2 + \delta$ (namely, it outputs 1 on $P(w_1)$ with probability 2δ more than on $P(w_0)$). We construct a straightline, black-box reduction R that uses A to distinguish two commitments to different values. R first receives a graph G and witnesses w_0 and w_1 from the adversary A. Next, R chooses a random edge $(i', j') \in E$ and random distinct colors for these vertices $c_{i'} \neq c_{j'} \in [3]$. R computes permutations π_0 and π_1 such that $\pi_0(w_0(\cdot))$ and $\pi_1(w_1(\cdot))$ are consistent with the colors $c_{i'}$ and $c_{j'}$. R then sends two sets of messages to a commitment challenger: the first consists of the colors for $\pi_0(w_0(k))$ for all $k \in U \setminus \{i', j'\}$, and the second consists of the colors for $\pi_1(w_1(k))$ for all $k \in U \setminus \{i', j'\}$. R generates commitments for $c_{i'}$ and c_j and then uses the commitments received from the commitment challenger for the other vertices, so R does not know whether it is using w_0 or w_1. A then asks to open a specific edge $(i, j) \in E$, and if (i, j) happens to be (i', j'), R opens the colors $c_{i'}, c_{j'}$. Otherwise, R aborts. If R didn't abort, the interaction is now over and A outputs a guess b^* for whether the witness was w_0 or w_1. R simply forwards this guess to the commitment challenger.

Note that by definition, R only queries A in a single session and only via black-box access. So, we only need to argue that R succeeds with better than $1/2$ probability assuming that A succeeds with $1/2 + \delta$ probability for some inverse polynomial δ. At a high level, this follows since A's view is identical to a random execution with either $P(w_0)$ or $P(w_1)$, assuming that R does not abort. The key point in arguing this is that any $b \in \{0, 1\}$, for any fixed edge (i', j') and fixed witness w_b, there is a 1–1 mapping between colors $c_{i'}, c_{j'}$ and permutations π_b over colors, so picking random colors for $c_{i'}, c_{j'}$ and computing the corresponding permutation w.r.t. w_b, is equivalent to picking a random permutation.

Next, since R chose (i', j') randomly and independent of A, the probability that R aborts because $(i', j') \neq (i, j)$ is at most $(1 - 1/|E|)$. So with probability $1/|E|$, A's guess at distinguishing w_0 from w_1 corresponds exactly to whether or not the commitment challenger chose the commitments for $\pi_0(w_0(\cdot))$ or $\pi_1(w_1(\cdot))$. It follows that R succeeds at distinguishing these two cases with probability $1/2 + \delta/|E|$. Further, we can do an additional hybrid over each of the elements in the set to distinguish two individual committed values with probability $1/2 + \delta/(|E| \cdot (|U| - 2))$.

For full details of the above high level argument, we refer the reader to the full paper [CFP22]. The main point is that since this new proof is a single-shot, straightline, black-box reduction, it immediately implies a universal reduction from WI to PRG security.

2.3   Impossibility of Hardness Amplification and Goldreich-Levin

Impossibility of Universal Hardness Amplification. (See Theorem 4) We start by giving an overview for why there is no universal black-box reduction for the proof of hardness amplification with black-box access to the function f. Let f be a one-way function, and define the n-fold direct product function $f^{(n)}$ such that $f^{(n)}(x_1, \ldots, x_n) = (f(x_1), \ldots, f(x_n))$. We show that this construction does not increase the security for generic functions f. Specifically, we consider generic security games C^f and $C^{(n),f}$ for the OWF security of an arbitrary function f and its n-fold product $f^{(n)}$. Suppose there exists a reduction R such that for any f and any augmented adversary (A, Nat) with advantage $a(\lambda)$ at inverting $f^{(n)}$, then the augmented adversary $(R^{(A,f)}, \mathsf{Nat})$ inverts f with advantage $\epsilon(\lambda, a)$. In this overview, we show that if $R^{(A,f)}$ only makes black-box use of the function f via oracle access to f, then it must satisfy $\epsilon(\lambda, a) \leq a + \mu(\lambda)$ for $a = 1/e$ and μ a negligible function.

Our high level approach is as follows. We will construct an augmented adversary (A, Nat) that has robust advantage roughly $1/e$, yet the answers by this attacker can be efficiently simulated in PPT. In more detail, consider some reduction $(R^{(A,f)}, \mathsf{Nat})$ that work for any function f. Such a reduction must also work for a random function $f : \{0,1\}^\lambda \to \{0,1\}^{3\lambda}$, and for random functions, we have the advantage that the reduction won't (except with negligible probability) be able to query the attacker on any point in the range of the function unless it has already queries f on the pre-image. So, it would seem that if we use such a random function, then we can easily emulate a perfect inverter (by simply looking at all the queries made by R to f). There is one main obstacle here: R actually gets some value y in the range of f as input (and its goal is to invert this point), and R could of course embed this y into its queries to (A, Nat). We overcome this issue by considering a particular "random-aborting" attacker (A, Nat) that (1) only inverts a $1 - 1/n$ fraction of all values y', and (2) never agrees to invert the same value y' twice. We can show that such an attacker succeeds in robustly inverting $f^{(n)}$ with probability roughly $1/e$. Intuitively, such an attacker "knows" how to invert f with probability $1 - 1/n$, but as we shall see, since (A, Nat) is stateful and never agrees to invert the same value twice we can show that (A, Nat) can only be used to invert f with probability roughly $1/e$. More precisely, we show how to correctly simulate this attacker with probability $1 - 1/e$ by a PPT simulator S that simply aborting whenever we see a query that contains a component y_i for which we do not know a pre-image (through one of the f queries made by R). Thus, if $(R^{(A,f)}, \mathsf{Nat})$ inverts a random function f with probability $\epsilon(\lambda, a(\lambda))$, it follows that $(R^{(A,f)}, S^f)$ will invert f with probability $\epsilon(\lambda, 1/e) - 1/e - \mathsf{negl}(\lambda)$. Since R, A, and S are efficient, this probability must be bounded by a negligible function, so $\epsilon(\lambda, 1/e) \leq 1/e + \mathsf{negl}(\lambda)$.

Let us proceed to defining the augmented adversary (A, Nat). The augmented adversary (A, Nat) interacts in the OWF security game of $f^{(n)}$, so A receives queries of the form $(y_1, \ldots, y_n)$. A will simply forward these queries to Nat, who responds with either $\bot$ or the correct inverse $(r_1, \ldots, r_n)$, based on the following procedure:

1. For each y_i in the query, if Nat has previously seen a query for y_i in ρ or if y_i is not in the image of f, it sets r_i to be $\bot$.
2. Next, it flips a coin and with probability roughly $1/n$ just sets r_i to be $\bot$
3. If r_i has not been set to $\bot$, Nat sets r_i to be any preimage in $f^{-1}(y_i)$.
4. Finally, if any r_i was set to $\bot$, Nat responds to the entire query with $\bot$. Otherwise, it responds with the inverse $(r_1, \ldots, r_n)$.

We argue that (A, Nat) will invert a *random* challenge $(f(x_1), \ldots, f(x_n))$ with constant probability, *for all possible prefixes* ρ. In particular, a random challenge $(y_1, \ldots, y_n)$ will always have that each y_i is in the image of f. Additionally, no matter what the history is, a random challenge will not collide with any past query with high probability (formally we need to restrict to only looking at the most recent $\lambda^{\log \lambda}$ queries in case ρ has super-polynomial length). So the only reason Nat outputs $\bot$ is if any of its coin flips tell it to set r_i to be $\bot$, but this happens with probability at most $1 - (1 - 1/n)^n \approx 1 - 1/e$. Thus, the augmented adversary (A, Nat) succeeds with probability roughly $1/e$.

We now argue that Nat can be efficiently simulated. The main reason is that because Nat only needs to reply to queries the first time it sees them, we only need to simulate *a single response* for the challenge $y = f(x)$ that the reduction receives. This is much easier than simulating multiple responses that may include y in various ways. Specifically, the simulator S simulates any queries that R makes to either Nat or f, without the use of Nat. Whenever S simulates a query to f, it records the responses before forwarding the reply back to R. To simulate a query $(y_1, \ldots, y_n)$ to Nat, S proceeds exactly as Nat except that it doesn't actually know how to invert f. Namely, it can still reject y_i values it has seen before, and flip a coin to ignore certain inputs. It tries to invert any y_i value it sees by looking at the queries R has made to f, and uses such a value if one exists.

It remains to argue that S diverges from the behavior of Nat with small probability. S diverges whenever R makes a query $(y_1, \ldots, y_n)$ where R has not queried some y_i before, or if y_i has multiple pre-images. But because f is a random function from λ to 3λ bits, the probability R can guess an element in the image of f without querying it is negligible (other than its input $y = f(x)$, and the probability that f is not injective is negligible). Thus, we only need to deal with when it queries $y = f(x)$ *for the first time*. But Nat outputs $\bot$ in that case with probability $\approx 1 - 1/e$, so S and Nat only diverge with probability roughly $1/e$!

Finally, it follows that if R, given access to Nat, inverts a random $(y_1, \ldots, y_n)$ with probability $1/e + 1/p(\lambda)$ for some polynomial p, then R given access to the simulator S will invert a random f with probability at least $1/p(\lambda)$, which is impossible. So $(R^{(A,f)}, \mathsf{Nat})$ must invert f with probability at most $\epsilon(\lambda, a) \leq a + \mu(\lambda)$ for $a = 1/e$ and some negligible function μ.

For the above proof, we note that we crucially rely on the fact that (A, Nat) is an augmented adversary because it only ever inverts individual y_i values that it has never seen before. Let us also point out that by setting the abort probability more carefully, we can make the proof go through also when are required to construct an attacker that succeeds with much higher probability a (and not just $1/e$). A rigorous proof is in the full paper.

Impossibility of a Universal Goldreich-Levin Theorem. (See Theorem 5) We briefly discuss the impossibility of a universal reduction for the Goldreich-Levin theorem. The high level idea and proof structure is similar to the impossibility of hardness amplification.

Recall that the Goldreich-Levin theorem shows that, for any one-way function g, the function $f(x, r) = (g(x), r)$ is a one-way function with hardcore predicate $h(x, r) = \langle x, r \rangle$ for $|x| = |r|$. Let us first outline why the security of the hardcore predicate h cannot be based on the OWF security of g via a universal reduction, when the reduction only has oracle access to the function g.

Similar to the above impossibility for hardness amplification, we construct an augmented adversary (A, Nat) with advantage a where Nat can be efficiently simulated by a machine S for a random function $g \colon \{0,1\}^\lambda \to \{0,1\}^{3\lambda}$. Nat only responds to queries of the form $(g(x), r)$ with the value of $h(x, r)$ (with probability roughly a) once per $g(x)$ value. Then, we construct S that simulates Nat (almost) perfectly except on the first query to the challenge $y = g(x)$ from the OWF challenger. However, since the output of Nat is a single bit, S can just guess what Nat would have output! It follows that S will simulate Nat with roughly $1/2$ probability, so if $(R^{(A,f)}, \mathsf{Nat})$ inverts g with probability $\epsilon(\lambda, a)$, then $(R^{(A,f)}, S^f)$ will do so with probability roughly $\epsilon(\lambda, a)/2$. Since R, A, and S are efficient, this implies that $\epsilon(\lambda, a)$ must be negligible.

Note that we did not use anything about $|r|$ or the structure of h in the above overview. In fact, we rule out any hardcore predicate h for constructions $f(x, r) = (g(x), r)$ for any $|r|$ (even no randomness). See the full paper.

2.4 Universal Reductions for Time-Evolving k-Window Natures, from Classical Non-adaptive Reductions

Let $k(\cdot)$ be any polynomial function. We here argue that if there exists a *non-adaptive*, straightline black-box reduction R from some game C to C', then there exists a universal reduction from C to C' w.r.t. time-evolving k-window Natures (see Theorem 6). For now, we focus on the simplified case where C and C' are 1-round games, but we consider a more general definition of a non-adaptive reductions in the full paper.

Recall that a straightline black-box reduction is one where the reduction R only makes black-box use of a classical, stateless adversary A. We say that such a reduction is non-adaptive if (for 1-round games) the reduction R after receiving a challenge message in C', generates m queries $q_1, \ldots, q_m$ for A in the game C, sends them all at once, receives the responses, and then responds to the challenger C'. Suppose there exists such a reduction R that has advantage ϵ in C' after making m non-adaptive queries to a classical adversary A with advantage a in C. Then for any augmented adversary (B, Nat) with robust advantage a, where Nat is additionally a *time-evolving k-window Nature*, we want to construct an augmented adversary (B', Nat) also with advantage close to ϵ. In particular, for any δ, we will construct B' such that (B', Nat) has robust advantage $\epsilon - \delta$. (This B', however, will have larger running time than R^B, where the running time depends on δ.)

As Nat is a time-evolving k-window Nature, we can essentially think of (B, Nat) as specifying ahead of time a sequence of independent, arbitrary algorithms $S_1, S_2, \ldots$ s.t. it uses S_i to respond to the ith query q_i. We achieve this as follows: in order for B' to be able to emulate such a sequence of attackers $S_1, S_2, \ldots$ using only interactive access to Nat, for each query q_i B' will first send k dummy messages to Nat (in essence resetting its state to be independent of the past, depending only on i). Subsequently, to generate a response for q_i, B' will invoke a fresh copy of B, communicate with Nat on behalf of B, send q_i to B, and reply with B's reply. However, this isn't enough, because each $S_i \in S_1, S_2, \ldots$ may respond differently as i increases (albeit each S_i still wins by robust winning). In other words, the augmented adversary changes over time. To apply the classical non-adaptive reduction R, we must somehow use (B, Nat) to emulate a classical adversary that responds to queries repeatedly according to the same distribution, because R might call its oracle multiple times.

Thus, we construct the universal reduction B' as follows. B' receives some challenge from C' and emulates R on this challenge to generate queries $q_1, \ldots, q_m$. B' then generates $m^2/\delta - m$ extra random "dummy" queries, call them $q_{m+1}, \ldots, q_{m^2/\delta}$. It then samples a random permutation $\pi \colon [m^2/\delta] \to [m^2/\delta]$ that it uses to permute the order of all the queries. For each $i \in [m^2/\delta]$, denote $q_i' = q_{\pi(i)}$. B' then uses $S_1, \ldots, S_{m^2/\delta}$ to respond to those queries, using each S_i to generate a response r_i' for q_i', in order. It then recovers the responses to the original queries by computing $r_i = r_{\pi(i)}'$ for each $i \in [m]$. R' can feed these to R in order to generate a response for the challenger C'. Importantly, B' is able to emulate $S_1, \ldots, S_{m^2/\delta}$ using a single interaction with the stateful Nat, as long as Nat is a time-evolving (k, μ)-window Nature.

At a high level, the reason the universal reduction B' works is that each response r_i is generated using a random S_j for $j \in [m^2/\delta]$. Thus, R's output should be statistically close to the output of R^A where A is a "classical" adversary A that samples a random $j \leftarrow [m^2/\delta]$ and responds with S_j. However, this isn't the case if there are any collisions on the set of m queries that R queries to this classical adversary A—in other words, if some $j \leftarrow [m^2/\delta]$ is chosen twice—but this bad event can be shown to happen only with probability at most δ. It follows that the output of (B', Nat) is at most δ-far from the output of R^A, so if R wins with probability ϵ, then (B', Nat) will win with probability at least $\epsilon - \delta$.

3   Defining Universal Reductions

In this section, we formally present the notion of a universal reduction. A more in depth study of these notions can be found in the full version [CFP22].

3.1   Preliminaries

We let $\mathbb{N} = \{1, 2, 3, \ldots\}$ denote the set of natural numbers, and for any $n \in \mathbb{N}$, we use $[n] = \{1, \ldots, n\}$ to denote the set from 1 to n.

Throughout, we use $\lambda \in \mathbb{N}$ to denote the security parameter. When we say that an event holds for *sufficiently large* $\lambda \in \mathbb{N}$ we mean that there exists an integer $N \in \mathbb{N}$ such that the event holds for all $\lambda \geq N$. In particular, for any function $f \colon \mathbb{N} \to \mathbb{N}$, the set $O(f)$ consists of all functions g such that there exists a constants c such that $g(\lambda) \leq c \cdot f(\lambda)$ for sufficiently large $\lambda \in \mathbb{N}$. We say that a function $f(\lambda)$ is polynomially-bounded if it is in the set $\lambda^{O(1)} = \mathrm{poly}(\lambda)$. We say that a function $\mu \colon \mathbb{N} \to \mathbb{R}$ is negligible if it is asymptotically smaller than any inverse-polynomial function, so for every constant $c > 0$, $\mu(\lambda) \leq \lambda^{-c}$ for sufficiently large $\lambda \in \mathbb{N}$. In this case, we say $\mu \in \mathsf{negl}(\lambda)$.

We use PPT to denote the acronym *probabilistic, polynomial time*. A uniform algorithm A is a constant-size Turing machine. We say that a function f is efficiently computable if there exists a uniform, polynomial-time algorithm A such that $A(x) = f(x)$ for all $x \in \{0,1\}^\lambda$. A non-uniform algorithm $A = \{A_\lambda\}_{\lambda \in \mathbb{N}}$ is a sequence of algorithms for all $\lambda \in \mathbb{N}$, and we assume for simplicity that A_λ always receives 1^λ as its first input. A non-uniform PPT algorithm is one where the description size of A_λ is bounded by a polynomial as a function of λ.

An interactive Turing machine (ITM) is an algorithm M that receives and sends messages to other ITMs. For two ITMs, A and B, we denote $\langle A(x), B(y) \rangle (z)$ to denote B's output in the interaction between A and B on private inputs x and y, respectively, and on common input z.

3.2   The Definition and Some Consequences

Towards this, let us first recall the standard notion of a *security game*, wherein an ITM *Challenger* C interacts with an ITM *Adversary* A: On common input 1^λ, C interacts with A until C outputs a bit $b \in \{0, 1\}$. If $b = 1$, we say that the adversary *wins*, and we say that A has advantage a if C outputs 1 with probability at least $a(\lambda)$ for all $\lambda \in \mathbb{N}$. The security game is fully specified by the challenger C, and in the sequel we will use security game and challenger interchangeably.

Whereas classically, the adversary is typically a PPT, or a non-uniform PPT, in our context, we will consider security games with respect to *augmented adversaries*: roughly speaking, a PPT attacker A that has access to some potentially unbounded Nature Nat (Fig. 1).

$$C \longleftrightarrow A \longleftrightarrow \mathsf{Nat}(\rho)$$

Fig. 1. *Execution in a nutshell.* The PPT challenger C plays an interactive security game with a PPT attacker A. To help with generating responses, A may send queries to a potentially unbounded Nature machine Nat. Note that Nat may have had previous interactions, which we specify using ρ, which comprises prior messages that Nat may have received, as well as any private coins that Nat may have flipped previously. When we omit ρ, we mean that Nat starts from the blank slate (i.e. no prior messages or coins).

Augmented Adversaries. In more detail, an augmented adversary (A, Nat) consists of a PPT ITM A, known as the *attacker*, and a stateful, possibly unbounded non-uniform ITM Nat, known as *Nature*. We think of A as the part of the augmented adversary that only uses "standard" computational resources, whereas Nat is a shared resource in the world that may have "magical" computational resources. Note that since Nat is a non-uniform ITM, it may take a non-uniform advice of arbitrary length. We assume that Nat halts on every input message.

Remark 1. All of our definitions—and proofs—work for more powerful Natures as well, even those that output an *arbitrary probability distribution* in response to any interaction prefix (as opposed to one being samplable by a TM). We define Nat as an ITM for convenience: It becomes easier to specify communication, randomness, views, etc. Furthermore, considering uncomputable Natures gives incomparable results: the feasibility results are stronger, but the impossibility results become weaker.

Interaction Model and Winning Security Games (Once). We consider executions of a security game C interacting with an augmented adversary (A, Nat). We use $\langle C \leftrightarrow A \leftrightarrow \mathsf{Nat} \rangle (1^\lambda)$ to denote an execution between C, A, and Nat, given the security parameter 1^λ as common input. In particular, the challenger C sends queries to and receives responses from the attacker A, who in turn sends queries to and receives responses from the Nature machine Nat. The execution ends when C halts outputting a bit $b \in \{0, 1\}$ representing the outcome of the security game. An ITM in this model is PPT if there is a polynomial upper bound—as a function of λ—on the number of steps it takes during the lifetime of any execution before halting. Formally, $\langle C \leftrightarrow A \leftrightarrow \mathsf{Nat} \rangle (1^\lambda)$ is a random variable over the joint views of C, A, Nat, where the randomness is over the coins of each party. Given an execution $\mathsf{exec} \in \mathsf{Supp}(\langle C \leftrightarrow A \leftrightarrow \mathsf{Nat} \rangle (1^\lambda))$, we let $\mathsf{out}_C[\mathsf{exec}]$ and $\mathsf{view}_C[\mathsf{exec}]$ denote C's output and view, respectively, in the execution exec.

Definition 4 (Winning Security Games). *Let $a \in [0, 1]$ and $\lambda \in \mathbb{N}$ be a security parameter. We say that an augmented adversary (A, Nat) has advantage a on λ for a security game C if*

$$\Pr\left[\mathsf{out}_C[\langle C \leftrightarrow A \leftrightarrow \mathsf{Nat} \rangle (1^\lambda)] = 1\right] \geq a.$$

Let $a : \mathbb{N} \to [0, 1]$. *The augmented adversary* (A, Nat) *has* advantage $a(\cdot)$ *for a security game* C *if for all security parameters* $\lambda \in \mathbb{N}$, (A, Nat) *has advantage* $a(\lambda)$ *for* C *on* λ.

Robust Winning. We will also be interested in executions involving Nat where Nat *has already had some prior interaction*; intuitively, we will want to capture a notion of what it means for (A, Nat) to "robustly" win in a security game— roughly speaking, that must (A, Nat) "wins" regardless of any prior interaction that Nat has had with the rest of the world.

We capture this by specifying an *interaction prefix* $\rho = (r, q_1, q_2, \ldots)$ for Nat at the beginning of an execution. We can think of ρ as specifying a finite sequence of queries $q_1, q_2, \ldots$ that Nat previously received, as well as the randomness r that Nat used to respond to those queries; thus ρ fully determines the past behavior and the current state of Nat. For any $\rho \in \{0, 1\}^*$ and security parameter $\lambda \in \mathbb{N}$, consider the interaction where Nat is initialized on input 1^λ, with (read-once) random tape prepopulated by r (followed by 0s), and where Nat is reactivated whenever it becomes idle, s.t. when Nat is activated for the ith time, its message tape is prepopulated with q_i (followed by 0s). Recall that an ITM enters an idle state whenever it is ready to receive the next message in the interaction. When there are no more queries in ρ to process, the random tape of Nat is then reset to uniform randomness. We then let $\mathsf{Nat}(1^\lambda, \rho)$ denote Nat in the state reached following the interaction specified by ρ and 1^λ. Let $\|\rho\|$ denote the number of queries sent to Nat in ρ. Finally, the notation $\langle C \leftrightarrow A \leftrightarrow \mathsf{Nat}(\rho) \rangle(1^\lambda)$ refers to an execution on input 1^λ where Nat starts in the state determined by ρ. If the prefix ρ is omitted, then Nat starts without any prior interaction.

We also define what it means to *concatenate* two prefixes $\rho \circ \rho'$, where $\rho = (r, q_1, q_2, \ldots)$ and $\rho' = (r', q_1', q_2', \ldots)$. Define r^* to be the contents of the random tape read by Nat in the interaction $\mathsf{Nat}(1^\lambda, \rho)$, including any 0s if r is too short, or trimming extraneous bits of r that $\mathsf{Nat}(1^\lambda, \rho)$ doesn't read if r is too long. Define $\rho \circ \rho' = (r^* \circ r', q_1, q_2, \ldots, q_1', q_2', \ldots)$, where $r^* \circ r'$ denotes string concatenation.

We are now ready to define what it means for an augmented adversary (A, Nat) to *robustly* win in a security game.

Definition 5 (Robust Winning). *Let* $a \in [0, 1]$ *and* $\lambda \in \mathbb{N}$ *be a security parameter. We say that an augmented adversary* (A, Nat) *has* robust advantage a *on* λ *for a security game* C *if for all* $\rho \in \{0, 1\}^*$, $(A, \mathsf{Nat}(\rho))$ *has advantage* $a(\lambda)$ *on* λ *for* C. *Let* $a : \mathbb{N} \to [0, 1]$. *The augmented adversary* (A, Nat) *has* robust advantage $a(\cdot)$ *for a security game* C *if for all* $\lambda \in \mathbb{N}$, (A, Nat) *has robust advantage* $a(\lambda)$ *for* C *on* λ.[9]

---

[9] In the definition of robust winning above, we require that the augmented adversary win a security game for *every* prefix ρ that Nat may have previously seen, even those containing exponentially many messages. A natural alternative is to consider a notion of robust winning that considers only those prefixes with poly(λ) many messages; indeed our impossibilities and feasibilities can both be made to work in that setting, but at the expense of definitional complexity.

Universal Reductions. We finally turn to defining the notion of a universal reduction. Roughly speaking, a universal reduction from security games C to C' guarantees that for every augmented adversary (A, Nat) that robustly wins C, there must exist an attacker A' (depending on A only) such that (A', Nat) robustly wins in C' using the same Nature.

Definition 6 (Universal Reductions). *Let* $\epsilon \colon \mathbb{N} \times [0,1] \to [0,1]$, C *and* C' *be security games. We say that there is an ϵ-universal reduction from C to C' if for all PPT A there exists a PPT A' such that for every augmented adversary (A, Nat) with robust advantage $a(\cdot)$ for C, (A', Nat) has robust advantage $\epsilon(\cdot, a(\cdot))$ for C'.*

Composability of Universal Reductions. We observe that the definition of a universal reduction easily composes:

Lemma 2 (Composition of Universal Reductions). *Let C_1, C_2, C_3 be security games. Suppose there exists an ϵ_1-universal reduction from C_2 to C_1, and an ϵ_2-universal reduction from C_3 to C_2. Then, there exists an $\epsilon^\star$-universal reduction from C_3 to C_1 where $\epsilon^\star(\lambda, a) = \epsilon_1(\lambda, \epsilon_2(\lambda, a))$ for all $\lambda \in \mathbb{N}$ and $a \in [0,1]$.*

Proof. Let (A_3, Nat) be any augmented adversary, and denote $a(\cdot)$ its robust advantage in C_3. Since there is a ϵ_2-universal reduction from C_3 to C_2, then there exists PPT A_2 s.t. (A_2, Nat) has robust advantage $\epsilon_2(\lambda, a(\lambda))$ in C_2 given security parameter λ for all $\lambda \in \mathbb{N}$. Since there is a ϵ_1-universal reduction from C_2 to C_1, then there must exist PPT A_1 s.t. (A_1, Nat) has robust advantage $\epsilon_1(\lambda, \epsilon_2(\lambda, a(\lambda)))$ in C_1 given security parameter λ for all $\lambda \in \mathbb{N}$.

We conclude that there thus exists a $\epsilon^\star$-universal reduction from C_3 to C_1 where $\epsilon^\star(\lambda, a) = \epsilon_1(\lambda, \epsilon_2(\lambda, a))$ for all $\lambda \in \mathbb{N}$ and $a \in [0,1]$. $\qquad\square$

Acknowledgements.. This work is supported in part by NSF CNS-2149305, NSF Award SATC-1704788, NSF Award RI-1703846, CNS-2128519, AFOSR Award FA9550-18-1-0267, and a JP Morgan Faculty Award. This material is based upon work supported by DARPA under Agreement No. HR00110C0086. Cody Freitag's work was done partially during an internship at NTT Research, and he is also supported in part by the National Science Foundation Graduate Research Fellowship under Grant No. DGE-2139899. Any opinions, findings and conclusions or recommendations expressed in this material are those of the author(s) and do not necessarily reflect the views of the NSF, the United States Government, or DARPA.

References

[AC02] Adcock, M., Cleve, R.: A quantum Goldreich-Levin Theorem with cryptographic applications. In: Alt, H., Ferreira, A. (eds.) STACS 2002. LNCS, vol. 2285, pp. 323–334. Springer, Heidelberg (2002). https://doi.org/10.1007/3-540-45841-7_26

[ARU14] Ambainis, A., Rosmanis, A., Unruh, D.: Quantum attacks on classical proof systems: the hardness of quantum rewinding. In 2014 IEEE 55th Annual Symposium on Foundations of Computer Science, pp. 474–483. IEEE (2014)

[BBF13] Baecher, P., Brzuska, C., Fischlin, M.: Notions of black-box reductions, revisited. In: Sako, K., Sarkar, P. (eds.) ASIACRYPT 2013. LNCS, vol. 8269, pp. 296–315. Springer, Heidelberg (2013). https://doi.org/10.1007/978-3-642-42033-7_16

[BBK22] Bitansky, N., Brakerski, Z., Kalai, Y.T.: Constructive post-quantum reductions. IACR Cryptol. ePrint Archive, p. 298 (2022)

[BDF+11] Boneh, D., Dagdelen, Ö., Fischlin, M., Lehmann, A., Schaffner, C., Zhandry, M.: Random oracles in a quantum world. In: Lee, D.H., Wang, X. (eds.) ASIACRYPT 2011. LNCS, vol. 7073, pp. 41–69. Springer, Heidelberg (2011). https://doi.org/10.1007/978-3-642-25385-0_3

[BG08] Barak, B., Goldreich, O.: Universal arguments and their applications. SIAM J. Comput. **38**(5), 1661–1694 (2008)

[BS20] Bitansky, N., Shmueli, O.: Post-quantum zero knowledge in constant rounds. In: Proceedings of the 52nd Annual ACM SIGACT Symposium on Theory of Computing, pp. 269–279 (2020)

[Can01] Canetti, R.: Universally composable security: a new paradigm for cryptographic protocols. In Proceedings 42nd IEEE Symposium on Foundations of Computer Science, pp. 136–145. IEEE (2001)

[CFP22] Chan, B., Freitag, C., Pass, R.: Universal reductions: Reductions relative to stateful oracles (2022). https://ia.cr/2022/156

[CMSZ21] Chiesa, A., Ma, F., Spooner, N., Zhandry, M.: Post-quantum succinct arguments: breaking the quantum rewinding barrier. In: FOCS, pp. 49–58. IEEE (2021)

[Die82] Dieks, D.G.B.J.: Communication by EPR devices. Phys. Lett. A **92**(6), 271–272 (1982)

[DN07] Dwork, C., Naor, M.: Zaps and their applications. SIAM J. Comput. **36**(6), 1513–1543 (2007)

[FS90] Feige, U., Shamir, A.: Witness indistinguishable and witness hiding protocols. In: Proceedings of the Twenty-second Annual ACM Symposium on Theory of Computing, pp. 416–426 (1990)

[GGM86] Goldreich, O., Goldwasser, S., Micali, S.: How to construct random functions. J. ACM **33**(4), 792–807 (1986)

[GL89] Goldreich, O., Levin, L.A.: A hard-core predicate for all one-way functions. In: Proceedings of the Twenty-First Annual ACM Symposium on Theory of Computing, pp. 25–32 (1989)

[GMR89] Goldwasser, S., Micali, S., Rackoff, C.: The knowledge complexity of interactive proof systems. SIAM J. Comput. **18**(1), 186–208 (1989)

[GMW91] Goldreich, O., Micali, S., Wigderson, A.: Proofs that yield nothing but their validity for all languages in NP have zero-knowledge proof systems. J. ACM **38**(3), 691–729 (1991)

[Gol07] Goldreich, O.: Foundations of Cryptography, vol. 1, Basic Tools. Cambridge University Press, Cambridge (2007)

[Gro96] Grover, L.K.: A fast quantum mechanical algorithm for database search. In: Proceedings of the Twenty-eighth Annual ACM Symposium on Theory of Computing, pp. 212–219 (1996)

[Hof11] Hofheinz, D.: Possibility and impossibility results for selective decommitments. J. Cryptol. **24**(3), 470–516 (2011)

[IR95] Impagliazzo, R., Rudich, S.: Limits on the provable consequences of one-way permutations. In: Proceedings of the Twenty-first Annual ACM Symposium on Theory of Computing, pp. 44–61 1989 (1995)

[Lam79]   Lamport, L.: Constructing digital signatures from a one-way function. Technical report (1979)

[LTW05]   Lin, H., Trevisan, L., Wee, H.: On hardness amplification of one-way functions. In: Kilian, J. (ed.) TCC 2005. LNCS, vol. 3378, pp. 34–49. Springer, Heidelberg (2005). https://doi.org/10.1007/978-3-540-30576-7_3

[Mah18]   Mahadev, U.: Classical verification of quantum computations. In: FOCS, pp. 259–267. IEEE Computer Society (2018)

[Mau02]   Maurer, U.: Indistinguishability of random systems. In: Knudsen, L.R. (ed.) EUROCRYPT 2002. LNCS, vol. 2332, pp. 110–132. Springer, Heidelberg (2002). https://doi.org/10.1007/3-540-46035-7_8

[Mau11]   Maurer, U.: Constructive cryptography – a new paradigm for security definitions and proofs. In: Mödersheim, S., Palamidessi, C. (eds.) TOSCA 2011. LNCS, vol. 6993, pp. 33–56. Springer, Heidelberg (2012). https://doi.org/10.1007/978-3-642-27375-9_3

[MP04]   Maurer, U., Pietrzak, K.: Composition of random systems: when two weak make one strong. In: Naor, M. (ed.) TCC 2004. LNCS, vol. 2951, pp. 410–427. Springer, Heidelberg (2004). https://doi.org/10.1007/978-3-540-24638-1_23

[MPR07]   Maurer, U., Pietrzak, K., Renner, R.: Indistinguishability amplification. In: Menezes, A. (ed.) CRYPTO 2007. LNCS, vol. 4622, pp. 130–149. Springer, Heidelberg (2007). https://doi.org/10.1007/978-3-540-74143-5_8

[MR11]   Maurer, U., Renner, R.: Abstract cryptography. In: Innovations in Computer Science, Citeseer (2011)

[Nao91]   Naor, M.: Bit commitment using pseudorandomness. J. Cryptol. 4(2), 151–158 (1991). https://doi.org/10.1007/BF00196774

[Pop05]   Popper, K.: The Logic of Scientific Discovery. Routledge, London (2005)

[Rog06]   Rogaway, P.: Formalizing human ignorance. In: Nguyen, P.Q. (ed.) VIETCRYPT 2006. LNCS, vol. 4341, pp. 211–228. Springer, Heidelberg (2006). https://doi.org/10.1007/11958239_14

[Sho94]   Shor, P.W.: Algorithms for quantum computation: discrete logarithms and factoring. In: Proceedings 35th Annual Symposium on Foundations of Computer Science, pp. 124–134. IEEE (1994)

[Unr12]   Unruh, D.: Quantum proofs of knowledge. In: Pointcheval, D., Johansson, T. (eds.) EUROCRYPT 2012. LNCS, vol. 7237, pp. 135–152. Springer, Heidelberg (2012). https://doi.org/10.1007/978-3-642-29011-4_10

[Unr16]   Unruh, D.: Computationally binding quantum commitments. In: Fischlin, M., Coron, J.-S. (eds.) EUROCRYPT 2016. LNCS, vol. 9666, pp. 497–527. Springer, Heidelberg (2016). https://doi.org/10.1007/978-3-662-49896-5_18

[Wat09]   Watrous, J.: Zero-knowledge against quantum attacks. SIAM J. Comput. 39(1), 25–58 (2009)

[WZ82]   Wootters, W.K., Zurek, W.H.: A single quantum cannot be cloned. Nature 299(5886), 802–803 (1982)

[Yao82]   Yao, A.C.: Theory and application of trapdoor functions. In: 23rd Annual Symposium on Foundations of Computer Science (SFCS 1982), pp. 80–91. IEEE (1982)

[Zha12]   Zhandry, M.: How to construct quantum random functions. In: FOCS, pp. 679–687. IEEE Computer Society (2012)

Permissionless Clock Synchronization with Public Setup

Juan Garay[1], Aggelos Kiayias[2], and Yu Shen[3(✉)]

[1] Texas A&M University, College Station, USA
garay@cse.tamu.edu
[2] University of Edinburgh and IOHK, Edinburgh, UK
aggelos.kiayias@ed.ac.uk
[3] University of Edinburgh, Edinburgh, UK
yu.shen@ed.ac.uk

Abstract. The permissionless clock synchronization problem asks how it is possible for a population of parties to maintain a system-wide synchronized clock, while their participation rate fluctuates—possibly very widely—over time. The underlying assumption is that parties experience the passage of time with roughly the same speed, but however they may disengage and engage with the protocol following arbitrary (and even chosen adversarially) participation patterns. This (classical) problem has received renewed attention due to the advent of blockchain protocols, and recently it has been solved in the setting of proof of stake, i.e., when parties are assumed to have access to a trusted PKI setup [Badertscher *et al.*, Eurocrypt '21].

In this work, we present the first proof-of-work (PoW)-based permissionless clock synchronization protocol. Our construction assumes a public setup (e.g., a CRS) and relies on an honest majority of computational power that, for the first time, is described in a fine-grain timing model that does not utilize a global clock that exports the current time to all parties. As a secondary result of independent interest, our protocol gives rise to the first PoW-based ledger consensus protocol that does not rely on an external clock for the time-stamping of transactions and adjustment of the PoW difficulty.

1 Introduction

In the classical clock synchronization problem, thoroughly studied over the past four decades by the distributed computing community—non-exhaustively, [1,8, 16,18–20,25,26]—, a set of processors, each one possessing a timer that is within a bounded rate of drift from "nominal time" (the real time—called Newtonian time in [8]), should realize logical clocks that are within a distance $\mathsf{Skew} \in \mathbb{N}$ of each other and within a linear envelope of nominal time. The typical threat

---

J. Garay—Research supported by NSF grants no. 2001082 and 2055694.
Y. Shen—Work supported by Input Output – IOHK through their funding of the Edinburgh Blockchain Technology Lab.

E. Kiltz and V. Vaikuntanathan (Eds.): TCC 2022, LNCS 13749, pp. 181–211, 2022.
https://doi.org/10.1007/978-3-031-22368-6_7

model involves a subset of parties who deviate arbitrarily either from correct protocol execution or in terms of their clock speed and may as a result prevent synchronization from happening. A clock synchronization protocol has parties exchanging messages to suitably adjust their clocks so that the synchronization condition is achieved.

Up until the work of [3] all prior work in clock synchronization assumed that the number of parties are known during the protocol execution (and available, unless they are assumed adversarial[1]). This standard assumption in Byzantine fault tolerance protocols was challenged first with the advent of the Bitcoin blockchain and related "permissionless" protocols. As exemplified in [11,12], the Bitcoin blockchain operates in a setting where the number of active parties may be unknown and continuously fluctuating throughout the protocol execution. While such results paved the way to rethink the problem of consensus in this setting (cf. [15,24]), near perfectly synchronized clocks remained a central assumption in all previous security analyses of blockchain protocols (cf. [4,10–12,22]).

In the setting where participation is dynamic and fluctuating over time, the adversary can introduce and remove honest parties at will without notifying the existing participants. As a result, existing clock synchronization algorithms (e.g., [1,20,25]) do not directly translate to such permissionless setting because they fundamentally rely on the fact that the parties are aware of the number of parties as well as of the number of tolerated corruptions/faults—i.e., they are able to *count*— and a different protocol design technique is needed.

The main challenge in this transient participation setting shifts from correcting the bounded-rate drift occurring between the ever connected honest parties over time to the task of bringing up to sync freshly joining parties who start without any information about nominal time, while accommodating for the fact that a (possibly large) number of honest parties is no longer active. In [3], assuming a so-called private-state setup [15] (specifically, a PKI), a protocol called "Ouroboros Chronos" is presented that can synthesize a notion of global time using a continuous flow of clock measurements that are provided by parties who only transiently participate in the protocol and their local clocks are assumed to be correct up to a bound. The level of participation fluctuates broadly with the only requirements that (i) it does not become negligible, and (ii) honest majority is preserved in terms of stake (all parties have a number of coins associated to their public keys that amount to their individual stake). Given this, their result leaves open the question of only utilizing a public(-state) setup.

To our knowledge, the only known result with a public setup in the permissionless setting, again from [3], is that parties may use a Nakamoto-style longest chain blockchain without difficulty adjustment and use the block index to define a concept of global time. The obvious downside of this idea is that the protocol execution speeds up and slows down as participation fluctuates and, most importantly, it will be entirely insecure when there is a steady increase (or

---

[1] We note that the problem of joining parties in the context of clock synchronization was considered, but only conditionally on the new party agreed upon and approved by a sufficient number of participants; see [16].

decrease) of participants, making the construction essentially only suitable for a static model where the number of parties (i.e., the computational power invested in the system for proof of work) remains fixed.

This motivates the current work, where the following open question is being tackled:

Is it possible for a dynamically changing population of peers to synchronize their clocks utilizing only a public setup and assuming PoW?

One apparent difficulty in answering this question is that using a blockchain protocol to derive consistency for clock adjustments runs into the complication that the blockchain protocol itself utilizes a clock to adjust the PoW difficulty at regular intervals. Indeed, the Bitcoin blockchain [21] relies fundamentally on a global clock being available to all parties.[2] It follows that this observation suggests also a secondary open question that will be tackled as well:

Is there a blockchain protocol in the PoW setting that has no dependency on a publicly accessible global clock?

1.1   Overview of Our Results

The clock synchronization problem asks parties to report clocks that satisfy two properties (cf. [8]) (i) *bounded skew:* the parties maintain logical clocks whose difference is upper bounded, and (ii) *linear envelope synchronization:* the logical clock reported by a party is always within a *linear envelope* of the nominal time. Note that we are interested in a formulation of this problem in a very general setting where some parties are adversarial and hence deviate from the protocol arbitrarily, while honest parties may come and go following arbitrary participation patterns. Given this setting we formulate the *desideratum* of a synchronized clock only with respect to a class of parties we call *alert*, which are honest parties that have also been online for a sufficiently long time to catch up with all protocol messages. More formally, the clock synchronization problem is stated as follows.

Definition 1 (Clock Synchronization). *There exist constants* Skew $\in \mathbb{N}$, shiftLB, shiftUB $\in (0, 1)$ *such that honest parties' logical clocks satisfy the following two properties:*

– **Bounded skews.** *Let* r_1, r_2 *be the reported logical clocks of two alert parties at any nominal time* r. *Then* $|r_1 - r_2| \leq$ Skew.

---

[2] The protocol implements such clock by having nodes querying other nodes in the network and possibly seeking user input—it has no way of deriving a clock from the protocol operation itself. See [12] for more details.

– *Linear envelope synchronization.* Each alert party's logical clock stays in a (U, L)-linear envelope[3] with respect to the nominal time r, where $U = 1/(1 - \mathsf{shiftUB})$ and $L = 1/(1 + \mathsf{shiftLB})$.

Solving the clock synchronization problem asks for a protocol that within a certain threat model achieves the two properties. This brings us to our first main result.

A Model for Permissionless Clock Synchronization in the PoW Setting. Our model (Sect. 2) simultaneously facilitates (i) the dynamic participation of parties, (ii) imperfect local clocks, and (iii) resource bounding by restricting parties' queries to a random oracle (cf. [13]). Specifically, we extend the previous model of the global imperfect clock of [3] to the PoW setting by introducing a random oracle functionality that apportions random oracle queries per unit of time between the honest parties and the adversary in a manner consistent with an honest majority assumption in terms of computational power. The concept of time provided by the imperfect local clock functionality of [3] enables parties to advance their local clocks and experience time at roughly the same speed (a maximum drift of Φ_{clock} is allowed). Note that the environment is allowed to introduce new parties and remove old parties at will, something that results in them being de-registered from the clock functionality; when this happens the clock functionality is not responsible for keeping them up to speed with the rest of the honest parties. In this way, parties can be seen as entirely transiently engaging with the protocol—each individual party may only engage for a small fraction of the total execution time as adaptively decided by the environment. Armed with our model, we then present our second main result.

A New Protocol for Permissionless Clock Synchronization in the PoW Model. We describe our new PoW-based clock synchronization protocol Timekeeper in Sect. 3. The construction is based on three key ingredients: (i) A mechanism that repurposes the concept of 2-for-1 PoWs introduced in [10] and subsequently used to achieve various properties such as fairness in [23] and high throughput in [5], to the setting of time-keeping by employing it to enable the collection of "timing beacons" from the active parties in a rolling window process; (ii) a PoW-based longest-chain type of blockchain that enables parties at regular intervals to reach consensus about the timing beacons that are shared and extract a suitable correction to their local clocks taking into account the arrivals of the beacons; and (iii) a novel target-recalculation function that can be thought of as the *reverse* of the one used in Bitcoin, that uses protocol recorded timestamps as a means to define the length of an epoch, and then uses the number of blocks produced in that period of time to adjust the PoW difficulty accordingly.

Putting these elements together, our clock synchronization protocol instructs parties when their local clock passes some specific moment (which happens periodically with respect to the interval length) to execute an adjustment on their

---

[3] A function $f : \mathbb{R} \to \mathbb{R}$ is within a (U, L)-linear envelope if and only if it holds that $L \cdot x \leq f(x) \leq U \cdot x$, for all x.

local clock based on the median value of the beacon timestamps and their corresponding arrival time. Moreover, towards the goal of letting newly joining parties become synchronized with the protocol time, we present a joining procedure which requires the fresh parties to passively listen to the protocol execution for a while and then synchronize with other honest participants.

Based on the ledger consensus function offered by our protocol it is easy to derive also the following result.

A New PoW-Based Blockchain Protocol Without a Global Clock. Given that our protocol is a Nakamoto-style "most-difficult chain" type of protocol that faclitates clock synchronization, it is easy to transform it to a full-fledged blockchain protocol that admits transactions as in Bitcoin script or Ethereum smart contracts. The resulting blockchain has the novel property that it does not depend on accessing a globally available clock. Instead, parties utilize their local clocks which may be drifting or be out of sync, but thanks to the synchronization (sub-)protocol that is offered by our construction they can adjust their local clocks periodically. This eliminates time as an attack vector in the context of PoW-based blockchain protocols and demonstrates that it is possible to achieve ledger consensus using merely local clocks in a fully dynamic setting where parties may come and go adaptively per the adversary's instructions.

Security Analysis. We present the full security analysis of Timekeeper in Sect. 4. As a high-level overview, we proceed to adapt the analytical toolset from [11,12] to the imperfect-local-clock model. Notably, we modify the concept of target recalculation epoch boundaries (from "point" to "zone") and the concept of isolated successes (which addresses the question of under what circumstances can a hash success guarantee the increase of accumulated difficulty). As an intermediate step, we study several predicates aiming at providing the "good" properties of an execution starting from the onset and until a given nominal round.

Our inductive-style proof works in the following manner. We prove that if at the onset, the PoW difficulty is appropriately set and the steady block-generation rate lasts during the whole clock synchronization interval, parties can maintain good skews after they enter the next interval and the shift value they compute to adjust their clocks is properly bounded. In addition, if good skews and certain time adjustment calculations are maintained during a target recalculation epoch, the block production rate will be properly controlled in the next epoch. To sum up, this guarantees that "good" properties can be achieved during the whole execution given a "safe" start and a bounded change in the number of parties (which can nevertheless still be exponential). We also provide an analysis of the joining procedure showing that joining parties starting with no *a-priori* knowledge of global time, can listen in and bootstrap their logical clock, turning themselves into *alert* parties being capable of fully engaging with the protocol.

In summary, Timekeeper solves the clock synchronization problem as defined above as follows.

Theorem (Theorem 3, informal). *Let Φ_{clock} be the maximum drift allowed on parties' local clocks and Δ the maximum (and unknown) message transmission delay. Then* Timekeeper *solves the clock synchronization problem assuming bounded dynamic participation and an honest majority in terms of random oracle queries, with parameter values*

$$\text{Skew} = 2\Phi, \quad \text{shiftLB} = 3\Phi/R, \quad \text{shiftUB} = 2\Phi/R,$$

where $\Phi = \Delta + \Phi_{\text{clock}}$ and $R \in \mathbb{N}^+$ is a parameter chosen sufficiently large w.r.t. the security parameter and reflects the time required for an honest party to become alert.

Organization of the Paper. The rest of the paper is organized as follows. In Sect. 2 we present our model, relevant definitions and building blocks. We describe our Timekeeper protocol in Sect. 3 and present the full analysis in Sect. 4. Detailed description of protocols, functionalities, and proofs can be found in the full version of the paper [14].

2   Model and Building Blocks

In this paper we adapt the timing and networking model of [3] to the setting of proof of work, obviating the requirement for a PKI as a setup assumption. In more detail, in the model there is an upper bound Δ in message transmission (cf. [4,9,12,22]), and parties do not have access to a global clock, but instead rely on their local clocks, whose drift is assumed to be upper-bounded by Φ_{clock}. What complicates matters is that the model supports dynamic participation where parties may join and leave during the protocol execution without warning (it is worth noting here that this is where the difficulty of our setting is derived from: indeed if all honest parties were online throughout then it would be trivial to implement a logical clock by incrementing a counter). For succinctness, we choose to express primitives and building blocks (see below) in our execution model utilizing the ideal functionality language of [7], but we do not pursue a composability analysis for our security properties, which are expressed in a game based manner as in [10,22].

2.1   Imperfect Local Clocks

As in [3], and as mentioned above, in this paper we remove the assumption that parties have access to a global clock, as in [4,10–12,22], and instead assume *imperfect local clocks*. In a nutshell, every honest party maintains a local clock variable by communicating with an imperfect local clock functionality $\mathcal{F}_{\text{ILCLOCK}}$. In contrast to the global-setup clock functionality in [17], where parties learn the exact global time and thus strong synchrony is guaranteed, parties registered with $\mathcal{F}_{\text{ILCLOCK}}$ will only receive "ticks" from the functionality to indicate that they should update their own clocks. In addition, $\mathcal{F}_{\text{ILClock}}$ issues "imperfect" ticks, i.e., the adversary is allowed to set a bounded drift to each party by manipulating its corresponding status variable in $\mathcal{F}_{\text{ILClock}}$. $\mathcal{F}_{\text{ILClock}}$ can be viewed as a variant from [3]'s with adaptations to provide a more natural clock model with real-word resources and in the proof-of-work setting.

For a detailed description of the functionality, see [14]. Here we just elaborate on the "imperfect" aspect of the clock and on the adversarial manipulation of clock drifts. Specifically, we allow the adversary to set some drifts to parties' local clocks, which will accelerate or stall their progress; such values are globally bounded by Φ_{clock}. This assumption allows local clocks to proceed at "roughly" the same speed.

Further, the adversary $\mathcal{A}$ can adaptively manipulate the drift of honest parties' clocks by sending CLOCK-FORWARD and CLOCK-BACKWARD messages to the functionality[4] after they conclude the current round. If $\mathcal{A}$ issues CLOCK-FORWARD for party P, it will enter a new local round before $\mathcal{F}_{\text{ILClock}}$ updates the nominal time, and this can be repeated as long as P's drift is not Φ_{clock} rounds larger than other honest parties. On the other hand, if $\mathcal{A}$ issues CLOCK-BACKWARD, it will set P's budget to a negative value, thus preventing $\mathcal{F}_{\text{ILClock}}$ from updating d_P at the end of the nominal round (d_P is the functionality variable that captures whether the party P has made its move for the clock tick). I.e., P will still be in the same logical round during these two nominal rounds. Again, this process can be repeated by $\mathcal{A}$ as long as the drift on P is not Φ_{clock} rounds smaller than others. As a consequence, the targeted party's local clock may remain static for several nominal rounds.

2.2   Other Core Functionalities

Common Reference String. We model a public-state setup by the CRS functionality $\mathcal{F}^{\mathcal{D}}_{\text{CRS}}$. The functionality is parameterized with some distribution $\mathcal{D}$ with sufficiently high entropy. Once $\mathcal{F}^{\mathcal{D}}_{\text{CRS}}$ receives (RETRIEVE, sid) from either the adversary $\mathcal{A}$ or a party P for the first time, it generates a string $d \leftarrow \mathcal{D}$ as the common reference string. In addition, $\mathcal{F}^{\mathcal{D}}_{\text{CRS}}$ will immediately send a message (RETRIEVED, sid) to functionality $\mathcal{W}(\mathcal{F}_{\text{RO}})$ (described next) to indicate that $\mathcal{W}(\mathcal{F}_{\text{RO}})$ should start to limit the adversarial RO queries. For all subsequent activations, $\mathcal{F}^{\mathcal{D}}_{\text{CRS}}$ simply returns d to the requester.

(Wrapped) Random Oracle. By convention, we model parties' calls to the hash function used to generated proofs of work as assuming access to a random oracle; this is captured by the functionality $\mathcal{F}_{\text{RO}}$. Notice that with regards to bounding access to real-world resources, functionality $\mathcal{F}_{\text{RO}}$ as defined fails to limit the adversary on making a certain number of queries per round. Hence, we adopt

---

[4] As such, our clock functionality is a more natural model of the real world compared to [3]'s, as it allows $\mathcal{A}$ to manipulate the clock in both directions, backward, and forward; in [3], only forward manipulation is allowed. Nonetheless, this does not result in a more powerful adversary.

a functionality wrapper [4,13] $\mathcal{W}(\mathcal{F}_{RO})$ that wraps the corresponding resource to capture such restrictions. We highlight that our wrapper $\mathcal{W}(\mathcal{F}_{RO})$ improves on previous wrappers in two aspects, in order to provide a more natural model of the real world: (1) We capture the pre-mining stage by letting the adversary query the RO with no restrictions (albeit polynomially bounded) before the CRS is released; (2) The wrapper limits adversarial access per nominal round by bounding the total number of queries that $\mathcal{A}$ can make. The second aspect allows us to dispose the "flat" computational model and define the computational power in terms of the number of RO queries per round, which makes it possible to further refine the notion of a "respecting environment" (see below) that is suited for imperfect local clocks.

Diffusion. We adopt the peer-to-peer communication functionality $\mathcal{F}_{Diffuse}^{\Delta}$ (cf. [3]), which guarantees that an honestly sent message will be delivered to all the protocol participants within Δ rounds. Moreover, for those adversarially generated messages, $\mathcal{F}_{Diffuse}^{\Delta}$ forces them to be delivered to all the honest parties within Δ rounds after they are learnt by at least one honest participant. This captures the natural behavior of honest parties that they will forward all the messages that they have not yet seen to their peers.

We refer to [14] for a detailed description of the above functionalities.

2.3 Dynamic Participation

The notion of a "respecting environment" was introduced in [11] to model the varying number of participants in a protocol execution. In [2,3], the notion of *dynamic participation* was introduced aiming at describing the protocol execution in a more realistic fashion. Here we present a further refined classification of possible *types* of honest parties. See Table 1.

Table 1. A classification of protocol participants.

Resource	Basic types of *honest* parties	
	Resource unavailable	Resource available
Random oracle $\mathcal{F}_{RO}$	*stalled*	*operational*
Network $\mathcal{F}_{Diffuse}^{\Delta}$	*offline*	*online*
Clock $\mathcal{F}_{ILCLOCK}$	*time-unaware*	*time-aware*
Synchronized state	*desynchronized*	*synchronized*

Consider an honest party P at a given point of the protocol execution. We say P is *operational* if P is registered with the random oracle $\mathcal{F}_{RO}$; otherwise, we say it is *stalled*. We say P is *online* if P is registered with the network; *offline* otherwise. We say P is *time-aware* if P is registered with the *imperfect* clock functionality $\mathcal{F}_{ILCLOCK}$; and *time-unaware* otherwise.

Further, we say P is *synchronized* if P has been participating in the protocol for sufficiently long time and achieves a "synchronized state" as well as a "synchronized clock." "Synchronized clock" means P holds a chain that shares a common prefix (cf. [10]) with other *synchronized* parties; "synchronized clock" refers to that P maintains a local clock with time close to other *synchronized* parties. Otherwise, P is *desynchronized*. Additionally, P is aware of whether it is synchronized or not, and maintains a local variable isSync serving as an indicator for other actions.

Based on the above classification, we now define the notion of *alert* parties:

$$alert \overset{\text{def}}{=} operational \land online \land time\text{-}aware \land synchronized.$$

In short, alert parties are those who have access to all the resources and are synchronized; this requires them to join the protocol execution passively for some period of time. They constitute the core set of parties that carry out the protocol.

In addition, we define *active* parties to include all parties that are alert, adversarial, and time-unaware.

$$active \overset{\text{def}}{=} alert \lor adversarial \lor time\text{-}unaware.$$

Respecting Environment in Terms of Computational Power. Next, we provide the following generalization of "respecting environment" to relate it to computational power as opposed to number of parties. Our assumption is that during the whole protocol execution, the honest computational power is higher than the adversarial one (cf. the "honest majority" condition in [10] and follow-ups). The computational power is captured by counting the number of RO (hash) queries that parties make in each round. Further, we restrict the environment to fluctuate the number of such queries in a certain limited fashion.

Definition 2. *For $\gamma \in \mathbb{R}^+$ we call the sequence $(h_r)_{r \in [0,B)}$, where $B \in \mathbb{N}$, (γ, s)-respecting if for any set $S \subseteq [0, B)$ of at most s consecutive integers, $\max_{r \in S} h_r \leq \gamma \cdot \min_{r \in S} h_r$.*

We say that *environment $\mathcal{Z}$ is (γ, s)-respecting* if for all $\mathcal{A}$ and coins for $\mathcal{Z}$ and $\mathcal{A}$ the sequence of honest hash queries (h_r) is (γ, s)-respecting.

Note that the notion of respecting environment here is different from the "flat" model adopted in [4, 10–12]. In a flat model, honest parties are assumed to have the same computational power, hence the total number of RO queries is a direct 1-to-1 map from the number of parties. The new respecting environment allows some subset of the honest parties to query the RO multiple times or stay stalled during a nominal round and hence it adapts to the "imperfect local clock" model used in this paper.

3   The Clock Synchronization Protocol with Public Setup

In this section we present the general approach and the various core building blocks of the new clock synchronization protocol—Timekeeper. For a complete description, refer to [14]. At a high level, Timekeeper is a Nakamoto-style PoW-based blockchain protocol together with time synchronization functionalities. Readers can think of it as a Bitcoin protocol with the following modifications:

- It replaces Bitcoin's original clock maintenance solution[5] with a new clock synchronization scheme, which requires parties to use 2-for-1 PoWs [10] to mine and emit clock synchronization beacons and include them in an upcoming block. Furthermore, protocol participants will periodically adjust their local clock values based on the beacons collected in the blockchain and their (local) receiving time.
- Events are triggered by counting the number of local rounds (which is different from the convention that events in PoW-based blockchains are triggered by the arrival of blocks). In other words, the protocol has a clock synchronization *interval* of length R and a target recalculation *epoch* of length M that are defined in terms of the number of rounds; in addition, M is a multiple of R. Both of these values are hardcoded in the protocol. More precisely, parties will call the synchronization procedure (see Sect. 3.3) when their local clock enters round $\langle \texttt{itvl}, \texttt{itvl} \cdot R \rangle$ (this represents the last round in interval $\texttt{itvl}$; see below for details on the round structure); and for target in the next epoch they will call the target recalculation function (details see Sect. 3.4) when their local clock enters $\langle \texttt{itvl}, \texttt{itvl} \cdot R \rangle$, where $(\texttt{itvl} \mod (M/R)) = 0$ (i.e., at the boundary of every (M/R) synchronization intervals).

See Fig. 1 for an illustration of the protocol execution.

Next, we present the basic components that are employed in Timekeeper.

3.1   Timekeeper Timestamps

As opposed to the conventional approach where blocks' timestamps are integer values, timestamps (both blocks' and beacon values) in Timekeeper are represented by a pair of values interval number and round number $\langle \texttt{itvl}, \texttt{r} \rangle \in \langle \mathbb{N}^+, \mathbb{N}^+ \rangle$. Note that (ideally) one synchronization interval would last for R

---

[5] In Bitcoin's original implementation, miners will adjust their time based on three different sources: (1) their local system clock; (2) the median of clock values from peers; (3) the human operator (if the first two disagrees).

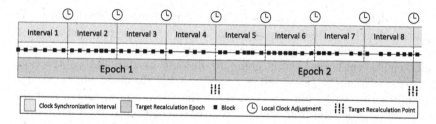

Fig. 1. An illustration of the clock synchronization protocol execution with one target recalculation epoch consisting of four clock synchronization intervals.

rounds (i.e., rounds $((i-1) \cdot R, i \cdot R]$ would belong to the i-th interval). However, in Timekeeper we let the lower bound be 0, which means that timestamps with a somewhat small round number are still valid. Specifically, a timestamp $\langle \mathtt{itvl}, \mathbf{r} \rangle$ is considered valid if and only if it satisfies the predicate $\mathsf{validTimestamp}(\mathtt{itvl}, \mathbf{r}) \triangleq \mathbf{r} \le \mathtt{itvl} \cdot R$. We note that this new treatment allows for some small distortion at the end of each interval—i.e., the round number of a few blocks at the beginning of the next interval may be smaller than the last block of the previous interval (we call these "retorted" timestamps); see Fig. 2.

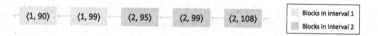

Fig. 2. An illustration of a segment of the blockchain with synchronization interval length R = 100. *Blocks can have timestamp values equal to blocks in the previous interval.*

Consider a chain of blocks in Timekeeper. Their timestamps should increase monotonically in terms of their interval number, and the round number in a single interval should also increase monotonically. More specifically, given two timestamps $\langle \mathtt{itvl}_i, \mathbf{r}_i \rangle, \langle \mathtt{itvl}_j, \mathbf{r}_j \rangle$ of two blocks $\mathcal{B}_i, \mathcal{B}_j$ respectively, if $\mathcal{B}_i$ is an ancestor block of $\mathcal{B}_j$, they should satisfy the following predicate:

$$\mathsf{validTimestampOrder}(\langle \mathtt{itvl}_i, \mathbf{r}_i \rangle, \langle \mathtt{itvl}_j, \mathbf{r}_j \rangle)$$

$$\triangleq \left\{ \begin{array}{c} \mathsf{validTimestamp}(\mathtt{itvl}_i, \mathbf{r}_i) \wedge \mathsf{validTimestamp}(\mathtt{itvl}_i, \mathbf{r}_i) \\ \wedge \left[(\mathtt{itvl}_i \le \mathtt{itvl}_j) \vee (\mathtt{itvl}_i = \mathtt{itvl}_j \wedge \mathbf{r}_i < \mathbf{r}_j) \right] \end{array} \right\}$$

Furthermore, we will overload the notation of comparison operators based on the valid order of timestamps. E.g., "$=$" will denote that two timestamps are identical, and $\langle \mathtt{itvl}_1, \mathbf{r}_1 \rangle < \langle \mathtt{itvl}_2, \mathbf{r}_2 \rangle$ if and only if $\mathsf{validTimestampOrder}(\langle \mathtt{itvl}_1, \mathbf{r}_1 \rangle, \langle \mathtt{itvl}_2, \mathbf{r}_2 \rangle)$ holds. Other operators $>, \le, \ge, \ne$ are defined similarly.

We also redefine "$+, -$" to describe the timestamp that is $k \in \mathbb{N}$ rounds before (resp., after) $\langle \texttt{itvl}, \texttt{r} \rangle$. Regarding addition, $\langle \texttt{itvl}, \texttt{r} \rangle + k = \langle \max\{\texttt{itvl}, \lceil (\texttt{r} + k)/\texttt{R} \rceil\}, \texttt{r} + k \rangle$. Intuitively, the additive operation simply adds k to $\texttt{r}$, and only increments $\texttt{itvl}$ when it is going to become invalid. For subtraction, $\langle \texttt{itvl}, \texttt{r} \rangle - k = \langle \max\{1, \lceil (\texttt{r} - k)/\texttt{R} \rceil\}, \max\{1, \texttt{r} - k\} \rangle$. In other words, regarding the subtraction operation, we only apply the operation on round, and the interval number is derived from the round after calculation. It does not output timestamps that are not "normally" belong to an interval. In case we do the subtraction operation for $k \geq \texttt{r}$, it will return $\langle 1, 1 \rangle$.

Timekeeper's new approach to timestamps raises questions regarding the "trimming" of blockchains by counting the number of rounds. Recall that in [10] the notation $\mathcal{C}^{\lceil k}$ represents the chain that results from removing the k rightmost blocks. In this paper, we overload this notation to denote the chain that results from removing blocks with timestamps in the last k rounds with respect to the current time. Specifically, for $\mathcal{C} = \mathcal{B}_1 \mathcal{B}_2 \dots \mathcal{B}_n$ and local time $\langle \texttt{itvl}, \texttt{r} \rangle$, $\mathcal{C}^{\lceil k} = \mathcal{B}_1 \mathcal{B}_2 \dots \mathcal{B}_m$ is the longest chain such that $\forall \mathcal{B} \in \mathcal{C}^{\lceil k}, \mathsf{Timestamp}(\mathcal{B}) < \langle \texttt{itvl}, \texttt{r} \rangle - k$. In other words, $\mathcal{B}_{m+1}$ is the first block (if it exists) such that $\mathsf{Timestamp}(\mathcal{B}_{m+1}) \geq \langle \texttt{itvl}, \texttt{r} \rangle - k$ holds.

3.2   2-for-1 Proofs of Work and Synchronization Beacons

2-for-1 PoW is a technique that allows protocols to utilize a single random oracle $H(\cdot)$ to compose two separate PoW sub-procedures involving two distinct and independent random oracles $H_0(\cdot), H_1(\cdot)$. It was first proposed in [10] in order to achieve a better/optimal corruption threshold (from one-third to one-half) for the solution of the traditional consensus problem using a blockchain.

We refer to [10] for more details, and here we present a simple implementation with the clock synchronization application in mind. In order to do the 2-for-1 mining, a party P prepares a composite input w that is a concatenation of two inputs w_0, w_1 of two different sub-procedures S_0, S_1, respectively. I.e., $w = w_0 \parallel w_1$. After selecting a nonce ctr, querying the random oracle with $ctr \parallel w$ and getting result u, P checks if $u < T$ which implies success in sub-procedure S_0; P also checks if $[u]^\mathsf{R} < T$ (where $[u]^\mathsf{R}$ denotes the reverse of a bitstring u) which indicates success in sub-procedure S_1. After successfully generating a PoW for S_0 (resp., S_1), in order to let parties others check validity, the proof will include the nonce and the entire composite input $ctr \parallel w$. Note that sub-procedure S_0 (resp., S_1) only cares about its corresponding part w_0 (resp., w_1), and treat the other part as dummy information.

The 2-for-1 PoW technique has several advantages when compared with the straightforward approach that would simply utilize two different random oracles. The most prominent advantage is that it prevents the adversary $\mathcal{A}$ from concentrating its computational power on one RO and thus gain advantage in the corresponding sub-procedure.

Synchronization Beacons. In addition to the conventional blocks constituting the blockchain, protocol participants in Timekeeper also produce another type of "tiny" blocks using 2-for-1 PoWs. We call these blocks *clock synchronization beacons* ("beacons" for short) since they are used to report parties' local time and synchronize their clocks.

In more detail, one clock synchronization beacon SB is a tuple with the following structure.

$$SB \triangleq \langle \langle \mathtt{itvl}, \mathrm{r} \rangle, P, \eta_{\mathtt{itvl}}, ctr, blockLabel \rangle,$$

where $\langle \mathtt{itvl}, \mathrm{r} \rangle$ is the local time SB reports; P denotes the identity of its miner; $\eta_{\mathtt{itvl}}$ is some fresh randomness in the current interval; ctr represents the nonce of the PoW and $blockLabel$ is the associated block input. Note that SB must record the identity of its miner because there might be multiple beacons, mined by different parties, reporting the same timestamp as well as nonce value; otherwise, it would be impossible for the parties to distinguish such beacons. Worse still, other participants would not be able to distinguish the same beacon SB when they receive SB multiple times. Regarding $\eta_{\mathtt{itvl}}$, it is a string associated with interval $\mathtt{itvl}$ for the purpose of preventing the adversary $\mathcal{A}$ from mining beacons with *future* timestamps. In other words, protocol participants (including $\mathcal{A}$) can only learn $\eta_{\mathtt{itvl}}$ after they have (almost) finished interval $\mathtt{itvl} - 1$. We present the structure of intervals in detail and how we compute $\eta_{\mathtt{itvl}}$ in Sect. 3.3 and treat it as a communal bitstring here. We note that parties can learn $\eta_{\mathtt{itvl}}$ from their local chain, and indeed SB does not need to include $\eta_{\mathtt{itvl}}$ (P can prune those beacons that are invalid with $\eta_{\mathtt{itvl}}$ in their local view). We keep $\eta_{\mathtt{itvl}}$ in the description for convenience.

Regarding the structure of a blockchain block $\mathcal{B}$, we adopt the similar structure as in [11] (with the dummy information in the 2-for-1 PoWs):

$$\mathcal{B} \triangleq \langle h, \mathtt{st}, \langle \mathtt{itvl}, \mathrm{r} \rangle, ctr, txLabel \rangle,$$

where h is the reference to the previous block, $\mathtt{st}$ the Merkle root of the block content, $\langle \mathtt{itvl}, \mathrm{r} \rangle$ its timestamp, ctr the nonce of PoW, and $txLabel$ the binded beacon input.

We are now ready to describe how the parties in Timekeeper do the 2-for-1 PoW mining. The composite input prepared in Timekeeper is different from the trivial instance above, in that the term $\langle \mathtt{itvl}, \mathrm{r} \rangle$ appears in both blocks and beacons. Hence, simply concatenating two inputs introduces redundant information in the PoW. When a party P is ready to perform the mining procedure, P binds the nonce, the blocks' input and beacon input together as

$$\langle ctr, h, \mathtt{st}, \langle \mathtt{itvl}, \mathrm{r} \rangle, P, \eta_{\mathsf{ep}}^{\mathcal{C}} \rangle$$

and hand them over to random oracle $\mathcal{F}_{\mathrm{RO}}$. Let u denote the result from $\mathcal{F}_{\mathrm{RO}}$. If $u < T$ (i.e., the block query succeeds), P finds a new block $\mathcal{B} = \langle h, \mathtt{st}, \langle \mathtt{itvl}, \mathrm{r} \rangle, ctr, txLabel \rangle$ where $txLabel := \langle P, \eta_{\mathsf{ep}}^{\mathcal{C}} \rangle$; if $[u]^{\mathrm{R}} < T$ (the beacon query succeeds), P gets a new beacon SB $= \langle \langle \mathtt{itvl}, \mathrm{r} \rangle, P, ctr, blockLabel \rangle$, where $blockLabel :=$

$\langle h, \mathsf{st} \rangle$. Note that for the sake of presentation, we reorder the content of blocks and beacons so that they are inconsistent with the input to the PoW.

After receiving the result from $\mathcal{F}_{\mathrm{RO}}$, P checks if it was able to successfully generate a new block. In addition, P checks if he successfully produces a beacon but only when P's local clock stays in the *beacon mining and inclusion* phase. Namely, P reports a timestamp that satisfies a certain criterion (details in Sect. 3.3).

3.3   Clock Synchronization Intervals and the Synchronization Procedure

As mentioned earlier, Timekeeper participants will periodically adjust their local clock. We call the time interval between two adjustment points[6] a *clock synchronization interval* (or "interval" for short). Ideally, one interval will last for R rounds. The actual number of local rounds that parties observe may differ according to the shift computed in the previous interval (we will show later that the shift computed in every interval is well-bounded). When party P's local clock gets to the last round of an interval, it will call the synchronization procedure (see below), which adjusts its local clock and gets the fresh randomness to run the next interval.

Interval Structure. Timekeeper divides one interval into three phases: (1) *view convergence*, (2) *beacon mining and inclusion* and (3) *beacon-set convergence*. The phase parties stay in depends on their local clocks. Furthermore, parties will keep track of the (local) arriving time of a synchronization beacon as long as it is online. In this section we describe these three phases as well as the bookkeeping function and explain the design intention behind them.

View Convergence. When a party P's local clock reports a time $\langle \mathsf{itvl}, \mathsf{r} \rangle$ such that $\mathsf{r} < (\mathsf{itvl} - 1) \cdot R + K$, P is in the *view convergence* phase. Note that this also includes rounds with potentially retorted timestamps. In this phase, if P is alert, it will try to mine the next block with the 2-for-1 PoW technique (i.e., the input information that P forwards to the $\mathcal{F}_{\mathrm{RO}}$ functionality does not need to be changed); nonetheless, P will not check if he successfully mines a beacon after P acquires the output. This is because all the beacons obtained in this phase are *invalid* in that they report an undesirable timestamp.

The general motivation for introducing the view convergence phase and letting parties wait for some period of time at the beginning of an interval is that we would like parties to start mining beacons with a *consistent* view of the previous interval. Since K is larger than the common prefix parameter (we will quantify K in later, in Sect. 4.2), at the end of the view convergence phase of interval $\mathsf{itvl} + 1$, alert parties will have a common view of interval itvl. In other words, they will agree on all the blocks in interval itvl, and the adversary $\mathcal{A}$ will not

---

[6] The first interval in particular lies between the beginning of the execution and the first time parties adjust their clock.

be able to apply any changes to these blocks. Hence, alert parties agree on the number of blocks in the previous interval, which decides the mining difficulty within the current interval. (This will used in our new target recalculation function, presented in Sect. 3.4.) Parties will mine beacons with the same difficulty, and this simplifies the protocol description as well as its analysis. Furthermore, alert parties will compute the same fresh randomness as

$$\eta_{\texttt{itvl}+1} \triangleq G(\eta_{\texttt{itvl}} \,\|\, (\texttt{itvl} + 1) \,\|\, v), \tag{1}$$

where v is the concatenation of all block hashes in interval $\texttt{itvl}$. Note that we adopt a different hash function $G(\cdot)$ (as opposed to $H(\cdot)$) to compute the next fresh randomness that is not used in the 2-for-1 PoW, which does not consume any queries to random oracle $\mathcal{F}_{\text{RO}}$.

Recall that by assumption the adversary $\mathcal{A}$ has full knowledge of the network, and hence it can learn all honest blocks from the previous interval immediately and manipulate the chain at will for up to a number of rounds bounded by the common prefix parameter, allowing $\mathcal{A}$ to mine the synchronization beacons before the alert parties start to mine. We call this period where $\mathcal{A}$ starts ahead of time the *pre-mining* stage. Nonetheless, we will show later that there will be at least one block generated by an alert party near the end of interval $\texttt{itvl}$, which prevents the adversary from pre-mining for too long a time.

Beacon Mining and Inclusion. When a party P's local clock is in rounds $\langle \texttt{itvl}, r \rangle$ satisfying $(\texttt{itvl} - 1) \cdot R + K \le r \le \texttt{itvl} \cdot R - K$, P is in the *beacon mining and inclusion* phase. Next, we define the predicate $I_{\text{sync}}(\texttt{itvl})$ to extract the set of timestamps in this phase. Formally,

$$I_{\text{sync}}(\texttt{itvl}) \triangleq \{(\texttt{itvl} - 1) \cdot R + K, \ldots, \texttt{itvl} \cdot R - K\}. \tag{2}$$

For convenience, we slightly overload this predicate. When the input is a timestamp, $I_{\text{sync}}(\langle \texttt{itvl}, r \rangle)$ outputs whether $\langle \texttt{itvl}, r \rangle$ stays in a beacon mining and inclusion phase. I.e., $I_{\text{sync}}(\langle \texttt{itvl}, r \rangle) = \textsf{true}$ if $r \in I_{\text{sync}}(\texttt{itvl})$, and $\textsf{false}$ otherwise.

After entering this phase, P will use a 2-for-1 PoW to mine both blocks and clock synchronization beacons. During interval $\texttt{itvl}$, the output will be a beacon which indicates its local time and value $\textsf{SB} \triangleq \langle \langle \texttt{itvl}, r \rangle, \textsf{P}, ctr, blockLabel \rangle$. Regarding the mining difficulty, Timekeeper will set the same target value for blocks and beacons[7]. In other words, the expected number of blocks and of beacons in this phase are equal.

After a beacon is successfully generated, it will be diffused into the network via $\mathcal{F}_{\text{Diffuse}}^{\text{sync}}$. P will include a beacon $\textsf{SB}$ into the pending block content if $\textsf{SB}$ is valid w.r.t. the current interval. Next, we describe how they check the validity of a beacon is checked. The format of a beacon $\textsf{SB}$ with respect to interval $\texttt{itvl}$ is correct if and only if it reports a timestamp $\langle \texttt{itvl}, r \rangle$ such that $r \in I_{\text{sync}}(\texttt{itvl})$.

---

[7] We will adopt the same target for simplicity. Indeed, maintaining a constant ratio between the difficulty level of blocks and that of beacons will work.

We say a beacon SB is *valid* w.r.t. *chain* $\mathcal{C}$ if and only if its format is correct and the hash value of SB (after concatenating with the fresh randomness in $\mathcal{C}$) is smaller than the corresponding mining target. P will try to include all the (valid) beacons mined in the current interval itvl with timestamps earlier than the current local time but which have not yet been included in the blockchain. Specifically, at round $\langle \text{itvl}, r \rangle$, all valid beacons recording timestamp $\langle \text{itvl}, u \rangle$ with $u \leq r$ will get into P's pending block content.

When P's local clock goes past the last round of beacon mining and inclusion phase, it stops checking the beacon hash output and it no longer includes beacons in the next block. Beacons that are generated and diffused right at the end of this phase get dropped.

Beacon-Set Convergence. The third and last phase—*beacon-set convergence*—consists of the last K rounds in an interval. In other words, a party P is in this phase when P reports a timestamp $\langle \text{itvl}, r \rangle$ with $r > \text{itvl} \cdot R - K$. During this phase, P behaves similar to the first phase. I.e., it will not check for the 2-for-1 PoW result to see if the beacon generation succeeds.

Parties have to wait for at least K rounds to ensure that they share a *consistent* view of the set of beacons included in the current interval (except with some negligible probability). This phase cannot be omitted since only when parties agree on the same beacon set can the synchronization procedure maintain the protocol's security properties (Sect. 4).

Beacon Arrival Booking. In order to adjust its clock, P also needs the local receiving time of all beacons that have been included in the chain. Hence, P will maintain a local registry that records the beacons it receives as well as their arrival time. More specifically, this local beacon ledger is an array of synchronization beacons. For each beacon SB, a pair $(a, \text{flag}) \in \langle \mathbb{N}^+, \mathbb{N}^+ \rangle \times \{\text{final}, \text{temp}\}$ is assigned to it. Consider a round $\langle \text{itvl}, r \rangle$ when P receives a beacon SB with $\text{Timestamp}(\text{SB}) = \langle \text{itvl}', r' \rangle$.

- If $\text{itvl}' \leq \text{itvl}$, which means the beacon SB is generated in the current or previous interval[8]. P will drop SB if it is not valid w.r.t. its localchain; otherwise, P will assign $(\langle \text{itvl}, r \rangle, \text{final})$ to SB. This means that all the information gathering regarding this beacon has been finalized and it is ready to be used.
- If $\text{itvl}' > \text{itvl}$, the beacon is generated in the future. P will assign $(\langle \text{itvl}, r \rangle, \text{temp})$ to SB, which indicates that modifications on the receiving time may be applied in the future. Note that parties may not know the fresh randomness in future intervals (for example, if they are newly joint parties and have not yet synchronized with the blockchain or they are alert but receive forthcoming beacons). Hence they cannot check the validity of beacons with temp flag. Nevertheless, invalid beacons would be excluded from the registry after P learns the upcoming fresh randomness.

---

[8] Beacons generated in previous intervals are stale in that P has already passed the synchronization point associated with these beacons, and they will never be used in the future. We list them for completeness.

If P receives multiple beacon messages with the same creator and time reported, P will adopt the first one it receives as its arrival time.

The Synchronization Procedure. At the end of an interval (i.e., when the local time reports $r = \texttt{itvl} \cdot R$), parties will use the beacons information to compute a value shift that indicates how much the logical clock should be adjusted. (See [14] for the complete specification.)

Adjusting the Local Clock. When a party P's local clock reaches round $\langle \texttt{itvl}, \texttt{itvl} \cdot R \rangle$ and P has finished the round's regular mining procedure, P will adjust its local clock based on the beacons recorded on chain and their local receiving time. More specifically, P will extract all the beacons from the beacon mining and inclusion phase, and compute the differences between their timestamp and local receiving time $\mathsf{Timestamp}(\mathsf{SB}) - \mathsf{arrivalTime}(\mathsf{SB})$. Since the timestamp of SB and its arrival time share the same interval index, we only need to compute the difference between their round numbers. Subsequently, all the beacons will be ordered based on this difference and a shift will be computed by selecting the median difference therein. Formally,

$$\mathsf{shift}^P_\texttt{itvl} \triangleq \mathsf{med}\{\mathsf{Timestamp}(\mathsf{SB}) - \mathsf{arrivalTime}(\mathsf{SB}) \mid \mathsf{SB} \in \mathcal{S}^P_\texttt{itvl}\}. \tag{3}$$

In case there are two median beacons $\mathsf{SB}_1, \mathsf{SB}_2$, parties will adjust $\mathsf{shift}^P_\texttt{itvl} \triangleq \lceil(\mathsf{Timestamp}(\mathsf{SB}_1) - \mathsf{arrivalTime}(\mathsf{SB}_1) + \mathsf{Timestamp}(\mathsf{SB}_2) - \mathsf{arrivalTime}(\mathsf{SB}_2))/2\rceil$. Afterwards, P will update its local clock to $\langle \texttt{itvl} + 1, r + \mathsf{shift} \rangle$. Later we show that this update strategy in the synchronization procedure allows parties' clocks to remain in a narrow interval and do not deviate too much from the nominal time.

Note that parties will enter local round $\langle \texttt{itvl}, r \rangle$ where $r = \texttt{itvl} \cdot R$ only once. If they enter some time $\langle \texttt{itvl}', r \rangle$ in the future, we will get $\texttt{itvl}' > \texttt{itvl}$ and they will never revert back.

Mining with Backward-Set Clocks. After the adjustment at the end of intervals, and shift is added to P's local clock, it may set its local time to values $\langle \texttt{itvl}, r \rangle$ such that $r \leq (\texttt{itvl} - 1) \cdot R$ (i.e., the retortion effect that was mentioned earlier). Nonetheless, P can continue to mine blocks with this timestamp and its local clock will eventually proceed to a time value of regular format (i.e., $r > (\texttt{itvl} - 1) \cdot R$).

We compare this treatment with the similar scenario in a PoS blockchain [3]. In [3], setting local clocks backward is never a problem since parties can keep silent during this period. Due to the nature of PoS-based blockchains, parties do not need to do anything if they are not assigned the leader slot. In our context, however, adopting the same 'silence' policy contradicts the basic nature of PoW-based blockchains as parties will forfeit the chance to extend their local chain. In other words, there is no point for an activate party to not make RO queries. This is taken care of by Timekeeper's timestamping scheme.

Updating the Beacon Arrival Time Registry. Notice that the beacon information stored in a party P's arrival time registry is closely related to which interval P stays in; after P enters the next interval, it needs to update the beacon bookkeeping. P will apply a shift computation for all beacons with flag temp. Furthermore, for those beacons that report a timestamp with interval equal to the incoming one, their flag will be set to final. In more detail, at the end of interval itvl, for all eligible SB in the beacon registry, their associated pair $(\langle \text{itvl}_{SB}, r_{SB} \rangle, \text{temp})$ will be updated to $(\langle \text{itvl}_{SB}, r_{SB} + \text{shift} \rangle, \text{final})$ if $\text{itvl}_{SB} = \text{itvl} + 1$. Note that for those beacons whose flags are set to final, P will removed all invalid ones from the registry after the update.

3.4   The Target Recalculation Function

If the mining target is not set appropriately ("appropriately" means that the block generation rate according to the current hashing power and target is somewhat steady; see [11]), PoW-based blockchain protocols fail to maintain any of the security properties in a permissionless environment. In Bitcoin, the target is adjusted after receiving the last block of the current epoch (and an epoch consists of 2016 blocks). Based on the time elapsed to mine these blocks, a new target is set based on the previous target value and the variation is proportional to the time elapsed. Note that Bitcoin's target recalculation function is not the only way to adjust the difficulty level. A large number of other recalculation functions have been proposed in alternate blockchains (e.g., Ethereum, Bitcoin Cash, Litecoin), with their security asserted by either theoretical analysis or empirical data.

In Timekeeper, we propose a new target recalculation function that is suitable for the new setting. Intuitively, our function is a reversed version of Bitcoin's original function, namely, protocol participants wait for some fixed number of rounds M (in their local view) to update the difficulty level. We call such M number of rounds a *target recalculation epoch*. Moreover, Timekeeper sets M as a multiple of R, which makes the target recalculation epoch consist of several clock synchronization intervals, and the start and end point of an epoch coincide with the start and end of different synchronization intervals. Recall that in the Timekeeper timestamp scheme introduced in Sect. 3.1, the first term in $\langle \text{itvl}, r \rangle$ does not directly reflect which target recalculation epoch it is in. For simplicity, we introduce function TargetRecalcEpoch that maps the protocol timestamp to the target recalculation epoch it belongs to:

$$\text{TargetRecalcEpoch}(\langle \text{itvl}, r \rangle) \triangleq \lceil \text{itvl}/(M/R) \rceil.$$

In addition, we introduce a function EpochBlocks which extracts all the blocks in chain $\mathcal{C}$ that belong to target recalculation epoch ep. Formally, given $\text{ep} \geq 1$,

$$\text{EpochBlocks}(\mathcal{C}, \text{ep}) \triangleq \{\mathcal{B} : \mathcal{B} \in \mathcal{C} \wedge \text{TargetRecalcEpoch}(\text{Timestamp}(\mathcal{B})) = \text{ep}\}.$$

Also for convenience, we let EpochBlockCount be a function that returns the number of blocks in chain $\mathcal{C}$ that belong to epoch ep. We also extend the input domain of epoch numbers to 0 and let it output Λ_{epoch} (the ideal number of blocks) to capture the fact that the target at the beginning of an execution is set appropriately and hence maintains the ideal block generation rate. Formally,

$$\mathsf{EpochBlockCount}(\mathcal{C}, \mathsf{ep}) \triangleq \begin{cases} |\mathsf{EpochBlocks}(\mathcal{C}, \mathsf{ep})| & \textit{if } \mathsf{ep} \geq 1 \\ \Lambda_{\mathsf{epoch}} & \textit{if } \mathsf{ep} = 0 \end{cases} \tag{4}$$

Going back to the algorithm, for the first epoch ($\mathsf{ep} = 1$) parties will adopt the target value of the genesis block (T_0). I.e., $T_1 = T_0$. Regarding other epochs ($\mathsf{ep} > 1$), parties will figure out how many blocks are produced in the previous epoch, and set the next target based on the previous one. This variation is proportional to the ratio of expected number of blocks Λ_{epoch} and the actual number. I.e., for epoch $\mathsf{ep} + 1$,

$$T_{\mathsf{ep}+1} \triangleq \frac{\Lambda_{\mathsf{epoch}}}{\Lambda} \cdot T_{\mathsf{ep}}, \quad \mathsf{ep} \in \mathbb{N}^+, \tag{5}$$

where Λ is the number of blocks in epoch ep—in other words, the size of $\mathsf{EpochBlocks}(\mathcal{C}, \mathsf{ep})$.

In order to prevent the "raising difficulty attack" [6], the maximal target variation in a single recalculation step still needs to be bounded (we denote this bound by τ). Specifically, if $\Lambda > \tau \cdot \Lambda_{\mathsf{epoch}}$, $T_{\mathsf{ep}+1}$ will be set as T_{ep}/τ; on the other hand, if $\Lambda < \Lambda_{\mathsf{epoch}}/\tau$, $T_{\mathsf{ep}+1}$ will be set as $\tau \cdot T_{\mathsf{ep}}$.

Remark 1. We observe that, compared to the Bitcoin case, the adversary $\mathcal{A}$ in Timekeeper is in a much worse position to carry out the raising difficulty attack. This is because in Bitcoin, in order to significantly raise the difficulty in the next epoch, $\mathcal{A}$ only needs to mine 2016 blocks with close timestamps; in the case of Timekeeper, however, the adversary has to mine $\tau \cdot \Lambda_{\mathsf{epoch}}$ blocks (with fake timestamps) in order to raise the same level of difficulty. The number of blocks that $\mathcal{A}$ needs to prepare is τ times larger than that in Bitcoin (assuming both protocols share the same number of expected blocks in an epoch).

3.5   Newly Joining Parties

Recall that Timekeeper runs in a permissionless environment where parties can join and leave at will. As such, it is essential that newly joining parties can learn the protocol time to become alert and participate in the core mining process. More specifically, after the joining procedure, newly joining party P's local clock should report a time in a sufficiently narrow interval with all other alert parties, at which point P can claim also being alert.

Based on the fine-grained classification of types of parties in our dynamic participation model (Sect. 2.3), newly joining parties can be classified into two types: (1) parties that are temporarily de-registered from $\mathcal{F}_{\mathrm{RO}}$, and (2) parties that start with bootstrapping from the genesis block, or parties that temporarily lose the network connection (i.e., de-registered from $\mathcal{F}_{\mathrm{Diffuse}}^{\Delta}$), or parties that are temporarily de-registered from $\mathcal{F}_{\mathrm{ILCLOCK}}$.

For parties that are stalled for a while, since they do not miss any clock tick or other necessary information from the network, they can easily re-join by simulating clock adjustments locally (details see [14]). For the rest of newly joining parties, they will be classified as de-synchronized (note that parties are aware of their synchronization status), and will run the joining procedure JoinProc, which we now describe.

Procedure JoinProc. In order to synchronize its clock, a newly joining party P needs to "listen" to the protocol for sufficiently long time. We describe the joining process below, which is similar to that in [3]. The main difference is that we adopt the heaviest-chain selection rule in order to adapt to the PoW context. The complete specification of this protocol is presented in [14], and the default parameters values are summarized in Table 2.

- **Phase A (state reset).** When all resources are available to P, after resetting all its local variables, P invokes the main round procedure triggering the join procedure.
- **Phase B (chain convergence, with parameter t_{off}).** In the second activation upon a MAINTAIN-LEDGER command, the party will jump to phase B and stay in phase B for t_{off} rounds. During this phase, the party applies the *heaviest-chain selection rule* maxvalid to filter its incoming chains. The motivation behind Phase B is to let P build a chain that shares a sufficiently long common prefix with all alert parties. Note that since P has not yet learnt the protocol time, it cannot filter out chains that should be put aside in the futureChains. Hence, the chain held by P may still contain a long suffix built entirely by the adversary. However, it can be guaranteed that this adversarial fork can happen for up to k rounds ahead. Thus, the beacons recorded before the fork can be used to compute the adjustment and their local arrival times will be reliable.
- **Phase C (beacon gathering, with parameter t_{gather}).** Once a party P has finished Phase B, it continues with Phase C, the beacon-gathering phase. During this phase, P continues to collect and filter chains as in Phase B. In addition, P now processes and bookkeeps the beacons received from $\mathcal{F}_{Diffuse}^{sync}$. At a high level, this phases' length parameter t_{gather} guarantees that: (1) enough beacons are recorded to compute a reliable time shift; (2) enough time has elapsed so that the blockchain reaches agreement on the set of (valid) beacons to use. At the end of Phase C, P is able to reliably judge valid arrival times.

Table 2. Parameters of the joining procedure and their corresponding phases.

Parameter	Default	Phase
t_{off}	2K	B
t_{gather}	5R/2	C
t_{pre}	3K	D

- **Phase D (shift computation, with parameter t_{pre}).** Since party P has now built a blockchain sharing a common prefix with any alert party, and has bookkeeped synchronization beacons for a sufficiently long time, P starts from the earliest interval i^* such that (1) the arrival times of all beacons included in blocks within the beacon mining and inclusion phase of interval i^* have been locally bookkeeped, and (2) all of these beacons arrived sufficiently later than the start of Phase C (parameterized by t_{pre} rounds). Based on this information, P computes the shift value as alert parties do at the boundary of synchronization interval i^*. P concludes Phase D when the adjusted time is a valid timestamp in interval $i^* + 1$ (in other words, r does not exceed $(i^* + 1)R$); otherwise, P updates the local arrival time of beacons with flag temp and repeats the above process with interval $i^* + 1$. We note that if Phase D involves the computation w.r.t. multiple intervals, the local time may temporarily be set as an invalid timestamp. Nevertheless, eventually after P has passed $(2K + 5R/2)$ (local) rounds, P will end up with a valid timestamp that with overwhelming probability is close enough to those of all alert parties.

4   Protocol Analysis

Our ultimate goal is to show that, at any point of the protocol's execution, the timestamps reported by all alert protocol participants of Timekeeper will satisfy the properties defined in Definition 1. We start off with some additional definitions and preliminary results.

4.1   Notation, Definitions and Preliminary Propositions

We note that several of the analytical tools proposed in [11,12] do not directly apply in the environment (with $\mathcal{F}_{ILCLOCK}$) where Timekeeper runs in. Therefore, we first extend and enhance these tools to adapt them to this new environment.

Our probability space is over all executions of length at most some polynomial in κ and λ; we use **Pr** to denote the probability measure of this space. Furthermore, let $\mathcal{E}$ be a random variable taking values on this space and with a distribution induced by the random coins of all entities (adversary, environment, parties) and the random oracle.

For the sake of convenience, we define a *nominal time* that coincides with the internal variable time in $\mathcal{F}_{ILCLOCK}$. Recall that time aims at recording how many times the functionality sends clock ticks to all registered honest parties.

Definition 3 (Nominal Time). *Given an execution of Timekeeper, any prefix of the execution can be mapped deterministically to an integer r, which we call nominal time, as follows: r is the value of variable time in the clock functionality at the final step of the execution prefix which is obtained by parsing the prefix from the genesis block and keeping track of the honest party set registered with the clock functionality (bootstrapped with the set of inaugural alert parties). (In case no honest party exists in the execution, r is undefined).*

Note that we adopt r to denote the nominal time, which is different from the protocol timestamp $\langle \texttt{itvl}, \texttt{r} \rangle$.

If at a nominal round r exactly h parties query the oracle with target T, the probability of at least one of them will succeed is

$$f(T, h) = 1 - (1 - pT)^h \le pTh, \text{ where } p = 1/2^\kappa.$$

During nominal round r, alert parties might be querying the random oracle for various targets. We denote by $T_r^{\min}$ and $T_r^{\max}$ the minimum and maximum of those targets. Moreover, the initial target T_0 implies in our model an initial estimate of the number of honest RO queries h_0; specifically, $h_0 = 2^\kappa \Lambda_{\text{epoch}}/(T_0 M)$, i.e., the number of parties it takes to produce Λ_{epoch} blocks of difficulty $1/T_0$ in time M. For convenience, we denote $f_0 = f(T_0, h_0)$ and simply refer to it as f. Also note that the ideal number of blocks $\Lambda_{\text{epoch}} = Mf$, so in the analysis we will use Mf to represent Λ_{epoch}.

"Good" Properties. Next, we present some definitions which will allow us to introduce a few ("good") properties, serving as an intermediate step towards proving the desired clock properties.

Let us consider the boundary of two target recalculation epochs. Recall that Bitcoin's target recalculation algorithm defines epoch in terms of the number of blocks (m blocks forms an epoch). Thus, a block with block height a multiple of m is the last block of an epoch. While it might be manipulated, its timestamp naturally becomes the proof that miners have adjusted their difficulty and entered the next epoch (known as the *target recalculation point* [11]). In contrast, Timekeeper adopts a new target recalculation function (see Sect. 3.4) that divides the epoch based on the parties' local view. While we can still define a target recalculation point based on one party's local view, parties can *never* agree on a point where they enter the next epoch based on nominal time.

In order to circumvent the above obstacle, we extend the notion of target recalculation point to target recalculation *zone*. See Fig. 3 for an illustration. Intuitively, a "target recalculation zone" w.r.t. epoch ep is a sequence of consecutive nominal rounds such that during these nominal rounds, at least one alert party crosses its own target recalculation point w.r.t. epoch ep. For convenience, we assume a "safe" start—i.e., the first epoch also has a target recalculation zone, and it naturally satisfies all good properties we will later define.

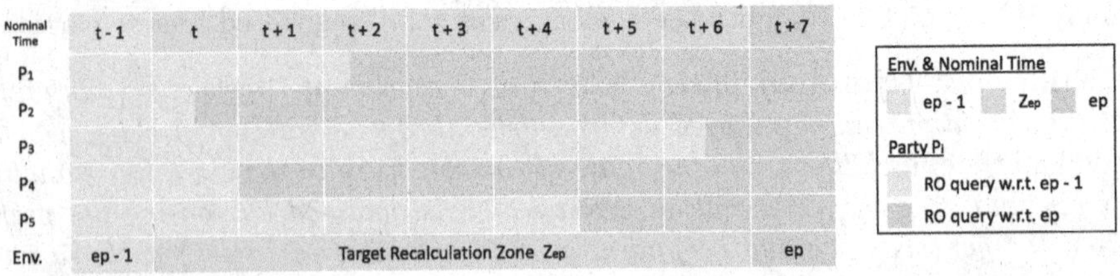

Fig. 3. An illustration of the target recalculation zone $Z_{\text{ep}} = \{t, \ldots, t + 6\}$.

Definition 4.

- *Nominal time r is good if $f/2\gamma^2 \leq ph_r T_r^{\min}$ and $ph_r T_r^{\max} \leq (1+\delta)\gamma^2 f$.*
- *Round $\langle \texttt{itvl}, r \rangle$ is a target-recalculation point w.r.t. epoch $\texttt{ep}$ if $(r = \texttt{itvl} \cdot R) \wedge [\texttt{itvl} \mod (M/R) = 0]$.*
- *A sequence of consecutive nominal rounds $Z_{\texttt{ep}} = \{r\}$ is a target recalculation zone w.r.t. target recalculation epoch $\texttt{ep}$ if during $Z_{\texttt{ep}}$ some subset of synchronized parties are in the logical round that is a target recalculation point w.r.t. $\texttt{ep} - 1$.*
- *A target-recalculation zone $Z_{\texttt{ep}}$ is good if for all $h_r, r \in Z_{\texttt{ep}}$ the target $T_{\texttt{ep}}$ satisfies $f/2\gamma \leq ph_r T_{\texttt{ep}} \leq (1+\delta)\gamma f$.*
- *A chain is good if all its target-recalculation zones are good.*
- *A chain is stale if for some nominal time u it does not contain an honest block computed after nominal time $u - \ell - 2\Delta - 2\Phi$.*
- *The blocklength of an epoch $\texttt{ep}$ on a chain $\mathcal{C}$ is the number of blocks in $\mathcal{C}$ with timestamp $\langle \texttt{itvl}, \cdot \rangle$ such that $\textsf{TargetRecalcEpoch}(\langle \texttt{itvl}, r \rangle) = \texttt{ep}$.*

We would like to prove that, at a certain nominal round r of the protocol execution, alert parties enjoy good properties on their local chains and reported timestamps. Towards this goal, we extract all chains that either belong to alert parties at r or have accumulated sufficient difficulty and thus might be adopted in the future. We denote this chain set by $\mathcal{S}_r$:

$$\mathcal{S}_r \triangleq \left\{ \mathcal{C} \in E_r \left| \begin{array}{l} \text{``}\mathcal{C} \text{ belongs to an alert party'' or} \\ \text{``}\exists \mathcal{C}' \in E_r \text{ that belongs to an alert party and} \\ \text{either } (\text{diff}(\mathcal{C}) > \text{diff}(\mathcal{C}')) \text{ or } (\text{diff}(\mathcal{C}) = \text{diff}(\mathcal{C}') \\ \text{and } \text{head}(\mathcal{C}) \text{ was computed no later than } \text{head}(\mathcal{C}'))\text{''} \end{array} \right. \right\}.$$

Next, we define a series of useful predicates with respect to the potential chain set $\mathcal{S}_r$ and parties' local clocks at nominal round r. Note that Φ is a constant that is the ideal maximal skew of all alert clocks, and $\Phi = \Delta + \Phi_{\text{clock}}$ where Δ is the network delay and Φ_{clock} is the maximal clock drift that $\mathcal{A}$ can set (see Sect. 2.1).

Definition 5. *For a nominal round r, let:*

- GOODCHAINS$(r) \triangleq$ *"For all $u \leq r$, every chain in $\mathcal{S}_u$ is good."*
- GOODROUND$(r) \triangleq$ *"All rounds $u \leq r$ are good."*
- NOSTALECHAINS$(r) \triangleq$ *"For all $u \leq r$, there are no stale chains in $\mathcal{S}_u$."*
- COMMONPREFIX$(r) \triangleq$ *"For all $u \leq r$ and $\mathcal{C}, \mathcal{C}' \in \mathcal{S}_r$, head$(\mathcal{C} \cap \mathcal{C}')$ was created after nominal round $u - \ell - 2\Delta - 2\Phi$."*
- BLOCKLENGTH$(r) \triangleq$ *"For all $u < r$ and $\mathcal{C} \in \mathcal{S}_u$, the blocklength Λ of any epoch $\texttt{ep}$ in $\mathcal{C}$ satisfies $\frac{1}{2(1+\delta)\gamma^2} \cdot mf \leq \Lambda \leq 2(1+\delta)\gamma^2 \cdot mf$*
- GOODBEACONS$(r) \triangleq$ *"For all $u < r$ and the beacon set $\mathcal{S}_{\texttt{itvl}}$ bookkeeped during any interval $\texttt{itvl}$, more than half of beacons within $\mathcal{S}_{\texttt{itvl}}$ are generated by honest parties".*

- GOODSHIFT$(r) \triangleq$ *"For all $u < r$, and the alert party P_i that adjusts its local clock at round u, P_i computes shift_i that $-2\Phi \leq \mathsf{shift}_i \leq \Phi$".*
- GOODSKEW$(r) \triangleq$ *"For all alert parties in nominal time r, their local time in this round differs by at most Φ if they are in the same interval or differs by at most 2Φ if they are in different intervals."* Formally,

$$\text{GOODSKEW}(r) :\Leftrightarrow \left(\forall \mathsf{P}_1, \mathsf{P}_2 \in \mathcal{P}_{\mathsf{alert}}[r] : \begin{array}{ll} |\mathbf{r}_1 - \mathbf{r}_2| \leq \Phi & \text{if } \mathtt{itvl}_1 = \mathtt{itvl}_2 \\ |\mathbf{r}_1 - \mathbf{r}_2| \leq 2\Phi & \text{if } \mathtt{itvl}_1 \neq \mathtt{itvl}_2 \end{array} \right)$$

where $\langle \mathtt{itvl}_1, \mathbf{r}_1 \rangle$ and $\langle \mathtt{itvl}_2, \mathbf{r}_2 \rangle$ are the timestamps that P_1 and P_2 reports during r[9].

Random Variables and (Δ, Φ)-Isolated Success. Next, for the purpose of estimating the difficulty acquired by honest parties during a sequence of rounds, we define the following random variables w.r.t. nominal round r.

- D_r: the sum of the difficulties of all blocks computed by alert parties at nominal round r.
- Y_r: the maximum difficulty among all blocks computed by alert parties at nominal round r.
- Q_r: equal to Y_r when $D_u = 0$ for all $r < u < r, + \Delta + \Phi$ and 0 otherwise.

We call a nominal round r such that $D_r > 0$ *successful* and one wherein $Q_r > 0$ *isolated successful*. An isolated successful round guarantees the irreversible progress of the honest parites.

We highlight that, under the imperfect local clock model $\mathcal{F}_{\mathrm{ILCLOCK}}$, the notion of an "isolated successful round" needs to be re-considered as parties' local clocks may span some consecutive rounds. Assuming a Φ-drift is maintained during the sequence of rounds we are interested in, an irreversible contribution to the chain happens when the (nominal) distance between such success and the following success is at least $\Phi + \Delta$ rounds. This is because the block producer may have a local clock that is already Φ rounds behind other alert parties, and it takes Δ rounds to diffuse the block. This cancels out other parties' successes for up to $\Phi + \Delta$ rounds. As a result, we call such event a (Δ, Φ)-*isolated successful*, which is the for the new formulation of Q_r (cf. [12]). Note that this (Δ, Φ)-isolated successful round is meaningful only when the protocol is able to maintain a Φ-bounded skew during the sequence of rounds we are considering.

Recall that the total number of hash queries alert parties (resp., the adversary) can make during nominal round r is denoted by h_r (resp., t_r). For a sequence of rounds S we write $n(S) = \sum_{r \in S} n_r$ and similarly, $t(S), D(S), Q(S)$.

Regarding the adversary $\mathcal{A}$, while $\mathcal{A}$ may query the random oracle for an arbitrarily low target and obtain blocks with arbitrarily high difficulty, we wish to upper-bound the difficulty it can accrue during a set of J queries. Consider a set of consecutive adversarial queries J and associate it with the target of

---

[9] If P passes multiple local rounds in nominal round r, we require that all of these timestamps should satisfy the predicate.

the first query (this target is denoted by $T(J)$). We define $A(J)$ and $B(J)$ to be equal to the sum of the difficulties of all blocks computed by the adversary during queries in J for target at least $T(J)/\tau$ and $T(J)$, respectively.

Let $\mathcal{E}_{r-1}$ fix the execution just before (nominal) round r. In particular, a value E_{r-1} of $\mathcal{E}_{r-1}$ determines the adversarial strategy and so determines the targets against which every party will query the oracle at round r and the number of parties h_r and t_r, but it does not determine D_r or Q_r. For an adversarial query j we will write $\mathcal{E}_{j-1}$ for the execution just before this query.

Blockchain Properties. We use blockchain properties as formulated in [10,11] as an intermediate step towards proving the clock properties and achieve our blockchain synchronizer. Next, we briefly describe these properties: common prefix, chain growth, chain quality and existential chain quality.

Notably, we consider common prefix in terms of number of rounds. I.e., honest parties will agree on a settled part of the blockchain with timestamps at most a given number of rounds before their local time.[10] Let $\mathcal{C}^{\lceil k}$ denote the chain resulting from removing all rightmost blocks with timestamp larger than $\mathbf{r} - k$, where $\mathbf{r}$ is the current (local) time. We can now define common prefix as follows.

– **Common Prefix** (with parameter $k \in \mathbb{N}$). For any two alert parties $\mathsf{P}_1, \mathsf{P}_2$ holding chains $\mathcal{C}_1, \mathcal{C}_2$ at rounds r_1, r_2, with $r_1 \leq r_2$, it holds that $\mathcal{C}_1^{\lceil k} \preccurlyeq \mathcal{C}_2$.

Regarding chain growth, the lemma below provides a lower bound on the irreversible progress of achieved by the honest parties regardless of any adversarial behavior. This lemma has appeared in previous analyses under varying settings, evolving from the synchronous network and static environment [10], to a dynamic environment [11], and further to a bounded-delay network setting [12]. The next lemma extends the chain growth property to a Δ-bounded network delay, Φ-bounded clock drift and dynamic environment.

Lemma 1 (Chain Growth). *Suppose that at nominal round u of an execution E an honest party diffuses a chain of difficulty d. Then, by (nominal) round v, every honest party has received a chain of difficulty at least $d + Q(S)$, where $S = [u + \Delta + \Phi, v - \Delta - \Phi]$.*

4.2 Protocol Parameters and Their Conditions

We summarize all Timekeeper parameters in Table 3 in Appendix A. It is worth noting that ϵ is a small constant regarding the quality of concentration of random variables (it will appear in the typical executions in Sect. 4.3). We introduce a parameter λ—which is related to the properties of the protocol—to simplify

---

[10] While most of the previous work considers common prefix in terms of number of blocks, we note that these two definitions are equivalent. This is due to the fact that if the protocol guarantees security, then the block generation rate is somewhat steady (cf. [11]) and thus the number of blocks generated during a period of time can be inferred from its length and the highest mining speed.

several expressions. Protocol parameter λ and the RO output length κ are the security parameters of Timekeeper.

In order to get desired convergence and perform meaningful analysis, we consider a sufficiently long consecutive sequence of at least

$$\ell = \frac{4(1+3\epsilon)}{\epsilon^2 f[1-(1+\delta)\gamma^2 f]^{\Delta+\Phi+1}} \cdot \max\{\Delta+\Phi, \tau\} \cdot \gamma^3 \cdot \lambda \qquad (6)$$

consecutive rounds.

We are now ready to discuss the conditions that protocol parameters should satisfy. We first quantify the length of a clock synchronization interval R, the length of a target recalculation interval M and the length of the convergence phase K. Specifically, we let one target recalculation epoch consists of 4 clock synchronization intervals, i.e., M = 4R; we set K = $\ell+2\Delta+4\Phi$ (this will coincide with our common prefix parameter and thus provide some desired properties).

Next, we will require that ℓ (defined in Eq. (6)) is appropriately small compared to the length of an epoch and of an interval (note that M = 4R).

$$\ell + 2\Delta + 7\Phi \le \epsilon M/(4\gamma) = \epsilon R/\gamma. \qquad (C1)$$

Further, we require that the advantage of the honest parties is large enough to absorb the errors introduced by ϵ (from the concentration of random variables) and $[1 - (1+\delta)\gamma^2 f]^{\Delta+\Phi}$ (from the network delay and clock skews).

$$[1 - (1+\delta)\gamma^2 f]^{\Delta+\Phi} \ge 1 - \epsilon \text{ and } \epsilon \le \delta/12 \le 1/12. \qquad (C2)$$

4.3 Typical Executions

We define the notion of *typical* executions following [11,12]. The idea here is that given a certain execution E, we compare the actual progress and the expected progress that parties will make under the success probabilities. If the difference and variance are reasonably small, and no bad events (see Definition 6) about the underlying hash function happen, we declare E *typical*.

Definition 6. *An insertion occurs when, given a chain C with two consecutive blocks B and B', a block B^* created after B' is such that B, B^*, B' form three consecutive blocks of a valid chain. A copy occurs if the same block exists in two different positions. A prediction occurs when a block extends one with later creation time.*

Note that in addition (compared to [11,12]), in Definition 7(a) we require that the difficulty of all blocks the alert parties can acquire during consecutive rounds S (i.e., $D(S)$) is well lower-bounded. This is because $D(S)$ also captures the beacon production process, where there is no loss incurred by the bounded-delay network as well as by skewed local clocks. Hence, a reasonably better lower-bound on $D(S)$ helps us get better results when arguing for the good properties of generated beacons by alert parties (Lemma 7).

Definition 7 (Typical Execution). *An execution E is typical if the following hold.*

(a) For any set S of at least ℓ consecutive good rounds,

$$(1 - \epsilon)[1 - (1 + \delta)\gamma^2 f]^\Delta ph(S) < Q(S) \leq D(S) < (1 + \epsilon)ph(S)$$
$$and \ D(S) > (1 - \epsilon)ph(S).$$

(b) For any set J of consecutive adversarial queries and $\alpha(J) = 2(\frac{1}{\epsilon} + \frac{1}{3})\lambda/T(J)$,

$$A(J) < p|J| + \max\{\epsilon p|J|, \tau\alpha(J)\} \ and \ B(J) < p|J| + \max\{\epsilon p|J|, \alpha(J)\}.$$

(c) No insertions, no copies, and no predictions occurred in E.

In the next lemma, we establish the quantitative relation between honest and adversarial hashing power during consecutive rounds with length at least ℓ, as well as the relationship between the total difficulty acquired by all parties $(D(S) + A(J))$ and their hashing power.

Lemma 2. *Consider a typical execution in a (γ, s)-respecting environment. Let $S = \{r : u \leq r \leq v\}$ be a set of at least ℓ consecutive good rounds and J the set of adversarial queries in $U = \{r : u - \Delta - \Phi \leq r \leq v + \Delta + \Phi\}$. We have*

(a) $(1 + \epsilon)p|J| \leq Q(S) \leq D(U) < (1 + 5\epsilon)Q(S)$.
(b) $T(J)A(J) < \epsilon M/4(1 + \delta)$ or $A(J) < (1 + \epsilon)p|J|$; $\tau T(J)B(J) < \epsilon M/4(1 + \delta)$ or $B(J) < (1 + \epsilon)p|J|$.
(c) If w is a good round such that $|w - r| \leq s$ for any $r \in S$, then $Q(S) > (1 - \epsilon)[1 - (1 + \delta)\gamma^2 f]^\Delta |S|pn_w/\gamma$. If in addition $T(J) \geq T_w^{\min}$, then $A(J) < (1 - \delta + 3\epsilon)Q(S)$.
(d) If w is a good round such that $|w - r| \leq s$ for any $r \in S$ and $T(J) \geq T_w^{\min}$, then $D(S) + A(J') < (1 + \epsilon)p(h(S) + |J'|)$ where J' denotes the set of adversarial queries in S.

We conclude that almost all executions (that are polynomially bounded by κ and λ) are typical.

Theorem 1. *Assuming the ITM system $(\mathcal{Z}, C)$ runs for L steps, the probability of the event "$\mathcal{E}$ is not typical" is bounded by $O(L^2)(e^{-\lambda} + 2^{-\kappa})$.*

4.4 Proof Roadmap

In the remainder of this section we present an overview of the analysis. Note that the predicates in Definition 5 are proved in an inductive way over the space of typical executions in a (γ, s)-respecting environment.

First, we focus on the steady block generation rate. For a warm-up, we argue that an adversarial fork cannot happen too long ago and then extract the common prefix parameter. Equipped with this knowledge, we show that if good skews and certain time adjustment calculations are maintained during a target recalculation epoch, the block production rate will be properly controlled in the next epoch.

Lemma 3. $\textsc{GoodRound}(r-1) \implies \textsc{NoStaleChains}(r)$.

Lemma 4. $\textsc{GoodRound}(r-1) \wedge \textsc{GoodSkew}(r-1) \implies \textsc{CommonPrefix}(r)$.

Lemma 5. $\textsc{GoodRound}(r-1) \wedge \textsc{GoodChains}(r-1) \wedge \textsc{GoodSkew}(r-1) \wedge \textsc{GoodShift}(r-1) \implies \textsc{BlockLength}(r)$.

Lemma 6. $\textsc{GoodRound}(r-1) \implies \textsc{GoodChains}(r)$.

Corollary 1. $\textsc{GoodRound}(r-1) \implies \textsc{GoodRound}(r)$.

Next, we move to the properties w.r.t. clocks. We argue that if at the onset, the PoW difficult is appropriately set and the steady block generating rate lasts during the whole clock synchronization interval, the beacon set used by parties to update their clock will be identical and the majority of these beacons will be produced and emitted by alert parties. For synchronized parties, this good beacon set implies that the differences between alert parties' local clocks are still narrow after they enter the next interval and that the shift value they computed is well-bounded. Furthermore, regarding newly joining parties, we also provide an analysis of the joining procedure showing that joining parties starting with no *a-priori* knowledge of the global time, they can listen in and bootstrap their logical clock and become alert parties. The above two aspects imply that a bounded skew is maintained over the whole execution.

Lemma 7. $\textsc{GoodRound}(r-1) \implies \textsc{GoodBeacons}(r)$.

Lemma 8. $\textsc{GoodSkew}(r-1) \implies \textsc{GoodShift}(r)$

Lemma 9. $\textsc{GoodSkew}(r-1) \wedge \textsc{GoodBeacons}(r-1) \implies \textsc{GoodSkew}(r)$.

To sum up, a "safe" start and a (γ, s)-respecting environment guarantee that good properties can be achieved during the whole execution.

Theorem 2. *For a typical execution in a* $(\gamma, M + 2(\ell + 2\Delta + 7\Phi))$-*respecting environment, if Condition C1 and Condition C2 are satisfied, then all predicates in Definition 5 hold.*

Finally, we work out the related parameters (in Theorem 3) and conclude that Timekeeper solves the clock synchronization problem.

Theorem 3. *Consider an execution of* Timekeeper *in a* $(\gamma, M + 2(\ell + 2\Delta + 7\Phi))$-*respecting environment. If Conditions (C1) and (C2) are satisfied, then the protocol achieves clock synchronization (Definition 1) with parameter values*

$$\text{Skew} = 2\Phi, \quad \text{shiftLB} = 3\Phi/R, \quad \text{shiftUB} = 2\Phi/R,$$

except with probability negligibly small in κ *and* λ.

A   Glossary

Table 3. Main parameters of Timekeeper.

Parameter	Description
h_r	The number of honest RO queries in (nominal) round r.
t_r	The number of RO queries by $\mathcal{A}$ in (nominal) round r.
δ	Advantage of honest parties ($t_r < (1 - \delta)h_r$ for all r).
f	The probability at least one honest RO query out of n_0 computes a block for target T_0.
R	The length of a clock synchronization interval in number of rounds.
M	The length of a target recalculation epoch in number of rounds.
K	The length of convergence phase in a clock synchronization interval in number of rounds.
Δ	Network delay in rounds.
Φ_{clock}	The upper bound of the drift that $\mathcal{A}$ can set.
Φ	The upper bound of the difference between honest parties' local clocks. We require that $\Phi = \Phi_{\text{clock}} + \Delta$.
κ	Security parameter; length of the hash function output.
(γ, s)	Respecting environment parameter.
ϵ	Quality of concentration of random variables.
λ	Related to the properties of the protocol

References

1. Abraham, I., Devadas, S., Dolev, D., Nayak, K., Ren, L.: Synchronous Byzantine agreement with expected $O(1)$ rounds, expected $O(n^2)$ communication, and optimal resilience. In: Goldberg, I., Moore, T. (eds.) FC 2019. LNCS, vol. 11598, pp. 320–334. Springer, Cham (2019). https://doi.org/10.1007/978-3-030-32101-7_20
2. Badertscher, C., Gaži, P., Kiayias, A., Russell, A., Zikas, V.: Ouroboros genesis: composable proof-of-stake blockchains with dynamic availability. In: Proceedings of the 2018 ACM SIGSAC Conference on Computer and Communications Security, CCS 2018, pp. 913–930. Association for Computing Machinery, New York (2018). https://doi.org/10.1145/3243734.3243848
3. Badertscher, C., Gaži, P., Kiayias, A., Russell, A., Zikas, V.: Dynamic ad hoc clock synchronization. In: Canteaut, A., Standaert, F.-X. (eds.) EUROCRYPT 2021. LNCS, vol. 12698, pp. 399–428. Springer, Cham (2021). https://doi.org/10.1007/978-3-030-77883-5_14
4. Badertscher, C., Maurer, U., Tschudi, D., Zikas, V.: Bitcoin as a transaction ledger: a composable treatment. In: Katz, J., Shacham, H. (eds.) CRYPTO 2017. LNCS, vol. 10401, pp. 324–356. Springer, Cham (2017). https://doi.org/10.1007/978-3-319-63688-7_11

5. Bagaria, V., Kannan, S., Tse, D., Fanti, G., Viswanath, P.: Prism: deconstructing the blockchain to approach physical limits. In: Proceedings of the 2019 ACM SIGSAC Conference on Computer and Communications Security, CCS 2019, pp. 585–602. Association for Computing Machinery, New York (2019). https://doi.org/10.1145/3319535.3363213

6. Bahack, L.: Theoretical bitcoin attacks with less than half of the computational power (draft). Cryptology ePrint Archive, Report 2013/868 (2013). https://ia.cr/2013/868

7. Canetti, R.: Universally composable security: a new paradigm for cryptographic protocols. In: 42nd Annual Symposium on Foundations of Computer Science, FOCS 2001, 14–17 October 2001, Las Vegas, Nevada, USA, pp. 136–145. IEEE Computer Society (2001). https://doi.org/10.1109/SFCS.2001.959888

8. Dolev, D., Halpern, J.Y., Strong, H.R.: On the possibility and impossibility of achieving clock synchronization. J. Comput. Syst. Sci. 32(2), 230–250 (1986). https://doi.org/10.1016/0022-0000(86)90028-0

9. Dwork, C., Lynch, N., Stockmeyer, L.: Consensus in the presence of partial synchrony. J. ACM 35(2), 288–323 (1988). https://doi.org/10.1145/42282.42283

10. Garay, J., Kiayias, A., Leonardos, N.: The bitcoin backbone protocol: analysis and applications. In: Oswald, E., Fischlin, M. (eds.) EUROCRYPT 2015. LNCS, vol. 9057, pp. 281–310. Springer, Heidelberg (2015). https://doi.org/10.1007/978-3-662-46803-6_10

11. Garay, J., Kiayias, A., Leonardos, N.: The bitcoin backbone protocol with chains of variable difficulty. In: Katz, J., Shacham, H. (eds.) CRYPTO 2017. LNCS, vol. 10401, pp. 291–323. Springer, Cham (2017). https://doi.org/10.1007/978-3-319-63688-7_10

12. Garay, J., Kiayias, A., Leonardos, N.: Full analysis of Nakamoto consensus in bounded-delay networks. Cryptology ePrint Archive, Report 2020/277 (2020). https://ia.cr/2020/277

13. Garay, J., Kiayias, A., Ostrovsky, R.M., Panagiotakos, G., Zikas, V.: Resource-restricted cryptography: revisiting MPC bounds in the proof-of-work era. In: Canteaut, A., Ishai, Y. (eds.) EUROCRYPT 2020. LNCS, vol. 12106, pp. 129–158. Springer, Cham (2020). https://doi.org/10.1007/978-3-030-45724-2_5

14. Garay, J., Kiayias, A., Shen, Y.: Permissionless clock synchronization with public setup. Cryptology ePrint Archive, Report 2022/1220 (2022). https://eprint.iacr.org/2022/1220

15. Garay, J., Kiayias, A.: SoK: a consensus taxonomy in the blockchain era. In: Jarecki, S. (ed.) CT-RSA 2020. LNCS, vol. 12006, pp. 284–318. Springer, Cham (2020). https://doi.org/10.1007/978-3-030-40186-3_13

16. Halpern, J.Y., Simons, B., Strong, R., Dolev, D.: Fault-tolerant clock synchronization. In: Proceedings of the Third Annual ACM Symposium on Principles of Distributed Computing, PODC 1984, pp. 89–102. Association for Computing Machinery, New York (1984). https://doi.org/10.1145/800222.806739

17. Katz, J., Maurer, U., Tackmann, B., Zikas, V.: Universally composable synchronous computation. In: Sahai, A. (ed.) TCC 2013. LNCS, vol. 7785, pp. 477–498. Springer, Heidelberg (2013). https://doi.org/10.1007/978-3-642-36594-2_27

18. Lamport, L.: Time, clocks, and the ordering of events in a distributed system. Commun. ACM 21(7), 558–565 (1978). https://doi.org/10.1145/359545.359563

19. Lamport, L., Melliar-Smith, P.M.: Byzantine clock synchronization. In: Proceedings of the Third Annual ACM Symposium on Principles of Distributed Computing, PODC 1984, pp. 68–74. Association for Computing Machinery, New York (1984). https://doi.org/10.1145/800222.806737

20. Lenzen, C., Loss, J.: Optimal clock synchronization with signatures. In: Proceedings of the 2022 ACM Symposium on Principles of Distributed Computing, PODC 2022, pp. 440–449. Association for Computing Machinery, New York (2022). https://doi.org/10.1145/3519270.3538444

21. Nakamoto, S.: Bitcoin: a peer-to-peer electronic cash system (2008). http://bitcoin.org/bitcoin.pdf

22. Pass, R., Seeman, L., Shelat, A.: Analysis of the blockchain protocol in asynchronous networks. In: Coron, J.-S., Nielsen, J.B. (eds.) EUROCRYPT 2017, Part II. LNCS, vol. 10211, pp. 643–673. Springer, Cham (2017). https://doi.org/10.1007/978-3-319-56614-6_22

23. Pass, R., Shi, E.: Fruitchains: a fair blockchain. In: Proceedings of the ACM Symposium on Principles of Distributed Computing, PODC 2017, pp. 315–324. Association for Computing Machinery, New York (2017). https://doi.org/10.1145/3087801.3087809

24. Pass, R., Shi, E.: Rethinking large-scale consensus. In: 30th IEEE Computer Security Foundations Symposium, CSF 2017, Santa Barbara, CA, USA, 21–25 August 2017, pp. 115–129. IEEE Computer Society (2017). https://doi.org/10.1109/CSF.2017.37

25. Srikanth, T.K., Toueg, S.: Optimal clock synchronization. J. ACM **34**(3), 626–645 (1987). https://doi.org/10.1145/28869.28876

26. Welch, J.L., Lynch, N.: A new fault-tolerant algorithm for clock synchronization. Inf. Comput. **77**(1), 1–36 (1988)

Beyond Uber: Instantiating Generic Groups via PGGs

Balthazar Bauer[1], Pooya Farshim[2], Patrick Harasser[3(✉)], and Adam O'Neill[4]

[1] IRIF, CNRS, Paris, France
`balthazar.bauer@ens.fr`
[2] IOHK and Durham University, Durham, UK
`pooya.farshim@gmail.com`
[3] Technische Universität Darmstadt, Darmstadt, Germany
`patrick.harasser@tu-darmstadt.de`
[4] Manning College of Information and Computer Sciences,
University of Massachusetts Amherst, Amherst, USA
`adamo@cs.umass.edu`

Abstract. The generic-group model (GGM) has been very successful in making the analyses of many cryptographic assumptions and protocols tractable. It is, however, well known that the GGM is "uninstantiable," i.e., there are protocols secure in the GGM that are insecure when using any real-world group. This motivates the study of standard-model notions formalizing that a real-world group in some sense "looks generic."

We introduce a standard-model definition called *pseudo-generic group (PGG)*, where we require exponentiations with base an (initially) unknown group generator to result in random-looking group elements. In essence, our framework delicately lifts the influential notion of Universal Computational Extractors of Bellare, Hoang, and Keelveedhi (BHK, CRYPTO 2013) to a setting where the underlying ideal reference object is a generic group. The definition we obtain simultaneously generalizes the Uber assumption family, as group exponents no longer need to be polynomially induced. At the core of our definitional contribution is a new notion of *algebraic unpredictability*, which reinterprets the standard Schwartz–Zippel lemma as a restriction on sources. We prove the soundness of our definition in the GGM with auxiliary-input (AI-GGM).

Our remaining results focus on applications of PGGs. We first show that PGGs are indeed a generalization of Uber. We then present a number of applications in settings where exponents are not polynomially induced. In particular we prove that simple variants of ElGamal meet several advanced security goals previously achieved only by complex and inefficient schemes. We also show that PGGs imply UCEs for split sources, which in turn are sufficient in several applications. As corollaries of our AI-GGM feasibility, we obtain the security of all these applications in the presence of preprocessing attacks.

Some of our implications utilize a novel type of hash function, which we call *linear-dependence destroyers* (LDDs) and use to convert standard into algebraic unpredictability. We give an LDD for low-degree sources,

E. Kiltz and V. Vaikuntanathan (Eds.): TCC 2022, LNCS 13749, pp. 212–242, 2022.
https://doi.org/10.1007/978-3-031-22368-6_8

and establish their plausibility for all sources by showing, via a compression argument, that random functions meet this definition.

1 Introduction

1.1 Background

IDEALIZED MODELS. A useful tool in cryptography are so-called idealized models of computation, which include the random-oracle, random-permutation, ideal-cipher, and generic-group models. In such models, all algorithms work relative to oracles that serve to implement some information-theoretically random reference object. Later, when a scheme defined in an idealized setting is used in practice, the oracles are heuristically instantiated by appropriate public, efficiently computable functions. On the one hand, idealized models are powerful because they limit the adversary's capabilities and make proofs tractable. On the other, they are subject to well-known uninstantiability results, which show the existence of (contrived) schemes that are secure in the idealized model, but provably insecure under any possible instantiation (see, e.g., [16,28,34,40]). This indicates that idealized models are not sound in general, yet "natural" applications (with the oracles appropriately instantiated) have withstood years of scrutiny.

THE GENERIC-GROUP MODEL. In this work, we mainly focus on the generic-group model (GGM), where a generic group is an idealization of a finite cyclic group. It was first defined by Nechaev [47] and later refined by Shoup [51], who considered random encodings of group elements.[1] More specifically, for a cyclic group $(G, \circ)$ of order p, Shoup's model considers a random injection $\tau \colon \mathbb{Z}_p \to S$, where $S \subseteq \{0,1\}^*$ with $|S| \geq p$. All algorithms run on input p and encodings of application-specific group elements. To perform group operations, algorithms can query a τ oracle and an operation oracle op defined as $\mathsf{op}(h_1, h_2) := \tau(\tau^{-1}(h_1) + \tau^{-1}(h_2))$ if $h_1, h_2 \in \mathsf{Rng}(\tau)$, and $\mathsf{op}(h_1, h_2) := \perp$ otherwise.

INSTANTIATING GENERIC GROUPS. In practice, a generic group is typically instantiated via an appropriate elliptic curve group. Indeed, for such groups no algorithms for solving discrete-logarithm-like problems more efficiently than the generic ones are known. Addressing the above-mentioned mismatch between idealized and instantiated schemes, we investigate what assumptions are being made when carrying out such an instantiation. Note that an indistinguishability-based approach formalizing the idea of "behaving like a generic group" would suffer from the same shortcomings known for random oracles [28].

This line of work has been carried out with considerable success for the random oracle model (ROM), where the ideal reference object is a random function (see, e.g., [11,25,55]). For generic groups on the other hand, the most compelling

---

[1] An alternative formulation of the GGM is given by Maurer [45]; we follow Shoup's presentation in this paper. Relations and comparisons between different flavors of the GGM are discussed in the recent work [56].

formulation so far of what assumption is being made when instantiating them is given by the so-called Uber assumption [19,21]. At a high level, the Uber assumption speaks to the hardness of distinguishing the exponentiation $g^{T(\mathbf{s})}$ of a polynomial evaluation $T(\mathbf{s})$ from random, given exponentiations $g^{R_1(\mathbf{s})}, \ldots, g^{R_n(\mathbf{s})}$ of other polynomial evaluations. This condition holds in generic groups, and must therefore be satisfied by any concrete group that aims to "faithfully" instantiate them. However, the Uber assumption is far from the most general (standard-model) property that might hold in generic groups and thus should also be satisfied by their real-world counterparts.

Indeed, we observe that in a wide range of advanced cryptographic protocols and primitives (such as security under bad randomness, deterministic encryption, leakage resilience, and code obfuscation to name a few), inputs may not be uniformly distributed and polynomially related, but follow distributions that are, for example, only assumed to have high entropy. The Uber assumption can fall short of providing means to prove security of practical schemes in such settings. Accordingly, the main question we ask is:

Are there standard-model properties that generalize the Uber assumption and allow instantiating generic groups in a broad range of applications?

We emphasize that our treatment is practice-oriented in that we aim for a notion that captures standard-model properties of groups that can be used to establish the standard-model security of *existing, practical* protocols in a variety of models. Further, the new definitions should combine, as far as possible, standard-model analyses with the ease of use offered by the GGM.

In order to develop the core ideas one step at a time, in this work we treat the case of simple (non-bilinear) groups[2] and focus on decisional problems. There are indeed multiple directions in which our work can be extended; we will briefly discuss some of these at the end of the Introduction.

1.2 Our Approach

Our approach is inspired by an existing framework that bridges the standard and idealized models of computation: Universal Computational Extractors (UCEs) of Bellare, Hoang, and Keelveedhi (BHK) [11], a security notion for hash functions which, at a high level, requires indistinguishability from a random oracle under unpredictable inputs. Indeed, their motivation is in some sense conceptually analogous to ours. To that end, we seek to extend UCEs to structured ideal primitives, and call the resulting security notion in the case of cyclic groups *pseudo-generic groups* (PGGs). Before presenting PGGs, we give a brief overview of UCEs and refer to Sect. 2 for formal definitions.

UNIVERSAL COMPUTATIONAL EXTRACTORS. Let H: $K \times D \to R$ be a keyed hash function. The UCE notion is defined via a game played by a source S and a distinguisher D: Sample a challenge bit $b \twoheadleftarrow \{0,1\}$, a hash key $hk \twoheadleftarrow K$, and a

---

[2] Similar work on the algebraic-group model (discussed later) was first carried out in simple groups [37] and later in bilinear ones [5].

RO $\rho: D \to R$. Then, $\mathcal{S}$ runs with access to an oracle HASH which, when queried on $x \in D$, returns $\mathsf{H}(hk, x)$ if $b = 1$, and $\rho(x)$ otherwise. Eventually, $\mathcal{S}$ outputs leakage L which is passed to $\mathcal{D}$, who is also given the hash key hk but no access to the hashing oracle. Distinguisher $\mathcal{D}$ must then guess b, and the requirement for H is that the advantage of every PPT $(\mathcal{S}, \mathcal{D})$ in this game is small.

Notice that for this definition to be meaningful, some restriction must be placed on $\mathcal{S}$ and $\mathcal{D}$: Without any additional requirement, $(\mathcal{S}, \mathcal{D})$ can win with overwhelming advantage by having $\mathcal{S}$ query HASH on any $x \in D$ with answer y, leak the pair (x, y) to $\mathcal{D}$, and then have $\mathcal{D}$ (who knows the hash key hk) check whether $y = \mathsf{H}(hk, x)$. To avoid such generic attacks, one requires $\mathcal{S}$ to be *unpredictable*, a notion formalized by asking that any predictor $\mathcal{P}$ have small advantage in the following game: Source $\mathcal{S}$ runs with access to a RO and produces leakage L. Then $\mathcal{P}$ runs on input L and wins if it can guess any of $\mathcal{S}$'s queries.

OUR NEW NOTION: PGG. To port the UCE definition to the context of cyclic groups, our first idea is to let a random group generator g play the role of the hash key, and to use exponentiation with base g in place of the hash.[3] The PGG security game for a group $(\mathsf{G}, \circ)$ then follows the UCE framework: Sample a secret bit $b \twoheadleftarrow \{0, 1\}$, a random generator $g \twoheadleftarrow \mathsf{G}$, and a generic-group encoding $\sigma: \mathbb{Z}_p \to \mathsf{G}$. Then, a source $\mathcal{S}$ interacts with an exponentiation oracle EXP which, on input $x \in \mathbb{Z}_p$, returns the real group element g^x if $b = 1$, and a generic element $\sigma(x)$ otherwise. The source can pass some leakage L to a distinguisher $\mathcal{D}$, who is also given the generator g but loses access to the oracle and has to guess b. As for UCEs, the requirement for G is that every such $(\mathcal{S}, \mathcal{D})$ has a small advantage in this game. Thus, the PGG notion captures the intuition that if an adversary does not know the random generator g of G, exponentiation with base g looks like it returns random elements from G.

As before, for this notion not to be void we must put restrictions on the queries that $\mathcal{S}$ is allowed to make. First, observe that $\mathcal{S}$ must be unpredictable, because without any such requirement $(\mathcal{S}, \mathcal{D})$ can mount the attack for UCEs sketched above. We argue now that due to the presence of a group structure on G that was missing in the UCE setting, further conditions are needed.

ALGEBRAIC UNPREDICTABILITY. An important question now is for what sources is PGG achievable in principle, meaning there are no "trivial" attacks. Recall that for UCEs the answer was unpredictable sources. In our context, unpredictability alone is not sufficient: Consider a source $\mathcal{S}$ that samples $x_1, x_2 \twoheadleftarrow \mathbb{Z}_p$, queries $h_i \leftarrow \text{EXP}(x_i)$, and computes $x_3 \leftarrow x_1 + x_2$ and $h'_3 \leftarrow h_1 \circ h_2$. It then queries $h_3 \leftarrow \text{EXP}(x_3)$ and passes the bit $(h_3 = h'_3)$ to $\mathcal{D}$, who simply returns it. The advantage of $(\mathcal{S}, \mathcal{D})$ in the PGG game is almost 1, even though $\mathcal{S}$ is unpredictable since x_1 and x_2 are random. The issue is that $\mathcal{S}$ can place unpredictable queries that satisfy a known linear relation and distinguish by checking if the corresponding relation holds for the oracle replies. Excluding this trivial/generic

---

[3] Recently, Bartusek, Ma, and Zhandry (BMZ) [4] studied the "fixed-generator" and "random-generator" settings in group-based assumptions. We necessarily work in the latter since, as we shall see, otherwise attacks arise.

attack motivates a more refined notion of unpredictability which we call *algebraic unpredictability*. In the corresponding game, the source S runs with access to the ideal exponentiation oracle while querying $x_1, \ldots, x_q$, and produces leakage L. Predictor P runs on input L and must guess a linear combination of the queries, i.e., outputs $(\alpha_0, \alpha_1, \ldots, \alpha_q)$ not all zero and wins if $\sum_{i=1}^{q} \alpha_i x_i = \alpha_0$.

This condition excludes the attack above, since P can output $(0, 1, 1, -1)$ to win the game. One might try to modify the attack and let the source leak (x_3, h_3) to D, who, given g, can compute g^{x_3} and compare it to h_3. But this also contradicts algebraic unpredictability, with a predictor returning $(x_3, 1, 1)$.

As we shall see in Sect. 3, due to the existence of obfuscation-based attacks (similar to those for UCEs [22]), algebraic unpredictability must be *statistical* in nature; that is, we allow the algebraic predictors to run in unbounded time.

PARALLEL STRUCTURE. It turns out that algebraic unpredictability by itself is not sufficient to rule out all generic attacks. Indeed, consider a source S that samples $x \leftarrow \mathbb{Z}_p$, queries $h_1 \leftarrow \text{EXP}(x)$ and $h_2 \leftarrow \text{EXP}(x^2)$, then computes $h_2' \leftarrow h_1^x$ and passes the bit $(h_2 = h_2')$ as leakage to D, who decides accordingly. Again, the advantage of (S, D) in the PGG game is almost 1, and now S is even algebraically unpredictable. The issue here is that S's queries satisfy a linear relation with coefficients that are themselves *unpredictable but known to* S (in this case, $x \cdot x - 1 \cdot x^2 = 0$), an attack vector not ruled out by algebraic unpredictability.

To address this problem, we consider *parallel sources*. Loosely speaking, this means that S's EXP queries are made in parallel by single-query sources $S_i(\text{st})$ which, other than receiving a common initial state, do not pass state among each other. Indeed, the attack above was possible because S could learn more than one oracle reply. Note that, in this example, although the queries x and x^2 are allowed, the equality check $h_2 = h_2'$ requires knowledge of h_2 and h_2' (related to different queries), and hence violates the definition of a parallel source.

RESTRICTED POST-PROCESSING. Surprisingly, even considering only parallel sources does not rule out all trivial attacks. Indeed, one can modify the source S from above and make it parallel by setting $\text{st} \leftarrow x$, having $S_1(\text{st})$ compute h_1 and h_2', and letting $S_2(\text{st})$ compute h_2. Leakage (h_2', h_2) is passed to D, which returns the bit $(h_2 = h_2')$. This attack works because each $S_i(\text{st})$ still allows arbitrary post-processing of its oracle response (here, computing the exponentiation of h_1). Accordingly, we further restrict the class of sources and consider algebraically unpredictable *masking* sources, which are parallel sources where each $S_i(\text{st})$ is allowed only *structured post-processing* of its oracle replies (e.g., no post-processing or at most one group operation).

SIMPLIFICATION. The nature of the EXP oracle allows us to both strengthen and simplify our notion: We consider a definition of PGG whereby the distinguisher no longer receives the random generator g, and accordingly modify algebraic unpredictability to hold with $\alpha_0 = 0$ only. This new version implies the old one, as g can be obtained by querying 1. Second, algebraic unpredictability holds for this source, as the non-simplified version allows for non-zero α_0.

GENERALIZING UBER. We give a formal definition of the resulting notion in Sect. 3. Note that our notion can indeed be seen as a generalization of Uber, whereby the exponents are no longer evaluations of polynomials but may come from arbitrarily correlated distributions, as long as they adhere to the requirements set above. In particular, linear independence between polynomially induced exponents is now generalized to algebraically unpredictable sources.

GGM FEASIBILITY. Analogously to BHK who showed a RO is a UCE, we show the soundness of our definition by proving that a generic group is PGG for algebraically unpredictable masking sources. (We adopt Shoup's model for generic groups here [50].) This turns out to be significantly more involved than in BHK. Typically, GGM proofs appeal to the Schwartz–Zippel lemma to carry out a lazy sampling of group elements. In our proof, we no longer use this lemma and instead rely on the *algebraic unpredictability* of sources to carry out a consistent lazy sampling. Here we use a weaker notion of *computational* algebraic unpredictability. (There is no contradiction with obfuscation-based attacks, as generic groups do not have compact representations.) A second feature of our proof is that we allow our sources to depend on the entire function table of the group encoding. This choice more accurately models computationally unbounded sources in the standard model, widens the applicability of PGGs, and due to the existence of arbitrary leakage from source, also captures the effects of preprocessing attacks (aka. auxiliary information) on the definition. We use the recent technique of decomposition of high-entropy distribution due to Coretti, Dodis, and Guo [29] to handle unbounded sources.

Our GGM feasibility result, beside showing that PGGs do not suffer from structural weaknesses exposed by generic attacks, places PGGs below the GGM in the hierarchy of assumptions on groups (cf. the so-called "layered approach" to security explained in [11])[4]. Indeed, using this result, one can establish security of an application in the GGM by first proving it secure under an appropriate PGG assumption (in the standard model), and then lifting the result to the GGM using the result above.

Finally, equipped with GGM feasibility, it is reasonable to conjecture that appropriate elliptic curve groups are indeed PGGs, thus allowing the framework to be applied to a variety of practical cryptosystems built using such groups.

AVOIDING UNINSTANTIABILITY. We note that PGGs circumvent a variety of uninstantiability techniques. Notably, the classical CGH-type uninstantiability results [27,34] are avoided due to the fact that the group elements are computed wrt. *high-entropy* exponents. Furthermore, attacks due to the existence of various forms of obfuscation are avoided by requiring that the algebraic unpredictability notion be *statistical*. An analogous approach has been used in works on UCEs to avoid uninstantiability [22].

---

[4] The idea is to have assumptions and models organized into a hierarchy, where higher levels justify lower ones and, conversely, proving a scheme secure at some level shows that it meets higher ones as well. This allows us to identify precisely how strong an assumption is needed for a given application. Moreover, proving security of a scheme at a lower level typically gives more insight into its inner workings.

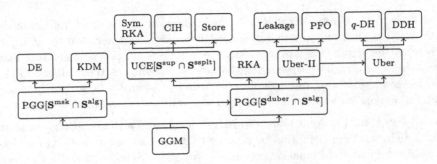

Fig. 1. Implications of PGGs. Here $\mathbf{S}^{\mathrm{ssplt}}$ denotes the class of simple split sources (see Sect. 6.2), CIH stands for correlated input hashing, and store for storage auditing protocols (see [11]). Results on DE (deterministic encryption), RKA and KDM or for ElGamal. Results for DE, RKA and UCE use LDDs if considering general sources.

We also note that Zhandry's recent AGM uninstantiability result [56] inherently relies on the fact that an algebraic adversary has to return a representation of the forged tag (which then either breaks DLP or compresses random strings). This does not carry over to PGGs because adversaries are not required to be algebraic in our setting.

1.3 Applications of Pseudo-Generic Groups

We demonstrate the applicability of our definition in three ways. First, we show that the Uber assumption holds in PGGs, thereby allowing us to recover all its applications within the PGG framework. For our second set of results, recall that there are several "advanced" security models for encryption, many of which have only been obtained via novel and often inefficient schemes. We demonstrate that PGGs enable proving (simple variants of) the classical *ElGamal encryption scheme* secure in a number of such advanced security models. According to the discussion above, this means that these notions can be safely assumed when ElGamal is implemented using suitable elliptic curve groups. Third, we show how to construct UCEs in PGGs. As before, this allows us to recover all their applications within the PGG framework. We refer to Fig. 1 for a schematic overview of our results.

PGGs GENERALIZE UBER. We prove that broad and even novel formulations of the Uber assumption hold in PGGs. The Uber assumption family [19,21] is an umbrella assumption that generalizes many hardness assumptions used to study the security of group-related schemes. Although it is commonly considered in bilinear groups, as previously mentioned, here we focus on simple groups. Nevertheless, proving that PGGs satisfy the Uber assumption allows us to recover all its applications within the PGG framework. For instance, all constructions whose security relies on the hardness of DDH (such as Diffie–Hellman key exchange, ElGamal encryption, and efficient PRFs [46]) or one of a number of closely related problems (e.g., q-DDHI, strong DDH, square DDH, and divisible DDH), or a randomized version of the recently introduced "Assumption 3" from [4], can be instantiated with PGGs. We further demonstrate that the Uber-II assumption, a variation of Uber with non-uniform exponents [25], also holds for PGGs. Specific instances of Uber-II have been used to build (composable) point-function obfuscation [15,26] and leakage-resilient PKE schemes [32].

We believe that PGGs better highlight the types of problems one expects to be hard in groups, as it places no restriction on how the exponents are sampled beyond the fact that certain trivial attacks are ruled out.

LINEAR DEPENDENCE DESTROYERS. For some of our further implications below, we require a particular type of hash function with domain and range $\mathbb{Z}_p$ we call *linear dependence destroyer* (LDD). LDDs are defined via a game played by a source $\mathcal{S}$ and a predictor $\mathcal{A}$. Source $\mathcal{S}$ specifies a tuple of hash inputs $(x_1, \ldots, x_q)$ and state information st without seeing the random hash key hk, whereas $\mathcal{A}$ gets st and hk and returns a tuple of coefficients $(\alpha_0, \alpha_1, \ldots, \alpha_q)$. Adversary $(\mathcal{S}, \mathcal{A})$ wins if $\sum_{i=1}^{q} \alpha_i \cdot \mathsf{H}(hk, x_i) = \alpha_0$, and H is an LDD if every $(\mathcal{S}, \mathcal{A})$ with $\mathcal{S}$ statistically unpredictable wins this game with negligible probability.

We show that the function $\mathsf{H}(hk, x) := 1/(x + hk)$ implicit in the work of Goyal, O'Neill, and Rao [39] is an LDD when $\mathcal{S}$ is a *low-degree source*. These are sources that compute their outputs as evaluations of low-degree polynomials on points with sufficient entropy. This result, in turn, enables proofs of security for applications that use LDDs for low-degree sources. The main step in our proof is that different polynomials with random constant terms (given by the hash key) are likely to be coprime. When this is the case, the numerator of the fraction $\sum_{i=1}^{q} \alpha_i/(P_i(s_1, \ldots, s_m) + hk) - \alpha_0$ is non-zero no matter the choice of $(\alpha_0, \alpha_1, \ldots, \alpha_q)$. Winning the LDD game is thus equivalent to $(s_1, \ldots, s_m)$ being a root of this numerator, which is unlikely by the Schwartz–Zippel lemma.

In fact, we conjecture that H is an LDD for *all* statistically unpredictable sources, not just for low-degree ones. To further lend plausibility to this notion, we also prove that a random function is an LDD, under mild restrictions on $\mathcal{S}$. To this end, we apply the compression technique originating from Gennaro and Trevisan [38] in a setting where *two* independent parties have full access to the code of the ideal object. The compression technique is commonly used in cryptography, and our extension may be of wider interest.

UCEs FOR SPLIT SOURCES. A natural question is how PGGs relate to the notion of UCEs. It seems that PGGs are harder to build because they have more structure. In other words, generic groups, which PGGs instantiate, seem stronger than random oracles, which UCEs instantiate. As our first application we show that, indeed, UCEs can be constructed from PGGs for dUber sources and LDDs. The constructed UCE is for statistically unpredictable split sources. A number of applications of UCEs, such as proofs of storage, correlated-input secure hashing, and RKA security for symmetric encryption, only rely on UCE for split sources. We note that a benefit of building UCEs from PGGs is that the construction may enjoy useful algebraic properties that constructions from

Table 1. Overview of applications of PGGs.

Application	PGG source	Other assumptions
Uber & Uber-II	dUber	–
RKA for ElGamal	dUber	LDD
KDM for ElGamal	Mask	–
Low-degree DE ElGamal	Mask	–
UCE for split sources	dUber	LDD
General DE for ElGamal	Mask	LDD

symmetric-key primitives do not. Once again, in the generic-group model, we show security against preprocessing attacks.

KEY-DEPENDENT MESSAGE SECURITY FOR ELGAMAL. Second, we show that PGGs enable proof of key-dependent message (KDM) security for a slightly tweaked version of ElGamal [17,24]. KDM security for ElGamal does not seem to be feasible using Uber (though less efficient constructions do exist, e.g., [3,20]). The KDM notion that we prove does not allow for adaptive queries, but it permits deriving key-dependent messages in an inefficient way. Furthermore, when combined with our GGM feasibility, we obtain KDM security against preprocessing attacks in the GGM.

HASH-THEN-ELGAMAL DETERMINISTIC PKE. Moving on, we prove that ElGamal admits full instantiation of its corresponding random-oracle-model Encrypt-With-Hash (EwH) deterministic encryption scheme [7], which replaces the coins in encryption with the hash of the message. Here we need that the hash function is an LDD. Preprocessing attacks are also accounted for in our definition and analysis. Note that a prior result of BHK [11] also implies security of ElGamal-based EwH, but uses an assumption on the hash that makes the result arguably tautological. It is also known how to instantiate EwH for schemes meeting "lossiness" assumptions [10,41]. Our result is the first that does not require such an assumption as it shifts the security assumption with non-uniform inputs from the hash function to the underlying group.

RELATED-KEY SECURITY. We also show that ElGamal offers a form of related-key attack (RKA) security, whereby secret keys (and their corresponding public keys) are generated from related random coins. RKA security was systematically studied by Bellare, Cash, and Miller [9] for PKEs. Under PGGs, and assuming LDDs (which for polynomially induced sources we show to exist) we can handle unpredictable related-key deriving functions that are claw-free (or more generally as long as the repetition pattern of secret keys does not affect unpredictability).

We summarize the above applications in Table 1. For each application, we record what type of source class is used in the reduction and whether the additional assumption of LDD is needed. For applications requiring LDDs we note that our results are modular wrt. the underlying source class. This means that for whatever source class we achieve LDDs, we also obtain an end application wrt. a corresponding source class. For example, low-degree LDDs (which we achieve unconditionally) translate to instantiations of UCEs and deterministic encryption wrt. low-degree sources and RKA security for low-degree related keys. The latter includes affine functions, which are often considered in the RKA literature.

We envision that several other security goals are also feasible under PGGs, of which we consider only a representative sample. Examples include security under bad randomness [8], joint RKA and KDM security [18], randomness-dependent message security [14], related-randomness security [48], and more generally application scenarios whereby the input distributions are not necessarily random and only guaranteed to come from high entropy distributions.

1.4   Other Related Work and Discussions

PUBLIC-SEED PSEUDORANDOM PERMUTATIONS. Soni and Tessaro [52] define a UCE-like, standard-model notion for random (two-sided) permutations called public-seed pseudorandom permutations (psPRPs). They provide constructions of UCEs from psPRPs (for a variety of sources) by showing, for example, that the five-round Feistel [52] and the more efficient Naor–Reingold construction [53] yield psPRPs when the round functions are UCEs. Our work continues these lines of research by extending the UCE approach to defining security from random oracles and random permutations to generic groups.

ALGEBRAIC GROUP MODEL. An intriguing notion that has recently received considerable attention is the algebraic group model (AGM) [5,37]. We observe that the AGM places restrictions on adversaries that are qualitatively different compared to PGGs: Algebraic adversaries must output a representation of returned group elements, which makes the AGM a powerful and useful model since this additional information allows to carry out certain reductions.[5] Restrictions on PGG adversaries on the other hand are of standard-model type.

Nevertheless, it would be interesting to study the relation between the two notions and also to knowledge assumptions. Following work on instantiating UCEs [23] and on constructing groups in which the AGM can be realized and the Uber assumption holds [1,2,42], another goal for future work is to construct PGGs from well-known assumptions (such as iO, dual-mode NIZKs, FHE, etc.).

EXTENSIONS OF PGGs. In this work, we develop the necessary techniques and set the stage for the pseudo-generic approach to group-related assumptions. In doing so, we leave a number of directions for future research.

A natural extension to our work would be to formulate analogous PGG-type notions for bilinear groups (as considered by Boyen for the Uber assumption [21] and extended via matrix DDH in [35]) or multi-linear groups. We anticipate further applications of this notion, as in the bilinear setting a host of schemes are only known to have a proof in the GGM and may be provable in PGGs.

---

[5] We note that our understanding of the role played by the AGM in assessing the hardness of group-related assumptions is evolving in light of recent works [43,56].

The matrix DDH assumption (MDDH) [35] considers matrix-vector multiplication in the exponent in multi-linear groups, where a matrix is sampled from a general distribution and the vector is uniform. However, this assumption is only studied for polynomially induced distributions. As such, MDDH is not a generalization of Uber in the sense of PGG to arbitrary distributions.

Certain applications require assumptions that lie beyond the reach of PGGs as currently formulated. PGGs do not capture applications where exponents may depend on a group generator that is not random (as, for example, in recent work on non-malleable point-function obfuscation [4,36,44]). The PGG framework also does not capture interactive [1] or knowledge-type [13] assumptions.

1.5   Structure of the Paper

In Sect. 2 we define the basic notation and recall the definition of UCEs. Section 3 contains our definitional contributions, where we define pseudo-generic groups, algebraically unpredictable and masking sources, and discuss the choices made in devising these notions. In Sect. 4 we prove that a generic group is a PGG, and then introduce LDDs and a candidate construction in Sect. 5. Section 6 contains the applications of PGGs. In Sect. 6.1 we show that an entropic variant of the decisional Uber assumption (and thus many implications thereof) holds in PGGs. Afterwards, we show how to apply PGG directly to the analysis of cryptosystems, by proving that PGGs and LDDs can be used to build UCEs for (simple) split sources. Further applications of PGGs are presented in the full version of the paper [6].

2   Preliminaries

Basic Notation. If $n \in \mathbb{N}$, we write $[n]$ for the set $\{1, \ldots, n\}$. Unless otherwise stated, an integer $p \in \mathbb{Z}$ is assumed to be prime, and we let $\mathbb{Z}_p$ denote the field of integers modulo p. We denote the set of all bit strings of finite length by $\{0,1\}^*$, and the empty string by ε. We use boldface characters $\mathbf{x} := (x_1, \ldots, x_n)$ to denote vectors and write $\mathbf{x}[i]$, with $i \in [n]$, to denote the ith entry x_i of $\mathbf{x}$. By $x \twoheadleftarrow \mathcal{S}$ we mean sampling x according to distribution $\mathcal{S}$. Similarly, $x \twoheadleftarrow S$ means sampling x uniformly at random from a finite set S. The cardinality of a set S is denoted $|S|$. We let $L \leftarrow []$ denote initializing an ordered list to empty, and $L : x$ denote appending an element x to the list L. A table T is a list of pairs (x, y), and we write $T[x] \leftarrow y$ to mean that the pair (x, y) is appended to T. We let $\mathsf{Dom}(T)$ denote the set of all values x such that $(x, y) \in T$ for some y, and similarly $\mathsf{Rng}(T)$ denote the set of all values y such that $(x, y) \in T$ for some x. For two sets D and R we denote by $\mathsf{Fun}(D, R)$ and $\mathsf{Inj}(D, R)$ the set of all functions and the set of all injections from D to R, respectively. When $|D| = |R|$, an injection is also a bijection.

MIN-ENTROPY. The min-entropy of a random variable $\mathcal{X}$ over a domain D is $\mathbf{H}_\infty(\mathcal{X}) := -\log \max_{x \in D} \Pr[\mathcal{X} = x]$. $\mathcal{X}$ is called a k-source if $\mathbf{H}_\infty(\mathcal{X}) \geq k$.

POLYNOMIALS AND RATIONAL FUNCTIONS. We let $\mathbb{F}[X_1,\ldots,X_m]$ be the ring of polynomials in $m \in \mathbb{N}$ variables over a field $\mathbb{F}$, and $\mathbb{F}(X_1,\ldots,X_m)$ be the field of rational functions of the form $R(X_1,\ldots,X_m) = \hat{R}(X_1,\ldots,X_m)/\check{R}(X_1,\ldots,X_m)$, with $\hat{R}, \check{R} \in \mathbb{F}[X_1,\ldots,X_m]$ and $\check{R} \neq 0$. Here, as usual, $\hat{R}$ is called the numerator and $\check{R}$ the denominator of R. If $0 \neq R \in \mathbb{F}[X_1,\ldots,X_m]$ is a polynomial, we denote its total degree by $\deg(R)$. We extend this notation to rational functions via $\deg(R) := \deg(\hat{R}) - \deg(\check{R})$ for every $0 \neq R = \hat{R}/\check{R}$. Observe that the degree of a rational function is well-defined, since it does not depend on its representation as a fraction of polynomials. Finally, if $R_1,\ldots,R_n \in \mathbb{F}(X_1,\ldots,X_m)$ such that $R_i \neq 0$ for every $i \in [n]$, we let $\deg(R_1,\ldots,R_n) := \max_{i\in[n]}\{\deg(R_i)\}$.

LINEAR DEPENDENCE. Let $R_1,\ldots,R_n,T \in \mathbb{F}(X_1,\ldots,X_m)$. We say that T is linearly dependent on $R_1,\ldots,R_n$ (over $\mathbb{F}$) if there exist $a_1,\ldots,a_n \in \mathbb{F}$ such that $T(X_1,\ldots,X_m) = \sum_{i=1}^n a_i \cdot R_i(X_1,\ldots,X_m)$.

HASH FUNCTION FAMILIES. A hash function family is a tuple of PPT algorithms $\mathsf{H} := (\mathsf{H.Setup}, \mathsf{H.KGen}, \mathsf{H.Eval})$. Here, algorithm $\mathsf{H.Setup}(1^\lambda)$ outputs a tuple π containing the descriptions of valid domain and range points D and R, as well as a key space K and other system-wide parameters. Algorithm $\mathsf{H.KGen}(\pi)$ is the hash key generation algorithm which returns a key $hk \in K$. The evaluation algorithm $\mathsf{H.Eval}(\pi, hk, x)$, called on a hash key hk and a domain point $x \in D$, outputs a point $y \in R$. To help readability, by slight abuse of notation we will simply write $\mathsf{H}(hk,x)$ in place of $\mathsf{H.Eval}(\pi,hk,x)$.

REMARK. Our definition of hash function families augments the usual syntax with a setup algorithm $\mathsf{H.Setup}$. Accordingly, we will extend the UCE definition to incorporate system parameters. Overloading notation, we allow $\mathsf{H.Setup}$ to alternatively take the description of a domain D and a range R as inputs, and let it return corresponding parameters π.

UNIVERSAL COMPUTATIONAL EXTRACTORS [11]. Let H be a hash function family. The advantage of a pair of PPT adversaries $(\mathcal{S},\mathcal{D})$ (called UCE source and UCE distinguisher) in the UCE game for H is defined as

$$\mathrm{Adv}^{\mathrm{uce}}_{\mathsf{H},\mathcal{S},\mathcal{D}}(\lambda) := 2 \cdot \Pr[\mathrm{UCE}^{\mathcal{S},\mathcal{D}}_{\mathsf{H}}(\lambda)] - 1,$$

where the UCE game is defined in Fig. 2 (left). We say that H is UCE[**S**] secure, if the advantage of any PPT $(\mathcal{S},\mathcal{D})$ with $\mathcal{S} \in \mathbf{S}$ in the UCE game for H is negligible. This is usually written as $\mathsf{H} \in \mathrm{UCE}[\mathbf{S}]$.

Without any restriction on the class of sources **S**, the UCE notion of security is unachievable [11]. BHK exclude trivial attacks by requiring that the source be *unpredictable*, meaning that it is hard to predict any of its oracle queries when observing the leakage L. Due to the obfuscation-based attack of [22], the flavor of unpredictability needs to be statistical. We recall the formal definition below.

(STATISTICALLY) UNPREDICTABLE SOURCES [11,22]. Let H be a hash function family and $\mathcal{S}$ a UCE source. We define the advantage of a (possibly unbounded) adversary $\mathcal{P}$ (called predictor) in the predictability game against $(\mathsf{H},\mathcal{S})$ as

$$\mathrm{Adv}^{\mathrm{pred}}_{\mathsf{H},\mathcal{S},\mathcal{P}}(\lambda) := \Pr[\mathrm{Pred}^{\mathcal{P}}_{\mathsf{H},\mathcal{S}}(\lambda)],$$

Game $\text{UCE}_H^{S,D}(\lambda)$:	Game $\text{Pred}_{H,S}^P(\lambda)$:	Game SZ_S^A:
$b \twoheadleftarrow \{0,1\}$	$Q \leftarrow []$	$(\pi := (p^\alpha, m, \text{st})) \twoheadleftarrow A_0$
$\pi \twoheadleftarrow \text{H.Setup}(1^\lambda)$	$\pi \twoheadleftarrow \text{H.Setup}(1^\lambda)$	for $i \in [m]$ do
$\rho \twoheadleftarrow \text{Fun}(D,R)$	$\rho \twoheadleftarrow \text{Fun}(D,R)$	$\quad (\mathbf{x}[i], \mathbf{z}[i]) \twoheadleftarrow S_i(\pi)$
$hk \twoheadleftarrow \text{H.KGen}(\pi)$	$L \twoheadleftarrow S^{\text{HASH}}(\pi)$	$(P,y) \twoheadleftarrow A_1(\pi, \mathbf{z})$
$L \twoheadleftarrow S^{\text{HASH}}(\pi)$	$x \twoheadleftarrow P(\pi, L)$	return $(y = P(\mathbf{x}))$
$b' \twoheadleftarrow D(\pi, hk, L)$	return $(x \in Q)$	
return $(b = b')$		
	Proc. $\text{HASH}(x)$:	Sources X_i / Z_i:
	$Q \leftarrow Q : x$	$(\pi := (p^\alpha, m, \text{st})) \twoheadleftarrow A_0$
Proc. $\text{HASH}(x)$:	return $\rho(x)$	$(x,z) \twoheadleftarrow S_i(\pi)$
if $(b = 0)$ then return $\rho(x)$		X_i : return x
else return $\text{H}(hk, x)$		Z_i : return z

Fig. 2. Left: The UCE game. **Center**: The unpredictability game. **Top right**: The Schwartz–Zippel game. **Bottom right**: The sources X_i and Z_i.

where the game Pred is defined in Fig. 2 (center). A source S is called statistically unpredictable if the above advantage is negligible for any (possibly unbounded) predictor P. The class of all statistically unpredictable sources is denoted $\mathbf{S}^{\text{sup}}$. We say that H is UCE secure if it is $\text{UCE}[\mathbf{S}^{\text{sup}}]$ secure.

SCHWARTZ–ZIPPEL LEMMA. We now recall the Schwartz–Zippel Lemma [33,49, 58], a simple yet powerful tool to bound the probability of finding a root of a non-zero polynomial when evaluating it at a random point. We also generalize the standard Schwartz–Zippel lemma and obtain a more general and game-based version of this result. In this variant, the points can be chosen according to distributions with enough min-entropy, and the polynomial picked given some leakage. This version may be more suitable for use in a cryptographic setting. A proof of the game-based Schwartz–Zippel lemma can be found in the full version of the paper [6].

Lemma 1 (Schwartz–Zippel). *Let* $\alpha, p \in \mathbb{N}$ *with* p *prime,* $S \subseteq \mathbb{F}_{p^\alpha}$, *and let* $0 \neq P(X_1, \ldots, X_m) \in \mathbb{F}_{p^\alpha}[X_1, \ldots, X_m]$. *Then*

$$\Pr_{x_1, \ldots, x_m \twoheadleftarrow S}[P(x_1, \ldots, x_m) = 0] \leq \frac{\deg(P)}{|S|}.$$

Lemma 2 (Game-based Schwartz–Zippel). *Let* $A = (A_0, A_1)$ *be a two-stage algorithm, where* A_0 *takes no input and returns a set of public parameters* $\pi := (p^\alpha, m, \text{st}) \in \mathbb{N}^2 \times \{0,1\}^*$ *with* $\alpha, p \in \mathbb{N}$ *and* p *prime, and* A_1 *takes* π *and values* $z_1, \ldots, z_m \in \{0,1\}^*$ *as input and returns a non-constant polynomial* $P(X_1, \ldots, X_m) \in \mathbb{F}_{p^\alpha}[X_1, \ldots, X_m]$ *with* $\deg(P) \leq d \in \mathbb{N}$ *and a value* $y \in \mathbb{F}_{p^\alpha}$. *Let* $S := \{S_i\}_{i \in \mathbb{N}}$ *be a family of sources, each taking* π *as input and returning values* $(x,z) \in \mathbb{F}_{p^\alpha} \times \{0,1\}^*$. *Then*

$$\Pr[\text{SZ}_S^A()] \leq d \cdot \mathop{\mathbb{E}}_{\substack{\pi \twoheadleftarrow A_0, \\ (x_1,z_1) \twoheadleftarrow S_1(\pi), \ldots, (x_m,z_m) \twoheadleftarrow S_m(\pi)}} \left[\frac{1}{2^{\min_{i \in [m]}\{\mathbf{H}_\infty(X_i|(A_0=\pi) \wedge (Z_i=z_i))\}}} \right],$$

where the game $\mathrm{SZ}_{\mathcal{S}}^{\mathcal{A}}()$ *is defined in Fig. 2 (top right), and the sources* $\mathcal{X}_i$ *and* $\mathcal{Z}_i$ *are given in Fig. 2 (bottom right).*

Observe that if $m = 1$, the expectation above is the prediction probability of $\mathcal{X}$ given $\mathcal{A}_0$ and $\mathcal{Z}$. In general, the minimum cannot be taken out of the expectation, because it reflects $\mathcal{A}$'s choices of which variables appear in P.

3   Pseudo-Generic Groups

We now formally define pseudo-generic groups (PGGs), where group elements are required to be indistinguishable from random, as long as their exponents satisfy a specific unpredictability condition. PGGs lift the definition of UCEs of Bellare, Hoang, and Keelveedhi [11] from the setting of hash functions to that of groups. In other words, the underlying ideal object in the PGG definition, from which a concrete group is supposed to be indistinguishable, is a generic group rather than a random oracle. We start by giving some background on computational group schemes and generic groups, and then proceed to defining PGGs.

COMPUTATIONAL GROUP SCHEMES [31]. A computational group scheme is a randomized algorithm Γ which, on input the security parameter 1^λ, outputs group parameters π consisting of a group operation $\circ$, an arbitrary group generator g, and a prime group order $p \in [2^{\lambda-1}, 2^\lambda)$. Implicit in these parameters is a set G such that $(\mathsf{G}, \circ)$ forms a cyclic group of order p with generator $g \in \mathsf{G}$. We write the sampling of group parameters as $(\pi := (\circ, g, p)) \twoheadleftarrow \Gamma(1^\lambda)$, with the understanding that π implicitly defines the underlying set G. As usual, the group operation gives rise to an exponentiation algorithm $\exp(h, x)$ whose output is denoted as h^x. We will often omit explicitly writing the operation $\circ$.

GENERIC GROUPS [45,47,51]. Given a group $(\mathsf{G}, \circ)$ of prime order p, the generic group on G is the uniform distribution over $\mathrm{Inj}(\mathbb{Z}_p, \mathsf{S})$, where $\mathsf{S} \subseteq \{0,1\}^*$ with $|\mathsf{S}| \geq p$. Recall that every map $\tau \in \mathrm{Inj}(\mathbb{Z}_p, \mathsf{S})$ allows one to define an associated group operation $\mathrm{op} \colon \mathsf{S} \times \mathsf{S} \to \mathsf{S} \cup \{\perp\}$ via $\mathrm{op}(h_1, h_2) := \tau(\tau^{-1}(h_1) + \tau^{-1}(h_2))$ if $h_1, h_2 \in \mathrm{Rng}(\tau)$, and $\mathrm{op}(h_1, h_2) := \perp$ otherwise. The generic group model is a model of computation in which all parties, honest or otherwise, are run on inputs p and encodings of application-specific elements, and have oracle access to a random encoding $\tau \in \mathrm{Inj}(\mathbb{Z}_p, \mathsf{S})$ and its associated operation oracle op.

PSEUDO-GENERIC GROUPS. Let Γ be a computational group scheme. We define the advantage of a pair of adversaries $(\mathcal{S}, \mathcal{D})$ (called PGG source and PGG distinguisher) in the PGG game for Γ as

$$\mathrm{Adv}_{\Gamma, \mathcal{S}, \mathcal{D}}^{\mathrm{pgg}}(\lambda) := 2 \cdot \Pr[\mathrm{PGG}_{\Gamma}^{\mathcal{S}, \mathcal{D}}(\lambda)] - 1,$$

where the PGG game is defined in Fig. 3 (left).[6] We say that Γ is PGG[S] secure if the advantage of any $(\mathcal{S}, \mathcal{D})$ with $\mathcal{S} \in \mathsf{S}$ and $\mathcal{D}$ a PPT algorithm in the PGG game is negligible. We denote this as $\Gamma \in$ PGG[S].

---

[6] Note that σ can be lazily sampled, so that the game runs in polynomial time.

Game $\mathrm{PGG}_\Gamma^{\mathcal{S},\mathcal{D}}(\lambda)$:	Game $\mathrm{AlgPred}_{\Gamma,\mathcal{S}}^{\mathcal{P}}(\lambda)$:	Masking source $\mathcal{S}^{\mathrm{Exp}}(\pi)$:
$b \twoheadleftarrow \{0,1\}$	$Q \leftarrow [\,]$	$(\mathbf{x},\mathbf{m},L) \twoheadleftarrow \bar{\mathcal{S}}(\pi)$
$(\pi := (\circ, g_0, p)) \twoheadleftarrow \Gamma(1^\lambda)$	$(\pi := (\circ, g_0, p)) \twoheadleftarrow \Gamma(1^\lambda)$	for $i = 1$ to $|\mathbf{m}|$ do
$r \twoheadleftarrow \mathbb{Z}_p^*;\ g \leftarrow g_0^r$	$\sigma \twoheadleftarrow \mathrm{Inj}(\mathbb{Z}_p, \mathsf{G})$	$\quad \mathbf{y}[i] \leftarrow \mathbf{m}[i] \circ \mathrm{Exp}(\mathbf{x}[i])$
$\sigma \twoheadleftarrow \mathrm{Inj}(\mathbb{Z}_p, \mathsf{G})$	$L \twoheadleftarrow \mathcal{S}^{\mathrm{Exp}}(\pi)$	return $(\mathbf{y}, L)$
$L \twoheadleftarrow \mathcal{S}^{\mathrm{Exp}}(\pi)$	$(\alpha_1, \ldots, \alpha_q) \twoheadleftarrow \mathcal{P}(\pi, L)$	
$b' \twoheadleftarrow \mathcal{D}(\pi, L)$	$[x_1, \ldots, x_q] \leftarrow Q$	dUber source $\mathcal{S}^{\mathrm{Exp}}(\pi)$:
return $(b = b')$	return $(\sum_{i=1}^q \alpha_i x_i = 0)$	$(\mathbf{x}, L) \twoheadleftarrow \bar{\mathcal{S}}(\pi)$
		for $i = 1$ to $|\mathbf{x}|$ do
		$\quad \mathbf{y}[i] \leftarrow \mathrm{Exp}(\mathbf{x}[i])$
Proc. $\mathrm{Exp}(x)$:	Proc. $\mathrm{Exp}(x)$:	return $(\mathbf{y}, L)$
if $(b = 0)$ then return $\sigma(x)$	$Q \leftarrow Q : x$	
else return g^x	return $\sigma(x)$	

Fig. 3. Left: The PGG game. **Center:** The algebraic unpredictability game. **Top right:** A generic masking source. **Bottom right:** A generic dUber source.

Recall from our earlier discussion that, similarly to UCEs and psPRPs, this notion of security is not achievable without restrictions on the class of PGG sources **S**. As a first step towards excluding trivial attacks, we introduce the notion of *algebraic unpredictability*, the core definition which allows us to extend UCE-type security notions beyond unstructured primitives (like hash functions and permutations). We require that no predictor be able to guess a non-trivial linear combination between the points queried by the source, as formalized below.

ALGEBRAICALLY UNPREDICTABLE SOURCES. Let Γ be a computational group scheme and $\mathcal{S}$ a PGG source, and assume that the leakage L produced by $\mathcal{S}$ encodes the number of Exp queries made by $\mathcal{S}$. We define the advantage of a (possibly unbounded) algorithm $\mathcal{P}$ (called predictor) in the algebraic unpredictability game against $(\Gamma, \mathcal{S})$ as

$$\mathrm{Adv}_{\Gamma,\mathcal{S},\mathcal{P}}^{\mathrm{alg\text{-}pred}}(\lambda) := \Pr[\mathrm{AlgPred}_{\Gamma,\mathcal{S}}^{\mathcal{P}}(\lambda)]\,,$$

where the game AlgPred is defined in Fig. 3 (center). We require that the output of $\mathcal{P}$ be different from the trivial all-zero tuple. A source $\mathcal{S}$ is called statistically algebraically unpredictable if the above advantage is negligible for any (possibly unbounded) predictor $\mathcal{P}$. We denote the class of all statistically algebraically unpredictable sources by $\mathbf{S}^{\mathrm{alg}}$. Observe that any such source must output distinct points (with high probability).

MASKING AND DUBER SOURCES. Algebraic unpredictability turns out to be insufficient to rule out all trivial attacks, as explained earlier. We thus restrict the set of sources for which we require PGG security even further and consider the class $\mathbf{S}^{\mathrm{msk}}$ of *masking* sources. These are sources $\mathcal{S}$ for which there exists a (possibly unbounded) auxiliary algorithm $\bar{\mathcal{S}}$ with polynomially bounded output, such that $\mathcal{S}$ takes the form in Fig. 3 (top right). Here, $\bar{\mathcal{S}}$ returns vectors $\mathbf{x} \in \mathbb{Z}_p^q$ and $\mathbf{m} \in \mathsf{G}^q$ of the same length, and leakage L. Source $\mathcal{S}$ then queries Exp on all entries of $\mathbf{x}$, and multiplies the replies with the corresponding elements from $\mathbf{m}$. We also define the subclass $\mathbf{S}^{\mathrm{duber}} \subseteq \mathbf{S}^{\mathrm{msk}}$ of *distributional Uber* (dUber) sources, as shown in Fig. 3 (bottom right), where we require $\mathbf{m} = (1_\mathsf{G}, \ldots, 1_\mathsf{G})$. To simplify notation, we define sources $\mathcal{S}$ in these classes via their corresponding auxiliary algorithms $\bar{\mathcal{S}}$, and call them auxiliary masking (resp., dUber) sources. Notice that masking and dUber sources always reveal the number of EXP queries through their leakage via the length $|\mathbf{y}|$ of $\mathbf{y}$.

Focusing on masking sources, and dUber sources in particular, provides a new perspective to our contribution. Indeed, dUber sources generalize the adversary in the Uber assumption insofar as oracle queries are no longer obtained as polynomial evaluations on a product distribution, but from a general distribution. To avoid trivial attacks, the target polynomial in the Uber assumption must be linearly independent from the other ones, a requirement covered by algebraic unpredictability in this setting.

PGG SECURITY. We say that a computational group scheme Γ is PGG secure if it is $\mathrm{PGG}[\mathbf{S}^{\mathrm{alg}} \cap \mathbf{S}^{\mathrm{msk}}]$ secure. In order to establish confidence in this notion and show that it hides no other obvious structural weaknesses, we prove in Sect. 4 that PGG security is indeed achievable in the generic-group model. However, we note that, for specific applications, PGG security with respect to subclasses of $\mathbf{S}^{\mathrm{alg}} \cap \mathbf{S}^{\mathrm{msk}}$ may be sufficient. On the other hand, there may exist larger, or even incomparable source classes for which PGG security is also feasible.[7]

DEFINITIONAL CHOICES. Observe that, in the PGG game, the randomized group generator g plays the role of the hash key hk in the UCE game. The fact that g remains hidden from the source prevents it from trivially winning the PGG game by sampling $x \twoheadleftarrow \mathbb{Z}_p$, querying $h \leftarrow \mathrm{EXP}(x)$, and checking if $g^x = h$. Similarly, g (or r) cannot be given to the distinguisher $\mathcal{D}$, since the source could query $h \leftarrow \mathrm{EXP}(1)$, leak h to $\mathcal{D}$, who then checks if $g = h$ (resp., $g_0^r = h$).

Note also that the random injection σ that the game samples has G (the real group), and not some larger set S, as its range. This is needed because the source can check group elements for validity (e.g., using exponentiation to power $p - 1$, or directly via an element validity algorithm if such a procedure is available).

Also observe that the source does not get oracle access to the operation op defined by σ. The reason is that, with such access, once again trivial attacks arise: The source samples two random group elements, then multiplies them first using the op oracle and then again locally using the input group operation $\circ$, and finally checks if the results match.[8] Removing access to the operation oracle from $\mathcal{S}$ does not restrict our ability to prove security results in the PGG model, as we shall see in Sect. 6.

COMPUTATIONAL ALGEBRAIC UNPREDICTABILITY. In [22], Brzuska, Farshim and Mittelbach demonstrate an attack against UCEs with respect to a *computational* notion of unpredictability. The types of sources that we consider for PGG

---

[7] For instance, one could allow for more expressive forms of post-processing. However, we have not yet been able to find applications of this wider class of sources.

[8] On the other hand, it is unclear how to rule this attack out using an extended notion of algebraic unpredictability that takes operation queries into account.

are analogous to the so-called split UCE sources. As BFM discuss, their iO-based attack does not extend to such sources. However, under the existence of a plausible form of obfuscation, attacks arise. In more detail, if the function mapping x to the obfuscation of the circuit $C[x] \colon h \mapsto h^x$ is one-way, the following attack emerges: The dUber source picks $x \leftarrow \mathbb{Z}_p$, defines $\mathbf{x} \leftarrow (1, x)$, and sets L to be an obfuscation of $C[x]$. The distinguisher then returns $(\mathbf{y}[2] = L(\mathbf{y}[1]))$. For this reason we focus on statistical algebraic unpredictability.

Despite this attack, there *is* a benefit in considering a computational notion of algebraic unpredictability when it comes to the analysis in idealized models. Indeed, as we show, PGG with respect to this wider class of sources is achievable in the GGM, and thus a wider class of applications can be proven secure in the GGM. This does not contradict potential security in the standard model since PGG with respect to computational algebraic unpredictability may still exist for sources that take specific forms.

MULTI-BASE PGGs. For the UCE and psPRP notions, BHK and ST respectively considered multi-key extensions to cover a wider range of applications. These notions are not known to be equivalent to their simpler single-key counterparts. For pseudo-generic groups, on the other hand, a simple generator re-randomization argument shows that the multi-base and single-base notions are equivalent. We thus focus on the (single-base) PGG version above.

4   Generic Groups Are PGGs

In this section we show the feasibility of PGGs in the generic-group model. The importance of this result is that it rules out generic attacks against the PGG notion, thus forming a check on the soundness of the definitional framework. Furthermore, it automatically lifts the security of each of the applications of PGGs that we consider to the GGM, as long as algebraically unpredictable, masking sources are used. This is similar to the Uber assumption family, where one relies on a specific assumption within Uber, and *reuses* the GGM hardness proved once for the whole family. As discussed above, we show GGM hardness of PGGs for a *computational* notion of algebraic unpredictability, which widens its applicability.

DEFINITIONAL CHOICES. Before stating our result, we clarify what it means for a generic group to be PGG secure. The PGG and AlgPred games in the GGM for a group of size p with target set S are presented in Figs. 4 (left) and 4 (center), masking sources are given in Fig. 4 (right). We stress that the oracles τ and op defining the generic group and its operation are *independent* of the injection σ used to define PGG security—only the ranges of the two encodings coincide, since, as in the standard model, σ must take values in the group (which is given by $\mathsf{Rng}(\tau)$ in the GGM). Advantage terms are defined as usual.

Recall that masking sources can be unbounded, which means that they are allowed an unlimited amount of group operations. Following [4], we mirror this in the GGM by giving $\mathcal{S}$ the entire function table of τ. Distinguisher $\mathcal{D}$ on the

Game $\mathrm{PGG}_{p,\mathsf{S}}^{\mathcal{S},\mathcal{D}}$:	Game $\mathrm{AlgPred}_{p,\mathsf{S},\mathcal{S}}^{\mathcal{P}}$:	Masking source $\mathcal{S}^{\mathrm{Exp}}(\tau)$:
$b \twoheadleftarrow \{0,1\}; r \twoheadleftarrow \mathbb{Z}_p^*$	$Q \leftarrow []$	$(\mathbf{x}, \mathbf{m}, \bar{L}) \twoheadleftarrow \bar{\mathcal{S}}(\tau)$
$\tau \twoheadleftarrow \mathrm{Inj}(\mathbb{Z}_p, \mathsf{S})$	$\tau \twoheadleftarrow \mathrm{Inj}(\mathbb{Z}_p, \mathsf{S})$	for $i = 1$ to $|\mathbf{m}|$ do
$\sigma \twoheadleftarrow \mathrm{Inj}(\mathbb{Z}_p, \mathrm{Rng}(\tau))$	$\sigma \twoheadleftarrow \mathrm{Inj}(\mathbb{Z}_p, \mathrm{Rng}(\tau))$	$\quad \mathbf{y}[i] \leftarrow \mathsf{op}(\mathbf{m}[i], \mathrm{Exp}(\mathbf{x}[i]))$
$L \twoheadleftarrow \mathcal{S}^{\mathrm{Exp}}(\tau)$	$L \twoheadleftarrow \mathcal{S}^{\mathrm{Exp}}(\tau)$	return $(\mathbf{y}, \bar{L})$
$b' \twoheadleftarrow \mathcal{D}^{\tau,\mathsf{op}}(L)$	$(\alpha_1, \ldots, \alpha_q) \twoheadleftarrow \mathcal{P}^{\tau,\mathsf{op}}(L)$	
return $(b = b')$	$[x_1, \ldots, x_q] \leftarrow Q$	Comm. proc. $\mathsf{op}(h_1, h_2)$:
	return $(\sum_{i=1}^q \alpha_i x_i = 0)$	return $\tau(\tau^{-1}(h_1) + \tau^{-1}(h_2))$
Proc. $\mathrm{Exp}(x)$:		
if $(b = 0)$ then	Proc. $\mathrm{Exp}(x)$:	
$\quad$ return $\sigma(x)$	$Q \leftarrow Q : x$	
else return $\tau(rx)$	return $\sigma(x)$	

Fig. 4. Left: The PGG game in the GGM. **Center:** The AlgPred game in the GGM. **Right:** A masking source $\mathcal{S}$ in the GGM. In all games, $|\mathsf{S}| \geq p$, and without loss of generality, all algorithms know p.

other hand is bounded, which means that it is only given oracles for τ and op and that the leakage L must be short. This choice of modeling more accurately reflects unbounded sources in the GGM by allowing an arbitrary number of group operations. Furthermore, it allows us to derive security in the presence of preprocessing attackers, as our sources can leak information about τ to the distinguisher.[9]

We are now ready to state the main result of this section. We only give an overview of the proof here, and provide the formal details in the full version [6].

Theorem 1 (GGM feasibility). *Let* $(\mathsf{G}, \circ)$ *be a group of order* p, *and* S *a set with* $|\mathsf{S}| \geq p$. *Then the generic group on* G *is* $\mathrm{PGG}[\mathsf{S}^{\mathrm{alg}} \cap \mathsf{S}^{\mathrm{msk}}]$ *secure. More precisely, for every adversary* $(\mathcal{S}, \mathcal{D})$ *in the PGG game with* $\mathcal{S} \in \mathsf{S}^{\mathrm{alg}} \cap \mathsf{S}^{\mathrm{msk}}$, *there exists a predictor* $\mathcal{P}$ *in the game AlgPred such that*

$$\mathrm{Adv}_{p,\mathsf{S},\mathcal{S},\mathcal{D}}^{\mathrm{pgg}} \leq \mathcal{O}\left(T^2 \cdot \mathrm{Adv}_{p,\mathsf{S},\mathcal{S},\mathcal{P}}^{\mathrm{alg}} + \sqrt{\frac{ST^2}{p}}\right),$$

where $S := 2q_{\mathcal{S}}(\lfloor \log p \rfloor + 1) + \ell + \lfloor \log q_{\mathcal{S}} \rfloor + \lfloor \log \ell \rfloor + 2$ *and* $T := q_{\mathcal{S}} + q_{\mathcal{D},\tau} + q_{\mathcal{D},\mathsf{op}}$. *Here* $q_{\mathcal{S}}$, $q_{\mathcal{D},\tau}$, *and* $q_{\mathcal{D},\mathsf{op}}$ *are upper bounds on the number of queries made by* $\mathcal{S}$ *and* $\mathcal{D}$ *to their respective oracles,* ℓ *is an upper bound on the length of the leakage* $\bar{L}$ *returned by* $\mathcal{S}$, *and we assume* $T \leq \sqrt{Sp}$.

Proof Overview. Fix any $(\mathcal{S}, \mathcal{D})$ as in the statement of the theorem. Without loss of generality, assume that $\mathcal{S}$ always returns exactly S bits (this can be achieved by padding the leakage $\bar{L}$ returned by $\mathcal{S}$). We use the game-playing framework and consider the following sequence of games:

---

[9] In particular, this model allows a restricted class of sources that leak arbitrary information (without any unpredictability requirements), as long as the sampling of the exponents is unpredictable (e.g., random, as is the case for the DLP).

Game_0 is the PGG game for $(\mathcal{S}, \mathcal{D})$ with respect to $b = 1$, i.e., where the oracle EXP uses the generic group injection τ.

Game_1 is the same as Game_0, but we additionally require that the queries $\mathcal{S}$ makes to the EXP oracle be all distinct. The distinguishing probability can be bounded by reducing to the algebraic unpredictability of a predictor that picks two coordinates i and j of $\mathbf{y}$ at random, and returns the zero vector with ± 1 at positions i and j.

Game_2 is the same as Game_1, but we use the "bit-fixing lemma" [4, Lemma 9] (with $\gamma := 1/p$) to resample τ right after the execution of $\bar{\mathcal{S}}$, whose output is treated as leakage. Also, we do not sample the new injection all at once, but implement it via lazy sampling. The loss in this transition is given by Lemma 9 in [4].

Game_3 is the same as Game_2, but we replace the randomly chosen exponent $r \twoheadleftarrow \mathbb{Z}_p^*$ with a formal variable R. We also start to lazy sample the new encoding σ with the values returned by EXP. The last two games are only different if, at the end of the execution of $\mathcal{D}$ in Game_3, $\mathcal{D}$ has queried two different polynomials that coincide when evaluated on a random $r \in \mathbb{Z}_p^*$, or if either $\mathcal{S}$ or $\mathcal{D}$ have made a query that belongs to the set of fixed points. All these events are bounded by the Schwartz–Zippel lemma: It is at this step that we use the fact that PGG is defined wrt. a random group generator.

Game_4 is the same as Game_3, but for every EXP query $\mathbf{x}[j]$, instead of saving an entry for $R\mathbf{x}[j]$ to the encoding table, we index it with a different and independent variable Z_j. This game is indistinguishable from the preceding one unless, at the end of the execution of $\mathcal{D}$ in Game_4, $\mathcal{D}$ has queried two distinct polynomials that coincide when evaluated on $(R\mathbf{x}[1], \ldots, R\mathbf{x}[q])$. Any such collision yields a non-trivial linear relation among the entries of $\mathbf{x}$. It is at this step that we appeal to the algebraic unpredictability of the source $\mathcal{S}$.

Game_5 is the same as Game_4, but we evaluate the variables Z_j at random values $c_j \twoheadleftarrow \mathbb{Z}_p$. The two games are close up to a Schwartz–Zippel term.

Game_6 is the same as Game_5, but we insist that the values c_j be pairwise distinct. The distinguishing probability can be bounded by a collision argument.

Game_7 is the same as Game_6, but we do not populate the encoding table in oracle calls to EXP. By construction, the last two games are indistinguishable.

Game_8 is the same as Game_7, but when we lazily sample replies to EXP queries, we do so consistently with σ rather than τ. Notice that the EXP oracle now only depends on σ and is completely decoupled from τ. The two games are close because the sets from where we sample have a large overlap.

Game_9 is the same as Game_8, but we undo lazy sampling of σ and instead sample it all at once. Also, we again use the bit-fixing lemma [4, Lemma 9] to undo resampling of τ. Since we are essentially reverting the second game hop from above, the distinguishing advantage can be bounded as before.

Game_{10} is the same as Game_9, but we remove the constraint that all queries $\mathcal{S}$ makes are pairwise different. Doing so, we have obtained the PGG game with $b = 0$, i.e., where the oracle EXP uses an independent encoding σ. Again, the distinguishing advantage here is the same as in the first game hop.

Collecting the terms above, we obtain

$$\mathrm{Adv}^{\mathrm{pgg}}_{p,\mathsf{S},\mathcal{S},\mathcal{D}} \leq 3\,T^2 \cdot \mathrm{Adv}^{\mathrm{alg}}_{p,\mathsf{S},\mathcal{S},\mathcal{P}} + \frac{26\,T^2}{p} + 36\,T\left(\frac{S}{P} + \frac{P}{p}\right),$$

where $\mathcal{P}$ is a predictor against algebraic unpredictability of $\mathcal{S}$ and $P \in \mathbb{N}$ an arbitrary number (coming from the application of the bit-fixing lemma). Setting $P :\approx \sqrt{Sp}$ to minimize the term on the right, we obtain the claimed result. $\square$

UBER WITH PREPROCESSING. Looking ahead, we observe that Uber and Uber-II sources are statistically algebraically unpredictable (even in the GGM) and, in particular, their algebraic unpredictability bound does not depend on the number of queries made by the predictor to the generic group oracles. This in turn implies that when the above theorem is applied to the Uber and Uber-II sources (with q polynomials of degree at most d and at most T generic group and operation queries) we obtain $\mathrm{Adv}^{\mathrm{dua\text{-}ii}}_{p,\mathcal{A}} \leq \tilde{O}\left(d(T+q)^2/p + \sqrt{S(T+q)^2/p}\right)$ in the GGM. When setting $q = 4$ and $d = 2$, the bound matches that established for the DDH problem [29, 30].

DISCUSSION ON DDH-II. As a second corollary, we obtain the hardness of the r-DDH-II assumption[10] in the GGM (here "r" stands for randomized generator). This result was also established by Bartusek, Ma, and Zhandry (BMZ) [4, Theorem 12]. Our proof, besides establishing the hardness of a winder class of assumption, is more modular and also avoids asymptotics. Furthermore, since our feasibility only relies on *computational* algebraic unpredictability, it can be applied in a setting where some group elements are directly leaked to the distinguisher.

5   From Simple to Algebraic Unpredictability: LDDs

We define a new type of hash function family called *linear-dependence destroyer* (LDD) that is useful for building schemes secure in PGGs. Intuitively, LDDs are hash functions with domain and range $\mathbb{Z}_p$ that remove, in a statistical sense, any linear dependence among a list of distinct but potentially correlated values.

LINEAR-DEPENDENCE DESTROYERS (LDDs). Let H be a hash function family with domain and range $\mathbb{Z}_p$ for some prime p. We define the advantage of a pair of adversaries $(\mathcal{S}, \mathcal{A})$ in the LDD game for H as

$$\mathrm{Adv}^{\mathrm{ldd}}_{\mathsf{H},\mathcal{S},\mathcal{A}}(\lambda) := \Pr[\mathrm{LDD}^{\mathcal{S},\mathcal{A}}_{\mathsf{H}}(\lambda)],$$

where the LDD game is defined in Fig. 5 (top left). We require that the outputs of $\mathcal{S}$ be pairwise distinct and the output of $\mathcal{A}$ be different from the all-zero tuple. We say that H is LDD[**S**] secure if the advantage of any $(\mathcal{S}, \mathcal{A})$ in the LDD game is negligible, with $\mathcal{S} \in \mathbf{S}$ and $\mathcal{A}$ a PPT machine. We write this as $\mathsf{H} \in \mathrm{LDD}[\mathbf{S}]$.

---

[10] Distinguish (g, g^x, g^y, g^{xy}) from (g, g^x, g^y, g^z) for a random generator g, unpredictable x, and random y and z.

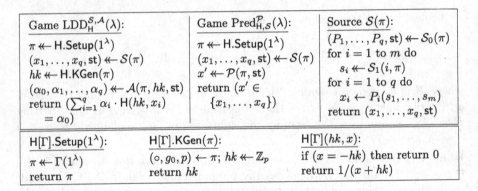

Fig. 5. Top left: The LDD game. **Top center:** The predictability game. **Top right:** Structure of a low-degree LDD source. **Bottom:** Candidate construction of an LDD family H[Γ] from a computational group scheme Γ.

We call an LDD source $\mathcal{S}$ statistically unpredictable if

$$\mathrm{Adv}^{\mathrm{pred}}_{\mathsf{H},\mathcal{S},\mathcal{P}}(\lambda) := \Pr[\mathrm{Pred}^{\mathcal{P}}_{\mathsf{H},\mathcal{S}}(\lambda)]$$

is negligible for any (possibly unbounded) predictor $\mathcal{P}$, where the game Pred is defined in Fig. 5 (top center). We denote the class of all statistically unpredictable LDD sources by $\mathbf{S}^{\mathrm{sup}}$. We say that H is an LDD if it is LDD[$\mathbf{S}^{\mathrm{sup}}$] secure.

In the full version of this work we show that, for a computational group scheme Γ, the hash function family H[Γ] with domain and range $\mathbb{Z}_p$ defined in Fig. 5 (bottom) is an LDD for the class of *low-degree sources* $\mathbf{S}^{\mathrm{low}}$. These are sources that compute their output as evaluations of low-degree polynomials on high-entropy points, as in Fig. 5 (top right). We present an informal statement of our theorem in the following, and refer the reader to the full version [6] for formal definitions and proofs.

Theorem 2 ((Informal) LDD for low-degree sources). *Let Γ be a computational group scheme, and let* H[Γ] *be the hash function family defined in Fig. 5 (bottom). Then* H[Γ] $\in$ LDD[$\mathbf{S}^{\mathrm{low}}$].

We were unable to prove that this construction is an LDD for *all* unpredictable sources, though we have not been able to break it either. We conjecture that LDDs exist for *all* statistically unpredictable sources, and not just for low-degree ones. More strongly, we conjecture that the hash function H[Γ] defined in Fig. 5 (bottom) is LDD secure for all statistically unpredictable sources. We emphasize that LDD is an *information-theoretic* notion and thus unconditional constructions (as for randomness extractors) may exist. We note that positive results for smaller classes of sources are also meaningful, as they would translate, via our constructions and proofs, into deterministic PKE, UCEs, and RKA-secure encryption.

As evidence towards the first conjecture, we can easily prove that a random oracle $\rho: \mathbb{Z}_p^2 \to \mathbb{Z}_p$ is an LDD, if all algorithms only get polynomially bounded oracle access to ρ (rather than the entire function table). Assume that $\mathcal{A}$ makes at most n queries, and let E denote the event that $\mathcal{A}$ queries ρ on one of the points $(hk, x_1), \ldots, (hk, x_q)$. Then we can build a predictor $\mathcal{P}$ such that $\Pr[E] \leq n \cdot \Pr[\mathrm{Pred}^{\mathcal{P}}_{\rho, \mathcal{S}}(p)]$, which is small by unpredictability of $\mathcal{S}$. If E does not occur, then the equation $\sum_{i=1}^{q} \alpha_i \cdot \mathsf{H}(hk, x_i) = \alpha_0$ is satisfied with probability at most $1/p$, because at least one coefficient α_j, $1 \leq j \leq q$, is non-zero, and thus the random-looking value $\mathsf{H}(hk, x_j)$ is determined by the winning condition.

We provide a stronger feasibility result for LDDs by showing that random functions are LDDs for any unpredictable source, even when *both* the source $\mathcal{S}$ and the adversary $\mathcal{A}$ have *full access* to the table of the random function.[11] This result would thus establish the existence of LDDs, similarly to that for other information-theoretic objects such as randomness extractors. At a very high level, we prove this result in two steps: First, we decompose arbitrary high-entropy sources into a convex combination of flat sources (i.e., sources that are uniform on subsets of the support of the distribution). This is a standard technique in the study of randomness extractors [54]. Second, we apply a *compression-style* argument [38] to show that any predictor that has a high LDD-advantage against unpredictable sources can be used to compress the random function. The complete proof is rather technical, and we refer to the full version [6] for a more detailed overview as well as the formal details.

6   Applications of PGGs

We now explore some examples of how PGGs can be used to prove the hardness of group-based assumptions and the security of practical cryptosystems under a variety of notions. As our first application, we prove that the decisional Uber assumption (DUA) family holds in PGGs. In doing so we also capture all of its implications. We then turn our attention to applications which do not seem to fall under the umbrella of the DUA. In the interest of space, we show here only how to construct UCEs from PGGs and LDDs. Further applications, namely KDM-CPA and RKA-CPA security of (modified versions of) ElGamal, and security of the ElGamal-with-Hash deterministic encryption scheme, are discussed in the full version [6]. Interestingly, all these applications enjoy reductions under PGGs which furthermore retain to a large extent the simplicity of proofs in the GGM. Standard-model constructions of such schemes under Uber (for example, the KDM-secure PKE scheme of Boneh et al. [20]) are often substantially more complex and less efficient.

6.1   Uber Assumptions in PGGs

The Uber assumption family [19, 21] is an umbrella assumption that generalizes many hardness assumptions used to analyze the security of concrete cryptosystems. It has been formalized for both simple and bilinear groups, and has been

---

[11] Accordingly, we also impose a statistical notion of unpredictability on sources by giving predictors access to the full table.

$$\boxed{\begin{array}{l}
\text{Game DUA-II}_\Gamma^{\mathcal{A}}(\lambda): \\[4pt]
d \twoheadleftarrow \{0,1\};\ (\pi := (\circ, g_0, p)) \twoheadleftarrow \Gamma(1^\lambda);\ r \twoheadleftarrow \mathbb{Z}_p^*;\ g \leftarrow g_0^r \\
(R_1, \ldots, R_n, T, \mathsf{st}) \twoheadleftarrow \mathcal{A}_0(\pi);\ R_{n+1} \leftarrow T \\
\text{for } i = 1 \text{ to } m \text{ do } \mathbf{s}[i] \twoheadleftarrow \mathcal{A}_1(i, \pi) \\
\text{if } (\exists i \in [n+1])(\check{R}_i(\mathbf{s}) = 0) \text{ then return true} \\
\text{for } i = 1 \text{ to } n \text{ do } h_i \leftarrow g^{R_i(\mathbf{s})} \\
\text{if } (d = 0) \text{ then } r' \twoheadleftarrow \mathbb{Z}_p \text{ else } r' \leftarrow T(\mathbf{s}) \\
h \leftarrow g^{r'};\ d' \twoheadleftarrow \mathcal{A}_2(\pi, h_1, \ldots, h_n, h, \mathsf{st});\ \text{return } (d = d')
\end{array}}$$

Fig. 6. The decisional Uber assumption II (DUA-II) game. Here, m is an upper bound on the number of variables of the R_i, $i \in [n+1]$. The (ordinary) decisional Uber assumption (DUA) is a special case of DUA-II where $\mathcal{A}_1(i, \pi)$ is the uniform distribution over $\mathbb{Z}_p$ for all $i \in [m]$ and all π.

shown to hold in (bilinear) generic groups [19]. In this work we focus on simple (i.e., non-bilinear) groups and show that Uber assumptions for them fall within the PGG framework. More precisely, we show that non-interactive, generator-independent Uber assumptions hold for PGGs.

We present an entropic generalization of the decisional version of the Uber assumption, which we call DUA-II, and show that it holds for PGGs. Loosely speaking, DUA-II extends DUA by sampling the inputs to the polynomials from independent, high-entropy distributions, rather than uniformly at random. Restricted versions of DUA-II and applications thereof have previously appeared in the literature. (See, for example, Canetti's DDH-II assumption [25].)

DECISIONAL UBER ASSUMPTION II (DUA-II). Let Γ be a computational group scheme. We define the advantage of an adversary $\mathcal{A} = (\mathcal{A}_0, \mathcal{A}_1, \mathcal{A}_2)$ in the DUA-II game for Γ as

$$\mathrm{Adv}_{\Gamma, \mathcal{A}}^{\mathrm{dua\text{-}ii}}(\lambda) := 2 \cdot \Pr[\text{DUA-II}_\Gamma^{\mathcal{A}}(\lambda)] - 1,$$

where the DUA-II game is defined in Fig. 6. Here, $\mathcal{A}_0$ and $\mathcal{A}_1$ can be unbounded with polynomially bounded output, and $\mathcal{A}_2$ is PPT. We require that T be linearly independent from $R_1, \ldots, R_n$, and that $\mathbf{H}_\infty(\mathcal{A}_1(i, \pi)) = \omega(\log \lambda)$ for every $i \in \mathbb{N}$ and every $\pi \twoheadleftarrow \Gamma(1^\lambda)$. We say that Γ is DUA-II secure if, for any $\mathcal{A}$ as above, the advantage of $\mathcal{A}$ in the DUA-II game for Γ is negligible.

Notice that we can assume without loss of generality that the rational functions $R_1, \ldots, R_n$ returned by $\mathcal{A}_0$ are linearly independent. Indeed, linear (in)dependence can be checked by computing $D := \mathrm{lcm}(\check{R}_1, \ldots, \check{R}_n)$, then writing a generic linear combination $\sum_{i=1}^n a_i \cdot R_i D = 0$, and then solving the ensuing linear system for $(a_1, \ldots, a_n)$. This yields a nonzero solution if and only if $R_1, \ldots, R_n$ are linearly dependent. Now observe that if R_k is linearly dependent on $R_1, \ldots, R_{k-1}$, then $g^{R_k(\mathbf{x})}$ can be computed directly by $\mathcal{A}_2$ (who knows $g^{R_1(\mathbf{x})}, \ldots, g^{R_{k-1}(\mathbf{x})}$) before guessing d', without having to rely on the challenger.

We now show that the Uber-II assumption holds in pseudo-generic groups. (We thus recover several cryptographic applications that fall under the reach of

Uber and Uber-II.) We only give an informal statement and a proof sketch here, and refer to the full version [6] for the formal statement and a full proof.

Theorem 3 ((Informal) PGG $\implies$ DUA-II). *Let Γ be a computational group scheme. If Γ is $\mathrm{PGG}[\mathbf{S}^{\mathrm{alg}} \cap \mathbf{S}^{\mathrm{duber}}]$ secure, then it is DUA-II secure.*

Proof Overview. Given an adversary $\mathcal{A} = (\mathcal{A}_0, \mathcal{A}_1, \mathcal{A}_2)$ in the DUA-II game, consider a PGG adversary $(\mathcal{S}, \mathcal{D})$ defined as follows: Source $\mathcal{S}$ runs $\mathcal{A}_0$ and $\mathcal{A}_1$, and queries EXP on $R_1(\mathbf{s}), \ldots, R_n(\mathbf{s}), r'$, where r' is either $T(\mathbf{s})$ or a random value, the choice being made at random. Distinguisher $\mathcal{D}$ then runs $\mathcal{A}_2$ and checks if it did predict the choice made by $\mathcal{S}$. By construction, $\mathcal{S}$ is a dUber source.

By direct inspection, the game $\mathrm{PGG}_\Gamma^{\mathcal{S},\mathcal{D}}(\lambda)$ with challenge bit $b = 1$ coincides with the game DUA-II$_\Gamma^{\mathcal{A}}(\lambda)$. On the other hand, when $b = 0$, the probability of $(\mathcal{S}, \mathcal{D})$ winning the PGG game is negligible. This follows from a bad event analysis: We transition to a game where $r' \neq R_i(\mathbf{s})$ for all $i \in [n]$. Given that σ is a random injection, we can then move to a game where the corresponding reply is picked at random, independently of the random choice of $\mathcal{S}$, so that $\mathcal{A}$ has no advantage in this game.

For algebraic unpredictability, let $\mathcal{P}$ be any predictor that returns a linear combination of the queries with coefficients $\alpha_1, \ldots, \alpha_n, \alpha_{n+1}$ given the leakage computed using the ideal EXP oracle. We again transition to a game where the EXP queries are pairwise distinct, and then replace the answers with pairwise different random elements that are independent of $\mathbf{s}$. Winning the algebraic unpredictability game then means that $\mathbf{s}$ (which $\mathcal{P}$ now knows nothing about) is a root of $\alpha_1 R_1 + \cdots + \alpha_n R_n + \alpha_{n+1} r'$, which is unlikely by Schwartz–Zippel. □

6.2 Building UCEs

In this section we show how to construct UCEs based on PGGs and LDDs. We consider UCEs for statistically unpredictable and *split* sources [11], whose definition we recall below; see Fig. 7 (left). Split sources are required to make distinct queries to prevent iO-based attacks. BHK use split sources to prove security of a number of applications, including RKA security, point-function obfuscation, and storage-auditing protocols, as well as several other applications that rely on computationally unpredictable split sources.

As can be seen in Fig. 7 (left), a split UCE source allows for limited post-processing of the outputs of the hash. This feature of split sources, however, is *not* used in any of its applications: The very simple $\mathcal{S}_1$ that merely returns $\mathbf{y}$ is sufficient for proving the security of the applications that BHK consider for split sources.[12] Our result in this section allows to recover applications of UCEs with respect to split sources (with a trivial $\mathcal{S}_1$) under PGGs and LDDs.[13]

---

[12] Interestingly, this simplification provides another avenue to circumvent iO-based attacks that exploit repetitions in $\mathbf{x}$.

[13] We note, however, that in iterative constructions of block-ciphers from hash functions [12], or indeed in domain extenders for hash functions [52], adaptive calls to the hash function seem to be necessary.

Split source $\mathcal{S}^{\text{HASH}}(\pi)$:	H.Setup(1^λ):	H.KGen(π):
$(\mathbf{x}, L_0) \twoheadleftarrow \mathcal{S}_0(\pi)$	$(\circ, g_0, p) \twoheadleftarrow \Gamma(1^\lambda)$	$(\pi_{\text{ldd}}, \circ, g, p) \leftarrow \pi$
for $i = 1$ to $|\mathbf{x}|$ do	$r \twoheadleftarrow \mathbb{Z}_p^*; \; g \leftarrow g_0^r$	$s \twoheadleftarrow \mathbb{Z}_p^*; \; h \leftarrow g^s$
$\quad \mathbf{y}[i] \leftarrow \text{HASH}(\mathbf{x}[i])$	$\pi_{\text{ldd}} \twoheadleftarrow \text{H}_{\text{ldd}}.\text{Setup}(\mathbb{Z}_p, \mathbb{Z}_p)$	$hk \twoheadleftarrow \text{H}_{\text{ldd}}.\text{KGen}(\pi_{\text{ldd}})$
$L_1 \twoheadleftarrow \mathcal{S}_1(\pi, \mathbf{y})$	$\pi \leftarrow (\pi_{\text{ldd}}, \circ, g, p)$	return (h, hk)
$L \leftarrow (L_0, L_1)$	return π	
return L		H$((h, hk), x)$:
		$\quad y \leftarrow \text{H}_{\text{ldd}}(hk, x)$
		$\quad$ return h^y

Fig. 7. *Left*: Structure of the split source $\mathcal{S} = \text{Splt}[\mathcal{S}_0, \mathcal{S}_1]$ associated to $\mathcal{S}_0$ and $\mathcal{S}_1$. In simple split sources, $\mathcal{S}_1$ returns $L_1 = \mathbf{y}$. *Right*: A UCE built from a PGG and an LDD hash function.

Our construction of UCEs from PGGs is inspired by the correlated-input (CI) secure hash of Goyal, O'Neill, and Rao (GOR) [39], where outputs of a hash function are required to look random on high-entropy, but possibly correlated, inputs. GOR show that the hash function which maps $x \mapsto g^{1/(x+hk)}$, where $hk \twoheadleftarrow \mathbb{Z}_p$ is the hash key, is non-adaptively CI secure for polynomially induced correlations under the q-DDH assumption. This assumption falls within Uber and thus together with Theorem 3, we re-obtain this result. This, however, falls short of achieving split UCE security, since the hash inputs are polynomially induced.

We make progress towards building fully secure UCEs from group-based assumptions. We present our construction in a modular way in terms of an underlying LDD as shown in Fig. 7 (right). (The GOR hash is that associated with the conjectural LDD $(hk, x) \mapsto 1/(x + hk)$.) Based on the conjectural existence of LDDs for all unpredictable sources, we obtain a fully secure UCE (beyond polynomial sources) for all statistically unpredictable and split sources. As for KDM security, in the GGM, we can account for preprocessing too.

Looking ahead into the proof, there is a close correspondence between the class of sources for which one achieves LDD security and UCE security. That is, if LDDs for a certain (e.g., low-degree) class of sources can be built, this would translate into UCE security for an analogous source class. Thus, we obtain an unconditional result for low-degree sources (since Theorem 2 shows that $1/(x + hk)$ is an LDD for low-degree sources).

SPLIT SOURCES. A UCE source $\mathcal{S}$ is called *split* if there exist PPT algorithms $\mathcal{S}_0$ and $\mathcal{S}_1$ such that $\mathcal{S}$ takes the form in Fig. 7 (left). Here, $\mathcal{S}_0$ returns a vector $\mathbf{x}$ whose entries are required to be pairwise distinct, and some leakage L_0. We write $\mathcal{S} = \text{Splt}[\mathcal{S}_0, \mathcal{S}_1]$ if $\mathcal{S}$ is a split source constructed from algorithms $\mathcal{S}_0$ and $\mathcal{S}_1$ as above, and we denote by $\mathbf{S}^{\text{splt}}$ the class of all such split sources. We further define the class $\mathbf{S}^{\text{ssplt}} \subseteq \mathbf{S}^{\text{splt}}$ of *simple split sources*, which are split sources where $\mathcal{S}_1$ simply returns $L_1 = \mathbf{y}$.

Theorem 4 (PGG $\wedge$ LDD $\implies$ UCE[$\mathbf{S}^{\text{sup}} \cap \mathbf{S}^{\text{ssplt}}$]). *Let Γ be a computational group scheme, H_{ldd} a hash function family, and H the hash function family based*

Auxiliary dUber source $\bar{S}'(\pi)$:	PGG distinguisher $\mathcal{D}'(\pi, (\mathbf{y}', L'))$:
$(\circ, g_0, p) \leftarrow \pi$; $r', s' \twoheadleftarrow \mathbb{Z}_p^*$; $g' \leftarrow g_0^{r'}$	$n + 1 \leftarrow |\mathbf{y}'|$
$\pi_{\mathsf{ldd}} \twoheadleftarrow \mathsf{H}_{\mathsf{ldd}}.\mathsf{Setup}(\mathbb{Z}_p, \mathbb{Z}_p)$	$h \leftarrow \mathbf{y}'[n+1]$
$\pi' \leftarrow (\pi_{\mathsf{ldd}}, \circ, g', p)$	$(L_0, \pi', hk) \leftarrow L'$
$hk \twoheadleftarrow \mathsf{H}_{\mathsf{ldd}}.\mathsf{KGen}(\pi_{\mathsf{ldd}})$	$\mathbf{y} \leftarrow \mathbf{y}'[1..n]$; $L \leftarrow (L_0, \mathbf{y})$
$(\mathbf{x}, L_0) \twoheadleftarrow S_0(\pi')$; $n \leftarrow |\mathbf{x}|$; $L' \leftarrow (L_0, \pi', hk)$	$b' \twoheadleftarrow \mathcal{D}(\pi', (h, hk), L)$
for $i = 1$ to n do $\mathbf{x}'[i] \leftarrow s' \cdot \mathsf{H}_{\mathsf{ldd}}(hk, \mathbf{x}[i])$	return b'
$\mathbf{x}'[n+1] \leftarrow s'$	
return $(\mathbf{x}', L')$	

Fig. 8. Reduction from a UCE adversary $(S, \mathcal{D})$ to a PGG adversary $(S', \mathcal{D}')$.

on Γ and $\mathsf{H}_{\mathsf{ldd}}$ as defined in Fig. 7 (right). If Γ is $\mathrm{PGG}[\mathbf{S}^{\mathsf{alg}} \cap \mathbf{S}^{\mathsf{duber}}]$ secure and $\mathsf{H}_{\mathsf{ldd}}$ is $\mathrm{LDD}[\mathbf{S}^{\mathsf{sup}}]$ secure, then H is $\mathrm{UCE}[\mathbf{S}^{\mathsf{sup}} \cap \mathbf{S}^{\mathsf{ssplt}}]$ secure. More precisely, for any adversary $(S, \mathcal{D})$ in the UCE game for H, there are an adversary $(S', \mathcal{D}')$ in the PGG game for Γ, and LDD source S and adversary $\mathcal{A}_{\mathsf{cr}}$ such that

$$\mathrm{Adv}_{\mathsf{H},S,\mathcal{D}}^{\mathsf{uce}}(\lambda) \leq 2 \cdot \mathrm{Adv}_{\Gamma,S',\mathcal{D}'}^{\mathsf{pgg}}(\lambda) + q(\lambda)^2 \cdot \mathrm{Adv}_{\mathsf{H}_{\mathsf{ldd}},S,\mathcal{A}_{\mathsf{cr}}}^{\mathsf{ldd}}(\lambda) + \frac{q(\lambda)^2}{2^{\lambda-1}}.$$

Here, $q(\lambda)$ is an upper bound on the number of queries made by S to its HASH oracle. Algorithm S' makes at most $q(\lambda) + 1$ queries to its EXP oracle and runs in similar time, and algorithm $\mathcal{D}'$ runs in similar time to $\mathcal{D}$.

Furthermore, $S' \in \mathbf{S}^{\mathsf{alg}} \cap \mathbf{S}^{\mathsf{duber}}$ is algebraically unpredictable. More precisely, for any PGG algebraic predictor $\mathcal{P}'$ there is an LDD adversary $\mathcal{A}$ for $\mathsf{H}_{\mathsf{ldd}}$ such that

$$\mathrm{Adv}_{\Gamma,S',\mathcal{P}'}^{\mathsf{alg\text{-}pred}}(\lambda) \leq \mathrm{Adv}_{\mathsf{H}_{\mathsf{ldd}},S,\mathcal{A}}^{\mathsf{ldd}}(\lambda) + \frac{q(\lambda)^2}{2} \cdot \mathrm{Adv}_{\mathsf{H}_{\mathsf{ldd}},S,\mathcal{A}_{\mathsf{cr}}}^{\mathsf{ldd}}(\lambda).$$

Moreover, $S \in \mathbf{S}^{\mathsf{sup}}$. That is for any predictor $\mathcal{P}''$, there is a predictor $\mathcal{P}$ against the original UCE source S in the Pred game such that

$$\mathrm{Adv}_{\mathsf{H}_{\mathsf{ldd}},S,\mathcal{P}''}^{\mathsf{pred}}(\lambda) \leq \mathrm{Adv}_{\mathsf{H},S,\mathcal{P}}^{\mathsf{pred}}(\lambda).$$

Proof Overview. Let $(S, \mathcal{D})$ be PPT adversaries against UCE security of H. We build $(S', \mathcal{D}')$ against the PGG security of the underlying group as shown in Fig. 8.

ADVANTAGE BOUND. Let b denote the challenge bit in the PGG game. Then it is easy to see that

$$\Pr\left[\mathrm{PGG}_{\Gamma}^{S',\mathcal{D}'}(\lambda) \mid b = 1\right] = \Pr\left[\mathrm{UCE}_{\mathsf{H}}^{S,\mathcal{D}}(\lambda) \mid b = 1\right].$$

Indeed, when $b = 1$ the exponentiation oracle is implemented via the real group operations. Parameter π' contains a random generator $g' = g_0^{r'}$. Hash values are computed with respect to $h = g_0^{rs'} = g_0^{r' \cdot rs'/r'}$. This means that the exponent of the first element of the hash key is rs'/r', which results in a random group element. Thus the UCE source and distinguisher are run as they would be in the UCE game with respect to the real hash function.

We next claim that

$$\Pr\left[\text{PGG}_\Gamma^{\mathcal{S}',\mathcal{D}'}(\lambda)\,\middle|\,b=0\right] \leq \Pr\left[\text{UCE}_\mathsf{H}^{\mathcal{S},\mathcal{D}}(\lambda)\,\middle|\,b \doteq 0\right]$$
$$+q(\lambda)^2 \cdot \text{Adv}_{\mathsf{H}_{\text{ldd}},\mathcal{S},\mathcal{A}_{\text{cr}}}^{\text{ldd}}(\lambda) + \frac{q(\lambda)^2}{2^\lambda}.$$

This claim follows from the fact that when $b = 0$ the EXP oracle returns random values subject to injectivity. We now transition to a game where EXP implements a random function. Using the random-function/random-permutation switching lemma, we incur an additive loss of $q(\lambda)^2/2^\lambda$. We modify this game further and replace the random function with a forgetful random function. The two games are identical unless there is a collision in the inputs to the random function. We may bound the probability of this event via the collision probability of the LDD, which itself can be bounded in terms of the LDD advantage: consider an adversary $\mathcal{A}_{\text{cr}}$ that picks two indices, sets their coefficients to $+1$ and -1, the rest of the coefficients to 0, and $\alpha_0 = 0$. The LDD source here is identical to the UCE source. Thus any LDD predictor can be converted into a UCE predictor: simply ignore the hash values and run the LDD predictor. This justifies the final inequality in the theorem.

The final game that we arrive at is equivalent to the UCE game with respect to a random oracle (recall that the source outputs distinct inputs).

ALGEBRAIC UNPREDICTABILITY. We now show that the PGG source constructed above is algebraically unpredictable. Consider a modified algebraic prediction game whereby EXP returns random group elements, still subject to injectivity but not respecting equality across inputs. These two games are identical unless there is a collision among the inputs. We may bound the probability of collision via the LDD adversary $\mathcal{A}_{\text{cr}}$ as above. This incurs a loss of $q(\lambda)^2/2$ times LDD advantage of $\mathcal{A}_{\text{cr}}$.

We now rely on the LDD security of the hash function to bound the probability of winning the *modified* algebraic predictability. Suppose there exists an algebraic predictor $\mathcal{P}'$ against PGG source $\mathcal{S}'$. We construct an LDD source $\mathcal{S}''$ and an LDD adversary $\mathcal{A}$ as follows. Source $\mathcal{S}$ runs $\mathcal{S}'$, which is itself running $\mathcal{S}$ and hence is identical to $\mathcal{S}$. (This source is unpredictable as shown above.) Adversary $\mathcal{A}$ receives a hash key and leakage, and simulates the group elements that the algebraic predictor $\mathcal{P}'$ in the modified game expects randomly but subject to injectivity. Together with the collision bound above, this establishes the second inequality stated in the theorem.

REMARK. We note that the above proof can be easily extended to *multi-key* UCEs [11, Figure 8] for split sources by generating multiple hash keys and hash public keys via re-randomization. BHK conjectured that UCE and multi-key UCE are in general equivalent, which remains open.

An alternative construction of UCEs from PGGs would first compute g^{rx} and then chop half of the output bits so that group operations on hash outputs are no longer possible. (This was previously suggested, for example, as a way to build a RO in the GGM by Zhandry and Zhang [57].) An analysis of this construction may be made possible in the PGG framework by defining new sources that permit different forms of post-processing.

Acknowledgments. We thank Sogol Mazaheri for collaborating in the early stages of this work. We also thank anonymous reviewers who helped improve the presentation of our results. Pooya Farshim was supported in part by EPSRC grant EP/V034065/1. Patrick Harasser was funded by the Deutsche Forschungsgemeinschaft (DFG) – SFB 1119 – 236615297. Adam O'Neill is supported in part by a gift from Cisco.

References

1. Agrikola, T., Hofheinz, D.: Interactively secure groups from obfuscation. In: Abdalla, M., Dahab, R. (eds.) PKC 2018, Part II. LNCS, vol. 10770, pp. 341–370. Springer, Cham (2018). https://doi.org/10.1007/978-3-319-76581-5_12
2. Agrikola, T., Hofheinz, D., Kastner, J.: On instantiating the algebraic group model from falsifiable assumptions. In: Canteaut, A., Ishai, Y. (eds.) EUROCRYPT 2020, Part II. LNCS, vol. 12106, pp. 96–126. Springer, Cham (2020). https://doi.org/10.1007/978-3-030-45724-2_4
3. Applebaum, B.: Key-dependent message security: generic amplification and completeness. In: Paterson, K.G. (ed.) EUROCRYPT 2011. LNCS, vol. 6632, pp. 527–546. Springer, Heidelberg (2011). https://doi.org/10.1007/978-3-642-20465-4_29
4. Bartusek, J., Ma, F., Zhandry, M.: The distinction between fixed and random generators in group-based assumptions. In: Boldyreva, A., Micciancio, D. (eds.) CRYPTO 2019, Part II. LNCS, vol. 11693, pp. 801–830. Springer, Cham (2019). https://doi.org/10.1007/978-3-030-26951-7_27
5. Bauer, B., Fuchsbauer, G., Loss, J.: A classification of computational assumptions in the algebraic group model. In: Micciancio, D., Ristenpart, T. (eds.) CRYPTO 2020, Part II. LNCS, vol. 12171, pp. 121–151. Springer, Cham (2020). https://doi.org/10.1007/978-3-030-56880-1_5
6. Bauer, B., Farshim, P., Harasser, P., O'Neill, A.: Beyond Uber: Instantiating Generic Groups via PGGs. Cryptology ePrint Archive, Paper 2022/1502 (2022)
7. Bellare, M., Boldyreva, A., O'Neill, A.: Deterministic and efficiently searchable encryption. In: Menezes, A. (ed.) CRYPTO 2007. LNCS, vol. 4622, pp. 535–552. Springer, Heidelberg (2007). https://doi.org/10.1007/978-3-540-74143-5_30
8. Bellare, M., Brakerski, Z., Naor, M., Ristenpart, T., Segev, G., Shacham, H., Yilek, S.: Hedged public-key encryption: how to protect against bad randomness. In: Matsui, M. (ed.) ASIACRYPT 2009. LNCS, vol. 5912, pp. 232–249. Springer, Heidelberg (2009). https://doi.org/10.1007/978-3-642-10366-7_14
9. Bellare, M., Cash, D., Miller, R.: Cryptography secure against related-key attacks and tampering. In: Lee, D.H., Wang, X. (eds.) ASIACRYPT 2011. LNCS, vol. 7073, pp. 486–503. Springer, Heidelberg (2011). https://doi.org/10.1007/978-3-642-25385-0_26
10. Bellare, M., Hoang, V.T.: Resisting randomness subversion: fast deterministic and hedged public-key encryption in the standard model. In: Oswald, E., Fischlin, M. (eds.) EUROCRYPT 2015, Part II. LNCS, vol. 9057, pp. 627–656. Springer, Heidelberg (2015). https://doi.org/10.1007/978-3-662-46803-6_21

11. Bellare, M., Hoang, V.T., Keelveedhi, S.: Instantiating random oracles via UCEs. In: Canetti, R., Garay, J.A. (eds.) CRYPTO 2013, Part II. LNCS, vol. 8043, pp. 398–415. Springer, Heidelberg (2013). https://doi.org/10.1007/978-3-642-40084-1_23

12. Bellare, M., Hoang, V.T., Keelveedhi, S.: Cryptography from compression functions: the UCE bridge to the ROM. In: Garay, J.A., Gennaro, R. (eds.) CRYPTO 2014, Part I. LNCS, vol. 8616, pp. 169–187. Springer, Heidelberg (2014). https://doi.org/10.1007/978-3-662-44371-2_10

13. Bellare, M., Palacio, A.: The knowledge-of-exponent assumptions and 3-round zero-knowledge protocols. In: Franklin, M. (ed.) CRYPTO 2004. LNCS, vol. 3152, pp. 273–289. Springer, Heidelberg (2004). https://doi.org/10.1007/978-3-540-28628-8_17

14. Birrell, E., Chung, K.-M., Pass, R., Telang, S.: Randomness-dependent message security. In: Sahai, A. (ed.) TCC 2013. LNCS, vol. 7785, pp. 700–720. Springer, Heidelberg (2013). https://doi.org/10.1007/978-3-642-36594-2_39

15. Bitansky, N., Canetti, R.: On strong simulation and composable point obfuscation. In: Rabin, T. (ed.) CRYPTO 2010. LNCS, vol. 6223, pp. 520–537. Springer, Heidelberg (2010). https://doi.org/10.1007/978-3-642-14623-7_28

16. Black, J.: The ideal-cipher model, revisited: an uninstantiable blockcipher-based hash function. In: Robshaw, M. (ed.) FSE 2006. LNCS, vol. 4047, pp. 328–340. Springer, Heidelberg (2006). https://doi.org/10.1007/11799313_21

17. Black, J., Rogaway, P., Shrimpton, T.: Encryption-scheme security in the presence of key-dependent messages. In: Nyberg, K., Heys, H. (eds.) SAC 2002. LNCS, vol. 2595, pp. 62–75. Springer, Heidelberg (2003). https://doi.org/10.1007/3-540-36492-7_6

18. Böhl, F., Davies, G.T., Hofheinz, D.: Encryption schemes secure under related-key and key-dependent message attacks. In: Krawczyk, H. (ed.) PKC 2014. LNCS, vol. 8383, pp. 483–500. Springer, Heidelberg (2014). https://doi.org/10.1007/978-3-642-54631-0_28

19. Boneh, D., Boyen, X., Goh, E.-J.: Hierarchical identity based encryption with constant size ciphertext. In: Cramer, R. (ed.) EUROCRYPT 2005. LNCS, vol. 3494, pp. 440–456. Springer, Heidelberg (2005). https://doi.org/10.1007/11426639_26

20. Boneh, D., Halevi, S., Hamburg, M., Ostrovsky, R.: Circular-secure encryption from decision Diffie-Hellman. In: Wagner, D. (ed.) CRYPTO 2008. LNCS, vol. 5157, pp. 108–125. Springer, Heidelberg (2008). https://doi.org/10.1007/978-3-540-85174-5_7

21. Boyen, X.: The uber-assumption family (invited talk). In: Galbraith, S.D., Paterson, K.G. (eds.) Pairing 2008. LNCS, vol. 5209, pp. 39–56. Springer, Heidelberg (2008). https://doi.org/10.1007/978-3-540-85538-5_3

22. Brzuska, C., Farshim, P., Mittelbach, A.: Indistinguishability obfuscation and UCEs: the case of computationally unpredictable sources. In: Garay, J.A., Gennaro, R. (eds.) CRYPTO 2014, Part I. LNCS, vol. 8616, pp. 188–205. Springer, Heidelberg (2014). https://doi.org/10.1007/978-3-662-44371-2_11

23. Brzuska, C., Mittelbach, A.: Using Indistinguishability Obfuscation via UCEs. In: Sarkar, P., Iwata, T. (eds.) ASIACRYPT 2014, Part II. LNCS, vol. 8874, pp. 122–141. Springer, Heidelberg (2014). https://doi.org/10.1007/978-3-662-45608-8_7

24. Camenisch, J., Lysyanskaya, A.: An efficient system for non-transferable anonymous credentials with optional anonymity revocation. In: Pfitzmann, B. (ed.) EUROCRYPT 2001. LNCS, vol. 2045, pp. 93–118. Springer, Heidelberg (2001). https://doi.org/10.1007/3-540-44987-6_7

25. Canetti, R.: Towards realizing random oracles: hash functions that hide all partial information. In: Kaliski, B.S. (ed.) CRYPTO 1997. LNCS, vol. 1294, pp. 455–469. Springer, Heidelberg (1997). https://doi.org/10.1007/BFb0052255

26. Canetti, R., Dakdouk, R.R.: Obfuscating point functions with multibit output. In: Smart, N. (ed.) EUROCRYPT 2008. LNCS, vol. 4965, pp. 489–508. Springer, Heidelberg (2008). https://doi.org/10.1007/978-3-540-78967-3_28

27. Canetti, R., Goldreich, O., Halevi, S.: The random oracle methodology, revisited (preliminary version). In: 30th ACM STOC (1998)

28. Canetti, R., Goldreich, O., Halevi, S. : The random oracle methodology, revisited. J. ACM 51(4) (2004)

29. Coretti, S., Dodis, Y., Guo, S.: Non-Uniform bounds in the random-permutation, ideal-cipher, and generic-group models. In: Shacham, H., Boldyreva, A. (eds.) CRYPTO 2018, Part I. LNCS, vol. 10991, pp. 693–721. Springer, Cham (2018). https://doi.org/10.1007/978-3-319-96884-1_23

30. Corrigan-Gibbs, H., Kogan, D.: The discrete-logarithm problem with preprocessing. In: Nielsen, J.B., Rijmen, V. (eds.) EUROCRYPT 2018, Part II. LNCS, vol. 10821, pp. 415–447. Springer, Cham (2018). https://doi.org/10.1007/978-3-319-78375-8_14

31. Cramer, R., Shoup, V.: A practical public key cryptosystem provably secure against adaptive chosen ciphertext attack. In: Krawczyk, H. (ed.) CRYPTO 1998. LNCS, vol. 1462, pp. 13–25. Springer, Heidelberg (1998). https://doi.org/10.1007/BFb0055717

32. Damgård, I., Hazay, C., Zottarel, A.: Short paper on the generic hardness of DDH-II (2014)

33. Demillo, R.A., Lipton, R.J.: A probabilistic remark on algebraic program testing. Inf. Process. Lett. 7(4) (1978)

34. Dent, A.W.: Adapting the weaknesses of the random oracle model to the generic group model. In: Zheng, Y. (ed.) ASIACRYPT 2002. LNCS, vol. 2501, pp. 100–109. Springer, Heidelberg (2002). https://doi.org/10.1007/3-540-36178-2_6

35. Escala, A., Herold, G., Kiltz, E., Ràfols, C., Villar, J.: An algebraic framework for Diffie-Hellman assumptions. In: Canetti, R., Garay, J.A. (eds.) CRYPTO 2013, Part II. LNCS, vol. 8043, pp. 129–147. Springer, Heidelberg (2013). https://doi.org/10.1007/978-3-642-40084-1_8

36. Fenteany, P., Fuller, B.: Same point composable and nonmalleable obfuscated point functions. In: Conti, M., Zhou, J., Casalicchio, E., Spognardi, A. (eds.) ACNS 2020, Part II. LNCS, vol. 12147, pp. 124–144. Springer, Cham (2020). https://doi.org/10.1007/978-3-030-57878-7_7

37. Fuchsbauer, G., Kiltz, E., Loss, J.: The algebraic group model and its applications. In: Shacham, H., Boldyreva, A. (eds.) CRYPTO 2018, Part II. LNCS, vol. 10992, pp. 33–62. Springer, Cham (2018). https://doi.org/10.1007/978-3-319-96881-0_2

38. Gennaro, R. , Trevisan, L.: Lower bounds on the efficiency of generic cryptographic constructions. In: 41st FOCS (2000)

39. Goyal, V., O'Neill, A., Rao, V.: Correlated-input secure hash functions. In: Ishai, Y. (ed.) TCC 2011. LNCS, vol. 6597, pp. 182–200. Springer, Heidelberg (2011). https://doi.org/10.1007/978-3-642-19571-6_12

40. Green, M.D., Katz, J., Malozemoff, A.J., Zhou, H.-S.: A unified approach to idealized model separations via indistinguishability obfuscation. In: Zikas, V., De Prisco, R. (eds.) SCN 2016. LNCS, vol. 9841, pp. 587–603. Springer, Cham (2016). https://doi.org/10.1007/978-3-319-44618-9_31

41. Hemenway, B., Ostrovsky, R.: Building lossy trapdoor functions from lossy encryption. In: Sako, K., Sarkar, P. (eds.) ASIACRYPT 2013, Part II. LNCS, vol. 8270, pp. 241–260. Springer, Heidelberg (2013). https://doi.org/10.1007/978-3-642-42045-0_13

42. Kästner, J., Pan, J.: Towards instantiating the algebraic group model. Cryptology ePrint Archive, Report 2019/1018 (2019)

43. Katz, J., Zhang, C., Zhou, H.-S.: An analysis of the algebraic group model. Cryptology ePrint Archive, Report 2022/210 (2022)

44. Komargodski, I., Yogev, E.: Another step towards realizing random oracles: nonmalleable point obfuscation. In: Nielsen, J.B., Rijmen, V. (eds.) EUROCRYPT 2018, Part I. LNCS, vol. 10820, pp. 259–279. Springer, Cham (2018). https://doi.org/10.1007/978-3-319-78381-9_10

45. Maurer, U.: Abstract models of computation in cryptography (invited paper). In: Smart, N.P. (ed.) Cryptography and Coding 2005. LNCS, vol. 3796, pp. 1–12. Springer, Heidelberg (2005). https://doi.org/10.1007/11586821_1

46. Naor, M., Reingold, O.: Number-theoretic constructions of efficient pseudo-random functions. In: 38th FOCS (1997)

47. Nechaev, V.I.: Complexity of a determinate algorithm for the discrete logarithm. Math. Notes 55(2) (1994)

48. Paterson, K.G., Schuldt, J.C.N., Sibborn, D.L.: Related randomness attacks for public key encryption. In: Krawczyk, H. (ed.) PKC 2014. LNCS, vol. 8383, pp. 465–482. Springer, Heidelberg (2014). https://doi.org/10.1007/978-3-642-54631-0_27

49. Schwartz, J.T.: Fast probabilistic algorithms for verification of polynomial identities. J. Assoc. Comput. Mach. 27(4) (1980)

50. Shoup, V.: On fast and provably secure message authentication based on universal hashing. In: Koblitz, N. (ed.) CRYPTO 1996. LNCS, vol. 1109, pp. 313–328. Springer, Heidelberg (1996). https://doi.org/10.1007/3-540-68697-5_24

51. Shoup, V.: Lower bounds for discrete logarithms and related problems. In: Fumy, W. (ed.) EUROCRYPT 1997. LNCS, vol. 1233, pp. 256–266. Springer, Heidelberg (1997). https://doi.org/10.1007/3-540-69053-0_18

52. Soni, P., Tessaro, S.: Public-seed pseudorandom permutations. In: Coron, J.-S., Nielsen, J.B. (eds.) EUROCRYPT 2017, Part II. LNCS, vol. 10211, pp. 412–441. Springer, Cham (2017). https://doi.org/10.1007/978-3-319-56614-6_14

53. Soni, P., Tessaro, S.: Naor-Reingold goes public: the complexity of known-key security. In: Nielsen, J.B., Rijmen, V. (eds.) EUROCRYPT 2018, Part III. LNCS, vol. 10822, pp. 653–684. Springer, Cham (2018). https://doi.org/10.1007/978-3-319-78372-7_21

54. Vadhan, S.P.: Pseudorandomness. Now Publishers (2012)

55. Zhandry, M.: The magic of ELFs. In: Robshaw, M., Katz, J. (eds.) CRYPTO 2016, Part I. LNCS, vol. 9814, pp. 479–508. Springer, Heidelberg (2016). https://doi.org/10.1007/978-3-662-53018-4_18

56. Zhandry, M.: To label, or not to label (in generic groups). In: Dodis, Y., Shrimpton, T. (eds.) CRYPTO 2022. LNCS, vol. 13509, pp. 66–96. Springer, Cham (2022). https://doi.org/10.1007/978-3-031-15982-4_3

57. Zhandry, M., Zhang, C.: The relationship between idealized models under computationally bounded adversaries. Cryptology ePrint Archive, Report 2021/240 (2021)

58. Zippel, R.: Probabilistic algorithms for sparse polynomials. In: Ng, E.W. (ed.) Symbolic and Algebraic Computation. LNCS, vol. 72, pp. 216–226. Springer, Heidelberg (1979). https://doi.org/10.1007/3-540-09519-5_73

Author Index

Printed in the United States
by Baker & Taylor Publisher Services